CW00542086

Advance Praise

"Rainer Zitelmann has achieved what almost no researcher before him has managed: His doctoral thesis lifts the lid on Germany's super rich, exploring the previously largely unexamined world of millionaires and multimillionaires. Zitelmann conducted in-depth interviews with 45 multi-millionaires and billionaires ... and it is particularly interesting to read how their parents dealt with the subject of money."

FOCUS MONEY-Online

"This is a unique fascinating book that you cant put down after you pick it up. It is loaded with fascinating information on the thoughts and actions of leaders in industry who became extremely wealthy."

Gary Latham,
Secretary of State Professor of Organizational Effectiveness,
Rotman School of Management, University of Toronto

Published by
LID Publishing Limited
The Record Hall, Studio 204,
16-16a Baldwins Gardens,
London EC1N 7RJ, UK

524 Broadway, 11th Floor, Suite 08-120,
New York, NY 10012, US

info@lidpublishing.com
www.lidpublishing.com

A member of:

www.businesspublishersroundtable.com

Printed in Great Britain by TJ International
ISBN: 978-1-911498-68-1

Translation: Sebastian Taylor
Proofreading: Silke Lührmann
Cover and page design: Matthew Renaudin

Rainer Zitelmann

The Wealth Elite

A groundbreaking study of
the psychology of the super rich

LONDON   NEW YORK   SHANGHAI
MADRID   BARCELONA   BOGOTA
MEXICO CITY   MONTERREY   BUENOS AIRES

Contents

Preface

The large number of popular 'wealth-creation' books are evidence of just how many people are interested in this topic. Oddly enough, scholars do not seem to share the same level of interest. I have read many of these popular books and, although I have learned quite a bit from them, the lack of empirical or scholarly studies on the subject has always struck me as a gap that needed to be filled. It was only during my own research for a book on the topic, *Reich werden und bleiben*,[1] a few years ago that I became aware that the first scholarly investigations of the various pathways to wealth were being carried out. However, these works primarily focused on higher-than-average earners or those who had achieved an affluent standard of living.

In contrast, scholarly investigations into the truly rich and the super rich – i.e. those who possess fortunes in the tens or hundreds of millions – were still conspicuous by their absence.

For this book, I succeeded in convincing 45 wealthy people to talk to me. Although they are, by any objective measure, extremely rich, most of them would not describe themselves as 'super rich'. One billionaire even told me, "I'm not really all that rich. There are others who are far richer, like Warren Buffett." He pointed out that according to the *Forbes* list of the wealthiest people in the world, there are several hundred individuals who are far richer than him. This was no false modesty, but simply evidence of a common tendency of individuals in this category of wealth to measure themselves against those at the top. I could not stop myself from reminding him that there are still 7.3 billion people who are poorer than him.

Without exception, the interviewees were entrepreneurs or investors and, in advance of the interviews, I studied the substantial – and overwhelmingly American – literature in the field of entrepreneurship research, seeking inspiration in the hope of arriving at appropriate questions for this book. I would like to thank my interviewees for their great candour. One of them, to whom I had sent a summary of the most important sections of our interview, wrote to me:

"As I was reading the transcript, there were moments when I was a bit shocked by my own remarks. But it *must have been* me who said all these things... I'm sure that what you recorded provides a pretty clear outline of my personality.

All of this will guide my actions in the future. It is as if you had 'filmed' my most intimate internal thoughts and reflections."

The interviews were conducted in person between September 2015 and March 2016, and each lasted between one and two hours. The transcripts fill 1,740 pages. In addition, every interviewee (with one exception) took a personality test consisting of 50 questions.

The results of the interviews are presented in Part B of this book. Readers who are primarily interested in these results can go straight to page 140. The second section of this book is certainly the more entertaining and, even within the scholarly framework of this work, some of the findings are sure to raise a smile or two. Part A is intended for those who are interested in entrepreneurship and academic wealth research, along with the methodologies used in this field, and for those who are curious to find out more about current scholarly discussions. Nevertheless, it is not absolutely necessary to read Part A in order to fully appreciate Part B.

This work explores the personalities and patterns of behaviour exhibited by wealthy individuals. Books that address this matter, whether as popular how-to books or as scholarly works, tend to raise certain expectations in their readers, many of whom are looking for insights, instructions, or even recipes on how to become rich. It is certainly true that my interviewees revealed patterns of behaviour, personality traits, and strategies that have helped them build their wealth. However, popular wealth-creation literature[2] makes the mistake of assuming that identifying similarities between wealthy people is enough to derive action plans that will unfailingly lead to wealth.

My interviewees have all attained great wealth, and their answers to my questions clearly demonstrate that the personality traits and patterns of behaviour described in this book have played a significant role in their extraordinary economic success. However, this is a study based on methods of qualitative social research and, as such, the interview subjects do not constitute a representative sample. Above all, their answers were not tested against a control group consisting of non-wealthy individuals.

While the behavioural patterns described here have contributed to the enormous financial success of these particular individuals, the very same behavioural patterns – such as elevated risk propensity, high levels of optimism, clear focus, swimming against the current of majority opinion and making many decisions

---

1   Rainer Zitelmann, *Reich werden und bleiben: Ihr Wegweiser zur finanziellen Freiheit*
     (Munich: FinanzBuch Verlag 2015).

2   See, for instance, T. Harv Eker, *Secrets of the Millionaire Mind: Mastering the Inner Game of Wealth*
     (New York: Harper International, 2007); Martin S. Fridson, *How to Be a Billionaire: Proven Strategies from the Titans
     of Wealth* (New York: John Wiley & Sons, 2000); Napoleon Hill, *Think and Grow Rich: Instant Aid to Riches –
     New and Revised Edition* (New York: Wilshire Book Co, 1966); Robert T. Kiyosaki and Sharon L. Lechter,
     Rich Dad Poor Dad: What the Rich Teach Their Kids about Money that the Poor and Middle Class Do Not!
     (New York: Tech Press, Inc., 1998); Bodo Schäfer, *Der Weg zur finanziellen Freiheit. In sieben Jahren die erste Million*
     (Frankfurt-am-Main: Campus Verlag, 1998).

from the 'gut' – can also lead to failure. In all likelihood – as my interviews also demonstrate – the fact that these individuals have been able to sustain their success over such an extended period of time, and to consolidate and grow their fortunes, is largely due to the control they eventually learned to exert over their innate, above-average risk propensity. Otherwise, the same behavioural patterns and personality traits that initially led to their success may well have caused them to fail at a later date – in which case they would never have become the subject of this or any other research into successful individuals. Before jumping to any conclusions, though, readers should consider this book in its entirety and, in particular, the qualifying comments in Chapter 21 regarding the limits of the conclusions drawn by this study.

This work was originally submitted to the Faculty of Economics and Social Sciences at the University of Potsdam in the winter term of 2016/2017 as a doctoral dissertation and was awarded the distinction 'magna cum laude'. I would like to thank Prof. Dr. Wolfgang Lauterbach, who initiated and guided me during my research. It was his research project "Wealth in Germany", the first empirical research project to address the genesis of wealth in Germany, that first introduced me to the field of academic wealth research. I would additionally like to thank Prof. Dr. Gerd Habermann, who also guided my work and provided me with access to some of my interviewees.

Dr. Rainer Zitelmann

Introduction

According to a study published in 2015, among all billionaires, the proportion whose wealth is self-made grew globally from 43% to 66% between 1995 and 2014.[3] This trend makes an enquiry into the personality traits and strategies that enable individuals to rise and join the ranks of the wealth elite increasingly relevant.

In recent years, the academic discipline of wealth research has become well established, and several doctoral dissertations and collections of essays have been published on this topic. One gap in the research relates to the group that will be referred to in this book as the 'wealth elite' or 'ultra-high-net-worth individuals' (UHNWIs). These are individuals who have accumulated net assets in the tens or hundreds of millions. There are hardly any findings that relate to the creation of wealth within this group, or to the personality traits and behavioural patterns that have enabled their economic success.

Additionally, academic wealth researchers have so far failed to give due consideration to the findings of another research field, namely entrepreneurship research. This comes as something of a surprise, as the results of entrepreneurship research are also of great interest to academic wealth researchers, because – as is shown in Chapter 1 – a substantial majority of wealthy people became wealthy as entrepreneurs. In particular, academic wealth researchers have so far failed to fully exploit the broad spectrum of research on the correlation between specific personality traits and entrepreneurial success.

This book aims to fill these research gaps. The author carried out 45 interviews with individuals whose net worth ranged between EUR 10 million and 30 million in the lowest category, rising into the hundreds of millions, and even several billion euros, in the highest category. Two thirds of the interviewees have net assets of between EUR 30 million and 1 billion. An overwhelming majority are self-made millionaires. The group also includes a few UHNWIs who initially inherited assets and went on to multiply their fortunes many times over.

---

3   *Billionaires: Master Architects of Great Wealth and Lasting Legacies* (UBS and PwC, 2015), 13.

In contrast, individuals whose wealth is primarily the result of inheritance or gifts are not relevant to the research questions explored in this book.

The interviews proved to be so fruitful because a great deal of effort was initially made in developing appropriate questions. This involved a comprehensive evaluation of research findings from various fields, including academic wealth research, entrepreneurship research, and behavioural economics.

Part A of this book, which details the state of the current scholarly research in the field, will allow the reader to gain an understanding of how the questions for the interviews were developed. Existing gaps in the research are outlined, questions are developed, and research methodologies are described. This process of reappraising the existing research, of developing research questions, and of considering appropriate methodologies is what led to the formulation of guidelines for the subsequent interviews.

It is, however, beyond the scope of this introduction to discuss details of the results of the literature review presented in great depth in Part A. The investigation was guided by the key question of the personality traits and behavioural patterns of UHNWIs. The interview questions were developed in order to understand the behavioural patterns, and to reveal the attitudes and attributes that were a condition for the exceptional economic success of these wealthy individuals.

To do this, it was important to find out more about the interviewees' social backgrounds, their formative years, their educations, and the formal and informal learning processes that shaped them. Is there a correlation between their formal education and the degree of wealth they went on to attain? Or did informal learning processes – for example, through competitive sports or early entrepreneurial activities – play a more important role? Is it possible to substantiate findings from entrepreneurship research suggesting that entrepreneurialism is already evident in youth?

Moreover, it is worth exploring what caused these people – all of whom are entrepreneurs and investors – at some point in their lives to choose self-employment over a career in an existing organization, and to accept the high risks associated with that choice. Was it, as some studies claim, an inability to fit into existing structures and assimilate into hierarchies that led these people to found their own businesses?

The extent to which goal-setting has played a role in the financial success of these individuals was an equally important line of investigation. Was it the case, as is unanimously claimed by popular wealth-creation books, that these people first set themselves the definite goal of becoming rich at some point? Or did they simply become wealthy as a by-product of their entrepreneurial activities, without this being their initial, primary goal?

And what do these individuals value most about the opportunities that their wealth offers, once they have become rich? Do they appreciate their financial freedom and independence – or is security more important to them? How important is it that they can afford beautiful and expensive things and – in spite of the envy many complain of – that they enjoy societal recognition?

Which special abilities and talents have played a role in the economic success of these entrepreneurs and investors? It is certainly interesting to consider the importance of an individual's sales skills.

And how do these people make decisions? Are they guided by strictly rational analysis, or rather by intuition or 'gut instinct'? What risks are they willing to take? In relation to risk propensity, are there differences between the nascent stages of self-employment and the later stages, when they are expanding their companies or continuing with their entrepreneurial endeavours? Did they really understand the risks they were taking in the same ways as others would?

This has a direct bearing on the role played by optimism and over-optimism. Almost all of these individuals see themselves as exceptionally optimistic – but what do they really mean by 'optimism'? And to what extent do they reflect on the risks associated with over-optimism, which are frequently highlighted in behavioural economics – because over-optimism can lead entrepreneurs to take unreasonable risks?

Finally, what role does the tendency to go your own way play for these individuals, to buck majority opinion and at times to swim against the tide? How important is their ability to deal with conflict? This question leads directly to the personality traits formulated by the Big Five model: Neuroticism, Extroversion, Openness to Experience, Conscientiousness, and Agreeableness. All of the interviewees, with one exception, completed a personality test to measure just how strongly developed these personality traits were.

During their long careers as entrepreneurs and investors, they also had to overcome crises and setbacks. How did they deal with these setbacks psychologically? Do common behavioural patterns exist in relation to how these individuals reacted to setbacks?

These questions were derived from various sources. In addition to the field of academic wealth research, these sources primarily included the American entrepreneurship research and behavioural economics. Moreover, questions arose from the evaluation of the biographies and autobiographies of successful people – a topic upon which the author published a book in 2012.[4] It seemed highly likely that the 45 interviewees would demonstrate both similarities and differences. To what extent do identical behavioural patterns emerge, and to what extent do the interviewees differ?

The individuals who are the subject of this work, namely those with net assets in the tens and hundreds of millions, represent such a small societal group that even

---

4   Rainer Zitelmann, *Dare to Be Different and Grow Rich* (Mumbai: Indus Source Books, 2012).

a sample of 20,000 respondents – as used by the Socio-Economic Panel – would include far too few of them to produce methodologically sound findings.[5] For this reason, standardized approaches based on quantitative methods were ruled out for this research. A qualitative approach based on guided interviews was selected instead. This means that a structure was developed to serve as a framework for the interviews, to guarantee that the questions and topics determined in advance would be raised during the interviews.

These types of guided interviews strike a balance between so-called narrative interviews, where the interviewer provides impulses for anecdotes while at the same time remaining as uninvolved as possible during the interview, and standardized approaches, where interviewees are asked identically worded questions in a precisely defined sequence.

Too often interviews with corporate executives and entrepreneurs show that interviewers have not sufficiently considered the methodological problems arising when their interviewees supply only socially acceptable answers. There is, however, a real danger that entrepreneurs, who are so used to producing positive soundbites in official statements, will almost habitually speak in polished clichés. This danger is all the greater the more general the wording of the questions and the less critical the interviewer. The problem is exacerbated if an interviewer subsequently sends the interview transcripts to the interviewee for approval. For these reasons, the author decided to carry out guided interviews without asking the interviewees to approve the transcripts of the recorded interviews.[6] The statements quoted in the second part of this work have been translated as faithfully as possible to the interviewees' original wording, although some minor editing has been carried out in the interest of readability for this English version.

HOW THIS BOOK IS STRUCTURED

Part A describes the current state of the existing research, defines the central questions of this work, and outlines the methodological approach used. Part B evaluates the interviews with the 45 UHNWIs.

Chapter 1 discusses the state of existing academic wealth research, summarizes the most important findings, and outlines gaps in the research. Chapter 2 takes a critical look at the usage and definition of the term 'economic elite' in many elite studies. Previous research into economic elites has placed far too much emphasis on employed executives in leadership positions while almost completely ignoring independent entrepreneurs and investors. There are good reasons why the economic elite should be divided into two categories. It is the wealth elite, as a distinct subgroup of the economic elite, that constitutes the subject of this work.

Chapter 3 describes the current state of entrepreneurship research. As early as the beginning of the 20th century, authors who explored the phenomenon of entrepreneurship, most notably Werner Sombart and Joseph Schumpeter, placed great emphasis on the importance of psychological issues. Today, there is a broad spectrum of research into the psychology of entrepreneurs, especially in the United States, which is discussed in Section 3.2. These efforts focus on the substantial findings of research into the personalities of entrepreneurs.

Chapter 4 deals with behavioural economics and learning theories, to the extent that they are relevant to entrepreneurial success. These include both 'explicit' and 'implicit' learning. Implicit learning, which is the basis for 'implicit knowledge', plays a particularly important role for entrepreneurs, as existing research has shown, and this is clearly confirmed by this book's interviews with UHNWIs.

A number of topics recur throughout Chapters 1 to 4. It would be quite surprising if this were not the case, particularly as the questions and topics for the interviews were deliberately developed from a wide variety of sources. A number of these topics, such as goal-setting and nonconformism, can be found in early entrepreneurship research and have come to feature prominently in recent entrepreneurship research, as well as in scholarly works in the field of behavioural economics.

Chapter 5 considers the role of chance or 'luck'. Both factors are frequently mentioned by successful individuals, and there are studies that ascribe a far greater role to these two factors than is the case in this book. What social and psychological explanations are there to account for why successful people emphatically point to luck or chance?

Chapter 6 examines personality theories, with a particular focus on the Big Five personality traits. This chapter also discusses the author's reasons for exploring traits beyond those specified by the Big Five personality theory, such as risk propensity, in the interviews.

Chapter 7 focuses on methodology. First, an overview of the variety of possible approaches to qualitative interviews is provided, followed by an explanation of the choice of guided interviews as the most suitable model for this research. Moreover, the above-mentioned problem of social desirability bias, which is frequently underestimated in research on entrepreneurs and elites, is discussed in particular detail.

Finally, Part B provides an evaluation of the 45 interviews with UHNWIs. This extensive material has been organized by topic. The interviewees' verbatim responses are presented at length, because one of the key objectives of this work is to reconstruct the perspectives of the interviewees while at the same time gaining as authentic an insight into their mindsets and behavioural patterns as possible.

---

5   Markus M. Grabka, "Verteilung und Struktur des Reichtums in Deutschland," in *Reichtum, Philanthropie und Zivilgesellschaft*, edited by Wolfgang Lauterbach, Michael Hartmann, and Miriam Ströing (Wiesbaden: Springer VS, 2014), 31.

6   A summary of the interviews was sent to most of the interviewees, with the express and strictly formulated request not to make any changes (except in the case of clear factual errors, for example when a number had been misunderstood). Only in one case did an interviewee make extensive corrections, although these did nothing to falsify the original statements.

PART A

Review of
existing research,
research questions,
and methodology

Review of Academic Wealth Research

"The discussion about what actually constitutes wealth is only just beginning," the economist Irene Becker asserted in 2003.[7] Among the points she singled out for criticism was the fact that the debate surrounding wealth has always focused on income, while ignoring wealth. "It is only when a high net income coincides with a high level of wealth that one can assume a material position that is sustainably sufficient to enable an elevated standard of living, and which guarantees the associated degree of security that is a qualitative characteristic of richness."[8]

In 2002, the sociologist Peter Imbusch stated that it was not only that detailed knowledge and information were lacking in the field of academic wealth research (namely who should actually be classified as wealthy and how they live) but, in addition, "opinions diverge on even the most basic questions: how do we define wealth? At what point is someone rich and how do we even measure their wealth?"[9] In contrast to poverty research, Imbusch complains that empirical findings in the field of academic wealth research are particularly unclear, contradictory, and incomplete.[10]

Commenting on the – in his opinion – alleged failings of sociology, Imbusch contends that wealth does not constitute a genuine sociological category and that the wealthy never used to be regarded as an identifiable object of study for sociologists.[11] One reason for this, he argues, is that the upper classes or elites are, numerically speaking, a relatively small group, and it would therefore make sense for sociologists to focus their work more on other groups.[12] In and of itself, this line of argument fails to convince. After all, sociologists frequently engage in intensive research into minority groups, many of which have no more members than 'the wealthy' – however one chooses to define that term.[13]

Imbusch continues: "Varied investigations into specific facets of wealth notwithstanding, it must be noted that sociology has so far failed to focus its research efforts on wealth." He blames this on the fragmentary state of existing empirical findings in relation to wealth as well as on the fact that "the wealthy and their wealth have proven to be an especially unwieldy object of investigation".[14]

Imbusch raises another interesting point, namely the commingling of research interests and judgements based on normative values, especially on this topic.

Wealth poses particular challenges for sociologists, not least because its normative dimensions make the subject area particularly vulnerable to a mixture of descriptive and judgemental analysis.[15]

Even ten years after researchers such as Becker and Imbusch had pointed out the gap in the existing research, their successors were still complaining about a lack of scholarly attention to the wealthy. "Scholars", observed Melanie Böwing-Schmalenbrock in 2012, "have largely ignored the subject of wealth... It could well be that no single discipline viewed itself as responsible for carrying out research into wealth. Even today, the topic is not firmly anchored in any one field, rather it moves between disciplines."[16] In the future, though, she expects that academic wealth research could well establish itself as a distinct, interdisciplinary discipline.[17]

Böwing-Schmalenbrock's claim still applies today, although her doctoral thesis – regarded as the very first scholarly monograph on the subject of empirical academic wealth research in Germany – has made a significant contribution towards closing that gap. In addition, numerous papers have appeared in collected editions and further projects are currently in the pipeline. Academic wealth research encompasses a broad range of questions and research strategies:

1. For decades now, studies have focused on issues surrounding the equality of wealth distribution – although these have largely proceeded from a normative standpoint. This approach has not been concerned with investigating the genesis of individual wealth; rather – often with clear, specifically political intentions –

---

7   Irene Becker, "Die Reichen und ihr Reichtum," in *Oberschichten – Eliten – Herrschende Klassen*, edited by Stefan Hradil and Peter Imbusch (Wiesbaden: Springer Fachmedien, 2003), 73.

8   Ibid., 74.

9   Peter Imbusch, "Reichtum als Lebensstil," in *Theorien des Reichtums*, edited by Ernst-Ulrich Huster and Fritz Rüdiger Volz (Hamburg: LIT Verlag, 2002), 213.

10 Ibid., 214–215.

11 Ibid., 215.

12 Ibid., 216.

13 One such example is transgender research. This concerns a group that, according to estimates published by the Transgender Identity and Intersex Association of Germany, comprises between 20,000 and 80,000 people (DW, "Transgender in Deutschland," last modified 13 May 2014, http://www.dw.com/de/transgender-in-deutschland/a-17630664). Although this group is small in absolute terms, there has been extensive academic study on this topic; see for instance the work of Gesa Lindemann, *Das paradoxe Geschlecht: Transsexualität im Spannungsfeld von Körper, Leib und Gefühl* (Wiesbaden: VS Verlag, 2011). There are likely to be a similar number of rockers in Germany, as there are around 1,000 clubs, each with between 10 and 20 members; see Dagobert Ernst, "Die meisten Rocker sind friedlich," *Der Westen* (2012, accessed 27 October 2017, http://www.derwesten.de/region/rhein_ruhr/die-meisten-rocker-sind-friedlich-id6396863.html). Rockers have also become the subject of sociological research, see for instance the doctoral dissertation written by Martin G. Opitz, "Rocker im Spannungsfeld zwischen Clubinteressen und Gesellschaftsnormen, Constance 1990" (PhD diss., Universität Bremen, 1989).

14 Imbusch, "Reichtum als Lebensstil," 217.

15 Ibid., 217.

16 Melanie Böwing-Schmalenbrock, *Wege zum Reichtum: Die Bedeutung von Erbschaften, Erwerbstätigkeit und Persönlichkeit für die Entstehung von Reichtum* (Wiesbaden: Springer VS, 2012), 47.

17 Ibid., 254.

it has investigated whether wealth has been 'fairly' distributed throughout society. To demonstrate this point, let us briefly consider two collections of essays published in 1993 and 2002 respectively. In 1997, Ernst-Ulrich Huster published a collection of essays under the title *Wealth in Germany. The beneficiaries of social polarization*. The unifying theme in this collection was the constant complaint about the unjust distribution of wealth. "Wealth and Prosperity at the Cost of the Poor" was the title of one essay, while another was headed "Wealth is Masculine, what else!" The editor magnanimously conceded: "Of course, the liberal democratic state's presumption of injustice [sic!] towards every citizen applies equally to higher earners and commercial enterprises."[18] By using such language, it is clear that the rich are being assigned the role of the accused – for, even if "presumption of injustice" is a Freudian slip in the German original, and is supposed to read "presumption of innocence," the latter only makes sense in relation to a group or an individual accused of a crime. In their preface to the 2002 collection *Theories of Wealth*, Huster and Volz state: "Huster's criticism is not related to wealth and the rich; his – political and politological! – critique is aimed at societal developments and the forces that seek to decouple the entire economic sphere, conceptually as well as practically and politically, from its involvement in social processes, from its grounding in normative discourse and from its dependency on fundamental social consensus, thereby submitting economics (and wealth) to a purely economic logic and jurisdiction inspired by the spirit of neoliberalism."[19] Both the above-mentioned collections are dominated by essays that address the distribution of wealth from the perspective of inequality. In contrast, questions regarding the accumulation of wealth at an individual level are hardly thematized. The same applies to a volume published by three Swiss sociologists in 2010 and entitled *How the Rich Think and Act*, which focused on the milieu of the rich, on tax policies, and on theoretical approaches to the topic of wealth. The most revealing aspect of the collection was the interviews that were carried out with millionaires.[20] The interviews addressed a range of topics, including the respondents' views on the causes of the recent financial crisis, how the rich lobby for their own interests, how "innovative and socially responsible" they are, etc.[21] The subject of the genesis of their wealth played an extremely subordinate role, and only a handful of pages were devoted to an outright superficial treatment of this question.

2. In conjunction with the four poverty and wealth reports published by Germany's federal government in 2001, 2005, 2008, and 2013,[22] a broad range of empirical work has been carried out and published. However, this research has overwhelmingly focused on trends in income distribution. In the majority of cases, references to wealth or the rich relate to those earning 200 or 300% of national net equivalent incomes.

3. The past few years have also seen the establishment of a research field investigating the links between wealth and philanthropy. In Germany, this research has largely been initiated or carried out by Thomas Druyen and Wolfgang Lauterbach, who have examined the reasons for, objectives of, and extent of wealthy individuals' engagement in philanthropy, such as making donations and establishing charitable foundations.[23]

Thomas Druyen divides the academic wealth research into the following sub-areas:[24]

A. Wealth (social structural research)
  - Distribution
  - Genesis
  - Use.
B. Wealth (cultural research)
  - Familial and entrepreneurial networks
  - Social engagement
  - Attitudes and lifestyles.
C. Wealth psychology / ethical wealth
  - Psychological types
  - Personality traits
  - Empathy and morals.

A majority of the lines of questioning presented in 1 to 3, along with those under A to C, are at best tangentially relevant to the subject of this book. This book is not devoted to questions relating to the equality of wealth distribution, nor does it examine

---

18 Ernst-Ulrich Huster, "Enttabuisierung der sozialen Distanz: Reichtum in Deutschland," in *Reichtum in Deutschland: Die Gewinner in der sozialen Polarisierung*, edited by Ernst-Ulrich Huster (Frankfurt-am-Main: Campus Verlag, 1997), 16.

19 Ernst-Ulrich Huster and Fritz Rüdiger Volz (eds.), *Theorien des Reichtums* (Hamburg: LIT Verlag, 2002), 9.

20 In this collection, 100 interviews are referred to, of which extracts from 40 are published. It is, however, clear that not every interviewee is a millionaire. Ueli Mäder, Ganga Jey Aratnam, and Sarah Schillinger, *Wie Reiche denken und lenken: Reichtum in der Schweiz – Geschichte, Fakten, Gespräche* (Zürich: Rotpunktverlag, 2010), 167 et seq.

21 Ibid., 167 et seq.

22 See for instance Deutscher Bundestag, "Lebenslagen in Deutschland: Dritter Armuts- und Reichtumsbericht der Bundesregierung" (Paper 16/9915, 2008); Deutscher Bundestag, "Lebenslagen in Deutschland: Erster Armuts- und Reichtumsbericht der Bundesregierung" (Paper 14/5990, 2001); Deutscher Bundestag, "Lebenslagen in Deutschland: Zweiter Armuts- und Reichtumsbericht der Bundesregierung" (Paper 15/5015, 2005).

23 For instance, see the articles in the collection Thomas Druyen, Wolfgang Lauterbach, and Matthias Grundmann (eds.), *Reichtum und Vermögen* [Wealth and Fortune]: *Zur gesellschaftlichen Bedeutung der Reichtums- und Vermögensforschung* (Wiesbaden: Springer VS, 2009); Wolfgang Lauterbach, Thomas Druyen, and Matthias Grundmann (eds.), *Vermögen in Deutschland* [Wealth in Germany]: *Heterogenität und Verantwortung* (Wiesbaden: Springer VS, 2011); Wolfgang Lauterbach, Michael Hartmann, and Miriam Ströing, *Reichtum, Philanthropie und Zivilgesellschaft* [Wealth, Philanthropy and Civil Society] (Wiesbaden: Springer VS, 2014).

24 Thomas Druyen, "Über die Studie 'Vermögen in Deutschland' und die vermögenskulturelle Zukunft," in *Vermögen in Deutschland: Heterogenität und Verantwortung*, edited by Wolfgang Lauterbach, Thomas Druyen, and Matthias Grundmann (Wiesbaden: Springer VS, 2011), 215.

the income rich in the sense described above. Similarly, questions regarding the social engagement of the rich, or the subject of wealth and philanthropy, along with the lifestyles and milieus of the rich, are expressly not addressed in this work. For this reason, it is not necessary to outline the state of current research in these fields.

Instead, this study focuses on the topic of the genesis of wealth, which was also addressed in the work of Böwing-Schmalenbrock. As her doctoral dissertation, produced as part of the "Wealth in Germany" study, has the strongest empirical foundation of the research in this field, the methodology and findings of her work will be presented in more detail below – supplemented by the findings published in a selection of essays and articles over the past few years that also deal with this subject.

The central focus of Böwing-Schmalenbrock's work is the sources of and factors behind the genesis of wealth. The sources of wealth are largely identified as either paid work or inheritance, and the factors are primarily individual characteristics, in particular personality traits.[25] One of the work's central premises, which has also been adopted for this book, is the importance of the role of the individual, i.e. their personality traits and decision-making, as a decisive factor in the genesis of wealth: "The actors and their individual characteristics are an inordinately crucial factor in the genesis of wealth; wealth is created as the result of individual wealth-building processes, which are actively influenced by the individuals concerned. The genesis of private household wealth therefore constitutes a complex, but freely accessible process of formation that only takes place as a result of the actions and decisions of the persons within the household."[26]

Böwing-Schmalenbrock distinguishes her approach from sociological mobility research. Her studies have "focused on developments within individual lives rather than on intra-generational comparisons". Her work is therefore concerned with intra-generational, rather than inter-generational, mobility processes.[27] She is convinced – rightly so – that, "above all, mobility is predicated on personality. Insofar as individuals are able to participate in the identification and exploitation of opportunities, the creation of wealth should be understood as a relatively open mobility process."[28]

Böwing-Schmalenbrock's insistence that wealth has its roots either in paid work or in inheritance, estates or gifts does, however, need to be modified or supplemented.[29] Admittedly, she does concede that "a third source is existing wealth, provided this is autonomously multiplied". However, in her view, this should be treated "more as a secondary source, rather than a primary one". Income from capital is therefore treated as a secondary factor in the genesis of wealth, not as its source.[30]

This line of argument fails to convince. It is ultimately irrelevant whether wealth has its origins in paid work or investments. There are wealthy individuals who have accumulated a greater proportion of their wealth from investments than from any form of employment – billionaires such as Warren Buffett and George Soros. But even among the individuals interviewed by Böwing-Schmalenbrock, whose fortunes were, in the median, approximately EUR 1.4 million,[31] as many as 48% stated that real estate was an 'important' source of their wealth, and one in ten described real estate as the 'most important' aspect of their personal wealth-building. And a total of 20% described stock market gains as an 'important' factor in wealth-building, although in this case only 2.4% stated that this was the 'most important' factor in building their wealth.[32]

Böwing-Schmalenbrock's initial hypothesis therefore needs to be modified, not least in light of her own research findings, to reflect the fact that wealth is built and accumulated by individuals:

- From paid work (includes every form of paid work, i.e. employment and self-employment, and is used in direct contrast to inheritance and gifts)
- From investments
- From inheritance/gifts.

The basis of Böwing-Schmalenbrock's study was the aforementioned research project "Wealth in Germany"; initiated by Wolfgang Lauterbach at the University of Potsdam. Interviews were carried out with 472 respondents, whose wealth averaged EUR 2.3 million, with a median fortune of EUR 1.4 million.[33] This was a pioneering research project, as, "for the very first time, data was collected on a primary statistical basis, which, due to the large number of cases and the survey's contents, progressed far beyond individualized studies and employed a standardized research instrument and clear focus to survey wealthy persons and households regarding the composition and scale of their financial assets."[34]

In other words, the focus of the study was not on UHNWIs but on the 'millionaires next door'. Böwing-Schmalenbrock describes a three-tiered 'pyramid of prosperity'. At the lowest level, the determining factor is annual net income – the lower threshold here is EUR 54,320, which is 200% of the average net disposable household income in Germany. The pyramid's upper tiers are defined in terms of financial assets – here, the author distinguishes between 'fragile wealth' (total assets of at least EUR 1.2 million) and 'stable wealth' (total assets of at least EUR 2.4 million).[35]

---

25   Böwing-Schmalenbrock, *Wege zum Reichtum*, 15.

26   Ibid., 16–17.

27   Ibid., 66.

28   Ibid., 67.

29   Ibid., 67.

30   Ibid., 16.

31   Ibid., 139.

32   Ibid., 174.

33   Ibid., 139.

34   Klaus Kortmann, "Vermögen in Deutschland: Die methodischen Anlagen der Untersuchung," in *Vermögen in Deutschland: Heterogenität und Verantwortung*, edited by Wolfgang Lauterbach, Thomas Druyen, and Matthias Grundmann (Wiesbaden: Springer VS, 2011), 15.

35   Böwing-Schmalenbrock, *Wege zum Reichtum*, 45.

Böwing-Schmalenbrock defines wealth as, "income generated by a household's assets [that] at least matches the household income required to live comfortably."[36] Of course, this depends largely on assumptions made in relation to interest rates and returns on investments. Böwing-Schmalenbrock assumes a return of 4.5% per annum. According to her definition, and a target net income of EUR 54,320, she arrives at a requirement for assets worth at least EUR 1.2 million. However, a return of 4.5% per year would appear to be somewhat unrealistic. After all – depending on whether a person generates the lion's share of their income from returns on capital investments, which would be subject to withholding tax in Germany, or rental income from property, which would be assessed according to an individual's personal rate of income tax – the long-term pre-tax returns on these investments would have to average between 6 and 8.5% in order to achieve a post-tax return of 4.5%.[37] The minimum threshold for a definition of wealth must clearly be set significantly higher than the level Böwing-Schmalenbrock has stipulated.

These qualifications are, however, not intended to devalue the important contribution made by the Wealth in Germany project. Its work is groundbreaking not least because of its systematic and empirical investigation of the genesis of wealth. This laid the foundations for further work – including this book. The key findings of the Wealth in Germany study are:

1. The most important prerequisite for accumulating substantial wealth from paid work is self-employment, i.e. engaging in an activity as a freelance professional or, in particular, on an entrepreneurial basis. "Above all, entrepreneurship is a guarantee of very large wealth and assets. Enormous increases in average wealth are observed as the degree of entrepreneurship grows. Households that become rich in this way have fortunes that are, on average, EUR 2.5 million higher than households for which this factor plays no role."[38] Households where entrepreneurship has played a decisive role in the accumulation of wealth and assets are twice as likely to place in the highest level of wealth, rather than in the middle level.[39]

2. Studies have shown that employment rarely lead to wealth.[40] Inheritance certainly contributes to the genesis of wealth, although its role remains subordinate to the role of paid work. In over half of rich households, paid work played a more significant role than inheritance.

3. "As the scale of wealth increases, personality traits gain in importance while the other individual aspects become less significant."[41] The study advances two arguments to support the assumption that, as wealth increases, the relevance of an individual's personality profile becomes more relevant. "Firstly, the appropriate personality profile increases the likelihood of an individual taking a path that will lead them to higher levels of wealth. Secondly, personality becomes even more relevant once the majority of significant hurdles have been overcome – which is increasingly the case as higher levels of wealth are achieved."[42]

4. Böwing-Schmalenbrock shows that – compared to the middle classes – the rich exhibit a far greater Openness to Experience among their personality traits. Another characteristic is their lower Agreeableness.[43] She also found strong similarities between the personality traits of persons who belong to the middle class and persons who became wealthy as a result of employment. "Only the self-employed occupy a special position; the detailed personality profile presented here is particularly applicable to this group and they differ greatly from the middle strata of society, as well as from other wealthy individuals."[44]

In summary, entrepreneurship and a very specific personality structure, which differs significantly from those of other groups (setting aside transfers of wealth for the time being), are the decisive factors in the genesis of wealth. In her concluding remarks, Böwing-Schmalenbrock therefore points out the direction in which further research is required: "Substantively, there is above all a need to focus on personality traits on the one hand, and self-employment on the other, since both directly support the creation of stable wealth."[45]

One hypothesis that can be derived from Böwing-Schmalenbrock's work is this: the richer a researcher's subjects, the greater the significance of both entrepreneurship and personality traits as sources of wealth. The implication of this inference is that research into the subject of entrepreneurship is of relevance to this book, in particular to the extent that it establishes a correlation between personality traits and entrepreneurial success. This is all the more relevant here, as this book is not concerned with the genesis of wealth as such, but with the genesis of wealth among UHNWIs. In addition, and in contrast to the approach taken by Böwing-Schmalenbrock, persons who have accumulated wealth primarily as a result of inheritance are not the subject of this book.

Analyses carried out by Wolfgang Lauterbach confirm that the influence of entrepreneurship grows with the level of wealth achieved. Lauterbach compared the proportions of entrepreneurs in the middle class (median wealth of EUR 160,000),

---

36   Ibid., 45.

37   According to Böwing-Schmalenbrock, ibid., the 4.5% originated in a different study (published in 2001), which refers to estimates from the German Central Bank, although without indicating an exact source. It is probable that the figure was put forward in the 1990s – and was unrealistic even then, especially if the returns are assumed to be so stable as to generate regular and reliable income.

38   Böwing-Schmalenbrock, *Wege zum Reichtum*, 187.

39   Ibid., 199.

40   Ibid., 203.

41   Ibid., 239.

42   Ibid., 126.

43   Ibid., 238.

44   Ibid., 242.

45   Ibid., 254.

among affluents (median wealth of EUR 750,000), among high-net-worth individuals (HNWIs; median wealth of EUR 3.4 million), among the 100 richest Germans (median wealth of EUR 1.5 billion), and among the 100 richest individuals in the world (median wealth of EUR 10.5 billion). Among the affluents, 37.8% were classified as entrepreneurs; among the HNWIs, 64.6% belonged to this group; and 98% of the 100 richest Germans were entrepreneurs, as were 95.2% of the world's 100 richest individuals.[46] "Empiric evidence shows that self-employment is a necessary prerequisite for the accumulation of wealth. Wealth is hardly ever achieved as a result of dependent employment."[47] Lauterbach goes as far as to claim that "entrepreneurship is absolutely necessary for the accumulation of extraordinary wealth".[48]

Lauterbach and Tarvenkorn confirm that personality traits have a decisive role to play. "As the process of individualization in modern society increasingly dismantles the class structure, the greater becomes the importance of – alongside structural factors – personal qualities such as 'Openness to Experience' or 'Risk Propensity', for instance in the field of investments. The nature of an individual's actions – whether, for example, risk-averse or risk-seeking – is determined by his or her personality."[49]

In the United States, entrepreneurship is the subject of intensive research, as will be shown in Chapter 3, while academic wealth research in its strictest sense is still less well developed than one would perhaps expect. Over many years, the field has been dominated by normative treatises – even those produced by social scientists – that have been more polemical than enlightening in nature. Published in 1968, Ferdinand Lundberg's *The Rich and the Super-Rich* attracted a great deal of attention. Lundberg, at the time a professor of social philosophy at New York University, stated: "As to the general human type of American wealth-builder, new and old, it can be said that he is usually an extrovert, given to little reflectiveness until perhaps he approaches senility. He is more often unschooled than schooled, and unread, and has for the most part a naive view of the world and his role in it. … By his position alone he is alienated."[50] Most of the 'capitalists' that make up the *Fortune* list could easily be described as "truants from high culture".[51]

Not quite as polemical, but approaching the subject from a similar standpoint, is the book *Wealth and Democracy: A Political History of the American Rich*. The book castigates "market theology"[52] together with growing inequality and the increasing influence of the rich in the political sphere. In contrast, Chrystia Freeland's *Plutocrats: The Rise of the New Global Super-Rich and the Fall of Everyone Else* is far more informative. Freeland describes the emergence of a new global elite that is different from previous generations' plutocrats in that it is largely made up of the "working rich"[53] and very often self-made billionaires. Although Freeland is politically overtly critical of the super rich, she does state: "The bulk of their wealth is generally the fruit of hustle, intelligence and a lot of luck. … Being self-made is central to the self-image of today's global plutocrats."[54]

Very few empirical studies into the genesis of wealth have been carried out in the United States. The American sociologists Paul G. Schervish, Platon E. Coutsoukis, and Ethan Lewis conducted interviews with 130 US millionaires between 1985 and 1987, publishing them in a single volume titled *Gospels of Wealth*. They argued that in order for researchers to be able to explore the self-image of the rich, the rich themselves should first be allowed to speak without immediately facing criticism. "Conspiracy analyses are 'structural' criticisms derived from an often well-meaning yet too facile attempt to uncover the 'true' motivations and purposes which the wealthy are said to hide beneath a veil of self-serving testimony."[55] The collection contained the life stories of millionaires, told in their own words, without any intervention from the scholars or any attempt to develop hypotheses or draw conclusions in relation to the genesis of wealth.

The work of the scholar Thomas J. Stanley has been particularly widely circulated in the United States. In his book *The Millionaire Mind*, which was published in 2000, he reported in extensive detail on the findings of his research. In 1998 he interviewed 733 millionaires. Those he surveyed had an average net fortune of USD 9.2 million and a median wealth of USD 4.3 million. The average household income was reported as USD 749,000, and the median value was USD 436,000. Only 8% of those he surveyed had inherited more than 50% of their wealth, whereas 61% had never received inheritances or gifts.[56] The survey was carried out using a catalogue of 277 questions.[57]

Once again, among the working professionals, self-employment was the dominant occupational category. Of those surveyed, 32% were entrepreneurs, 16% were senior executives, 10% were attorneys, and 9% were physicians. The remainder comprised

46 Wolfgang Lauterbach, "Reiche Parallelwelten? Soziale Mobilität in Deutschland bei Wohlhabenden und Reichen," in *Reichtum, Philanthropie und Zivilgesellschaft*, edited by Wolfgang Lauterbach, Michael Hartmann, and Miriam Ströing (Wiesbaden: Springer VS, 2014), 91.

47 Ibid., 94.

48 Ibid., 92.

49 Wolfgang Lauterbach and Alexander Tarvenkorn, "Homogenität und Heterogenität von Reichen im Vergleich zur gesellschaftlichen Mitte," in *Vermögen in Deutschland: Heterogenität und Verantwortung*, edited by Wolfgang Lauterbach, Thomas Druyen, and Matthias Grundmann (Wiesbaden: Springer VS, 2011), 74.

50 Ferdinand Lundberg, *The Rich and the Super-Rich: A Study in the Power of Money Today* (New York: Lyle Stuart, 1968), 70–71.

51 Ibid., 68.

52 Kevin Philipps, *Wealth and Democracy: A Political History of the American Rich* (New York: Broadway Books, 2002), 422.

53 Chrystia Freeland, *Plutocrats: The Rise of the New Global Super-Rich and the Fall of Everyone Else* (New York: Penguin Press, 2012), 42.

54 Ibid., 45.

55 Paul G. Schervish, Platon E. Coutsoukis, and Ethan Lewis, *Gospels of Wealth: How the Rich Portray Their Lives* (Westport: Praeger Publishers, 1994), 268.

56 Thomas J. Stanley, *The Millionaire Mind* (New York: Bantam Books, 2001), 17.

57 Ibid., 16.

groups such as sales professionals, architects, professors, corporate middle managers, and housewives.[58] Those with the highest levels of net wealth were the entrepreneurs. The study's key findings were:

1. Making the right career choice plays a crucial role.[59] "After studying millionaires for more than 20 years, I have concluded that if you make one major decision correctly, you can become economically productive. If you are creative enough to select the ideal vocation, you can win, win big-time. The really brilliant millionaires are those who selected a vocation … that has few competitors but generates high profits."[60] Intelligence and education play a subordinate role in achieving financial success. Many very well-educated people, those with exceptional qualifications, make the mistake of joining major companies or large legal practices, where they have to engage in intense competition with other very highly qualified competitors. "But they forgot one thing: choice of vocation. Where you will fight is much more important in winning than what you do once the dogfight begins. Even some of the best and brightest MBA students I have ever taught lost most of their dogfights. Why not select a vocation and target where you can more easily emerge as the winner?"[61]

2. Intellectual aptitude and exceptional academic qualifications are not decisive factors in achieving financial success. The average SAT score of all millionaires was 1,190. The highest test scores were achieved, as one would expect, by attorneys and physicians, followed by entrepreneurs, who were nevertheless significantly richer than the freelance professionals.[62] An SAT score of 1,190 may well be above average, but it is nowhere near sufficient to gain admittance to one of America's top-rated colleges. In the survey, the millionaires were asked to assess the importance of a catalogue of factors for their success. Only 20% said that a high IQ or superior intellect were of major importance. Of the 30 success factors nominated by the survey's respondents, having a high IQ was ranked 21st. Only 15% said that attending a top-rated college with a high final grade had been very important, which placed this factor in 23rd place. The final spot in the ranking, 30th place, was occupied by graduation near/at top of the class. Only 11% of participants viewed this as a major factor in their financial success.[63] Notably, among the entrepreneurs, the richest group among the survey's participants, the belief that social skills are more important than superior intellect prevailed: 16% of this group viewed a high IQ or superior intellect as a key factor in their success, 12% believed that attending a top-rated college was important, and a mere 5% said graduation near/at top of the class. In comparison, 34% of attorneys (i.e. more than twice the proportion among entrepreneurs) rated a high IQ or superior intellect as a key success factor, 18% highlighted their degree from a top-rated college, and 26% of the attorneys (five times as many as among

the entrepreneurs) stated: graduation near/at top of the class. In contrast, 45% of entrepreneurs mentioned the ability to sell as being very important, while only 16% of attorneys took the same view.[64] Stanley concluded that "it would be a bad idea to try to compete in the same vocational area with the whiz kids from your school."[65] Competition with other highly intelligent individuals is much higher in professions such as law or medicine, which subsequently reduces the likelihood of exceptional financial success.

3. 'Creative intelligence' is key to financial success. The following is a comparison between the percentage of entrepreneurs (and in brackets the percentage of attorneys) who agreed that the following factors played a decisive role in their financial success: seeing opportunities others do not see: 42 (19); finding a profitable niche: 35 (14).[66]

4. A willingness to take financial risks is highly relevant in any explanation of economic success. The higher their net wealth, the greater the extent to which the survey's participants agreed with this assessment. Among the respondents with net fortunes of below USD 1 million (in addition to the 733 millionaires, a further 268 persons with wealth below this threshold were interviewed), only 18% supported this opinion; among those with a net wealth of between USD 2 million and 5 million, 28% answered in the affirmative, and, among those with net wealth of more than USD 10 million, 41% agreed. Stanley was careful to point out that this did not mean that the richer participants in his study took a reckless approach to risk. It is interesting, for instance, to note that within the group of persons with assets worth less than USD 1 million, almost half (47%) had bought a lottery ticket at some point during the preceding 12 months, whereas only 20% of those with USD 10 or more million had done the same.[67]

5. In this and other books, Stanley makes a clear distinction between those who earn large salaries but at the same time spend a lot (UAW: under-accumulator of wealth) and those who save a great deal of money and thereby accumulate a real fortune (PAW: prodigious accumulator of wealth). He demonstrates that – depending upon their approach to saving – among persons with almost

---

58   Ibid., 19.
59   Ibid., 33.
60   Ibid., 31.
61   Ibid., 32.
62   Ibid., 23.
63   Ibid., 45.
64   Ibid., 50.
65   Ibid., 71.
66   Ibid., 74.
67   Ibid., 155.

identical incomes (annual incomes of USD 730,000 respectively 715,000) the net worth of the PAWs amounted to USD 7.5 million and that of the UAWs to just USD 400,000.[68]

Beyond the sphere of scholarly research, there have been decades of popular wealth-creation literature.[69] The number of how-to books on the subject of 'getting rich' is very large indeed, but the genre can essentially be divided into two categories:

1. The titles of many how-to and popular science books promise insights into getting rich, when actually they are mainly about investing (primarily in stocks) or stock market strategies.
2. The rest of this literature tends to focus on the mental capacity required to become rich, or strategies to become rich.

The books mentioned in point 1 are not helpful in developing questions and hypotheses for this book. The findings of academic wealth research show that only 2.4% of millionaires in Germany claim that stock market profits were the major source of their wealth.[70] In the United States, stock market culture is far more prevalent than in Germany, but even there, at the height of the stock market euphoria in 1998, only 12% of those interviewed said that stock market investments were the reason for their financial success. Respondents in this American survey were allowed to select multiple responses and ranked stocks 27 out of the 30 most important factors in their success.[71]

An evaluation of the *Forbes* list of the richest Americans at the end of the 1990s concluded that not a single individual had ever made it onto the billionaires' list as a result of speculating with securities or passive stock investments.[72] Although seven Americans who owed their wealth to investments were included, these investments did not involve passive stock investments. Rather they were figures such as Carl Icahn, who specialized in hostile takeovers, buying and reselling entire companies, etc. "Even the man commonly (and with considerable justice) described as the world's greatest investor, Warren Buffett, ranks among the billionaires largely because of his corporate activism, rather than his passive investing ... While the 'Sage of Omaha' takes no direct role in the management of Berkshire Hathaway's operating companies, he sets broad strategies and closely monitors each unit's managers."[73] A glance at the list of the wealthiest Germans shows that, yes, there are entrepreneurs and inheritors, but there is nobody who built their wealth primarily by investing in the stock market.[74]

The wealth-creation guides mentioned in point 2 above focus primarily on the mental preconditions required to create wealth. From the large number of books in this category, one has been selected for extensive analysis because of its widespread influence and the impact it has had on the genre. Napoleon Hill's *Think and Grow Rich*, which has sold more than 60 million copies around the world since its publication in 1937, is the epitome of the classic self-help wealth-creation literature. Hill was born in Virginia in 1883.[75] He studied law at Georgetown University before working as a journalist. Robert L. Taylor, the then governor of Tennessee and owner of *Bob Taylor's Magazine*, was made aware of Hill's newspaper articles and commissioned him to write a series of short biographies of famous Americans. The steel magnate Andrew Carnegie was Hill's first subject. He encouraged Hill to interview the 500 most successful men in the United States and to use his findings to develop a method that would lead to success. The men Hill got to know in the course of this endeavour included Henry Ford, George Eastman, Thomas Alva Edison, Frank Winfield Woolworth, J. P. Morgan, and Harvey Firestone. Although his was not a scholarly work, some of Hill's ideas led to lines of questioning for the interviews presented here to determine whether UHNWIs ever applied the kind of mental techniques described and recommended by Hill.

Hill's most important hypothesis is: "When you begin to think and grow rich, you will observe that riches begin with a state of mind, with definiteness of purpose, with little or no hard work."[76] According to Hill, only those driven by an unquenchable desire for wealth will become rich. This puts him in contradiction with the many wealthy people who claim that wealth is more a by-product – often at least partially unintended or unavoidable – than the original driving motive of their success. Hill emphasizes, "But desiring riches with a state of mind that becomes an obsession, then planning definite ways and means to acquire riches, and backing those plans with persistence which *does not recognize failure*, will bring riches."[77]

Hill claimed that wealth can only be achieved by committing yourself, in writing, to achieving a specific financial target within a specifically defined period of time. In his book, Hill developed the steps required to become rich:[78]

---

68   Thomas J. Stanley and William D. Danko, *The Millionaire Next Door* (Atlanta: Longstreet Press, 1996), 92.

69   For many more examples, see Eker, *Secrets of the Millionaire Mind*; Fridson, *How to Be a Billionaire*; Hill, *Think and Grow Rich*; Kiyosaki and Lechter, *Rich Dad Poor Dad*; Schäfer, "Der Weg zur finanziellen Freiheit."

70   Böwing-Schmalenbrock, *Wege zum Reichtum*, 174.

71   Stanley, *The Millionaire Mind*, 45.

72   Fridson, *How to Be a Billionaire*, 14.

73   Ibid., 16.

74   See Manager-Magazin, "The 500 Richest Germans," 12 October 2015.

75   These and subsequent biographical details are from Wikipedia and from Hill, *Think and Grow Rich*, 297–298.

76   Ibid., 25.

77   Ibid., 35.

78   For the following, see ibid., 36.

1. The financial target needs to be precisely defined
2. It needs to be clear what someone intends to give in return, as well as the exact time by which they want to reach their goals
3. A plan must be produced and its implementation begun immediately
4. Everything needs to be documented, and the written goals must be read aloud every morning and every evening: "As you read—see and feel and believe yourself already in possession of the money."

According to Hill, the process of transforming a wish into a reality – such as wealth – is based on the consistent application of autosuggestion, which provides access to the subconscious mind and enables its power to be used. He emphasizes that all the other techniques recommended in his book are mere tools that enable access to the energy of the subconscious. Hill encouraged his readers to follow the above-mentioned steps, to imagine their financial goals twice a day, and to load these goals with emotion. "Your subconscious mind recognizes and acts only upon thoughts which have been well-mixed with emotion or feeling."[79] The "repetition of affirmation of orders to your subconscious mind is the only known method of voluntary development of the emotion of faith" and is the only way to anchor goals in the subconscious.[80]

Hill assumes that it is not enough to set a goal; rather, a goal needs to be anchored in the subconscious mind. He claims that the subconscious has access to more information than the conscious. If you are successful in anchoring a goal, then a way will be found to achieve this goal. Hill describes this approach: "The human mind is constantly attracting vibrations which harmonize with that which dominates the mind. Any thought, idea, plan, or purpose which one *holds* in one's mind attracts a host of its relatives, adds these 'relatives' to its own force, and grows until it becomes the dominating, motivating master of the individual in whose mind it has been housed."[81] In another passage, Hill states that the subconscious mind "receives and files sense impressions or thoughts, regardless of their nature. You may voluntarily plant in your subconscious mind any plan, thought, or purpose which you desire to translate into its physical or monetary equivalent."[82]

Hill argues that this is most effective when someone is able to visualize clearly that their financial goals have already been reached. He suggests that the subconscious can be tricked in this way. "To make this 'deceit' more realistic, conduct yourself just as you would if you were already in possession of the material thing which you are demanding when you call upon your subconscious mind."[83] Hill challenges his readers to visualize the sum of money they most desire and to imagine that they have already achieved their goal. This effort will create a tension between the inner and outer reality, which the subconscious will want to bridge sooner or later.[84]

Another of Hill's hypotheses states that every failure can be transformed into a great success and that every disadvantage can be turned into an advantage of at least equal proportions: "every failure brings with it the seed of an equivalent success".[85] According to Hill, 500 of the most successful men in the United States explained that their greatest successes often happened immediately after a failure.[86] Of course, this did not (necessarily) happen automatically. Hill suggested that it is possible to learn "the art of converting defeat into the stepping stones to opportunity".[87] The most significant realization is that "every failure brings with it the seed of an equivalent advantage".[88] Hill's book inspired an entire genre of literature on wealth creation, and established mental factors as central in the creation and accumulation of wealth.

While academic wealth research is still in its formative stages, and the question of the creation of wealth for HNWIs has tended to be the subject of popular self-help books rather than empirical scholarly examination, there is a more established tradition of elite research, one strand of which focuses on economic elites.

---

79   Ibid., 74.
80   Ibid., 52.
81   Ibid., 56.
82   Ibid., 226.
83   Ibid., 53.
84   Ibid., 76–77.
85   Ibid., 39.
86   Ibid., 21.
87   Ibid., 25.
88   Ibid., 175.

2 Defining The Wealth Elite

Whenever the term 'elite' is used in scholarly literature, make a point of stating that it has no uniform definition. "There is not much consensus among West German elite researchers," observed Wolfgang Felber in 1986. "The only characteristic that all authors have assigned to elites is, as Endruweit quite correctly stated, the quality of having been selected. An elite only includes those people who, having been subjected to a particular selection process, have proven themselves superior to other members of a social system in regard to certain characteristics ... Except for the quality of having been selected, there is no other characteristic assigned to the elite by all of the authors."[89]

In 2004, Barbara Wasner came to a similar conclusion: "With regards to the definition of the elite, there is currently only a very narrow degree of consensus between the varying elite theories. All assume that elites are comprised of individuals who have been subjected to a selection process (in whatever form). They are regarded (often positively) as a minority. Beyond these fundamental considerations, however, there is little agreement between the various theorists."[90]

In 2003, Beate Krais identified two constitutive elements of the term 'elite': the selection process based on particular personal achievement and societal recognition of this achievement as success. "The key element of this concept of membership of an elite is the personally attributable achievement, rather than a title or a privilege granted at birth. The elite is therefore comprised of those individuals who have delivered the highest level of performance according to the standards of the respective selection process." In addition, a second criterion must also be fulfilled: "the public recognition of an ... achievement, of *success*. It is therefore crucial that this is an achievement that is firstly recognized by society as meaningful and, secondly, that this is publicly praised, that it is accepted as a success."[91]

In 2004, Viktoria Kaina found that "still no consensus has been reached with regards to who belongs to a given society's elites and why an individual is counted among the elite." The "most general understanding of elites" concerns "a small number of individuals who have become grouped together via a process of selection and competition, the same process which both warrants and justifies their elevated position within society".[92]

In 2006, Armin Nassehi stated that the social science discourse surrounding the field of elite research was stuck on attempting to define "the subject's essential features". Scholars in the field were unable to rely on any consensus, or even a clear idea of the composition of elites and the best approach to researching them. "The elite discourse appears to be primarily, or at least to a large extent, concerned with first defining in conceptual terms exactly what this term could signify. There is near consensus regarding whether there are actually elites, less consensus on whether elites are actually needed, and hardly any consensus as to what distinguishes them."[93]

Two years later, Christine Kestel stated that the term 'elite' was "problematic because it is such an ambiguous term".[94] She described a "confusion of different definitions all attempting to come to terms with reality,"[95] and affirmed: "It is, however, possible to arrive at a lowest common denominator, to formulate the core concept of the term elite, which at least *also* means that an elite is a social subject that emerges as the product of a selection process and then becomes visible to others as a minority exerting a certain influence on societal developments." She conceded, however, that this was "a lowest common denominator defined in extremely vague terms".[96]

As demonstrated above, scholars have repeatedly found that there is hardly any consensus regarding a definition of 'elite'. This applies to research carried out in the United States as much as in Germany. The American sociologist Shamus Rahman Khan stated in 2012 that defining the term 'elite' is no easy task as, "scholars in this area rarely define their term, and thus there is little agreement on (or even discussion about) a definition". Khan himself provides a general definition of elites as "those who have vastly disproportionate control over or access to a resource".[97]

In 2006, Herfried Münkler, Grit Straßenberger, and Matthias Bohlender observed that the problem of providing a definition starts with the "dual meaning" of the term 'elite': "It is both a social-analytic and a political-polemic category.

---

89   W. Felber, *Eliteforschung in der Bundesrepublik Deutschland* (Wiesbaden: Springer Fachmedien, 1986), 19.

90   Barbara Wasner, *Eliten in Europa: Einführung in Theorien, Konzepte und Befunde* (Wiesbaden: Springer Fachmedien, 2006), 16.

91   Beate Krais, "Begriffliche und theoretische Zugänge zu den 'oberen Rängen' der Gesellschaft," in *Oberschichten – Eliten – Herrschende Klassen*, edited by Stefan Hradil and Peter Imbusch (Wiesbaden: Springer Fachmedien,, 2003), 38.

92   Viktoria Kaina, "Deutschlands Eliten zwischen Kontinuität und Wandel. Empirische Befunde zu Rekrutierungswegen, Karrierepfaden und Kommunikationsmustern," *Aus Politik und Zeitgeschichte B* 10 (2004), 8.

93   Armin Nassehi, "Differenzierungseliten in der 'Gesellschaft der Gegenwarten," in *Deutschlands Eliten im Wandel*, edited by Herfried Münkler, Grit Straßenberger, and Matthias Bohlender (Frankfurt-am-Main: Campus Verlag, 2006), 255.

94   Christine Kestel, "Über Elite: Form und Funktion von Elite-Kommunikation in der Gesellschaft der Gegenwarten" (PhD diss., Ludwig-Maximilians-Universität Munich, 2008), 16.

95   Ibid., 24.

96   Ibid., 45.

97   Shamus Rahman Khan, "The Sociology of Elites," *Annual Review of Sociology* 38 (2012), 362.

Its use is principally liable to ambiguity due to the desire to either define elite normatively or describe it assertively."[98] In this book the term is used as a social-analytic descriptive term and not as a normative term.

Felber proposed a further distinction concerning the term 'elite', differentiating between whether the assignment to an elite is made on the basis of subjective or objective characteristics. "'Subjective' criteria are those that focus on the facts of consciousness; accordingly, the individuals who belong to an elite are those that are believed to belong to the elite. In contrast, 'objective' criteria relate to characteristics that exist independently of the consciousness of those involved; the individuals who belong to the elite belong because they possess these characteristics, irrespective of whether those involved are conscious of this fact or not."[99] In this book, the term 'wealth elite' is used objectively – namely, irrespective of whether the individuals who belong to the elite would describe themselves as belonging to the elite or not. Whether someone perceives themselves as being a member of an elite is, therefore, not a determining factor in whether they are identified as belonging to an elite.

The functionalist approach dominates in contemporary research. This approach dispenses with the concept of a single, unified elite, instead identifying a number of competing functional elites. In modern societies "there is no longer one pyramid with one apex but a number of pyramids, each with its own elite at the top".[100] These social spheres include, for example, the political, the economic, the scientific, the religious, and the cultural elites. The 1995 Potsdam Elite Study distinguished between functional elites in the major spheres of politics, public administration, business and the economy, trade associations, unions, mass media, science, the military, and culture.[101]

2.1. WHO ARE THE ECONOMIC ELITE?

As early as 1962, Ralf Dahrendorf pointed to the ambiguity of the terms 'elites' and 'ruling groups'. In reality, he observed, the upper stratum of every society comprises a "minimum of three aggregates or quasi-groups":[102]
- The upper status group
- The economic upper class
- The ruling class or power elite.

"The most decisive criterion for belonging to the economic upper class is not economic power; rather it is the assets or income associated with a particular rank or position within society. One could say that this refers to the highest tax bracket – except that the opportunities of legal, quasi-legal and illegal tax evasion make this definition too imprecise."[103] Apart from the fact that there is no such thing as legal tax evasion (tax evasion is always illegal; perhaps Dahrendorf meant to refer to legal tax-avoidance schemes, which are largely irrelevant in Germany today), his use of the term is simply too broad to serve as a workable definition of the functional elite in the economic sphere.

However, Dahrendorf is correct in his assertion that the exercise of power should not necessarily be regarded as constitutive in defining the economic elite. In effect, he states that those who belong to the economic elite *may* be in a position to exercise power – whether at a national or a municipal level – as a result of belonging to this elite. According to this approach, however, the exercise of power is not a constitutive characteristic of membership in the elite.

This approach differs from other approaches (see below) that view the exercise of power as an essential prerequisite for membership in an elite. Whereas Dahrendorf defines the term very broadly, encompassing a not insubstantial section of society (today this would include everyone in Germany subjected to an income tax rate of 45%), other authors are too restrictive and narrow in defining the term 'economic elite', asserting that the potential to exert political influence is the determining characteristic of membership.

The 1995 Potsdam Elite Study defined the elite in terms of the "extent to which they exert a decisive influence on key decision-making processes that relate to society as a whole".[104] What is meant by 'society as a whole' remains unclear. Is influence on political decisions taken at a national level a necessary precondition of membership in the elite, or is it enough, for example, to be in a position to exert influence on key decisions taken at the municipal level of a major metropolis?

The Potsdam Elite Study defined company size (measured by turnover) as most important selection criterion for top position holders within the economy.[105] The study primarily focused on the management boards (and to some extent the supervisory boards) of major companies and banks.[106] As a result, the term 'economic elite' was largely restricted to salaried executives. Entrepreneurs, who represent a key cadre of the economic elite, were – along with investors – largely excluded, as the management boards of major companies typically consist of salaried executives rather than entrepreneurs.

---

98   Herfried Münkler, Grit Straßenberger, and Matthias Bohlender, "Einleitung," in *Dies: Deutschlands Eliten im Wandel* (Frankfurt-am-Main: Campus Verlag, 2006), 13.

99   Felber, *Eliteforschung*, 20.

100   Michael Hartmann, *The Sociology of Elites* (New York: Routledge, 2006), 105.

101   Bürklin, *Einleitung*, Wilhelm Bürklin et al, Eliten in Deutschland. Rekrutierung und Integration, Wiesbaden 1997, 17.

102   Ralf Dahrendorf, "Eine neue deutsche Oberschicht?" *Die neue Gesellschaft* 9 (1962), 18.

103   Ibid., 19.

104   Jörg Machatzke, "Die Potsdamer Elitestudie: Positionsauswahl und Ausschöpfung," in *Eliten in Deutschland: Rekrutierung und Integration*, edited by Wilhelm Bürklin, and Hilke Rebenstorf (Wiesbaden: Springer Fachmedien, 1997), 35.

105   Ibid., 43.

106   Ibid., 44–45.

Applying Dahrendorf's 'wealth and income' criteria, the group of salaried executives (members of the management boards of large corporations) is only a small minority of the economic upper class, which does not even include the highest net worth individuals. As the findings of academic wealth researchers demonstrate, a majority of UHNWIs are entrepreneurs rather than salaried executives. As shown above, the higher the level of wealth, the more evident this becomes.

When income rather than wealth is considered, management board members in major companies (who constitute a large percentage of respondents in traditional elite studies) actually represent an atypical minority of those in the highest income bracket. In 2011, 16,341 individuals in Germany declared a taxable income of more than EUR 1 million.[107] Salaried executives can only achieve such incomes when they are on the management boards of leading companies – examples include the board members of DAX companies (i.e. the index of the 30 largest companies listed on Germany's stock market), who earned an average of EUR 5.86 million in 2015.[108] A majority of MDAX (Germany's second major stock index, for the next 50 largest companies) board members are also income millionaires.[109] Nevertheless, as only 80 companies are listed on the DAX and MDAX, the number of income millionaires is only in the triple-digit range.

The Potsdam Elite Study was a comprehensive survey and its respondents included 539 members of the management boards of major companies and 338 top position holders within large financial institutions.[110] Among these were executive board members from leading companies, many of whom were income millionaires. Income and wealth were not applied as selection criteria for the study; rather these 877 persons were characterized by the fact that they occupied leadership positions within large commercial enterprises. Even if all of these individuals qualified as income millionaires – which is not the case – they would still only represent a minority of some 5% of all income millionaires in Germany. There are no statistics concerning the professions of income millionaires, but every indication is that a large majority of income millionaires are entrepreneurs rather than salaried executives in leadership positions within large commercial enterprises. There are many entrepreneurs in small and medium-sized enterprises with incomes (especially dividends) that far exceed the total remuneration (salary plus bonus) paid to major companies' executive board members. The highest level of the upper class, as defined by Dahrendorf's 'wealth/income' criterion, is equally excluded when the scope of research is exclusively limited to executive board members of major companies.

It therefore makes sense to consider the economic elite in terms of two subcategories, the second category of which is the subject of this book:

1. Top position holders in large companies who, in all likelihood, can exert influence on political decisions at a national level because of their positions and the size of their companies. This group is largely composed of salaried executives.

These are traditionally the focus of most studies of the economic elite, such as those by Bourdieu, Hartmann, and the Potsdam Elite Study.

2. The wealth elite, i.e. those who are at the apex of the wealth pyramid but who are not necessarily able to exert political influence at a national level. In a majority of cases, this group is composed of entrepreneurs and investors.

Academic wealth research focuses on the latter group. Is the term 'elite' even applicable in this context? If exerting a decisive influence on key societal decisions is viewed as a fundamental criterion, as was the case for the authors of the Potsdam Elite Study, certainly not. This book, however, follows the approach adopted by Dahrendorf, who correctly ignored power as a criterion in his definition of the term 'economic elite', preferring to employ wealth and income as a defining characteristic of membership of the economic elite instead.

Employing the other definitions of the term 'elite', as cited above, the wealth elite, as defined here, is unquestionably an elite. UHNWIs have achieved their status by passing through an economic selection process. The individuals comprising this group represent an elite because "their performance in a defined selection process was superior in relation to specific characteristics than the performance of all other members of the social system".[111] The specific characteristic is wealth, and the selection process is the market. This is at least the case for the large group of self-made UHNWIs among the subjects of this book. This is also the case, at least in part, for those who have inherited their fortunes. Maintaining (and especially increasing) an inherited fortune represents a significant economic achievement in itself. The above definition from Rahman ("those who have vastly dispropor-tionate control over or access to a resource"[112]) applies equally to the wealth elite. The resource, in this case, is wealth.

The process by which the wealth elite are selected is very different from the selection process by which an individual rises to a leadership position within a large company. Whereas a leadership position within a large company is normally regarded as the culmination of a career within the company, the economic selection

---

107 Statista, "Anzahl der Einkommensteuerpflichtigen mit mindestens einer Million Euro Einkünften in Deutschland von 2004 bis 2013," last modified 2017, https://de.statista.com/statistik/daten/studie/162287/umfrage/einkommensmillion-aere-in-deutschland. In 2011, 12,374 persons earned between EUR 1 million and 2.5 million, 2,567 earned between EUR 2.5 million and 5 million, and 1,400 earned more than EUR 5 million.

108 "Auf den nachfolgenden Seiten erhalten Sie folgende Vergütungsinformationen auf Basis der Geschäftsberichte 2014 bzw. 2015," accessed 27 October 2017, http://www.hkp.com/cms/upload/press/20160330_Pressegespraech_DAX_GB-Auswertung_2015_Tabellen.pdf

109 "Die Top-Verdiener im MDax," last modified 15 May 2014, http://www.wiwo.de/finanzen/boerse/vorstandsvergue-tung-die-top-verdiener-im-mdax/9897550.html.

110 Machatzke, "Die Potsdamer Elitestudie," 44–46.

111 Felber, Eliteforschung, 19.

112 Khan, "The Sociology of Elites," 362.

process for the wealth elite follows entirely different rules. What counts is the actual economic achievement, including founding and successfully establishing a (typically small or medium-sized) enterprise, or the profitability of investment activity, such as in the real estate market.

How broadly should the term 'wealth elite' be defined? In this book, the term is used in reference to persons with a net worth of at least EUR 10 million.[113] This group is, admittedly, heterogeneous, encompassing HNWIs with net fortunes of EUR 10 million and individuals with fortunes in the billions of euros, with very different financial resources, lifestyles, and political influence. However, what the members of this group do have in common is that they do not have to work in order to make a living – although a significant majority of the members of this group choose to do so.

When invested at a net interest rate of 3% per annum, EUR 10 million generates a monthly income of EUR 25,000. Consuming this capital in its entirety over a 40-year period would allow an annual expenditure of EUR 250,000. The possibilities available to such individuals are therefore fundamentally different from those available to the "millionaire next door",[114] who does not belong to the wealth elite, as the income from the assumed 3% interest per annum only amounts to EUR 2,500 per month, which falls far short of fulfilling the lifestyle expectations of a member of the wealth elite.

Members of the wealth elite are objectively characterized by a high degree of financial freedom beyond the means of the "millionaire next door". On a subjective level, many members of the wealth elite also define themselves by the fact that the income generated by their fortunes relieves them of any economic necessity to pursue paid work and allows them to enjoy a high standard of living.

2.2. THE ROLE OF HABITUS FOR ADVANCING INTO THE ECONOMIC ELITE

Limiting the scope of the term 'economic elite' to the senior executives of major corporations has far-reaching consequences, particularly with regards to the findings that relate to an elite's recruitment mechanisms and to social mobility. The factors that will enable a person to rise to join the ranks of the economic elite are largely dependent upon the exact definition of that term. If the scope of the term is drawn to primarily include the senior executives of major corporations, then the elite's recruitment mechanisms will differ significantly from those employed by the wealth elite as defined above.

One key focus of the work of Pierre Bourdieu is the reproduction mechanisms employed by the ruling class.[115] In addition to formal educational qualifications, Bourdieu identifies 'habitus', above all, as playing a key role. He defines habitus as "a socially constituted system of structured and structuring dispositions, acquired in practice and constantly aimed at practical functions".[116] This includes an individual's style of dress, the hobbies and leisure activities they favour, their mode of speech, the social circles in which they move, the sports they practice, the general knowledge they possess, and, ultimately, the self-confidence they exhibit.

Differences in habitus, according to Bourdieu, demarcate the various classes within a society. "Each class condition is defined … by everything which distinguishes it from what it is not and especially from everything it is opposed to; social identity is defined and asserted through difference. This means that inevitably inscribed within the dispositions of the habitus is the whole structure of the system of conditions, as it presents itself in the experience of a life-condition occupying a particular position within that structure."[117]

According to Bourdieu, there are two forms in which history is objectified or embodied: objectivity in institutions and objectivity in the human organism, i.e. habitus.[118] Habitus is assigned a particularly central importance: individuals are born into specific class groups within society and, from childhood onwards, learn particular behaviours and, from their parents and social environments, assimilate modes of comporting and articulating themselves, and develop specific taste preferences. These behaviours and preferences combine to create a lifestyle in keeping with their specific class group and the group's individual members, and to differentiate their class group from other social strata. "Taste, the propensity and capacity to appropriate (materially or symbolically) a given class of classified, classifying objects or practices, is the generative formula of life-style, a unitary set of distinctive preferences which express the same expressive intention in the specific logic of each of the symbolic sub-spaces, furniture, clothing, language or body hexis."[119]

For Bourdieu and the theorists who followed him, habitus functions, above all, as a key mechanism in the reproduction of elite structures: whoever has, as a result of their socialization, internalized the habitus of the elite, has, from the outset, a decisive advantage over those who have not been socialized in this way. "The individual's past, which has shaped and informed their habitus, continues to exert an influence as habitus by producing orientations, attitudes, and modes of action which lead the individuals back to the social spaces determined by their social class. They remain in their class group and reproduce their class group in their practices."[120]

---

113   See Section 7.2 for a more detailed explanation.

114   Stanley and Danko, *The Millionaire Next Door.*

115   Regarding this and the following see Pierre Bourdieu, *Distinction: A Social Critique of the Judgement of Taste* (Abingdon: Routledge, 2010); Hartmann, *The Sociology of Elites,* 46–54.

116   Bourdieu and Wacquant quoted in Hartmann, *The Sociology of Elites,* 115.

117   Bourdieu, *Distinction,* 171–172.

118   Beate Krais and Gunter Gebauer, *Habitus* (Bielefeld: Transcript Verlag, 2016), 34.

119   Bourdieu, *Distinction,* 169.

120   Krais and Gebauer, *Habitus,* 34.

For his empirical research, Bourdieu developed a questionnaire in which, for example, he asked respondents about the furniture they owned; the hobbies they pursued; their favourite musicians, singers, writers, artists, and films; their taste in clothing; and the food they served to guests.[121] The totality of these preferences defines the lifestyles that distinguish the classes and groups within a society from one another.

Michael Hartmann placed particular emphasis on the relevance of habitus in relation to the recruitment of elites in Germany. He found that major corporations in Germany used four key personality traits to identify their desired habitus:[122]

- Intimate knowledge of required codes of dress and etiquette
- Broad-based general education
- An entrepreneurial attitude, including an optimistic outlook on life
- Supreme self-assurance in appearance and manner.

Upwardly mobile social climbers, in Hartmann's view, very often exhibit a lack of the necessary, or at least desired, confidence in their bearing and behaviour, and at the same time lack the ability to skilfully question the official canon and dominating behavioural codes, or to simply break them should the situation arise. This self-assurance, which includes a playful attitude to established rules and codes, constitutes "the central difference between those who belong and those who would only like to belong".[123]

Hartmann points to the – subconscious – selection mechanisms in which habitus plays a key role to explain why the members of the economic elite are primarily recruited from among the bourgeoisie and grand bourgeoisie. He identifies a key quality that is essential for any prospective appointee to the executive board or senior management of a major company: habitual similarities to those who already occupy such positions. "Since decisions bearing on top positions in large corporations are made by a very small circle of people, and since the procedure involved is not particularly formalized, the key factor here is similarity with the so-called 'decision makers', i.e. to seem to be 'cut from the same cloth'. These decisions are based far less on rational criteria than is generally assumed."[124]

In order to support his line of argument, Hartmann examined the career prospects of the group with the highest educational qualification, a PhD. He reasoned that, if it is only through variations in qualifications that social background plays a role in an individual's ascent to the ranks of the elite, then limiting his research to those with identical qualifications should neutralize this factor. As he himself proved, this is, however, not the case: "Of those from the working class or middle class who obtained a PhD ... only 9.3%, i.e. approximately one in eleven, managed to reach the top level of senior management. Among those from the upper social echelons, the proportion rises to 13.1%, which means that one in eight succeeded, and those hailing from the grand bourgeoisie have a one-in-four chance of making it to the highest strata of the German economy."[125]

Hartmann examined the social backgrounds, educations, and career paths of those individuals who had obtained a PhD in the fields of engineering, law, or economics in the years 1955, 1965, 1975, or 1985 and gone on to work in business, politics, the legal professions, or academia. Hartmann limited his study to these three subject areas (i.e. engineering, law, and economics) because, as he pointed out, 90% of Germany's executives had studied one of these three subjects, and the same subject areas also dominated in the fields of politics and public administration. In the business world, nearly half of all top-level executives with PhDs held this qualification in one of these three subjects.[126]

Hartmann's study found that there is a very strong correlation between social background and appointments to executive management positions within the German economy. Social selection was shown to function not only on the basis of the unequal educational opportunities of the different social classes and groups but also in a very direct way. "Although each of the PhD graduates included in the study had gained the highest, and at the same time most socially selective, qualification, their career chances in Germany's business world, and thereby their prospects of attaining a position within the German economic elite, were distributed unequally according to their social background. Despite the intense selection process they had already undergone in attaining their doctorates, they were then subjected to a further social selection process, entirely independent of their academic qualifications, as they sought leadership positions within Germany's largest companies."[127]

Following Bourdieu, Hartmann argues that the habitus developed within social milieus makes a key difference. "At the highest levels of society, people are simply 'more self-assured' because of their intimate familiarity with the terrain from childhood onwards. In place of this confidence, individuals who have reached adulthood within the ranks of the broader social classes exhibit a degree of 'unsteadiness', which arises from their lack of knowledge or familiarity with the milieus of the economic elite."[128]

These findings are indeed convincing – for the group examined by Hartmann. The fundamental weakness of his approach, however, lies in his one-sided definition of the economic elite. Hartmann's broader definition of the economic elite

---

121 Bourdieu, *Distinction*, 513 et seq.

122 Hartmann, *The Sociology of Elites*, 82.

123 Ibid., 82.

124 Ibid., 81.

125 Michael Hartmann, *Der Mythos von den Leistungseliten: Spitzenkarrieren und soziale Herkunft in Wirtschaft, Politik, Justiz und Wissenschaft* (Frankfurt-am-Main: Campus Verlag, 2002), 65.

126 Ibid., 23.

127 Ibid., 71.

128 Ibid., 168.

includes all of those who occupy executive management positions in one of Germany's major companies. He then goes on to define the economic elite in narrower terms as those who occupy the highest management positions in world-class corporations.[129] The higher an individual's position within the economy, the greater the weighted importance of an individual's social background, Hartmann concluded. His hypothesis regarding the crucial importance of social selection applied in particular to the upper echelons of executive management within large corporations.[130]

This means, however, that Hartmann's study was explicitly limited to salaried executives within large corporations. Self-employed entrepreneurs, who often earn far more than executives, were largely ignored by the study, except for those owners of large companies who also occupied formal senior management positions within their own companies. However, this is only true for a very small number of the major corporations included in Hartmann's study.

There is much evidence to support the view that social mobility occurs to a far greater extent within the field of entrepreneurship than is the case among the board members of major German companies. Hartmann argued that social selection exerts a greater influence in the world of business than is the case in other elite segments. He explained this difference as follows: "The children of the grand bourgeoisie" prioritize positions within the business world over those in legal professions or politics because they are "generally drawn to positions promising the greatest power and the highest incomes".[131] Whether it is true that leadership positions within the world of commerce really do offer a greater degree of power than equivalent positions within the political sphere is open to debate. That this pathway offers greater earning potential is, however, an inarguable fact. What Hartmann, nevertheless, fails to consider is that, in many cases, entrepreneurs earn far more than salaried executives, even those at the highest levels. Those who desire wealth, as has been repeatedly demonstrated by the findings of the academic wealth-research studies outlined above, only have a minimal chance of achieving their goals as employees. The overwhelming majority of the wealthy and high-income earners are entrepreneurs, mainly owners of small and medium-sized enterprises.

The findings of Hartmann's study are clearly plausible with regard to elite recruitment within major companies. Admittance to the highest echelons of management is the crowning achievement of a decades-long career and is ultimately decided by the individuals who comprise a company's supervisory board. In this respect, a strongly subjective factor does indeed play a major role, as Hartmann and other scholars who emphasize the importance of habitus rightly point out.

However, the selection process for the wealth elite is quite different – the interviews presented in Part B of this book demonstrate just how different. One extreme example concerns an interviewee who experienced significant difficulties when learning to read and write and struggled to complete basic secondary education.

This did not stop him from amassing a fortune worth several hundred million euros, although it would certainly have proved an obstacle to gaining a seat on the board of one of Germany's major corporations. Section 9.1 will provide a detailed examination of the social recruitment mechanisms of the wealth elite.

As this study demonstrates, many entrepreneurs and ultra-wealthy individuals come from the middle classes. Many of the personality traits exhibited by entrepreneurs would not be especially conducive to pursuing a career within a major corporation. Whereas, for instance, a willingness to conform is seen as a positive characteristic in any individual's ascent to a company's top management, entrepreneurs are often nonconformists and have, in many cases, pursued self-employment precisely because they recognized that their personalities or formal educational qualifications would make it impossible for them to achieve a successful career or ascend to the executive management of a large corporation (for more on this, see Section 10.1). There is much evidence to support the assumption that someone like Steve Jobs would never have been able to enjoy a successful career within the rigidly prescribed structures of a major company, because his patterns of behaviour would not be compatible with the requirements associated with an appointment to an executive board.[132] He was forced to establish his own company in order to make his mark on the world and achieve success.

The selection mechanisms employed by companies when making appointments to their executive boards and the selection mechanisms acting on company founders are of an entirely different nature. Whether or not an individual succeeds in advancing to the ranks of the wealth elite is not decided by the benevolence of a committee or the goodwill of a mentor; it is decided by the market. And whether or not, for example, a real estate investor attains wealth is equally independent of any boardroom decisions – it is the result of whether they have made intelligent investment decisions or not. This suggests that habitus and formal educational qualifications play a more subordinate role in an individual's ascent to the ranks of the wealth elite than they do in an individual's rise to the upper echelons of management within a large corporation.

This clearly demonstrates the consequences of a too-narrow definition of the term 'economic elite' to encompass only the highest position holders in major companies. Studies that are limited to the totality of these individuals (executive board members of major companies), while largely excluding entrepreneurs and successful investors as well as the wealth elite as a whole, produce findings that

---

129   Ibid., 63.

130   Ibid., 87.

131   Ibid., 174.

132   For more on the behaviour patterns of Steve Jobs, see Jeffrey S. Young and William L. Simon, *iCon Steve Jobs: The Greatest Second Act in the History of Business* (New Jersey: John Wiley & Sons, 2005), 77, 184–185, 235–236.

are skewed in a single direction (solely reflecting the realities of a single subgroup) in relation to the reproduction mechanisms employed by the economic elite.

The following chapter will present the findings of entrepreneurship research – a discipline that, unlike traditional elite research, does not concern itself with the top executives of world-class large corporations, but instead considers the specific factors for entrepreneurial success. As entrepreneurs are the most significant group among the wealthy, it is certainly well worth devoting attention to entrepreneurship research.

Review of Entrepreneurship Research

3

3.1. SOMBART, SCHUMPETER, AND KIRZNER ON THE ROLE OF THE ENTREPRENEUR

Werner Sombart was one of the first scholars to consider the entrepreneur as a type with a particular focus on psychological aspects. In his work *The Quintessence of Capitalism: A Study of the History and Psychology of the Modern Business Man* (1913), he distinguished three 'mental traits' that he considered important for a successful entrepreneur:

1. The 'conqueror'. The entrepreneur has to have the ability to make plans and a strong will to carry them out. In Sombart's definition, this distinguishes him from a mere inventor, who is satisfied with having made a discovery. The entrepreneur also has to have the capacity to carry his scheme through and the diligent application not to turn away from his goal. His characteristics also include having the "determination and strength to break down any obstacle that stands in his way. But he must be a conqueror also in his ability to take high risks and to stake his all in order to achieve greatly."[133]
2. The 'organizer'. The entrepreneur has to have the ability to bring large numbers of people together into a happy, successful creative force.[134]
3. The 'trader'. What Sombart describes as a 'trader', we would more likely call a talented salesperson today. The entrepreneur has to "confer with another, and, by making the best of your own case and demonstrating the weakness of his, get him to adopt what you propose. Negotiation is but an intellectual sparring match."[135] This ability is always required, be it in order to attract good employees, sell products, or prove your negotiating talent, as the steel magnate Andrew Carnegie did

---

133   Werner Sombart, *The Quintessence of Capitalism: A Study of the History and Psychology of the Modern Business Man* (London: T. Fisher Unwin, Ltd., 1915), 52–53.

134   Ibid., 53.

135   Ibid., 54.

when he was consulting with the banker J. P. Morgan about a billion-dollar buyout. The core of the matter, Sombart argues, is always to convince the buyer of the advantages of the contract.[136] "To arouse interest, to win confidence, to stir up the desire to purchase … How he reaches it is immaterial, so long as he does reach it by any method except the appeal to force. He must make the other party eager to complete the bargain. The trader must work by suggestion."[137]

The entrepreneur has to have a predisposition for instinctively right and apt actions. These types of aptitudes are evident in some people; in others they are absent or very weak.[138] The natural entrepreneur is quick to understand, sure of their judgement of other people, and rich in ideas, inspiration, and a certain kind of "vivid imagination".[139] The entrepreneurial undertaking has to "be something demanding in its nature, something that makes a lazy pause on the oven bench a torment". The most important characteristics for an entrepreneur are determination, persistence, perseverance, restlessness, purposefulness, boldness, and daring.[140] Sombart mentions a comparison frequently drawn between entrepreneurs and artists, which he regards as misleading. The entrepreneur "works towards a goal; to the artist an end in view is an abomination. The former is dominated by his intellect, the latter by his emotions. The former is hard where the latter is delicate and tender. The undertaker is practical and businesslike, the artist is the most impractical and unbusinesslike fellow in the world. The undertaker's eyes look without to the macrocosm beyond, the artist's gaze is fixed on the microcosm within."[141]

Regardless of his personal views on the matter, the entrepreneur's most important intrinsic motivation is the pursuit of profit – because it is the essential necessity of his action. "In the soul of the modern business man there is a desire to achieve bigger and bigger things, and this forces him to be constantly undertaking more and more. But why? Principally because he wants more profit. Not that profit-chasing is the chiefest motive in his soul. The condition of things forces profit-chasing upon him. All successful capitalist enterprises must necessarily work to provide a surplus. It matters not how the individual capitalist regards the surplus – whether he contents himself with the mere acquisition of gold, or whether he aims at power, or is satisfied as long as he is occupied, or even desires to utilize the surplus in schemes for social reform. In any event, he must make a profit; his enterprise must be gainful."[142]

In his work *Der Moderne Kapitalismus*, Sombart emphasizes the importance of the role of the individual, which plays a much greater role in capitalism than in earlier economic systems. "In the beginning, [is] the 'creative act' of the individual; a 'daring', 'entrepreneurial' man, who courageously decides to leave the well-worn path of traditional economic management and strike a new way … The genesis of capitalism is a history of personalities."[143]

The inner structure of the capitalist economic system implies "that the power of decision and action of a few is given more freedom than in other economic systems.

Therefore you can say that the very capitalist economy grew to its entire form from the creative initiative of the few."[144] It would be a great mistake to assume that the importance of human personality has diminished in the 'mechanized world'. "The exact opposite is the case: the importance of the individual, admittedly an outstanding one, is greater today in economic life than ever before."[145] This is why, especially in the United States, personalities are highly regarded in economic life: "not the companies, not the families, not the capital, but at last the individual is the driving force in the economy".[146]

In some respects, the following statements by Sombart are reminiscent of Schumpeter. "What differentiates the capitalist from the feudal entrepreneur is this: he acts much more subversively and transformatively." The capitalist entrepreneur breaks with old traditions; he pushes through the barriers of the old economy; "he is a destroyer and creator in one". He yanks entire populations from their habitual forms of existence. "Even when history does not confirm this: our insight into the essence of human nature would lead us to conclude: such different thinkers, such innovators, such disruptors, such creators were always only individuals, were always only a few."[147]

Sombart describes the psychological disposition of the entrepreneur as follows: the "will to succeed, that means: the efforts to reach great economic success: a sentiment that, for example, is typical for all Americans, from the trust magnates all the way to the lowest errand boys".[148] The new type of entrepreneur is "free from concern for family tradition, for commerce, for business customs".[149] Sombart strongly disagrees with Max Weber's theory of the Protestant roots of capitalism and emphasizes that the modern entrepreneur is characterized by the fact that he, "with few exceptions, is freed from the very tedious obligations to religion and morality anchored in religion." It is only this secularization of the capitalist soul "that gives all of the demons of passion free rein".[150]

---

136 Ibid., 54–55.

137 Ibid., 55.

138 Ibid., 201.

139 Ibid., 204.

140 Ibid., 203.

141 Ibid., 204.

142 Ibid., 347–348. Similar to Werner Sombart, *Der moderne Kapitalismus, Vol. 3: Die vorkapitalistische Wirtschaft,* second half-volume (Munich: Duncker & Humblot, 1927), 36–37: "I have denoted this mediatization of the subjective purpose of the capitalist entrepreneur in the capitalist enterprise as the objectification of the striving for profit."

143 Werner Sombart, *Der moderne Kapitalismus, Vol. 1: Die vorkapitalistische Wirtschaft* (Munich: Duncker & Humblot, 1916), 836.

144 Sombart, *Der moderne Kapitalismus,* Vol. 3, 12.

145 Ibid., 40.

146 Ibid., 41.

147 Sombart, *Der moderne Kapitalismus,* Vol. 1, 837.

148 Sombart, *Der moderne Kapitalismus,* Vol. 3, 27.

149 Ibid., 29.

150 Ibid., 30.

Sombart's greatest achievement was to shift the focus onto the entrepreneur's personality, whose importance he repeatedly emphasized. In particular, he recognized the important role played by sales skills in the entrepreneur's success – an aspect far too often neglected by later generations of scholars.

In his 1911 work *The Theory of Economic Development*,[151] Joseph Schumpeter extensively dealt with the psychology of the entrepreneur. Of central importance is the insight that entrepreneurs do not let social norms govern their actions to the same extent as others do. Although he did not use this specific term, Schumpeter essentially characterized successful entrepreneurs as nonconformists.

"Any deviating conduct by a member of a social group is condemned," says Schumpeter. This condemnation could lead to 'social ostracism'".[152] This is why the majority conforms, but there will always be other individuals who are incited by the shocked reactions of those around them and who "for this very reason behave with disregard for social norms".[153]

The person who wants to do something "new and unusual" not only has to reckon with external resistance "but also to overcome his own ingrained resistance".[154] The type of entrepreneur described by Schumpeter swims "against the stream".[155] In contrast to hedonistic, passive people, this type of entrepreneur struggles "against those 'bonds', a struggle to which not all are suited".[156] "The fact that something has not yet been done is irrelevant to him as a counterargument. He does not feel the inhibitions which otherwise constrain the behaviour of economic agents."[157]

This type "draws other conclusions from the data of the world around him than those drawn by the mass of static economic agents".[158] This entrepreneurial type is "quite indifferent ... to what his peers and superiors would have to say about his business".[159]

Schumpeter asks what drives an entrepreneur to act in this way. He firmly challenges the assumption "that striving for the satisfaction of desires in the form of the consumption of goods" is the primary economic drive of enterprise.[160] Even when the entrepreneur has already amassed significant capital, he dedicates all his energy to acquiring even greater amounts of goods. Given the fact that above a certain income level – which differs from individual to individual – "the intensity of these as yet unfulfilled desires loses its potency", consumption in itself is not a strong enough goal to explain the actions of the entrepreneur.[161]

Schumpeter proves that mere consumerism cannot be the entrepreneur's primary driving force. Although entrepreneurs live in luxury, this is not what motivates their ambition.[162] Whether consciously or unconsciously, these people are driven by two motives: the joy of having a powerful position in society and the joy of the creative process.[163] Schumpeter does not deny that the desire to satisfy certain consumption desires can drive the entrepreneur. "On some occasions we will recognize the desire to satisfy wants, while on others we will recognize social power as the motive. To a certain extent, of course, both motives must act together.

It is also the case that every millionaire, should he lose his millions, would first work towards satisfying basic wants."[164] However, Schumpeter argues that economics has so far underestimated the motive of striving for power.

Schumpeter makes a key observation, namely that the entrepreneur sees the goods he acquires (essentially, financial means) "as an outward sign of hard-fought victories" and that the wealth achieved as a result of his economic striving "can be its own reward".[165] The gains that he makes are "largely not consumed, rather they are reinvested in new economic ventures".[166] The entrepreneur is driven "to experiment and to place his mark on the economic sphere".[167] In contrast, the great masses have no such inclination "to experiment with innovations" as is characteristic of the entrepreneur.[168]

According to Schumpeter, weak people labour through completing conventional and repetitive tasks. "The strong retain a power surplus – he seeks to bring about change for change's sake, always carrying out new plan after new plan, ad infinitum. In contrast, the activity as such becomes an end in and of itself, without the need for any further impulse: The joy of doing, without any other motive, is certainly a psychological reality."[169] These types of people have an impetus to steadily push forwards, without any limits. They only stop "when the strength of their bodies is exhausted, or when external obstacles prove to be insurmountable, never as a result of having satisfied their needs".[170]

151　This book was first published in 1911 as *Theorie der wirtschaftlichen Entwicklung*. The first English edition was published in 1934 and corresponds to the third German edition, which contained a completely rewritten second chapter. The quotes that appear here are taken from the second chapter of the original German edition and have been translated for this book.

152　Joseph Schumpeter, *Theorie der wirtschaftlichen Entwicklung* (Leipzig: Duncker & Humblot, 1912), 118.

153　Ibid., 119.

154　Ibid., 120.

155　Ibid., 121.

156　Ibid., 128.

157　Ibid., 132.

158　Ibid., 152.

159　Ibid., 163–164.

160　Ibid., 134.

161　Ibid., 135.

162　Ibid., 137.

163　Ibid., 138.

164　Ibid., 140.

165　Ibid., 141.

166　Ibid., 191.

167　Ibid., 143.

168　Ibid., 162.

169　Ibid., 145.

170　Ibid., 146.

As time has passed, these thoughts have proved to be even more current than Schumpeter himself envisaged. In his work *Capitalism, Socialism and Democracy* (1942), he presented an argument that events of the following decades failed to confirm: that the social function of the entrepreneur, as he described it, "is losing importance and is bound to lose it at an accelerating rate in the future". He predicted that technical advancements would increasingly become the preserve of educated specialists who supply what is demanded of them and make sure that it works as it should. Additionally, according to Schumpeter, personality and willpower counted less in a world that had grown accustomed to economic changes and took them for granted instead of offering resistance.[171] Economic progress had demonstrated a tendency to become "depersonalized and automatized".[172] This, he argued, would make traditional entrepreneurs increasingly expendable as their role became obsolete.[173]

The entrepreneur theory of Israel Kirzner, a theorist of the Austrian School of Economics and a student of Ludwig von Mises, points to similarities as well as differences with Schumpeter. "In many respects the picture of the entrepreneur which I have sought to delineate," Kirzner emphasizes in his work *Competition & Entrepreneurship* (1973), "bears much resemblance to that elaborated by Schumpeter".[174] Kirzner describes the following as a characteristic of the Schumpeterian entrepreneur: "[His] alertness to unnoticed opportunities has enabled him to depart from the routine repetitive working of widely known opportunities ... is closely parallel to my own distinction".[175]

Nevertheless, Kirzner stresses an important difference in understanding the role of the entrepreneur. While Schumpeter strongly emphasizes the innovative destroyer, Kirzner promotes the ability of the entrepreneur to recognize opportunities in the market and to thereby restore market equilibrium. Schumpeter focuses on the disruption of equilibrium in a given market, while Kirzner considers the question of how this equilibrium became established in the first place. "For me the important feature of entrepreneurship is not so much the ability to break away from routine as the ability to perceive new opportunities which others have not yet noticed."[176] According to Kirzner, Schumpeter sees the entrepreneur more in the role of a destroyer of equilibrium. "By contrast my own treatment of the entrepreneur emphasizes the equilibrating aspects of his role."[177]

Kirzner is firmly critical of the view of economics put forwards by Lionel Robbins, who defined it as a behavioural science that examines the relationship of goals and scarce resources with alternative uses. "It is my position that this analytical vision of economizing, maximizing, or efficiency-intent individual market participants is, in significant respects, misleadingly incomplete."[178]

In Kirzner's image of an entrepreneur, the concept of 'alertness', of always having an eye on new opportunities, plays the central role. He introduces the notion of the 'pure entrepreneur',[179] which does not represent an actual, empirically existing person but is an abstracted combination of the constitutive, specific characteristics of the entrepreneur, taken from all of the different roles that real entrepreneurs simultaneously adopt. According to his definition, this pure entrepreneur is a decision-maker whose sole role is to discover opportunities that have not yet been recognized.[180]

Pure entrepreneurs start without any means; they generate profit by recognizing opportunities. "Purely entrepreneurial decisions are by definition reserved for decision-makers who own nothing at all."[181] Of course, this does not mean that the real-life entrepreneur does not own anything, but this is a necessary mental construct for Kirzner, in seeking to understand their specific role.

Jesus Huerta de Soto, who makes reference to Kirzner, accentuates these thoughts when he states that entrepreneurial profit, "in a sense, arises out of nothing, ... which we will refer to as 'pure entrepreneurial profit'. To derive entrepreneurial profit, one needs no prior means, but only to exercise entrepreneurship well."[182]

Kirzner's approach follows Mises, in that it is an 'arbitrage' theory of profit.[183] This first requires the acknowledgement of limited knowledge. This recognizes that the opportunity of making purely commercial gains only comes about because of the incompleteness of market participants' knowledge. "These opportunities can be seized by anyone discovering their existence before others have done so."[184] This is a marked departure from Schumpeter. For Kirzner, the entrepreneur is not necessarily the source of innovations. "I view the entrepreneur not as a source of innovative ideas ex nihilo, but as being alert to the opportunities that exist already and are waiting to be noticed."[185]

An interesting thought is rooted in the work of both Mises and Huerta de Soto. Huerta de Soto also emphasized the importance of alertness that had been

---

171   Joseph Schumpeter, *Capitalism, Socialism and Democracy* (London: George Allen & Unwin Publishers, 1976), 132–133.

172   Ibid., 133.

173   Ibid., 134.

174   Israel Kirzner, *Competition & Entrepreneurship* (Chicago: The University of Chicago Press, 1973), 79.

175   Ibid., 79.

176   Ibid., 81.

177   Ibid., 73.

178   Ibid., 32–33.

179   Ibid., 39.

180   Ibid., 39.

181   Ibid., 47.

182   Jesus Huerta de Soto, *Socialism, Economic Calculation, and Entrepreneurship* (Cheltenham: Edward Elgar Publishing, 2010), 24.

183   Kirzner, *Competition & Entrepreneurship*, 85.

184   Ibid., 67.

185   Ibid., 74.

so strongly stressed by Kirzner, adding, "a striking similarity exists between the alertness a historian must show when selecting and interpreting the important past events which interest him, and the alertness an entrepreneur must show concerning the events he believes will occur in the future. This is why Mises asserts that historians and entrepreneurs employ very similar approaches." Huerta de Soto refers to a remark by Mises, who "goes so far as to define the 'entrepreneur' as someone who looks into the future with the eyes of a historian".[186]

Huerta de Soto summarizes the task of the entrepreneur, as presented by Mises, Kirzner, and other representatives of the Austrian School – in contrast to the traditional definition by Lionel Robbins – as follows: "Entrepreneurship, or human action, does not fundamentally consist of the optimal allocation of given means to ends which are also given. Instead, … it basically involves perceiving, determining, and recognizing the ends and means, that is, actively and creatively seeking and discovering new ends and means."[187]

The works of Sombart, Schumpeter, and Kirzner contain many points of reference for questions raised by this book. All three strongly emphasize the role of individual personality and the personality traits of the entrepreneur, which are accorded a much greater degree of importance than was the case in earlier economic eras. Sombart and particularly Schumpeter emphasize the role of the entrepreneur as a nonconformist who takes a stand against majority opinion. Sombart, to a greater extent than the others, points to willpower as one of the most important characteristics that a successful entrepreneur must have in order to aim for ambitious goals, and also highlights the importance of sales talent. In contrast, 'alertness' is paramount for Kirzner, by which he means the ability of the entrepreneur to generate profit by discovering opportunities not yet discovered by others.

3.2. AMERICAN AND GERMAN RESEARCH ON ENTREPRENEURIAL PERSONALITY TRAITS AND GOAL-SETTING

There are already – independent of entrepreneurship research, which is discussed below – numerous studies that have investigated the relationship between personality and professional success. 'Personality' is a key concept in the field of entrepreneurship research. Personality is defined as the totality of all characteristics that remain stable over time and make a person distinctive and unique – this term is addressed in detail in Chapter 6.

Studies have found evidence that individuals who possess the characteristics of conscientiousness, extroversion, emotional stability, and low levels of agreeableness are more successful in their careers than individuals for whom this is not the case.[188]

In the United States, there is a broad range of research into the motivation, objectives, and personality traits of entrepreneurs. In recent years, a number of studies on the same subject have been conducted in Germany as well. In a majority of cases, these have involved empirical research, based on interviews with entrepreneurs. In the United States, entrepreneurship research has existed as a discipline since the 1960s and in 2008 there were as many as 401 professorships of entrepreneurship research at American universities.[189]

A comparative empirical study of successful and unsuccessful company founders, published in Austria in 1986, is interesting in that it directly compared 62 successful company founders with 63 unsuccessful company founders.[190] Although the author mainly focused on the importance of socio-demographic attributes, such as age, family life cycle, gender, and education, the analysis of motivational structures revealed that successful company founders identified the pursuit of achievement, the pursuit of success, and the pursuit of innovation as the most important motivating factors. Unsuccessful company founders, on the other hand, were primarily motivated by the desire for a new role, the desire for independence, and the pursuit of wealth.[191]

Of greater relevance to the subject of this work are the hypotheses and findings of a doctoral dissertation on the psychological factors affecting company founders and entrepreneurial success, published in 2004.[192] Andreas Utsch interviewed several hundred small-scale entrepreneurs (founders and owners of companies with at most 50 employees) in Germany. Admittedly, it must be assumed that only a very small proportion of the interviewed entrepreneurs were multi-millionaires. Nevertheless, some of the lines of questioning, methodological approaches, and theories developed throughout Utsch's doctoral dissertation are of general interest to entrepreneurship researchers, as he examines the link between certain personality traits relevant to entrepreneurial activity and entrepreneurial success. Basing his approach on existing – primarily American – entrepreneurship research, Utsch developed a catalogue of questions and hypotheses, which he then used to test which personality traits were most relevant to entrepreneurship.

---

186 Huerta de Soto, *Socialism*, 19.

187 Ibid., 51.

188 See also Timothy A. Judge and John D. Kammeyer-Mueller, "Personality and Career Success," in *Handbook of Career Studies*, edited by Hugh Gunz and Maury Peiperl (Los Angeles: Sage Publications, 2007), 61–66.

189 Michael Faschingbauer, *Effectuation: Wie erfolgreiche Unternehmer denken, entscheiden und handeln*, 2nd ed. (Stuttgart: Schäffer-Poeschel Verlag, 2013), 245.

190 Gerhard Plaschka, *Unternehmenserfolg: Eine vergleichende empirische Untersuchung von erfolgreichen und nicht erfolgreichen Unternehmensgründern* (Vienna: Service Fachverlag an der Wirtschaftsuniversität Wien, 1986), 67.

191 Ibid., 147.

192 Andreas Utsch, "Psychologische Einflussgrößen von Unternehmensgründung und Unternehmenserfolg" (PhD diss., Justus-Liebig-Universität Gießen, 2004).

Several studies of the relationship between entrepreneurial success and specific personality traits suggest that the following attributes are associated with entrepreneurial success:[193]
- Commitment
- Creativity
- A high degree of extroversion
- Low levels of agreeableness.

Other studies have shown that the following personality traits correlate strongly with entrepreneurial success:[194]
- Orientation towards action after suffering disappointments (the entrepreneur remains able to act, even after failure)
- Internal locus of control (the conviction "I hold my destiny in my own two hands")
- Optimism (the expectation that the future holds positive things in store)
- Self-efficacy (the expectation that tasks can be performed successfully, even in difficult circumstances).

A meta-analytical review by Hao Zhao and Scott E. Seibert in 2006 revealed significant differences between entrepreneurs and executives in four of the Big Five personality traits. The study showed that entrepreneurs scored higher on Conscientiousness and Openness to Experience, whereas they scored lower on Neuroticism and Agreeableness. The study found no variation for Extroversion.[195]

A German comparative survey of 153 individuals, which included self-employed, partially self-employed, and fully employed respondents, confirmed that the need for achievement and the strength of one's internal locus of control are core conditional factors for self-employment. The study reported significant variations between self-employed respondents and employees.[196]

In 2007, Andreas Rauch and Michael Frese established that there was a growing interest among researchers in the psychology of entrepreneurship. They also pointed to deficits in previous research. For instance, they claimed, researchers had so far only ever looked to identify linear relationships between personality traits and entrepreneurial success. Rauch and Frese argued that drawing parallels between broadly defined personality traits and entrepreneurial success makes little sense. In reality, they contested, the direct correlations are mostly weak. Their effect is based much more on the fact that they influence very specific characteristics that Rauch and Frese consider decisive for entrepreneurial success. These more specific characteristics and attributes include need for achievement, risk-taking, innovativeness, autonomy, locus of control, and self-efficacy.[197]

According to Rauch and Frese, meta-analyses demonstrate the strong correlation between performance orientation and entrepreneurial success.[198] Studies on the connection between innovativeness and the desire for autonomy have also reported a correlation with entrepreneurial achievement, whereas the often-postulated relationship between the internal locus of control and entrepreneurial success is weaker. The clearest correlation, as revealed by the meta-analyses, is between entrepreneurial success and the expression of self-efficacy.[199] Rauch and Frese found that the individual personality traits were often only relatively weakly correlated with entrepreneurial success, which came as no surprise to the authors. After all, they argued, it is not a single personality characteristic but a specific combination of several such characteristics that is responsible for success.[200] They believe that the correlations between personality traits and entrepreneurial success are best measured in relation to small and medium-sized companies as the entrepreneur, and their personality, naturally plays a greater role in small and medium-sized enterprises than in a larger company.[201]

In Germany, several waves of surveys carried out by the German Socio-Economic Panel (SOEP)[202] between 2000 and 2009 have been analysed in order to determine the personality profile of self-employed people. This analysis considered the Big Five personality traits – Openness to Experience, Conscientiousness, Extroversion, Agreeableness, and Emotional Stability – together with locus of control (internal–external), risk attitude, patience, and impulsiveness.[203] According to this study, the personality profile of self-employed individuals is quite different from that of dependent employees. "The self-employed score an average of 36% higher for the trait 'openness to experience' than the standard deviation for this trait among the non-self-employed. Extroversion is approximately 21% higher than the standard deviation." There were much smaller deviations in relation to the other dimensions

193   See also Eva Schmitt-Rodermund and Rainer K. Silbereisen, "Erfolg von Unternehmern: Die Rolle von Persönlichkeit und familiärer Sozialisation," in *Unternehmerisch erfolgreiches Handeln*, edited by Klaus Moser, Bernad Batinic, and Jeanette Zempel (Göttingen: Verlag für Angewandte Psychologie, 1999), 118.

194   Sigrun Göbel and Michael Frese, "Persönlichkeit, Strategien und Erfolg bei Kleinunternehmern [Personality, Strategies and the Success of Small Businesses]," in *Unternehmerisch erfolgreiches Handeln*, edited by Klaus Moser, Bernad Batinic, and Jeanette Zempel (Göttingen: Verlag für Angewandte Psychologie, 1999), 101.

195   Hao Zhao and Scott E. Seibert, "The Big Five Personality Dimensions and Entrepreneurial Status: A Meta-Analytical Review," *Journal of Applied Psychology* 91, no. 2 (2006), 259.

196   Günther F. Müller, "Dispositionelle und biographische Bedingungen beruflicher Selbständigkeit," in *Unternehmerisch erfolgreiches Handeln*, edited by Klaus Moser, Bernad Batinic, and Jeanette Zempel (Göttingen: Verlag für Angewandte Psychologie, 1999), 187.

197   Andreas Rauch and Michael Frese, *Born to Be an Entrepreneur?, Revisting the Personality Approach to Entrepreneuship* 47. https://www.researchgate.net/publication/270820381_Born_to_Be_an_Entrepreneur_Revisiting_the_Personality_Approach_to_Entrepreneurship

198   Ibid., 49.

199   Ibid., 53.

200   Ibid., 54.

201   Ibid., 57.

202   The SOEP is a representative longitudinal survey of 12,000 private households in Germany, carried out annually by the German Institute for Economic Research.

203   Maro Caliendo, Frank Fossen, and Alexander Kritikos, "Selbstständige sind anders: Persönlichkeit beeinflusst unternehmerisches Handeln," *Wochenbericht des DIW Berlin* 11 (2011), 5.

of the Big Five personality test. Nevertheless, the entrepreneurs were much more open to risk than the non-entrepreneurs (40% of the standard deviation). The internal locus of control – in contrast with the external locus of control – is also much stronger for self-employed people.[204]

3.2.A. QUESTIONS AND METHODOLOGICAL CHALLENGES

There are two different questions to ask with regard to the connection between personality traits and motivations on the one hand, and entrepreneurial success on the other. Firstly, which personality traits increase the likelihood that an individual will become an entrepreneur – that is, will become self-employed? Secondly, are there any correlations between these personality traits and the degree of entrepreneurial success an individual will achieve? "There should be different processes by which a person decides to become an entrepreneur and by which a person achieves entrepreneurial success."[205]

This raises numerous methodological questions. How to measure success (turnover, number of employees, other business performance indicators) is one question; another question relates to just how general or specific the personality traits under examination are. Researchers have found that personality traits frequently do not correlate directly with entrepreneurial success. Instead, Rauch and Frese point to the fact that "their effects are mediated by more specific, proximal processes, such as motives, cognitive processes, or self-regulatory processes".[206]

One methodological problem is that many studies solely test for linear relationships between personality variables and success. However, Rauch and Frese stress the importance of testing for non-linear relationships as well. For example, they point out that it is entirely possible that some entrepreneurs are *overly* willing to take risks, *overly* ambitious, *overly* optimistic, etc. "In contrast to achievement tests (such as cognitive ability), more of the same thing may not be a good thing at all. Thus, we urge future researchers to test for non-linear relationships."[207]

3.2.B. ATTITUDES TO RISK AND RISK PERCEPTION

The importance of non-linear relationships is especially relevant to examinations of the correlation between risk propensity and entrepreneurship. This issue has interested researchers since the 1920s and 1930s. Representatives of the Chicago School of Economics, such as Frank H. Knight, defined entrepreneurs primarily as bearers of risk.[208] The school's proponents understood entrepreneurial thought and action above all as the assumption of risk. "An entrepreneur is a bearer of uncertainty and an allocator of resources."[209]

Empirical studies into the relationship between risk propensity and entrepreneurial success are inconclusive, as established in 1991 by Elizabeth Chell, Jean Haworth, and Sally Brearley.[210] It appears that an elevated propensity for risk tends to correlate with the decision to become an entrepreneur, but there is no indication that this is a predictor of entrepreneurial success. In 1999, Eva Schmitt-Rodermund and Rainer K. Silbereisen pointed out that the few studies to directly examine the relationship between risk propensity and entrepreneurial success made no distinction between successful versus insolvent and rapidly growing versus slowly growing companies with regard to entrepreneurial risk propensity. They did, however, suggest "correlations during the business-creation process",[211] which may show that a high risk propensity is a prerequisite for setting up a company, but not for entrepreneurial success.

In 1998, Rauch and Frese reported the results of research demonstrating that successful entrepreneurs accepted moderate levels of risk. While too little risk was not challenging enough for them, excessive levels of risk were also to be avoided. Other studies concluded that a willingness to take risks only correlates to a small degree with entrepreneurial success, whereas excessive risk-taking correlates strongly with entrepreneurial failure.[212]

An American meta-analysis published by Rauch and Frese in 2000 suggests that there is a non-linear relationship between risk propensity and success. To a certain extent, a willingness to take risks correlates positively with success, but an even greater propensity for risk-taking has negative effects. In deciding to become an entrepreneur, the propensity for risk-taking plays a role, whereas, in terms of entrepreneurial success, it can be harmful. "To become an entrepreneur is risky but doing business in a risky way might be dangerous."[213] A number of studies even showed that "risk-taking is negatively associated with business success".[214]

According to Rauch and Frese in 2007, meta-analyses proved that there is a correlation between risk propensity and entrepreneurial success, albeit a weak one. "It is also smaller in comparison to other personality traits. Therefore, we suggest

204   Ibid., 6.

205   Andreas Rauch and Michael Frese, "Psychological Approaches to Entrepreneurial Success: A General Model and an Overview of Findings," in *International Review of Industrial and Organizational Psychology*, edited by C.L. Cooper and I.T. Robertson (Chichester: Wiley, 2000), unnumbered.

206   Rauch and Frese, *Born to Be an Entrepreneur?*, 57.

207   Ibid., 43.

208   See also Stefan Lackner, *Voraussetzungen und Erfolgsfaktoren unternehmerischen Denkens und Handelns: Eine empirische Analyse mittelständischer Unternehmen* (Hamburg: Verlag Dr. Kovac, 2002), 18 et seq.

209   Ibid., 21.

210   Elizabeth Chell, Jean Haworth, and Sally Brearley, *The Entrepreneurial Personality: Concepts, Cases and Categories* (London: Routledge, 1991), 42 et seq.

211   Schmitt-Rodermund and Silbereisen, "Erfolg von Unternehmern," 117.

212   Andreas Rauch and Michael Frese, "Was wissen wir über die Psychologie erfolgreichen Unternehmertums? Ein Literaturüberblick," in *Erfolgreiche Unternehmensgründer: Psychologische Analysen und praktische Anleitungen für Unternehmer in Ost- und Westdeutschland*, edited by Michael Frese (Göttingen: Verlag für Angewandte Psychologie, 1998), 13.

213   Rauch and Frese, "Psychological Approaches," unnumbered.

214   Ibid., unnumbered

to test in the future, whether the curvilinear relationship between entrepreneurs' risk taking, business creation, and success appears to be true."[215]

It is also worth investigating whether entrepreneurs are even able to view their own behaviours – which others may perceive as risky – in the same terms. "From an observer's perspective a behaviour might be judged to be highly risky while a business owner might judge the same behaviour as an attempt to minimize risk."[216] As Locke and Baum observe, "entrepreneurs do not experience their ventures as highly risky, as compared, say, to how an outsider would experience it. This is because entrepreneurs have high self-confidence; in relation to their perceived ability the venture may not seem risky. And if they possess genuine ability, the venture may not be objectively risky for them."[217]

Robert Hisrich, Janice Langan-Fox, and Sharon Grant also point to studies that show no difference between entrepreneurs and non-entrepreneurs with regard to their willingness or reluctance to consciously take risks. Rather, the two groups are distinguished by their subjective perception of risk. "The central thesis of this work is that entrepreneurs are characterized by lower risk perception, thus giving the illusion of greater risk tolerance. Research has shown that entrepreneurs categorize ambiguous business scenarios significantly more positively than do non-entrepreneurs." In addition, entrepreneurs rely more on heuristics in their decision-making, thus reducing their perception of risk. Without such "cognitive shortcuts", many entrepreneurial decisions would never even have been made.[218]

In 1999, Lowell W. Busenitz dealt extensively with the paradox that, in deciding to create a business, company founders tolerate high levels of risk, and yet many studies have failed to measure a significantly higher risk propensity among company founders than among other groups. For him, this raises the question as to why some entrepreneurs are willing to accept elevated levels of risk, although they did not differ in terms of their average risk propensity. In a study involving 176 company founders, Busenitz tested the hypothesis that "entrepreneurs use biases and heuristics more extensively in their decision making and, therefore, fail to fully acknowledge the risk associated with starting their own businesses".[219]

The study's findings confirmed the hypothesis. Company founders more frequently use heuristics and streamline their decision-making processes. Furthermore, Busenitz showed that company founders tended more towards over-optimism and (statistically invalid) generalizations than was the case for employed managers.[220] He concluded that they are not subjectively more willing to take risks; rather they do not adequately perceive their behaviours as risky. However, it is important to recognize that this study focused exclusively on the business-creation process.

So, does the same apply to established companies? Here too, outside parties may well view certain decisions as an expression of a pronounced risk propensity, while the company's entrepreneurial owner may not necessarily regard them as risky. Chell, Haworth, and Brearley point out that, from an entrepreneurial standpoint, the option of 'doing nothing' could also be viewed as highly risky and, in contrast, a behaviour that outsiders may view as highly risky could be viewed by the entrepreneur as a strategy to minimize risk.[221]

A comparative study of employees and self-employed people carried out in Germany between 2000 and 2009 confirmed the following correlation between risk orientation and the longevity of self-employment: "Very risk averse and very risk tolerant self-employed people are much more likely to abandon their entrepreneurial activities than those who take a moderate approach to risk (formally speaking, the probability of self-employment assumes an inverse 'bell curve' in relation to risk propensity)."[222] According to the study's authors, one possible explanation is that the probability of failure increases in proportion to the acceptance of elevated levels of risk, whereas projects that are not risky enough will only generate low incomes, reducing the appeal of self-employment in relation to employment.[223]

A survey of billionaires as part of a UBS and PwC study in 2015 concluded that billionaires had a different understanding of risk from other groups. The failure to exploit an opportunity could also be understood as a risk. "They're afraid to lose by not capturing an opportunity, tending not to worry about the downside of a new venture failing but instead being concerned about missing out on the upside."[224]

Therefore, the concept of risk played a major role in the interviews with entrepreneurs and investors conducted for this book. How do these individuals assess their own attitudes towards risk-taking? Had their propensity for taking risks changed during the course of their lives? Were they more tolerant of risk in the nascent stages of their entrepreneurship than later in their business lives? Is there a difference between their own perception of risk and the perceptions of others?

3.2.C. SELF-EFFICACY

The term 'self-efficacy' is a central concept in the social cognitive theory of Albert Bandura. The concept of self-efficacy "refers to people's perceptions of their own

---

215   Rauch and Frese, *Born to Be an Entrepreneur?*, 50.

216   Rauch and Frese, "Psychological Approaches," unnumbered

217   Edwin A. Locke and J. Robert Baum, "Entrepreneurial Motivation," in *The Psychology of Entrepreneurship*, edited by J. Robert Baum, Michael Frese, and Robert Baron (New York: Psychology Press Taylor & Francis Group, 2012), 99.

218   Robert Hisrich, Janice Langan-Fox, and Sharon Grant, "Entrepreneurship Research and Practice: A Call to Action for Psychology," *American Psychologist* 62, no. 6 (2007), 583.

219   Lowell W. Busenitz, "Entrepreneurial Risk and Strategic Decision Making: It's a Matter of Perspective," *Journal of Applied Behavioral Science* 35, no. 3 (1999), 326.

220   Ibid., 332.

221   Chell, Haworth, and Brearley, *The Entrepreneurial Personality*, 43.

222   Caliendo, Fossen, and Kritikos, "Selbstständige sind anders," 7.

223   Ibid., 7.

224   *Billionaires: Master Architects*, 15.

capabilities for action in future situations". According to this theory, individuals "with a higher sense of self-efficacy are more likely to decide to attempt difficult tasks, to persist in their efforts, to be calm rather than anxious during task performance, and to organize their thoughts in an analytical manner".[225]

The term also describes the degree to which an individual believes they can master a specific – even challenging – situation. At the two extremes of the self-efficacy scale are the convictions: "This is what I need to do and I can make it" (high self-efficacy) and "I'll never manage this. What will people think of me?" (low self-efficacy).[226] "In short, it was found that performance is affected not only by what one is trying to do (i.e., the goal), but also by how confident one is of being able to do it (i.e., self-efficacy)."[227]

As a predictor for entrepreneurial success, self-efficacy is appreciably more compelling than other personality traits tested so far. Empirical studies show that successful entrepreneurs possess higher degrees of self-efficacy than other groups. "Moreover, self-efficacy showed the highest correlation with success in a meta-analysis (corrected $r = .419$). Such a correlation is as high as the correlation between weight and height in US adults, one of the highest medical relationships."[228]

In a German study in which 98 small business owners were tested for 29 personality traits, there was no stronger correlation than that with self-efficacy ($r = .41$). In comparison, the correlation between success and risk propensity, at $r = .11$, had no significance.[229] In another study, entrepreneurs who scored highly for the characteristics of self-efficacy, need for dominance, and a strong internal locus of control were compared with other entrepreneurs who demonstrated much lower propensities in all three characteristics. Of the entrepreneurs who scored highly for self-efficacy, need for dominance, and a strong internal locus of control, 89% were successful, compared with only 11% of the entrepreneurs with lower scores.[230]

In a comparison of entrepreneurs and senior executives in eastern Germany, Utsch demonstrated that the greatest deviations were found in the variables self-efficacy, control aversion, and the need for achievement.[231] In a further study, which surveyed 201 entrepreneurs, significant correlations were identified between self-efficacy (negative: "When faced by a new task, I often doubt that I will be able to cope with it") and the company's growth in terms of employee numbers and profits.[232]

American studies have shown a strong correlation between 'entrepreneurial self-efficacy' and the success of a company, especially in its nascent stages. Entrepreneurial self-efficacy refers to "the strength of a person's belief that he or she is capable of successfully performing the various roles and tasks of entrepreneurship".[233] This sense of self-belief relates to innovation, risk acceptance, marketing, management, and finances.[234]

Bandura also highlighted the connection between self-efficacy and the magnitude of an individual's goals. "People who are beset with self-doubts about their capabilities do not go around setting challenging goals for themselves and sticking for long in the face of difficulties to the goals they adopted. People's belief in their capabilities influence the level of goals they set for themselves. The stronger the self-efficacy, the higher the goals people set for themselves."[235]

3.2.D. ACTION ORIENTATION AFTER FAILURE

Utsch identified a further key personality characteristic for entrepreneurs, 'action orientation', which is evident in the wake of failure. "Action orientation after failure means that people remain able and ready to take action immediately after suffering a setback or making a mistake."[236] Utsch's research revealed a strong correlation between action orientation after failure and the success of small businesses.[237]

A study published by Sigrun Göbel and Michael Frese found that, of 29 personality traits, only three correlated more strongly with entrepreneurial success than action orientation after failure.[238] Their conclusion: "An entrepreneur with a high score on this scale remains oriented to action after failure."[239] In a further study of entrepreneurs in western Germany, action orientation after failure was identified as an extremely important personality characteristic for business success.[240] A closely related characteristic of successful entrepreneurs is tenacity. "One trait that sets them apart from others is that they do not give up when things go wrong." Successful entrepreneurs get back on their feet after setbacks, because they ascribe their failures to either bad luck or a lack of effort on their own part.[241]

---

225   Daniel Cervone and Lawrence A. Pervin, *Personality: Theory and Research*, 12th ed. (New York: John Wiley & Sons, 2013), 436.

226   Ibid., 449–450.

227   Edwin A. Locke and Gary P. Latham, "Goal Setting Theory, 1990," in *New Developments in Goal Setting and Task Performance*, edited by Edwin A. Locke and Gary P. Latham (New York: Routledge Taylor & Francis Group, 2013), 11.

228   Rauch and Frese, *Born to Be an Entrepreneur?*, 53.

229   Göbel and Frese, "Persönlichkeit, Strategien," 101.

230   Sigrun Göbel, "Persönlichkeit, Handlungsstrategien und Erfolg," in *Erfolgreiche Unternehmensgründer: Psychologische Analysen und praktische Anleitungen für Unternehmer in Ost- und Westdeutschland*, edited by Michael Frese (Göttingen: Verlag für Angewandte Psychologie, 1998), 107.

231   Utsch, "Psychologische Einflussgrößen," 59.

232   Ibid., 108.

233   Chen, Greene, and Crick quoted in Locke and Baum, "Entrepreneurial Motivation," 98–99.

234   Locke and Baum, "Entrepreneurial Motivation," 99.

235   Albert Bandura, "The Role of Self-Efficacy in Goal-Based Motivation," in *New Developments in Goal Setting and Task Performance*, edited by Edwin A. Locke and Gary P. Latham (New York: Routledge Taylor & Francis Group, 2013), 151.

236   Utsch, "Psychologische Einflussgrößen," 102.

237   Ibid., 109.

238   Göbel and Frese, "Persönlichkeit, Strategien," 101.

239   Ibid., 96.

240   Göbel, "Persönlichkeit, Handlungsstrategien und Erfolg," 119.

241   Locke and Baum, "Entrepreneurial Motivation," 102.

Bandura shows the connection between self-efficacy, goal-setting, and reaction to failure. In psychological experiments, test subjects were told that they had failed to achieve a challenging goal. "Those who were dissatisfied with the substandard performance but judged themselves efficacious to meet the challenge redoubled their efforts ... Those who judged themselves inefficacious to meet the challenging goal and couldn't care less about their mediocre performance slackened their effort and just coasted along apathetically."[242]

This is confirmed by an analysis of the biographies of ultra-wealthy individuals. The life stories of the wealthy read, upon closer inspection, as a succession of serious problems and crises that, once overcome, enabled these individuals to ultimately achieve even greater success and propagate their wealth. Setbacks or crises often provided the impetus for even greater success in the future. Examples of specific reactions to such serious crises can be found in the biographies of John D. Rockefeller,[243] Ingvar Feodor Kamprad (IKEA),[244] Michael Bloomberg,[245] Warren Buffett,[246] and Walt Disney.[247]

This was an important line of questioning in the interviews in Part B of this book. How do entrepreneurs react to failure? How do they experience setbacks? Where do they lay the blame for their setbacks? How they ascribed blame, explained failures, and reacted to failures were all important questions.

3.2.E. THE IMPORTANCE OF SETTING GOALS AND PLANNING (GOAL-SETTING THEORY)

What role does goal-setting play in the success of wealthy people? This is one of the questions this book seeks to address. An analysis of the biographies of wealthy individuals reveals that they frequently emphasize very strongly the importance of setting goals that are extraordinary, challenging, and considered 'unrealistic' by most other people.[248] Examples of this can be seen in the biographies of Larry Page (Google),[249] Sam Walton (Walmart),[250] Richard Branson,[251] Ray Kroc (McDonald's),[252] Howard Schultz (Starbucks),[253] and Michael Dell (Dell Computers).[254]

The relevance of goal-setting to entrepreneurial success has also been examined by scholars. The theory of 'goal-setting' developed by Edwin A. Locke (University of Maryland) and Gary P. Latham (University of Toronto) is of central importance. In 1981, they published a review of the research findings on this topic from the 1970s. In 90% of the studies on this topic, they reported the following finding: "specific and challenging goals lead to higher performance than easy goals, 'do your best' goals, or no goals ... Goal setting is most likely to improve task performance when the goals are specific and sufficiently challenging."[255] They also examined how specific and how difficult the goals were to achieve. The result: more challenging and more specific goals lead to better results than easy and vaguely formulated goals.[256]

In a second comparative study, Locke and Latham summarized the results of numerous other studies on this topic from the 1980s. Some 400 empirical studies had been carried out up to 1990, and they confirmed two findings in particular:

- "There is a linear relationship between the degree of goal difficulty and performance." Locke and Latham found that the performance of the people with the highest goals was 250% greater than the performance of the people with the lowest goals.[257]
- "Specific, difficult goals lead to higher performance than no goals as well as vague, abstract goals such as 'do your best'." It was found that 51 of the 53 studies published up to 1990 confirmed that people who set specific and more ambitious goals were more successful than those who did not.[258]

Even in 1990, the basis for these findings was already very convincing – goal-setting theory was the inductively developed product of studies involving 40,000 participants in eight countries, both in field studies and experiments.[259]

Ambitious and specific goals are so important because, according to Locke and Latham, they focus an individual's attention on the activities that are relevant to the goal, and because individuals increase the intensity and the duration of the effort required to achieve their goals. They work harder and longer to achieve their goals than people who do not have such goals.[260]

---

242   Bandura, "The Role of Self-Efficacy," 149–150.

243   Ron Chernow, *Titan: The Life of John D. Rockefeller, Sr.* (New York: Vintage, 1998), 130 et seq., 554.

244   Rüdiger Jungbluth, *Die 11 Geheimnisse des IKEA-Erfolgs* (Frankfurt-am-Main: Bastei Lübbe, 2008), 75.

245   Michael Bloomberg, *Bloomberg by Bloomberg: With Invaluable Help from Matthew Winkler* (New York: John Wiley & Sons, 1997), 1 et seq.

246   Zitelmann, *Dare to Be Different and Grow Rich*, 36–40.

247   Ibid., 48–51.

248   Ibid., 1–21.

249   David A. Vise and Mark Malseed, *The Google Story* (New York: Dell Publishing, 2005), 11.

250   Sam Walton, *Made in America: My Story* (New York: Bantom Books, 1993), 15.

251   Richard Branson, *Screw It, Let's Do It: Lessons in Life and Business, Expanded* (London: Virgin Books, 2007), 196.

252   John F. Love, *McDonald's: Behind the Arches.* Rev. ed. (New York: Bantam Books, 1995), 23, 39–40, 45–47.

253   Howard Schultz and Dori Jones Yang, *Pour Your Heart Into It: How Starbucks Built a Company One Cup at a Time* (New York: Hyperion, 2007), 35–36, 42–44.

254   Lauri S. Friedmann, *Business Leaders* (Greensboro: Michael Dell, 2009), 79.

255   Edwin A. Locke, Karyll N. Shaw, Lise M. Saari, and Gary P. Latham, "Goal Setting and Task Performance: 1969–1980," *Psychological Bulletin* 90, no. 1 (1981), 125.

256   Ibid., 126–129.

257   Locke and Latham, "Goal Setting Theory, 1990," 5.

258   Ibid., 5.

259   Ibid., 11.

260   Ibid., 6.

Studies on other personality traits demonstrate the importance of the fact that successful people set their own ambitious and challenging goals. In a study of 91 salespeople, Murray R. Barrick, Michael K. Mount, and Judy P. Strauss showed that there is a close correlation between conscientiousness and success. The reason that conscientious salespeople were much more successful than others was primarily due to the more difficult goals they set for themselves. There was a clear correlation between the variables 'prior goal-setting' and 'goal commitment' and sales success.[261] "Our results show that autonomous goal setting and, to a lesser extent, goal commitment mediate the relationship between conscientiousness and two measures of job proficiency – supervisory ratings of job performance and sales volume. This indicates that highly conscientious individuals are more likely to set goals autonomously, to be committed to subsequent goals, and to perform better."[262] In essence, the importance of conscientiousness is secondary because, as shown by this study, conscientiousness only has an indirect link to success, via the process of setting ambitious goals. Salespeople are ideal subjects for the examination of the role played by personality traits, attitudes, and behaviours in relation to commercial success, as the direct impact of these qualities on their success is so easy to measure.

In 2013, Locke and Latham published a collection of 37 essays showing the development of research into this subject between 1990 and 2010. In addition to the 400 studies carried out prior to 1990, there were another 600 studies that confirmed the key assumptions of goal-setting theory and showed its usefulness for various disciplines.[263]

Steve Kerr and Douglas LePelley dealt with the question of how difficult goals must be in order to achieve optimal results. "Compared to easy goals, difficult goals are far more likely to generate sustained enthusiasm and higher levels of performance. However, this finding comes with an important caveat, namely, that the goals, though difficult, must be seen to be achievable by those who are supposed to attain them."[264] On the one hand, the failure to achieve overly ambitious, and therefore unattainable, goals could have the opposite effect, leading to frustration. On the other hand, Kerr and LePelley cite the example of General Electric, where Jack Welch used the strategy of 'stretch goals' to show that the formulation of 'impossible goals' could provide a significant stimulus. They quote Welch's assertion: "We have found that by reaching for what appears to be impossible, we often actually do the impossible; and even when we don't quite make it, we inevitably wind up doing much better than we would have done."[265]

In 2004, J. Robert Baum and Edwin A. Locke reported on research testing goal-setting theory for entrepreneurs. They empirically confirmed the following hypothesis, based on a survey of 229 entrepreneurs: "The higher the entrepreneur-CEO's goals for venture growth, the higher the subsequent venture growth will be."[266] The correlation between self-efficacy and the magnitude of the goals is evident and was also empirically proven. "The higher the entrepreneur-CEO's self-efficacy about venture growth, the higher the goals for subsequent venture growth will be."[267] This does not relate to the achievement of individual goals but to the growth of the entire company. The study provides impressive confirmation that ambitious, long-term goals have a significant impact on success. "Thus, we measured vision as a long-term goal, and the positive findings of this study for vision must be interpreted as support for the use of long-term goals."[268]

In 2013 Baum published another paper on "Goals and Entrepreneurship." Goal-setting theory has special value to the field of entrepreneurship research, he explained, "because it covers self-set goals and involves explicit, consciously chosen targets that are usually focused on performance".[269] Early-stage investors confirmed that most successful entrepreneurs begin with goals that are beyond the normal realms of possibility.[270] Baum cites numerous studies that prove that the expectation of goal-setting theory, whereby larger goals lead to better performance, are also empirically confirmed by entrepreneurship research.[271] "Multiple entrepreneurship studies support the view that entrepreneurs who set their own goals are motivated to attain higher performance than if they had no goals."[272]

According to Baum, entrepreneurs are visionaries who have the ability to recognize what might work in the future. However, the entrepreneurial vision should not be confused with formal 'vision statements' of the kind that are used to motivate employees or communicate externally. "The full vision, however, is inside the entrepreneur's head and is much more detailed than any one statement or slogan."[273]

In 2006, Robert A. Baron examined which cognitive factors play a role in identifying opportunities and developing ideas. For him, three factors, each functioning in close relationship to the others, stood out: "engaging in an active search

---

261   Murray R. Barrick, Michael K. Mount, and Judy P. Strauss, "Conscientiousness and Performance of Sales Representatives: Test of the Mediating Effects of Goal Setting," *Journal of Applied Psychology* 78, no. 5 (1993), 718.

262   Ibid., 719.

263   Edwin A. Locke and Gary P. Latham (eds.), *New Developments in Goal Setting and Task Performance* (New York, London, 2013), xi.

264   Steve Kerr and Douglas Lepelley, "Stretch Goals: Risks, Possibilities, and Best Practices," in *New Developments in Goal Setting and Task Performance*, edited by Edwin A. Locke and Gary P. Latham (New York: Routledge Taylor & Francis Group, 2013), 21.

265   Welch quoted in ibid., 29.

266   J. Robert Baum and Edwin A. Locke, "The Relationship of Entrepreneurial Traits, Skill, and Motivation to Subsequent Venture Growth," *Journal of Applied Psychology* 89 (2004), 590.

267   Ibid., 590.

268   Ibid., 596.

269   J. Robert Baum, "Goals and Entrepreneurship," in *New Developments in Goal Setting and Task Performance*, edited by Edwin A. Locke and Gary P. Latham (New York: Routledge Taylor & Francis Group, 2013), 462.

270   Ibid., 463.

271   Ibid., 463.

272   Ibid., 464.

273   Ibid., 468.

for opportunities; alertness to opportunities (the capacity to recognize them when they emerge); and prior knowledge of a market, industry, or customers as a basis for recognizing new opportunities in these areas".[274]

An important question for this book was therefore: Is it possible to confirm that UHNWIs set unusually ambitious goals for themselves? And, if so, what kind of goals do they set? How specific are their goals and what do they relate to? Did the interviewees formulate their goals in writing? Or was goal-setting potentially not as important as goal-setting theory assumes?

One approach, which was described by Gabriele Oettingen, Marion Wittchen, and Peter M. Gollwitzer as 'mental contrasting', has proven to be especially effective in the achievement of ambitious goals. The process of mentally contrasting a desired future with the limitations of the current reality is, as has been demonstrated by numerous psychological experiments, an effective method of self-regulation in attaining goals.[275] "The model of fantasy realization proposes that mentally contrasting a desired future with the reality that impedes its realization will create selective, that is, expectancy-dependent goal-commitments with subsequent goal striving and goal attainment."[276]

According to Gabriele Oettingen, Gaby Hönig, and Peter M. Gollwitzer, fantasies can be fulfilled only if first they are reformulated as goals and then, in a second step, the desired future is contrasted with the current reality.[277] Whether a goal is actually achieved or not is largely determined by the strength of an individual's 'goal commitment': "Commitment implies the extension of effort, over time, toward the accomplishment of an original goal and emphasizes an unwillingness to abandon or to lower the original goal."[278]

A further question relates to the relationship between goal-setting and planning. Michael Frese, Judith Stewart and Bettina Hannover pointed out that individuals differed in the extent to which they took their goals seriously and how strongly they acted in a goal-oriented manner. There was also a clear difference in how methodically they acted. Though connected, these are two different components: "The plan component and the goal component of action are conceptually distinct although probably empirically related. A person can be extremely goal oriented and still lack a precision of plans." Frese, Stewart, and Hannover refer to 'action styles', which they acknowledge can be learned at least to a certain degree.[279]

Plans are the connecting lines, the bridges between thoughts and actions, because they translate goals into actionable operations.[280] Frese makes an important distinction between his usage of 'plans' and the everyday meaning of the word. The 'plans' he is referring to do not necessarily have to be fully prepared or fleshed out in the strictest sense. In some cases, these plans might only exist as general ideas about how to proceed.[281] It may well be that an entrepreneur claims not to have a plan at all, believing that their actions are based only on intuition, whereas they are in fact acting in accordance with an unconscious plan at all times.[282]

Plans are important because they make people act, and they reduce the probability that an individual will lose sight of a goal.[283] However, plans do not only have positive functions; they can also be counterproductive, if, for example, they are too rigid and the entrepreneur clings to fixed plans even though, particularly in more chaotic situations, the ability to react more flexibly would be more appropriate.[284]

3.2.F. NONCONFORMISM, AGREEABLENESS, AND ASSERTIVENESS

As shown in Section 3.1, Schumpeter describes the entrepreneur as an outright nonconformist. The observations of the cognitive scientist Saras Sarasvathy confirm this view in some respects. She succeeded in "extracting key elements of expertise from experienced entrepreneurs". [285] The term 'effectuation' describes a certain type of thinking and acting that field research has identified in successful entrepreneurs.

The basis of Sarasvathy's studies was two lists of the 100 most successful entrepreneurs between 1960 and 1985, and another list of the winners of the Ernst & Young 'Entrepreneur of the Year' awards up to 1996. She interviewed 30 entrepreneurs, each of whom had more than ten years' experience of founding multiple businesses, who had founded enterprises with annual sales revenues of between USD 200 million and 6.5 billion, and who had successfully floated at least one of their companies on the stock exchange.[286] Presumably, many of these individuals are worth in the tens and hundreds of millions, although this was not the focus of Sarasvathy's studies.

One of Sarasvathy's key findings is that these entrepreneurs "systematically ignored essential elements that are commonly considered to be professional.

---

274   Robert A. Baron, "Opportunity Recognition as Pattern Recognition: How Entrepreneurs 'Connect the Dots' to Identify New Business Opportunities," *Academy of Management Perspectives* 20 (2006), 104.

275   Gabriele Oettingen, Marion Wittchen, and Peter M. Gollwitzer, "Regulating Goal Pursuit through Mental Contrasting with Implementation Intentions," in *New Developments in Goal Setting and Task Performance,* edited by Edwin A. Locke and Gary P. Latham (New York: Routledge Taylor & Francis Group, 2013), 523.

276   Ibid., 524.

277   Gabriele Oettingen, Gaby Hönig, and Peter M. Gollwitzer, "Effective Self-Regulation of Goal Attainment," *International Journal of Educational Research* 33 (2000).

278   John R. Hollenbeck and Howard J. Klein, "Goal Commitment and the Goal-Setting Process: Problems, Prospects, and Proposals for Future Research," *Journal of Applied Psychology* 72 (1987), 212.

279   Michael Frese, Judith Stewart, and Bettina Hannover, "Goal Orientation and Planfulness: Action Styles as Personality Concepts," *Journal of Personality and Social Psychology* 52 (1987), 1183.

280   Michael Frese, "The Psychological Actions and Entrepreneurial Success: An Action Theory Approach," in *The Psychology of Entrepreneurship,* edited by J. Robert Baum, Michael Frese, and Robert Baron (New York: Psychology Press Taylor & Francis Group, 2012), 157.

281   Ibid., 157.

282   Ibid., 158.

283   Ibid., 158.

284   Ibid., 159.

285   Faschingbauer, *Effectuation,* xv.

286   Saras D. Sarasvathy, *Effectuation: Elements of Entrepreneurial Expertise – New Horizons of Entrepreneurship* (Cheltenham: Edward Elger, 2008), 22–23.

A majority of them questioned the forecast data they were supplied with, thought well beyond the suggested target markets and primarily focused on their personal interests, their knowledge and their social network to shape their business ideas."[287]

Having an individual approach, Locke and Baum argue, is an important prerequisite for entrepreneurial success. "This means [entrepreneurs] often go against the status quo, defy tradition, or do what others claim is foolish, crazy, or impossible. Entrepreneurs, therefore, must not only be in charge, they must be independent thinkers. Regardless of whom they consult, they must rely in the end on their own judgement. The buck stops with them. Dependent, follower types cannot operate in such a role and do not seek to."[288]

Birger P. Priddat argues in a similar vein: "Entrepreneurs are atypical decision-makers, a minority … The innovative entrepreneur – who notoriously acts as an investor – is also characterized by the fact that he dares to approach uncertain situations, to set something new into the world, to operate within uncertainty. This is what makes him extraordinary, what makes him a nonconformist."[289] This nonconformism seems to be characteristic of entrepreneurs; it means "not acting like others think you should". Seen from the outside, the entrepreneur may even seem "a little crazy at times". But this is a "craziness but still within the sphere of conformity."[290]

Hisrich, Langan-Fox, and Grant go a step further. In line with several other authors, they refer to the 'dark side' of entrepreneurs. "Entrepreneurs 'break the mold' by rejecting society's prevailing norm of seeking employment with another organization or person. Many entrepreneurs are misfits, difficult employees who start their own firms because they are unwilling to submit to authority and find it difficult to work in a pre-structured environment."[291] However, this aspect of entrepreneurship has been neglected by scholarly research, argue Hisrich et al.[292]

In 1985, Manfred F. R. Kets de Vries published an essay entitled "The Dark Side of Entrepreneurship". He approvingly cites one entrepreneur who believes that "the entrepreneur who starts his own business generally does so because he is a difficult employee. He does not take kindly to suggestions or orders from other people and aspires most of all to run his own shop." He argues that, unlike employed executives, entrepreneurs are "suspicious about authority". Entrepreneurs are not willing to integrate into existing organizations or hierarchies. "Instead, they often experience structure as stifling. They find it very difficult to work with others in structured situations unless, of course, *they* created the structure and the work is done on *their* terms." They have become entrepreneurs because of their inability to submit to authority and their unwillingness to accept company rules.[293]

In 1996, Kets de Vries emphasized that the feeling of being different has an important influence on entrepreneurs.[294] "It also seems that many of these people cannot function in structured situations. They appear to be allergic to authority. They like to be in control."[295] Kets de Vries criticizes the fact that the traditional questions employed by surveys and interviews are not able to accurately assess the problematic psychopathology of entrepreneurs. He presents a case study of an entrepreneur whom he treated in his psychoanalytic practice. "The enterprise also symbolized his ability to rebel. Setting up an enterprise somehow became a personalized statement of separation. It would make him a person in his own right."[296] Personality traits that make an individual more difficult can have different impacts. On the one hand, they can damage an entrepreneur and their company, often with massive consequences. On the other hand, it also appears that "it is their mix of the creative and the irrational that makes many entrepreneurs so successful".[297]

Other studies confirm that entrepreneurs often do not accept social norms to the same extent as other people. In 1999, Elisabeth J. Teal and Archie B. Carroll published a study in which they positively tested the hypothesis "that entrepreneurs may exhibit moral reasoning skills at a slightly higher level than middle-level managers or the general adult population".[298]

Some evidence suggests that entrepreneurs are often difficult people. In the early 1980s, David McCelland had already developed the idea that 'affiliation', a component of 'Agreeableness', could hinder the career of an employed executive since they would have problems with difficult decisions that could lead to conflicts. Zhao and Seibert argued that this applies even more so to entrepreneurs. "Although the negative effects of Agreeableness appear to predominate for those performing managerial work in established organizations, we expect the negative effects to be even more detrimental for those in an entrepreneurial role." One reason for this is that "managers in established organizations who operate in an overly self-interested and disagreeable manner are likely to eventually suffer negative consequences from peers and supervisors. Entrepreneurs work in smaller organizations and they are less likely to be constrained by dense and interlocking social relationships."[299]

287   Faschingbauer, *Effectuation*, 248.

288   Locke and Baum, "Entrepreneurial Motivation," 97–98.

289   Birger P. Priddat, "Unternehmer als Cultural Entrepreneurs," in *Unternehmertum: Vom Nutzen und Nachteil einer riskanten Lebensform*, edited by Ludger Heidbrink and Peter Seele (Frankfurt-am-Main: Campus Verlag, 2010), 115.

290   Ibid., 122.

291   Hisrich, Langan-Fox, and Grant, "Entrepreneurship Research and Practice," 582.

292   Ibid., 582.

293   Manfred F. R. Kets de Vries, "The Dark Side of Entrepreneurship," *Harvard Business Review* (November 1985), accessed 27 October 2017, https://hbr.org/1985/11/the-dark-side-of-entrepreneurship/ar/1.

294   Manfred F. R. Kets de Vries, "The Anatomy of the Entrepreneur: Clinical Observations," *Human Relations* 49, no. 7 (1996), 856.

295   Ibid., 857.

296   Ibid., 871.

297   Ibid., 878.

298   Elisabeth J. Teal and Archie B. Carroll, "Moral Reasoning Skills: Are Entrepreneurs Different?", *Journal of Business Ethics* 19 (1999), 229.

299   Zhao and Seibert, "The Big Five," 261.

This hypothesis was confirmed by the evaluation of several studies according to which entrepreneurs show much less Agreeableness than managers.[300]

Analysis of the biographies of many rich people also reveals that they are often markedly confrontational and not very agreeable. Evidence of this can be found in the biographies of Jack Welch (General Electric),[301] Bill Gates (Microsoft),[302] Steve Jobs (Apple),[303] Rupert Murdoch,[304] David Ogilvy,[305] George Soros,[306] and Ray Kroc (McDonald's).[307]

One hypothesis put forward in this book is that a specific form of nonconformism is a characteristic of UHNWIs. Entrepreneurs and investors were asked whether they consciously contradicted popular opinion when making important decisions and what role this played in their financial success. They were also asked about the extent of their willingness to engage in confrontation. Anyone who is not willing to engage in conflict cannot compete in the market against competitors, just as they cannot assert themselves within their own company. In the interviews, interviewees were asked whether they assessed themselves as nonconformists and as willing to engage in conflict. The two aspects are closely related, as nonconformist behaviour often leads to conflict with others.

3.2.G. TYPOLOGY AND MODELS FOR SUCCESSFUL ENTREPRENEURS

John B. Miner devoted 20 years of research to studying the factors behind entrepreneurial success. His most important finding was: "First, there is not a single type of entrepreneur, but rather there are four different types, each with a distinct personality."[308] Miner argued that the idea of 'the entrepreneur' as one type of individual who possesses very specific personality traits is unfounded. Miner examined a total of 100 entrepreneurs, whom he interviewed extensively and tested for 18 personality traits. He concluded that there are four types of entrepreneurs, each of whom exhibits different personality traits and experiences success in different commercial arenas and situations:

1. The Personal Achiever. These are the individuals who set themselves goals, develop plans for achieving them, work hard, and are very good at managing difficult situations. They believe that their work should be guided by personal goals rather than those of others.[309] They also have a need to plan and set goals, and are characterized by a pronounced personal initiative.[310] They are strong individualists. In many cases, they became entrepreneurs because, as dependent employees, they did not have the freedom they needed to implement the ideas they believed in so strongly.[311] They are more successful with their own small- to medium-sized enterprises (with, for instance, fewer than 30 employees) than in larger enterprises.[312]

2. The Supersalesperson. "To succeed as entrepreneurs, supersalespeople need to use the selling route: spending as much time as possible selling and getting someone else to manage the business."[313] The supersalesperson entrepreneur is able to empathize with others, and achieves success primarily as a result of their social competences and sales talents, but they need to be partnered with a manager, as the organization of structured processes is not usually their strength. Often, supersalesperson entrepreneurs have been successful salespeople before starting out as entrepreneurs.[314]

3. The Real Manager. These individuals, above all, possess management skills. They achieve success when they start a large company where their management skills are required and of great advantage. Typically, these persons were previously employees working within large commercial organizations and companies.

4. The Expert Idea Generator. "Expert Idea Generators invent new products, find new niches, develop new processes, and generally find a way to outthink the competition."[315] These are visionaries, capable of generating ideas and transforming them into entrepreneurial success.

For 62% of the entrepreneurs surveyed by Miner, a single typology clearly dominated, while the remaining 38% were classed as 'complex entrepreneurs', which included several of these typologies. His most interesting finding: only one person combined all four typologies, while Miner was able to observe a combination of

---

300   Ibid., 264.

301   Welch, Jack, with John A. Byrne, *Jack: Straight from the Gut* (London: Warner Books, 2001), 98, 110, 120–121, 131, 138; Jack Welch and Suzy Welch, *Winning: The Answers – Confronting 74 of the Toughest Questions in Business Today* (New York: Warner Books, 2006), 58, 84, 86, 99.

302   James Wallace and Jim Erickson, *Bill Gates and the Making of the Microsoft Empire* (Chichester: Wiley, 1992), 50, 101, 149, 161–162, 266, 277 et seq., 293.

303   Young and Simon, *iCon Steve Jobs*, 177, 284–285, 235–236.

304   Michael Wolff, *The Man Who Owns the News: Inside the Secret World of Rupert Murdoch* (London: The Bodley Head, 2008), 18; 35.

305   Kenneth Roman, *The King of Madison Avenue: David Ogilvy and the Making of Modern Advertising* (New York: St. Martin's Griffin, 2009), 86–87, 171.

306   Robert Slater, *George Soros: The World's Most Influential Investor* (New York: McGraw-Hill Companies, 2009), 94, 114.

307   Love, *McDonald's*, 89 et seq., 102.

308   John B. Miner, *The 4 Routes to Entrepreneurial Success* (San Francisco: Berrett-Koehler Publishers, 1996), 1.

309   Ibid., 10.

310   Ibid., 9.

311   Ibid., 18.

312   Ibid., 31–32.

313   Ibid., 4.

314   Ibid., 43.

315   Ibid., 5.

two typologies in 27% of his subjects and a combination of three in 10% of the entrepreneurs he studied.[316]

It is also important to point out that entrepreneurs undergo different stages of development, during which a variety of personality traits come to the fore. This process was observed by Chell, Haworth, and Brearley, who published an evaluation of the entrepreneurial personality traits of 31 company founders. Their findings were published in 1991 as *The Entrepreneurial Personality*. They conducted 31 interviews and had the entrepreneurs fill out a questionnaire. Their questions included the degree to which the company's processes were formalized (for example, were there written strategic plans, or were plans made on a more informal basis? Was there a clearly defined hierarchy of roles within the organization? And were formal meetings held at regularly timetabled intervals?).[317] They distinguished between three stages of company development: start-ups, established enterprises, and professionally managed enterprises.[318] The authors also distinguished between four entrepreneurial types, namely the 'caretaker', the 'administrator', the 'quasi-entrepreneur', and the actual 'entrepreneur'.

The authors demonstrated that entrepreneurial behaviour can indeed alter at the different stages of an enterprise's development. "For example, the behavioural characteristics of the business owner can change during the life course. In particular, a person who may well have been classified as an entrepreneur in earlier years may be classified as a caretaker in later years as their energy levels, goals and motivations change."[319]

The research carried out by Miner and by Chell et al. is of relevance to this book for several reasons. It is evident that there is no single pathway to wealth. This raises the question: Are there characteristics or traits common to all people who achieve great wealth? Or is it possible to identify typologies or patterns that shape the process of wealth creation and accumulation? It seems unlikely that all UHNWIs possess exactly the same personality traits or have identical behaviour patterns. However, it is likely that certain patterns can be observed that are found in many wealthy people.

3.2.H. MOTIVATIONS FOR ENTREPRENEURSHIP AND THEIR CORRELATION WITH SUCCESS

Why do some people decide to become entrepreneurs? And do these reasons play a role in an individual's subsequent success as an entrepreneur?

In the United States in the mid-1980s, Stanley Cromie conducted interviews with 35 male and 34 female entrepreneurs to find out why they had opted for self-employment. 'Autonomy', 'achievement', 'job dissatisfaction', and 'money' were the dominant motivations; all other reasons were – at least for the male interviewees – much less important.[320] The motive of earning a great deal of money came across very clearly in the interviews and was explicitly formulated. "Many of the samples were quite explicit in expressing this need. They said things like,

... 'you will never make real money working for someone else' or 'I want to earn lots and lots of money.'[321]

Another survey of entrepreneurs and those who were seriously considering becoming self-employed, also conducted in the 1980s, revealed that 'greater financial rewards' (25%) was the number one reason, followed by 'desire to be own boss' (20%), 'personal challenge' (18%), 'desire to build something of your own' (16%), and 'frustrated with corporate life' (13%).[322]

In the mid-1980s, Gerhard Plaschka interviewed 299 successful and 63 unsuccessful entrepreneurs in Austria for his doctoral dissertation "Entrepreneurial Success: A Comparative, Empirical Study of Successful and Unsuccessful Company Founders". For successful entrepreneurs, the motivation 'to prove their own capability' was the most important, followed by 'carrying out their own ideas' and 'attaining the freedom to decide and act'. Financial motivations, such as reaching a 'performance-based income', striving for 'economic independence', and attaining a 'higher income' were in 6th, 9th, and 11th place of the 22 rankings.[323]

In the late 1980s, G.M. Naidu and Chem L. Narayana interviewed 83 entrepreneurs whose companies had received Small Business Administration awards for outstanding performance. The two most frequent motivations for becoming self-employed were the desire for independence (75%) and the goal of earning (more) money (52%).[324]

In the early 1990s, Sue Birley and Paul Westhead interviewed 405 owner-managers about the reasons why they had become self-employed. One of the primary reasons was the independence motive – for example, 'to have considerable freedom to adapt my own approach to my work' or 'to control my own time'. These were followed by financial motivations, such as 'to give myself, my spouse, and my children security' or 'desire to have high earnings'.[325] However, the study also revealed that the motivations behind an individual's decision to become self-employed did not have any bearing on whether they actually succeeded with their enterprise or not.

---

316   Ibid., 107.

317   Chell, Haworth, and Brearley, *The Entrepreneurial Personality*, 76.

318   Ibid., 151.

319   Ibid., 73.

320   Stanley Cromie, "Motivations of Aspiring Male and Female Entrepreneurs," *Journal of Occupational Behaviour* 8 (1987), 255.

321   Ibid., 257.

322   Robert Ronstadt, "The Decision *Not* to Become an Entrepreneur," in *Frontiers of Entrepreneurship Research*, edited by John A. Hornday, Jeffrey A. Timmins, and Karl H. Vesper, 192–212 (Massachusetts: Babson College, 1993), 195.

323   Plaschka, *Unternehmenserfolg*, 118.

324   G.M. Naidu and Chem L. Narayana, "Problem-Solving Skills and Growth in Successful Entrepreneurial Firms," in *Frontiers of Entrepreneurship Research*, edited by N.C. Churchill (1990), 93.

325   Sue Birley and Paul Westhead, "A Taxonomy of Business Start-Up Reasons and Their Impact on Firm Growth and Size," *Journal of Business Venturing* 9 (1994), 11.

In a paper published in 2000, Raphael Amit, Kenneth R. MacCrimmon, Charlene Zietsma, and John M. Oesch surveyed 51 owners of growth-oriented technology companies to ask the question "Does Money Matter?" As a control group, 28 senior executives from the same industry were also interviewed. The result of their work contradicts the assumption that money is the most important motive for starting a business. Nevertheless, the entrepreneurs believed that their chances of becoming rich by starting a business were considerably higher than if they had continued working as an employee. Interestingly, employed executives in the control group reported that they believed they would make more money as an executive than as an entrepeneur.[326]

However, studies investigating the motivations for starting a business have reported wildly differing results. In 2003, Nancy M. Carter, William B. Gartner, Kelly G. Shaver, and Elizabeth J. Gatewood reported a comparison of the motivations of 179 self-employed men and 205 self-employed women with a group of 89 female and 85 male employees. The main motive for the male and female entrepreneurs was the 'desire for independence', followed by the 'desire for financial success'.[327] The surprising result of the study was, however, that the reasons for their career choices did not differ significantly among entrepreneurs and employees. "Entrepreneurs were similar to non-entrepreneurs in the kinds of reasons they offered for career choice on self-realization, financial success, innovation, and independence ... Overall, these findings argue against considering entrepreneurs to be qualitatively different from individuals who pursue other career options."[328]

Locke and Baum conclude from the evaluation of several studies that independence may be relevant as a predictor of self-employment. However, this motive was less meaningful in regard to whether the entrepreneur would later enjoy actual success.[329]

Nathalie Galais' gave an overview of the status of research up to 1998. She evaluated 19 scientific papers in which various motivations were named, including:
- Desire for independence ('own boss', 'freedom', 'self-realization', 'personal development')
- Desire for recognition
- Desire for work satisfaction
- Desire to earn a lot of money (or 'prosperity', 'financial improvement', etc.)
- Dissatisfaction with previous working conditions.[330]

Galais herself conducted a survey of German entrepreneurs. For the West German entrepreneurs, the independence motive was also in the foreground ('desire to make their own decisions'). This was followed by the 'appeal of work activities', 'dissatisfaction with previous working conditions', and the 'desire to earn more money'.[331]

In 2009, Christina Stadler's doctoral dissertation examined the motivations of small and mid-sized entrepreneurs.[332] The most important motive, according to the findings of her work, was the 'joy of entrepreneurship'. These types of 'soft' factors have been given too little attention in the past.

Neither the American nor the German studies on the topic have concerned themselves with a discussion of the bias towards socially desirable answers. In both countries, idealistic motivations (desire for independence, self-realization, etc.) are socially more acceptable than talking about the desire for maximizing profits.

3.2.I. KEY INFLUENCES DURING CHILDHOOD AND ADOLESCENCE

Eva Schmitt-Rodermund reports in an essay on the findings of a long-term study. The survey was based on the Terman Study, which monitored 1,600 individuals in the Berkeley, California, area over 60 years. The boys and girls, selected as children, all possessed IQs of 130 or more and were born in the years around 1910. The first survey took place in 1922, the final survey in 1986. On the basis of the interviews carried out with the boys, in combination with the impressions provided by their parents, the author compared the boys who exhibited an entrepreneurial personality profile with the rest of their peers. "The boys classified as demonstrating entrepreneurial traits were those who scored highly for conscientiousness and hard work, extroversion and openness to experience, while scoring low for agreeableness and mental instability."[333] This profile corresponds with the above-mentioned studies on the personality profiles of entrepreneurs. The findings: "The more a boy identifies with entrepreneurial personality traits, the greater the likelihood that he will engage in entrepreneurial activities in adulthood, or join the executive or supervisory boards of commercial enterprises." The boys who were described by their parents as possessing the traits associated with entrepreneurial personalities were later twice as likely to become entrepreneurs or CEOs as those with different personality profiles.[334]

---

326 Raphael Amit, Kenneth R. MacCrimmon, Charlene Zietsma, and John M. Oesch, "Does Money Matter? Wealth Attainments as the Motive for Initiating Growth-Oriented Technology Ventures," *Journal of Business Venturing* 16 (2000), 120.

327 Nancy M. Carter, William B. Gartner, Kelly G. Shaver, and Elizabeth J. Gatewood, "The Career Reasons of Nascent Entrepreneurs," *Journal of Business Venturing* 18 (2003), 29.

328 Ibid., 31.

329 Locke and Baum, "Entrepreneurial Motivation," 108.

330 Nathalie Galais, "Motive und Beweggründe für die Selbständigkeit und ihre Bedeutung für den Erfolg," in *Erfolgreiche Unternehmensgründer: Psychologische Analysen und praktische Anleitungen für Unternehmer in Ost- und Westdeutschland*, edited by Michael Frese (Göttingen: Verlag für Angewandte Psychologie, 1998), 84.

331 Ibid., 85.

332 Christina Stadler, *Freude am Unternehmertum in kleineren und mittleren Unternehmen: Ergebnisse einer Quer- und Längsschnittanalyse* (Wiesbaden: Gabler Verlag, 2009).

333 Eva Schmitt-Rodermund, "Wer wird Unternehmer? Persönlichkeit, Erziehungsstil sowie frühe Interessen und Fähigkeiten als Vorläufer für unternehmerische Aktivität im Erwachsenenalter," *Wirtschaftspsychologie* 2 (2005), 13.

334 Ibid., 16.

In a cross-sectional study of adult entrepreneurs who were asked to retrospectively report on their childhoods and teenage years, the same correlations were reported.[335]

Furthermore, the study showed that individuals who went on to become entrepreneurs were more likely to have taken on leadership roles during their adolescence (student body president, official positions within sporting clubs or boy scouts, etc.) and were more likely to have invented something (such as new recipes or even their own constructions and devices) than other children and adolescents.[336] In addition, the study revealed that individuals who proceeded along an entrepreneurial path in later life were more likely to have read books on economic subjects during their earlier years, and more frequently expressed a desire to engage in independent entrepreneurship when asked about their future career plans.[337]

In 2012, Martin Obschonka, Rainer K. Silbereisen, and Eva Schmitt-Rodermund reported on a study involving 488 participants, which "found that ... early entrepreneurial competence in adolescence predicted business idea generation".[338] Participants were asked to recall the time when they were 14 or 15. They were asked whether they had been class representatives, whether they had published a school newspaper, whether they were the leader of a band, whether they had taken up leadership roles within youth organizations, etc. They were also asked how often they had created new technical devices and whether, at this age, they had already engaged in commercial interests, such as selling things to their friends. "As expected, early entrepreneurial competence in adolescence directly predicted entrepreneurial behaviour, which underscores the relevance of adolescent competence for adults' entrepreneurship."[339]

This research also provided another key finding: the children of entrepreneurial parents are far more likely than their peers to go on to become entrepreneurs themselves. Researchers examined whether high parental income or parental entrepreneurship is more likely to increase the likelihood of an individual becoming an entrepreneur in later life. This empirical study showed unequivocally "that having a parent who is an entrepreneur affects a child's entrepreneurial probability much more than having rich parents".[340]

A further study in the United States compared 102 individuals who had seriously considered the idea of setting up a business (but had subsequently not done so) with 208 entrepreneurs. The findings were interesting: "Nonstarts were asked whether their mothers or fathers were entrepreneurs, and if they had other 'entrepreneurial role models'. Some 44% had entrepreneurial fathers, 12% had entrepreneurial mothers, and 40% replied that they had an entrepreneurial role model." In comparison, 76% of active entrepreneurs had an entrepreneurial father and 25% had an entrepreneurial mother. Other studies carried out in the United States reported that some 60% of the sons of entrepreneurs have gone on to become entrepreneurs in their own right.[341]

In some interviews with millionaires, it becomes clear that adolescent competitive sport plays a crucial role in entrepreneurship. In a monograph concerning millionaires published in Switzerland in 2010, one of the interviewees reported: "At school, I was always in leadership positions, as class president and as captain of the school football team. I am convinced that this requires certain basic character traits."[342] One of the other interviewees had spent 12 years as a competitive athlete[343] and another had played for the Swiss national handball team.[344]

For this book, the interviewees were therefore asked whether they had been interested in commercial activities during their adolescence (e.g. producing or selling something) or whether they had engaged in competitive sport. This line of questioning is based on the assumption that these individuals, all of whom went on to amass significant wealth, had already demonstrated interests or skills in childhood that set them apart from their peers and became the basis for their entrepreneurial activities and financial success. In addition, it is interesting to find out whether they had specific childhood role models who exerted an influence on their subsequent career paths.

An analysis of the biographies of the wealthy also reveals that many of them were extremely rebellious children who often came into conflict with authority figures, in particular their parents and teachers.[345] Numerous examples of such childhood rebelliousness are found in the biographies of Steve Jobs,[346] Bill Gates,[347] Larry Ellison (Oracle),[348] Ted Turner (CNN),[349] Warren Buffett,[350] and the investor Prince Alwaleed.[351] It is for this very reason that the interviews also included questions on whether the UHNWIs had conflicts that arose with authority figures (primarily parents and teachers) that went beyond the scope of typical teenage conflicts.

---

335   See Eva Schmitt-Rodermund, "Pathways to Successful Entrepreneurship: Parenting, Personality, Competence, and Interests," *Journal of Vocational Behavior* 65 (2004).

336   Schmitt-Rodermund, "Wer wird Unternehmer?" 14–15.

337   Ibid., 17.

338   Martin Obschonka, Rainer K. Silbereisen, and Eva Schmitt-Rodermund, "Explaining Entrepreneurial Behavior: Dispositional Personality Traits, Growth of Personal Entrepreneurial Resources, and Business Idea Generation," *Career Development Quarterly* 60 (2012), 178.

339   Ibid., 187.

340   Erick Hurst and Annamaria Lusardi, "Liquidity Constraints and Entrepreneurship: Household Wealth, Parental Wealth, and the Transition In and Out of Entrepreneurship," *Journal of Political Economy* 112, no. 2 (2004), 15.

341   Ronstadt, "The Decision Not to Become an Entrepreneur," 200–201.

342   Mäder, Aratnam, and Schillinger, *Wie Reiche denken und lenken*, 183.

343   Ibid., 203.

344   Ibid., 207.

345   Zitelmann, *Dare to Be Different and Grow Rich*, 105–114.

346   Young and Simon, *iCon Steve Jobs*, 22 et seq., 42.

347   Wallace and Erickson, *Bill Gates*, 21–22, 38 et seq., 89 et seq.

348   Mike Wilson, *The Difference between God and Larry Ellison: Inside Oracle Corporation* (New York: Harper Business, 2002), 23–24.

349   Porter Bibb and Ted Turner, *It Ain't as Easy as It Looks* (Boulder: Atlantik Books, 1993), 18, 29–30.

350   Alice Schroeder, *The Snowball: Warren Buffett and the Business of Life* (London: Bloomsbury Publishers, 2008), 86–87

351   Riz Khan, *Alwaleed: Businessman, Billionaire, Prince* (London: Harper Collins, 2006), 22–33.

Questions Raised by Behavioural Economics and Learning Theories

4

Behavioural economics studies the effects of psychological, social, cognitive, and emotional factors on the economic decisions of individuals and institutions.

One of this book's hypotheses is that entrepreneurs usually do not act in accordance with the rational assumptions of classic economic theories. They do not typically base their decisions on probabilistic calculations and tend not to slavishly follow complex theoretical assumptions, preferring instead to act intuitively and rely largely on their gut feelings. This applies to entrepreneurs to a far greater extent than it does to employed executives, as entrepreneurs do not have to go to the same lengths to justify their decisions to others (e.g. committees, supervisory boards), and entrepreneurs are far less likely than employed executives to have business administration qualifications.

Classic economic theories base their assumptions on the model of *Homo economicus*, whose characteristics include unlimited rationality, willpower, and self-interest. Such simplified assumptions are important for building economic models but can only ever describe a limited slice of reality.[352] When critics of this approach point out that economic subjects do not behave according to these principles in the real world, their criticism falls short because the proponents of this approach have never claimed that they do.

In contrast, the research approach adopted by behavioural economics stresses that the real-life decision-making of individuals is plagued by irrationality, distorted perceptions, and systematic errors. In simplified terms, scholars working within the field show that economic subjects frequently fail to perceive reality correctly and are instead often governed by biases and emotions. Numerous experiments have shown that most people often rush to premature conclusions that violate all laws of logic and probability.[353]

Existing research demonstrates that people are governed by heuristics and biases, and that their perceptions and actions are based on constant distortions of reality, as they apply rules of thumb rather than logic and probability calculations. "This program of heuristics and bias", says Hanno Beck, "seems to brand man as a cognitive failure – how can we then explain the success that people demonstrate in solving the most complex tasks?"[354] Researchers such as Gerd Gigerenzer and Beck advocate a different view: heuristics could be interpreted as offering rapid, unconscious solutions that do not always result in mistakes and that, within the right environment, can bring about positive results.[355]

Their research shows that heuristics – i.e. the mental shortcuts and rules of thumb on which people commonly base their decisions – can sometimes make sense and should not be viewed disparagingly in comparison with analytical problem-solving strategies (i.e. those strategies that take full account of probability and logic). "With the aid of these heuristic techniques, and in spite of time constraints and a lack of information, it is possible to arrive at efficient decisions, the results of which can certainly be compared favourably with other, more formal, methods. They are quick because they do not rely on complicated calculations, and they are economic because they only require limited amounts of information, and can even achieve better results."[356]

Gigerenzer stresses the importance of the "intelligence of the unconscious", the power of which "is in knowing, without thinking, which rule is likely to work in which situation".[357] He claimed that it would be wrong to assume that intelligence is necessarily conscious or always dependent upon rational thought processes. Gigerenzer's core hypothesis is that apparent cognitive limitations demonstrated by economic theorists in a range of experiments often prove to be intelligent social judgements in the real world.[358] Beck points out that many of the economic institutions and policies created or implemented by humans were not the product of logical-constructivist thinking, but are actually the result of a spontaneous, evolutionary process. "They weren't the result of careful planning, they have become established because they proved to be superior over the course of centuries of field trials."[359]

In an uncertain world, claims Gigerenzer, complex decision-making methods, which require a greater degree of information and more extensive computation, often result in poorer decisions and can actually be damaging, primarily because they may raise unjustified expectations of certainty. Gigerenzer argues that, in order to make reliable decisions in an uncertain world, we have to ignore certain information, which is exactly what people do when they employ rules of thumb. These rules of thumb, or intuitions, allow us to save both time and effort, and make better decisions.[360]

---

352   Hanno Beck, *Behavioral Economics: Eine Einführung* (Wiesbaden: Springer Gabler, 2014), 6.
353   Ibid., 35.
354   Ibid., 76.
355   Ibid., 77.
356   Ibid., 84.
357   Gerd Gigerenzer, *Gut Feelings: The Intelligence of the Unconscious* (New York: Viking Penguin, 2007), 19.
358   Ibid., 103.
359   Beck, *Behavioral Economics*, 397.
360   Gerd Gigerenzer, *Risk Savvy: How to Make Good Decisions* (New York: Viking Penguin, 2014), 40.

Decisions based on heuristics are often superior because they concentrate on the limited information that is actually relevant, while ignoring superfluous input.[361]

Experiments have shown that it is sometimes better to spend less time and use less information, rather than expending more time and making use of more information. "*Less is more* means there is some range of information, time, or alternatives where a smaller amount is better."[362] Here is an example: Thomas Astebro and Samir Elhedhli showed that, when venture capitalists attempt to predict the chances of an early-stage venture being successful or not, more information does not necessarily lead to more certainty. In fact, the opposite is true. "The more information about the venture provided to the [venture capitalists], the less able they were at predicting outcomes … The results should bring support for the argument that simple, but not extremely simple, decision rules can perform well, especially because this test was performed on a large number of non-experimental decisions."[363]

4.1. THE ROLE OF 'GUT DECISIONS' AND INTUITION

Gigerenzer emphasizes the value of intuition. An intuition or a gut feeling, according to Gigerenzer, is a judgement:
1. Which appears quickly in our consciousness,
2. Whose underlying reasons we are not fully aware of, and
3. Which is strong enough to act upon.[364]

He describes this as a form of unconscious intelligence. "Most parts of our brain are unconscious, and we would be doomed without the vast experience stored there. Calculated intelligence may do the job for known risks, but in the face of uncertainty, intuition is indispensable."[365]

A study of 83 Nobel Prize winners in science and medicine revealed that 72 of them strongly emphasized the importance of intuition in their success.[366] In some cases, intuition will surface very suddenly, but sometimes it needs a certain incubation period. Konrad Lorenz, who won a Nobel Prize for medicine, used the following analogy: "If you press (too hard) … nothing comes of it. You must give a sort of mysterious pressure and then rest, and suddenly BING! … the solution comes."[367] Scholars who have studied this topic confirm: "A period away from concentrated problem solving may allow time for an unrecognized misleading assumption, dissolved in the way in which the problem has been formulated, to dissipate, thus opening up new lines of inquiry."[368]

Over the years, numerous studies have investigated the role played by intuition for entrepreneurs and employees in management positions. In a survey of 32 executives who worked for a large international technology service provider, there was not a single interviewee who admitted that they had *never* made a gut decision.

On the other hand, none of them admitted that they *always* trusted their gut feeling. A majority of surveyed executives claimed that they trusted their gut decisions in about 50% of cases.[369] In a survey of 50 senior executives working for a large international carmaker, 76% of those interviewed admitted that they overwhelmingly trusted gut decisions.[370] Weston H. Agor reports that he tested 2,000 executives, and his clear finding was: "Without exception, top managers in every organization examined are significantly different from middle and lower level managers in their ability to use intuition."[371]

According to Gigerenzer, his own studies suggest that the higher executives are in the company hierarchy, the more they trust their gut feelings. However, most said that if they had to justify their decisions to another person, they would conceal their intuition and rationalize their decisions.[372] In family-owned companies, on the other hand, confessing to gut feeling is not taboo: "They are less anxious about gut feelings; if an error occurs, employees are not likely fired on the spot."[373] Many executives would not stand by their intuition-based gut decisions because a rational justification would be expected of them. In addition, a group dynamic would not let an individual defend a decision based on an intuition that they couldn't explain.[374]

Alden M. Hayashi cites the CEO of a large American company in confirmation of the finding that intuition plays an ever more important role, the higher a manager has risen in a company's hierarchy. "Very often, people will do a brilliant job up through the middle management levels, where it's very heavily quantitative in terms of the decision-making. But then they reach senior management, where the problems get more complex and ambiguous, and we discover that their judgement or intuition is not what it should be. And when that happens, it's a problem; it's a big problem."[375]

---

361   Ibid., 31.

362   Gigerenzer, *Gut Feelings*, 37.

363   Thomas Astebro and Samir Elhedhli, "The Effectiveness of Simple Decision Heuristics: Forecasting Commercial Success for Early-Stage Ventures," *Management Science* 52, no. 3 (2006), 407.

364   Gigerenzer, *Risk Savvy*, 30.

365   Ibid., 30.

366   Guy Claxton, "Knowing Without Knowing Why," *The Psychologist* (May 1998), 219.

367   Lorenz quoted in ibid., 219.

368   Ibid., 219.

369   Gigerenzer, *Risk Savvy*, 108–110.

370   Ibid., 110.

371   Weston H. Agor, "Using Intuition to Manage Organizations in the Future," *Business Horizons* (July/August 1984), 51.

372   Gigerenzer, *Risk Savvy*, 112.

373   Ibid., 114.

374   Ibid., 108–109.

375   Cited in Alden M. Hayashi, "When to Trust Your Gut," *Harvard Business Review* (February 2001), 7.

The importance of heuristics and gut decisions goes well beyond the individual. They leave their mark on the entire company, as Gigerenzer shows. People in leadership positions have their own "rules of thumb, which they develop, often unconsciously, to help them make quick decisions". Even in cases where these rules of thumb are not intentionally implemented within the workplace, most employees would follow them unconsciously – and these rules remain in force, even long after the executive in question has left the company.[376] In some cases, such rules of thumb can even feed through an organization's entire corporate culture.

Timothy D. Wilson and Jonathan W. Schooler showed that introspection' does not necessarily lead to better decisions. They compared two groups. One made spontaneous decisions without reflecting on reasons. In contrast, the other group had to reflect extensively and justify why they came to a decision. The results of the quick and spontaneous decision process were better than the results achieved by those who had time to reflect on their reasons.[377] Of course, this does not necessarily apply to all decision-making processes. There are surely many decisions where lengthy deliberation and analysis will lead to better results. However, it is interesting that this cannot be generalized, but that there are also decisions that confirm the opposite – as shown by both authors.

Frank La Pira reports on a research project involving 16 intensive interviews and psychological tests with 'serial entrepreneurs'. The project focused on people who had founded several companies and included individuals who had founded between 3 and 17 companies each.[378] Serial entrepreneurs were asked specifically because they exhibited the lowest probability that their entrepreneurial success had been the result of happy accidents or external good fortune. Every person took a test, which can measure whether a person tends to make decisions based on analysis or on intuition. The "results indicate that the cohort of repeat entrepreneurs chosen for this study had a clear propensity for intuitive decision making. The repeat entrepreneur's mean score was significantly lower than [that of] managers and lower than that of general entrepreneurs."[379]

Risk aversion, attention to detail, and high regard for routines and rules were considered as characteristics of rational decision-making. In contrast, emotional decisions, passion, rash decisions, action orientation, spontaneity, and willingness to take risks were identified as markers of intuitive decision-making.[380] It is particularly noticeable that entrepreneurs stated that they looked at the big picture rather than the details. They claimed to trust their intuition and make emotional decisions more frequently. Additionally, they were more willing to take on risk and were more action oriented.[381] However, this does not mean that they abdicated logical, analytical considerations – one does not exclude the other.

Christopher W. Allinson, Elizabeth Chell, and John Hayes interviewed 156 highly successful entrepreneurs in Scotland and 546 employees in management positions in the United Kingdom. They also worked with the CSI test. "The results of this study offer support for the hypotheses that entrepreneurs (of high growth firms) are more intuitive than members of the general population and middle and junior managers, but that, in terms of cognitive style, they are similar to senior managers."[382]

Naresh Khatri and H. Alvin Ng attempted to pinpoint in more detail situations when gut decisions could pay off for a company. Their hypothesis was that gut decisions were more likely to pay off in uncertain and unstable situations than in stable, certain situations. They interviewed 281 individuals in management positions in the computer industry (unstable external situation), in banking (at that time, a fairly stable situation), and in utility companies (a stable external situation). Firstly, it is interesting to note that representatives from all three industries confirmed that intuitive decisions played an important role. On a scale of 1 to 7 (7 = strong agreement), the representatives from the utility companies reported 4.18, those in the banking sector reported 4.3, and those in the computer industry ranked the highest at 5.5.[383] The study revealed that intuitive decisions have a positive influence on a company's performance in an unstable situation, while they have a negative or negligible effect in a stable situation.[384]

Scholars have proposed various views on how gut feelings work and why intuitive decisions often prove superior to analytical decisions. Gigerenzer's approach, which stresses the importance of heuristics, has already been presented. However, there are other research approaches. "A second line of inquiry suggests that intuiting may involve the use of more complex, but still not consciously accessible, cognitive structures."[385] These researchers have extensively addressed the structures of expert knowledge and how these structures influence the quality of intuitive decision-making in a variety of fields.[386] According to their theory, the superiority of gut decisions is not primarily the result of heuristics, but the result of a very long, implicit learning process that an individual is not consciously aware of. In a split second, insights emerge as if from nowhere, stirred up by the recognition of patterns, which are, in turn,

---

376   Gigerenzer, *Gut Feelings*, 76.

377   Timothy D. Wilson and Jonathan W. Schooler, "Thinking Too Much: Introspection Can Reduce the Quality of Preferences and Decisions," *Journal of Personality and Social Psychology* 60, no. 2 (1991), 181 et seq.

378   Frank La Pira, "Entrepreneurial Intuition, an Empirical Approach," *Journal of Management and Marketing Research*, accessed 5 August 2016, http://www.aabri.com/manuscripts/10554.pdf, 5.

379   Ibid., 12.

380   Ibid., 18.

381   Ibid., 12.

382   Christopher W. Allinson, Elizabeth Chell, and John Hayes, "Intuition and Entrepreneurial Behaviour," *European Journal of Work and Organizational Psychology* 9, no. 1 (2009), 41.

383   Naresh Khatri and H. Alvin Ng, "The Role of Intuition in Strategic Decision Making," *Human Relations* 53, no. 1 (2000), 73.

384   Ibid., 75 et seq.

385   Erik Dane and Michael G. Pratt, "Exploring Intuition and Its Role in Managerial Decision Making," *Academy of Management Review* 32, no. 1 (2007), 37.

386   Ibid., 41.

the result of many years of experience. This is how chess players can intuitively identify and assess extraordinarily complex situations – by recognizing a pattern that they have encountered many times over their years of experience.

The set of questions about decision-making behaviour was of great importance for the interviews in this book. How strongly do individuals make decisions from the gut, which decisions are made using analytic faculties, and which are based on intuition? Did they later regret occasions when they had not trusted their gut feeling or had failed to follow their intuition?

4.2. OPTIMISM AND OVER-OPTIMISM

Behavioural economics also provides insight into another important question for this book, namely the role of optimism and over-optimism as contributing factors to the success or failure of entrepreneurs and investors. Over-optimism can be defined as a tendency of individuals to overestimate themselves regarding certain characteristics or abilities. Individuals frequently overestimate the contribution of their own performance to certain events, and believe that good things happen more frequently, or bad things less frequently, to them than to others.[387] "In terms of its consequences for decisions, the optimistic bias may well be the most significant of the cognitive biases," says Daniel Kahneman.[388] The effect of optimism and over-optimism is ambivalent, i.e. this attitude is often helpful, but can also sometimes be damaging.

As early as the end of the 1980s, Arnold C. Cooper, Carolyn Y. Woo, and William C. Dunkelberg showed how well developed over-optimism can be, based on a survey of 2,994 entrepreneurs, all of whom had recently started their enterprises. Although about two thirds of businesses founded at this time in the United States failed within four years,[389] 81% of the respondents put their personal odds for success at 70% or more, and 33% said their chance of failing was zero.[390] "Entrepreneurs who have already made the commitment to become business owners display a remarkable degree of optimism. Most see their own odds for success as extremely high, far higher than would seem justified by the historic experience of new firms."[391] The entrepreneurs were asked how they estimated the odds for success for other comparable companies. Here, too, their estimations were too optimistic, although not as optimistic as for their own company. "Entrepreneurs perceive their prospects for success as substantially better than those for similar businesses."[392]

The researchers also examined whether the degree of optimism stood in direct proportion to any specific characteristics or abilities exhibited by the respective business founder that would actually influence their prospects of success. No such connection was identified. The entrepreneurs were all equally optimistic, irrespective of whether this optimism was justified in their case or not. "Entrepreneurs' perceptions of their own chances for success do not seem to be systematically related to factors which previous research suggests might be associated with success."[393]

Based on a large number of empirical studies, Thomas Astebro, Holger Herz, Ramana Nanda, and Roberto A. Weber pointed out in 2014 that the median income of entrepreneurs in the United States was lower than the median income of employees. Only a very small number of entrepreneurs earned extremely high incomes, which distorted the group statistical average to a level above the median income. The group's median income was, however, lower than that of employees, and roughly 50% of all business founders had to give up within six years, while only 10% had achieved revenues of more than USD 1 million per year.[394] The authors' point is not just that a high percentage of entrepreneurs failed but also that many entrepreneurs generated very small incomes over a long period of time – low incomes that they paid for with high levels of risk. They tied their illiquid capital up in their companies, and the returns from their companies were no higher than the returns from highly diversified equity funds.[395] In principle, the authors believed that there could only really be three explanations for this:

1. That there is a portion of the population who are very willing to take on risk, and therefore become entrepreneurs
2. Levels of risk are falsely assessed due to over-optimism
3. The non-financial advantages of entrepreneurship (self-determination, control over one's own time) are the overwhelming motivations for entrepreneurship.[396]

The authors concluded that all three explanations were plausible but that the riddle of why people become entrepreneurs despite the objectively unfavourable risk–reward ratio remained unsolved.

Kahneman, who suggested that over-optimism was the explanation, showed that when presented with negative news and forecasts, specifically relating to their company, entrepreneurs are in no way disconcerted. In one experiment, inventors were given the results of an objective and expert analysis of the commercial odds of success of their ideas. Even those who were given the lowest chances of success

387   Beck, *Behavioral Economics*, 58.

388   Daniel Kahneman, *Thinking, Fast and Slow* (New York: Strauss and Giroux, 2011), 255.

389   Arnold C. Cooper, Carolyn Y. Woo, and William C. Dunkelberg, "Entrepreneurs' Perceived Chances for Success," *Journal of Business Venturing* 3 (1988), 99.

390   Ibid., 103.

391   Ibid., 106.

392   Ibid., 106.

393   Ibid., 106.

394   Thomas Astebro, Holger Herz, Ramana Nanda, and Roberto A. Weber, "Seeking the Roots of Entrepreneurship: Insights from Behavioral Economics," *Journal of Economic Perspectives* 28, no. 3 (2014), 51.

395   Ibid., 54.

396   Ibid., 54.

were not dissuaded in half of the cases. Later, only five of these 411 projects were actually successful. Some 47% of the inventors who were advised that their projects were unfeasible continued their efforts unchanged and doubled their losses, rather than throwing in the towel.[397]

According to Kahneman, it is important not to underestimate the role played by cognitive biases. For example, company founders frequently ignore their market competitors. "We focus on what we want to do and can do, neglecting the plans and skills of others."[398] This was demonstrated by Don A. Moore, John M. Oesch, and Charlene Zietsma in 2007. They interviewed 34 founders of high-tech companies, along with 20 employees who had seriously considered founding a company. In their over-optimism, the founders ignored all external factors (as did, interestingly, the non-founders), in particular whether there were serious competitors in their chosen markets. They were concerned exclusively with their own abilities and the factors that had a direct bearing on their own projects. This study showed that external factors played an incredibly small role in the decision to found a company or not. "Only 12% of total factor mentions focused on the external environment (13% for founders and 9% for non-founders), and of those, only 10% or 5% of total factor mentions, dealt with competition."[399]

Without great optimism, most entrepreneurs would never have become self-employed. Mathew L. A. Hayward, Dean A. Shepherd, and Dale Griffin argue that founders' over-optimism is a key explanation for why people found companies even though the probability of failure is so high. "Overconfidence, the central construct of our work, emerges as an enduring motor of the economic prosperity that excessive venture formation generates, and equally as a brake on that prosperity."[400] On the other hand, excessive optimism is often damaging, especially in difficult situations – such as when an entrepreneur or investor continues to inject their own money into their company when an objective observer would long have recognized just how hopeless the situation was.

In 2007, Manju Puri and David T. Robinson examined the ways in which optimism influences economic decisions. They found that "moderate optimism correlates to reasonably sensible economic decisions while extreme optimism correlates to seemingly irrational decisions".[401] Taking a large, random sampling of interviews, the two researchers examined how optimistic the individuals were and how economic and financial decision-making processes differed between moderate optimists and extreme optimists. "Moderate optimists display prudent financial habits: they are more likely to pay their credit card balances on time, they have long planning horizons, and they report that they save because saving is a good thing to do. Extreme optimists, however, have short planning horizons and are less likely to think saving is a good thing to do. Moderate optimists save more, extreme optimists save less."[402] There were a number of other significant differences. For example, moderate optimists worked much longer hours than extreme optimists did. The authors concluded:

"The idea that optimism can be both good and bad straddles two opposing views in the psychology literature. Our results suggest that many of the negative traits associated with behavioural biases may only be salient for those with extreme bias, and that modest amounts of behavioural bias, be it overconfidence, self-attribution bias, or optimism, may indeed be associated with seemingly reasonable decision-making."[403]

In 2009, Keith M. Hmieleski and Robert A. Baron published a study based on interviews with 207 founders. Their study closed a gap in the existing research because, at that time, there had been very few studies carried out on the correlation between the optimism of a company's founder and the eventual success of the company. The first important result of the study was that the entrepreneurs were, as a group, extremely optimistic. Their optimism was much more pronounced than in the average population.[404] While optimism appears to be a fundamental prerequisite for entrepreneurship, the survey from Hmieleski and Baron also shows a negative correlation between levels of optimism and the success of an entrepreneur. The authors measured the level of an entrepreneur's optimism on the one hand and indicators of the company's success (profit growth and growth of the number of employees) on the other hand. Since the degree of optimism for all interviewed entrepreneurs was very high in comparison with the average population, the authors assumed a non-linear relationship between optimism and company success. "The relationship between optimism and new venture performance may be positive up to moderate levels of optimism, but beyond this point, may become negative."[405]

Beck emphasizes that over-optimism should not always be viewed negatively. After all, he points out, it promotes entrepreneurship and enables motivated entrepreneurs to convince others (e.g. finance providers and stockholders) of their ideas. "It may be possible that it is exactly this overconfidence and over-optimism that moves people to great deeds – but it is the same phenomenon that makes them fail. When only five of 100 over-optimistic people succeed in breaking through, then this strategy has advanced humanity in an evolutionary sense – to the detriment of the other 95 over-optimists who failed."[406]

397   Kahneman, *Thinking*, 257.

398   Ibid., 259.

399   Don A. Moore, John M. Oesch, and Charlene Zietsma, "What Competition? Myopic Self-Focus in Market-Entry Decisions," *Organization Science* 18, no. 3 (2007), 444.

400   Mathew L. A. Hayward, Dean A. Shepherd, and Dale Griffin, "A Hubris Theory of Entrepreneurship," *Management Science* 52, no. 2 (2006), 169.

401   Manju Puri and David T. Robinson, "Optimism and Economic Choice," *Journal of Financial Economics* 86 (2007), 72.

402   Ibid., 73–74.

403   Ibid., 97.

404   Keith M. Hmieleski and Robert A. Baron, "Entrepreneurs' Optimism and New Venture Performance: A Social Cognitive Perspective," *Academy of Management Journal* 52, no. 3 (2009), 482.

405   Ibid., 482.

406   Beck, *Behavioral Economics*, 68.

Even if this is beneficial for society as a whole, on an individual level it still raises the question of how a person can protect themselves, at least to a certain degree, from damaging over-optimism. Is there a prescription against over-optimism? Kahneman is sceptical. The main obstacle, in his view, is that the subjective degree of conviction is determined by the coherence of the narrative that has been constructed, and not by the quality or quantity of objective information that supports it.[407]

There are, however, methods that can serve to correct over-optimism. Before starting a project, Garry Klein recommends practising an exercise in which a group of people, all of whom are very familiar with a plan, come together in a meeting, where they are given the following brief: "Imagine that we are a year into the future. We implemented the plan as it now exists. The outcome was a disaster. Please take five to 10 minutes to write a brief history of that disaster."[408] The key benefit of this 'premortem method' is that it allows doubt and it encourages the advocates of the decision to explore possible dangers that have not already been considered.[409]

A further line of questioning for the interviews that form Part B of this work was, therefore: How optimistic are the interviewees? And especially: How do they actually define optimism? Do they consider the risks of over-optimism or not? And, if so, how do they try to reduce the negative consequences? One indicator for over-optimism could be related to HNWIs' assessments of the risks of investing the lion's share of their capital into their own companies. Objectively this is a risk, because of the low level of diversification, but do they also think of it, subjectively, in these terms?

4.3. RISK PERCEPTION AND RISK ASSESSMENT

Over-optimism by definition often leads to a mistaken assessment of risk. "When they come together, the emotional, cognitive and social factors that support exaggerated optimism are a heady brew, which sometimes leads people to take risks that they would avoid if they knew the odds. There is no evidence that risk takers in the economic domain have an unusual appetite for gambles on high stakes; they are merely less aware of risks than more timid people are."[410]

Lowell W. Busenitz surveyed 176 entrepreneurs and 95 employees in management roles in large organizations. He came to the following conclusion: "entrepreneurs use biases and heuristics more, which is likely to lead them to perceive less risk in a given decision situation".[411] With his study, Busenitz sought to explain why some entrepreneurs are willing to accept higher levels of risk even though their risk propensity is no higher than that of others.[412] "Using their specific biases and heuristics to filter their decisions, entrepreneurs are likely to perceive less risk in chosen business opportunities ... Thus, it is not differences in risk propensity that distinguish entrepreneurs from managers in large organizations but differences in the ways they perceive and think about risk."[413] When asked whether they made their decisions on the basis of statistically proven processes or on the basis of rules of thumb, the entrepreneurs – with far greater frequency than the employees in management roles – exhibited a noticeable tendency towards rules of thumb. The study furthermore showed that entrepreneurs are also far more likely than managers to tend towards over-optimism.

4.4. NONCONFORMISM

Gigerenzer emphasizes the importance of imitation in human behaviour. Given the limitations on time and information, no human would ever possibly want to try to make all of their decisions on their own. In many cases, the wisest approach is to simply copy the behaviour of other people. Imitation is one of the key processes by which the vast store of cultural knowledge is successfully passed from one generation to the next.[414] Nevertheless, it is necessary to distinguish between two different types of imitation:
- "Do what the majority of your peers do"
- "Do what a successful person does".[415]

Imitating the majority may satisfy a person's instincts for social acceptance and create a "comfortable conformity,"[416] but if everyone restricted themselves to imitating others, change would be impossible.[417] The imitation of traditional behaviours tends to be successful when the pace of change is slow, and becomes futile when changes are happening quickly.[418] Even ignorance, in Gigerenzer's opinion, can serve as a factor in success – for example, when an agent is simply unaware of certain laws that govern the social world.[419] Incidentally, this explains why a number of lateral entrants and career changers are able to become more successful than those who have amassed extensive experience within a specific industry or sector.

---

407 Kahneman, *Thinking*, 264.
408 Ibid., 264.
409 Ibid., 264.
410 Ibid., 263.
411 Busenitz, "Entrepreneurial Risk," 325.
412 Ibid., 326.
413 Ibid., 327.
414 Gigerenzer, *Gut Feelings*, 216–218.
415 Ibid., 217.
416 Ibid., 218.
417 Ibid., 219.
418 Ibid., 219.
419 Ibid., 221.

Over-optimism, which numerous studies have identified as being especially pronounced among entrepreneurs, strongly correlates with nonconformism, as demonstrated by Antonio E. Bernardo and Ivo Welch in 2001. "Our main argument is that overconfident entrepreneurs (independent spirits, innovators, leaders, change agents, or even dissidents) are less likely to imitate their peers and more likely to explore their environment. Entrepreneurial activity can thus provide valuable additional information to their social group."[420] Although over-optimism, as a product of independent thought and action, often has negative consequences for entrepreneurs, it is beneficial for society as a whole, the authors argue. "When overconfident, entrepreneurial individuals instead follow their own information, downweighting the information in the herd, their actions in effect broadcast their private information to the rest of their group. Unknowingly, overconfident entrepreneurs behave altruistically, making irrational choices that are to their own detriment but help their groups."[421]

Some researchers view entrepreneurs in general as 'misfits'. In her book *Entrepreneurial Behavior*, Barbara J. Bird expresses the view that "entrepreneurs are frequently organizational 'misfits,' unable or unwilling to be supervised, managed or controlled by others or by systems. Instead of working for someone else, entrepreneurs choose to work for themselves. Instead of joining already existing organizations as employees, entrepreneurs (particularly founders) build organizations around themselves."[422]

One of the reasons why individuals choose to become entrepreneurs is that they were dissatisfied in their previous role as an employee.[423] Some researchers even go as far as to claim that individuals become entrepreneurs because they are in some way socially displaced – for example, because they are immigrants, employees who have lost their jobs, or in some way psychologically displaced.[424] Rebellion is an attitude demonstrated by many individuals who later become entrepreneurs. "Socially, the rebel resists authority and isolates himself. He sees himself and is seen by others as the misfit, the man who cannot take orders, who prefers to go it alone."[425]

George G. Brenkert pointed out that scholarly research repeatedly characterizes entrepreneurs as rule breakers. He provides detailed citations from the relevant literature:[426]

- "Rules are meant to be broken … I think you have to be of that mind to be an entrepreneur. If you're going to follow the rules, you might as well forget it, because the rules will beat you before you get started."
- "Entrepreneurs take risks – breaking rules, cutting across accepted boundaries, and going against the status quo."
- "One of the key principles of entrepreneurship – the business of breaking the settled mold – is the absence of clear and fast rules."

– "But entrepreneurs are different. They're not just willing to bend the rules; they revel in it. In fact, most start-up success stories I've heard contain at least one episode of an audacious entrepreneur using some outrageous tactic to swing a crucial deal or find the resources to get an idea off the drawing board."

In 1999, Geoff Williams used successful company founders as an example of how deliberate rule-breaking could pay off. He set out five rules and then provided examples of successful entrepreneurs who had broken these rules. "Listen to the experts. Have a business plan. Be adequately capitalized. Start a business in an industry you know. Don't launch a business in a crowded marketplace."[427]

The fact that entrepreneurs swim against the current and take positions that run counter to majority opinion was demonstrated in 2014 by Elizabeth Pontikes and William P. Barnett. They focused on the timing of companies' entry into a given market. They distinguished between organizations that enter markets under comparatively favourable conditions (such as in the wake of other organizations' successful initial public offerings (IPOs) or during a flood of venture capital funding) and organizations that enter markets under more difficult conditions (e.g. following negative events, such as the bankruptcy of one of a sector's market participants). They found that organizations that entered a target market in the wake of negative events enjoyed a greater degree of long-term success than those whose market entry was buoyed by positive market events.

The authors provided empirical data to prove their hypothesis, although there would also seem to be logical reasons for this. "Consensus about the meaning of salient events clears the way for those who conform to the prevailing view. Positive 'hype' about spectacular financing opportunities may dissuade people from critically questioning whether a market is a good fit for the organization. In contrast, when the consensus view is that a recent failure is evidence of deeper problems in a market, a nascent entrepreneur will be required to defend her nonconformist approach at every turn. A start-up that braves this process is especially capable."[428]

---

420   Antonio E. Bernardo and Ivo Welch, "On the Evolution of Overconfidence and Entrepreneurs," *Journal of Economics & Management Strategy* 10, no. 3 (2001), 302.

421   Ibid., 302.

422   Barbara J. Bird, *Entrepreneurial Behavior* (Glenview: Scott, Foresman and Company, 1989), 172.

423   Ibid., 61.

424   Ibid., 154–155.

425   Ibid., 123.

426   The following quotations – and many more – are found in George G. Brenkert, "Innovation, Rule Breaking and the Ethics of Entrepreneurship," *Journal of Business Venturing* (2008)

427   Geoff Williams, "No Rules," *Entrepreneur* (1999), accessed 27 October 2017, https://www.entrepreneur.com/article/18298.

428   Elizabeth G. Pontikes and William P. Barnett, "When to Be a Nonconformist Entrepreneur? Organizational Responses to Vital Events" (Working Paper 3003, Stanford Graduate School of Business, 2014), accessed 7 July 2015, https://www.gsb.stanford.edu/faculty-research/working-papers/when-be-nonconformist-entre-preneur-organizational-responses-vital, 26.

When a market is 'hot', an organization does not need to be as well positioned or viable in order to secure venture capital funding or transition to public ownership through an IPO. In contrast, when the consensus view of a market is negative, organizations and their business models are subjected to a greater degree of critical assessment and therefore have to be more viable if they are to successfully enter a market. "Organizations that move against the consensus and enter tainted categories after bankruptcies are especially likely to remain in the long-term … Yet organizations that are funded in these booms do not benefit as a result. To the contrary, being funded in a wave of venture capital activity does not bode well, indicating that the organization is less likely to end up going public in the end."[429]

These findings suggest that a nonconformist approach pays off in the long term. Bucking a trend, swimming against the current, breaking with the consensus – are these the qualities that explain why certain entrepreneurs and investors achieve success? In the interviews that form Part B of this book, the interviewees are asked to assess the extent to which their business and investment strategies went against the grain of prevailing moods or opinions, and whether they believe that this was a contributing factor to the success of their endeavours.

Zhen Zhang and Richard D. Arvey deal with the question of whether the nonconformism that is so characteristic among entrepreneurs was also evident during their childhoods or adolescence. They class entrepreneurs as rule breakers by definition. During childhood and adolescence, such rule-breaking is predominantly negative. These two researchers examined the biographies of 60 entrepreneurs and 105 managers and compared these with the average for the population as a whole. Moderate rule-breaking – which includes behaviour such as group fighting, the deliberate vandalism of school property, and school probation – occurred more frequently among young people who would later go on to become entrepreneurs than among the rest of the population, as well as occurring more frequently than among the group of employed managers.[430] More serious examples of juvenile delinquency, such as criminal offences, were seldom reported for young people, who later become entrepreneurs, possibly because severe rule-breaking could impede an individual's career attainment and have more serious and far-reaching consequences in their later professional life.[431]

They also found that negative forms of rule-breaking during puberty could have positive consequences during adulthood.[432] In addition, the researchers found that individuals who came into conflict with their schools or the legal system as juveniles generally possessed higher levels of risk propensity. Such individuals were less likely to expect that their negative behaviour would lead to negative consequences. "We argue that one of the underlying processes linking risk propensity and entrepreneurship is that people with high risk propensity are more likely to exhibit behavioural patterns of challenging the status quo and breaking established rules/mental frames in social contexts.

This behavioural pattern, in turn, can result in a higher probability of successfully grasping business opportunities and starting new ventures."[433] The researchers were able to successfully test this hypothesis.

This represented an interesting topic in relation to the interviews carried out within the framework of this book. The interviewees were asked whether they had exhibited a tendency to break rules and challenge authority during their teenage years. Did they engage in conflicts with authority figures, i.e. parents and teachers, to a greater extent than is typical during puberty?

There are inherent interconnections between several topics raised here, notably:
- Rule-breaking and nonconformism
- Risk propensity
- Over-optimism
- Gut decisions.

In 2006, Elizabeth W. Morrison provided empirical verification of the common-sense assumption that individuals who break rules in their companies tend to have higher risk propensities. "Risk-taking propensity is also likely to be relevant for understanding pro-social rule breaking. Individuals with high risk-taking propensity not only enjoy taking risks but overestimate the likelihood of success associated with risky courses of action and underestimate the likelihood of failure."[434] An empirical study published by Morrison confirms this hypothesis: "Risk-taking propensity, an individual-difference variable, also predicted the reported likelihood of pro-social rule breaking. Regardless of how much autonomy they had, and regardless of whether others always follow the rule, individuals who were more comfortable with risk reported a higher likelihood of breaking the rules than those who were more risk avoidant."[435]

This confirms the correlation between (over-)optimism, risk perception, nonconformism, and the willingness to break rules. However, there is also a link between these traits and the individual's propensity – or reluctance – to take decisions intuitively. Several studies verify that people who trust their intuition "tend to be less conformist."[436]

---

429   Ibid., 26–27.

430   Zhen Zhang and Richard D. Arvey, "Rule Breaking in Adolescence and Entrepreneurial Status: An Empirical Investigation," *Journal of Business Venturing* 24 (2009), 439.

431   Ibid., 443.

432   Ibid., 444.

433   Ibid., 437.

434   Elizabeth W. Morrison, "Doing the Job Well: An Investigation of Pro-Social Rule Breaking," *Journal of Management* 32, no. 10 (2006), 17.

435   Ibid., 22.

436   Allinson, Chell, and Hayes, "Intuition and Entrepreneurial Behaviour," 35.

4.5. EXPLICIT AND IMPLICIT LEARNING –
INFORMAL LEARNING

There are a number of competing approaches to explain entrepreneurial activity within the field of entrepreneurship research.[437] Economists primarily emphasize the role of the environment, market opportunities, and an entrepreneur's ability to allocate resources optimally. The second, more psychological, approach emphasizes the role of personality traits in entrepreneurial success. "Most writers in this approach would not allow for an experiential learning role to alter behaviour in entrepreneurship, since inherent personality characteristics cannot be taught."[438] David Deakins and Mark Freel chose not follow either of these approaches, dismissing the economists, who emphasize the role of external conditions, as well as the psychologists, who concentrate on personality traits. Instead, they highlight the importance of entrepreneurial learning for entrepreneurial success. Their central hypothesis is that an entrepreneur's, or an entrepreneurial team's, ability to learn is decisive for the growth process.[439]

But these approaches do not necessarily contradict each other. On the one hand, the economists are right to emphasize the key role of external conditions. However, since these are identical at a given time for all competing entrepreneurs, this does not explain why one entrepreneur is more successful than another. And, of course, personality traits also play an important role, as has been demonstrated by numerous studies. Still, this does not preclude the fact that the ability to learn is also a crucial factor. Rather, these abilities are connected. For example, a person who, due to their personality, is very open to new experiences is more ready to learn and more able to learn than a person who is not. And a person who is not as influenced by opinions, but tries out approaches that may well run counter to popular opinion, is more likely to have better learning experiences than a person who stays on the well-trodden path and conforms to accepted and established behaviours.

Deakins and Freel discuss the importance of learning theories and how they relate to entrepreneurial learning. In particular, three types of learning are highlighted:
- Learning by trial and error.
- Learning by imitation. "Imitative behaviour involves the observation of successful organisations and the adoption of those practices which it is believed are the key to the observed success."[440]
- Learning by networking.

In a case study, Deakins and Freel show that entrepreneurial learning, to a large extent, occurs experimentally.[441]

This book postulates that an above-average ability to learn is a decisive prerequisite for entrepreneurial success. Business models have to be adapted, and sometimes a complete pivot or reorientation is required, and all of this happens via a process of constant learning and responding to the environment. Entrepreneurs recognize what works and what does not. They can take on successful ideas from other market participants, rather than having to gain all of their experiences by trial and error.

In 1997, John E. Young and Donald L. Sexton explicitly addressed the following questions: "Why do entrepreneurs learn? What do they learn? How do they learn? When is their learning considered effective?"[442] First, they distinguished between explicit and implicit learning. Implicit learning is unconscious, and the entrepreneur either cannot, or cannot fully, express what they have learned. Implicit learning primarily relates to the acquisition of very complex information, and, unlike conscious learning, the process is not a result of systematically testing hypotheses.[443] The paper published by Young and Sexton, however, focuses on the explicit learning process of entrepreneurs.

The increasing ability to solve new and complex problems is core to the learning process. "The complex novel problem represents the most challenging learning situation to the entrepreneur."[444] The entrepreneur faces a constant barrage of new challenges, set either by the company itself or by the environment: requirements from banks, changing competition, issues within the company (recruitment, fluctuation), etc. As the entrepreneur does not have anyone above them to encourage their learning, they have to make their own decisions about the best way to learn – and whether to draw on outside support – in order to gain domain knowledge and other relevant expertise. "The authors believe that it is vital for entrepreneurs to develop and lay out specific learning plans if they are to be successful."[445]

In 1999, David Harper published the paper "How Entrepreneurs Learn: A Popperian Approach and Its Limitations". The author's focus is on entrepreneurial learning, which follows the model of knowledge discovery described by Karl Popper. "I focus upon entrepreneurs who learn from their mistakes and the refutation of their ideas. These 'Popperian' entrepreneurs, as I call them, artificially make the growth of their knowledge more intensive by consciously adopting

---

437 David Deakins and Mark Freel, "Entrepreneurial Learning and the Growth Process in SMEs," *Learning Organization* 5, no. 3 (1998), 146 et seq.

438 Ibid., 146.

439 Ibid., 153.

440 Ibid., 148.

441 Ibid., 153.

442 John E. Young and Donald L. Sexton, "Entrepreneurial Learning: A Conceptual Framework," *Journal of Enterprising Culture* 5, no. 3 (1997), 225.

443 Ibid., 226.

444 Ibid., 229.

445 Ibid., 241.

an overtly critical and systematic approach to problem-solving. Like scientists, these entrepreneurs carry out piecemeal experiments as a way of acquiring knowledge by comparing the results observed with the results expected."[446]

The approach adopted by this type of entrepreneur follows the scientific principles of first proposing a hypothesis, then testing it, and then either confirming it or rejecting it and starting over. The self-critical, self-reflective approach, which characterizes Popper's philosophy, is, according to Harper's hypothesis, also a prerequisite for successful entrepreneurial learning. 'Popperian' entrepreneurs "acknowledge the tentative and conjectural nature of all knowledge, including their own, and recognise that many entrepreneurial forays into the unknown turn out to be mistakes in their original form. They emphasize that since they can learn from their mistakes, it is desirable to discover their mistakes as fast as possible."[447]

Successful entrepreneurs who learn according to this model typically exhibit an undogmatic attitude. "Thus, Popperian entrepreneurs avoid dogmatic strategies for immunising their own ideas against refutation. In particular, they avoid:
- Introducing ad hoc solutions or hypotheses (e.g. substantial decline in market growth dismissed as normal seasonal fluctuation),
- Always adopting a sceptical attitude to the reliability of the experiment or experimenter (e.g. market research firm)."[448]

Harper assumes that entrepreneurial activity primarily consists of continually solving new problems at ever higher levels. "Entrepreneurial activity begins and ends with problems ... And even when succeeding in solving any particular market problem, the entrepreneur discovers new problems so that his or her learning process is conceivably without end."[449] It is also possible, for example, that new problems arise as the unintended side effect of solving previous problems.[450]

Harper concedes that Popper's approach of applying the scientific method of trial and error and hypothesis-testing to other areas of human activity – including entrepreneurial activity – is not uncontested. Nor does he claim that all entrepreneurs follow the approach he describes. "First, a Popperian approach to entrepreneurship requires only that a small minority of economic transactors be as sophisticated and open-minded in their decision-making as Popperian-like scientists."[451] Harper nevertheless suggests that those entrepreneurs who follow this learning method will ultimately be the most successful.[452]

Naidu and Narayana explored the importance of problem-solving abilities for entrepreneurs. They surveyed 83 entrepreneurs whose companies had received Small Business Administration awards for outstanding performance. Entrepreneurs were asked to list the major problems they had faced when setting up their companies. At the same time, they were asked whether, and to what extent, these problems still persisted. Each problem was classified as 'major problem', 'minor problem', or 'not a problem at all'. "Those who had the initial condition three (major problem) and moved to two (minor problem) or one (not a problem) in the current period, or who reported a 'minor problem' in the initial period and subsequently reported 'no problem' in the current period are classified as 'problem solvers'."[453]

The authors then looked at whether there was a correlation between the growth of the company (over a five-year period) and the entrepreneur's ability to solve problems. "In eleven out of the 34 problem areas, there were significant differences between 'problem solvers' and 'others' with respect to median growth. With respect to all eleven problem areas, 'problem solvers' had higher median growth than others."[454] The ability to solve problems clearly plays an important role in entrepreneurial success. Whether this is learned in a systematic way, as Harper suggests with his Popperian entrepreneur, is open to dispute. It seems more likely that implicit learning plays a more important role.

Arthur S. Reber has worked intensively in the field of implicit learning, which he claims leads to implicit, hidden knowledge. Implicit learning is characterized by two features:
- "It is an unconscious process"
- "It yields abstract knowledge".[455]

In her fundamental contribution to the field of implicit learning, Carol Augart Seger set out the following criteria: "What is learned (complex information, not simple associations), how it is learned (incidentally, not through hypothesis testing), the status of the information learned (unconscious, not verbalizable), and the neural bases of the learning (nonhippocampal)."[456]

Experiments examining the learning of grammar rules and probability calculations have demonstrated that "the operations of implicit learning are shown to take place independently of consciousness; their mental products have been demonstrated to be held tacitly; their functional controlling properties have been shown to operate largely outside awareness".[457] Intuition is characterized by the fact that the person knows

446   David A. Harper, "How Entrepreneurs Learn: A Popperian Approach and Its Limitations"
       (Working Paper prepared for the group in Research in Strategy, Process and Economic Organization,
       Department of Industrial Economics and Strategy, Copenhagen Business School, 1999), 11–12.
447   Ibid., 12.
448   Ibid., 13.
449   Ibid., 17.
450   Ibid., 18.
451   Ibid., 22.
452   Ibid., 23.
453   Naidu and Naranyana, "Problem-Solving Skills," 96.
454   Ibid., 96.
455   Arthur S. Reber, "Implicit Learning and Tacit Knowledge," *Journal of Experimental Psychology* 118, no. 3 (1989), 219.
456   Carol Augart Seger, "Implicit Learning," *Psychological Bulletin* 115, no. 2 (1994), 164.
457   Reber, "Implicit Learning," 233.

what is right or wrong, what is a suitable or unsuitable answer in a specific situation – but they are not aware themselves of the reason for this knowledge. Intuition, as defined by Reber, is the end result of an implicit learning experience.[458] This is especially important in relation to entrepreneurial learning, because the research constantly emphasizes the role of hidden knowledge for entrepreneurs.

According to Reber, in evolutionary terms, implicit learning precedes explicit learning. He claimed that this is an ability shared by all humans. Reber argues that there is – regardless of intelligence – only little difference between people's ability for implicit learning.[459] However, this hypothesis has since been disproved. The experiments conducted by Leanne S. Woolhouse and Rowan Bayne demonstrated that the ability for implicit learning differs significantly from person to person.[460]

Taken in conjunction with the studies that show that entrepreneurial success correlates strongly with the ability to make intuitive decisions, these findings clearly show just how important implicit learning is for entrepreneurs. As early as 1990, Charles W. Ginn and Donald L. Sexton published the findings of a study comparing 143 founders and CEOs of rapidly expanding enterprises with 150 founders and CEOs of enterprises that were expanding at an extremely slow pace. Using the Myers-Briggs Test, which measures a number of factors, including how well developed intuitive decision-making processes are, the researchers were able to demonstrate that almost 60% of the key decision-makers in rapidly expanding enterprises tended to arrive at their decisions intuitively, whereas this was only true for 14% of the decision-makers in slow-growth enterprises.[461] "The results indicate that founders of rapid-growth firms have psychological preferences that are significantly different from those of their slower-growth counterparts. Growth oriented founders prefer an intuitive approach or consideration of future possibilities when gathering information."[462]

The importance of implicit learning, which had already played an important role in Friedrich A. von Hayek's work, is today recognized as crucial to entrepreneurial learning. In 2010, in a paper titled "Hayek on Tacit Knowledge", Fuat Oguz demonstrated that 'tacit knowledge' was a concern in Hayek's early scholarly writing. "Yet, because of the lack of a theoretical structure to analyse this theme, Hayek was not able to deepen his work in this direction. As he moved to philosophy, he began to use the insights of Gestalt psychology."[463]

The term first came to prominence in Hayek's 1962 essay "Rules, Perception and Intelligibility". He starts his essay with the example of small children who are able to apply the rules of grammar and idiomatic language without consciously knowing them.[464] "The child who speaks grammatically without knowing the rules of grammar not only understands all the shades of meaning expressed by others through following the rules of grammar, but may also be able to correct a grammatical mistake in the speech of others."[465] Hayek points to the skills of a craftsman or athlete, commonly referred to as 'know-how'. "It is characteristic of these skills that we are usually not able to state explicitly (discursively) the manner of acting which is involved."[466] Oguz summarizes Hayek's view of tacit knowledge as being extremely difficult to articulate and as playing no role in cost–benefit analyses. "An entrepreneur's experience-based understanding of what distinguishes a profit opportunity from mere price differences is a good example of this kind of knowledge."[467]

More recently, the term 'tacit knowledge' was reintroduced by the Hungarian–British philosopher Michael Polanyi, who coined the much-quoted phrase "we can know more than we can tell"[468] in his book *The Tacit Dimension* (1966). For Polanyi, this represents a central problem of communication. "Our message had left something behind that we could not tell, and its reception must rely on it that the person addressed will discover that which we have not been able to communicate."[469] Polanyi clarifies the difference between implicit and explicit knowledge; between skill, on the one hand, and theoretical knowledge on the other. "The skill of a driver cannot be replaced by a thorough schooling in the theory of the motorcar; the knowledge I have of my own body differs altogether from the knowledge of its physiology; and the rules of rhyming and prosody do not tell me what a poem told me, without any knowledge of its rules."[470]

Georg Hans Neuweg illustrates the significance of Polanyi's epistemology and theory of knowledge to learning theory. He defines 'tacit knowing' as a synonym for intuitive skill. "'Tacit knowing' relates to the circumstances occurring *during* perception, judgement or action. In doing so, the subject does not think discursively, and does not provide self-instruction either before or during the performance. The subject perceives something, makes a judgement, expects something, has an idea, solves a problem, reaches a goal, makes a movement, etc. To the extent that the subject's conscious mind is not aware of the ongoing mental processes and the accompanying regulation of such processes, but rather only perceives the results

458   Ibid., 232.

459   Arthur S. Reber, Faye F. Walkenfeld, and Ruth Hernstadt, "Implicit and Explicit Learning: Individual Differences and IQ," *Journal of Experimental Psychology* 17, no. 5 (1991), 888 et seq.

460   Leanne S. Woolhouse and Rowan Bayne, "Personality and the Use of Intuition: Individual Differences in Strategy and Performance on an Implicit Learning Task," *European Journal of Personality* 14 (2000), 157 et seq.

461   Charles W. Ginn and Donald L. Sexton, "A Comparison of the Personality Type Dimensions of the 1987 Inc. 500 Company Founders/CEOs with Those of Slower-Growth Firms," *Journal of Business Venturing* 5 (1990), 323.

462   Ibid., 313.

463   Fuat Oguz, "Hayek on Tacit Knowledge," *Journal of Institutional Economics* 6, no. 2 (2010), 162.

464   Friedrich August von Hayek, "Rules, Perception and Intelligibility," in *Studies in Philosophy, Politics and Economics* (London: Routledge & Kegan Paul, 1967), 43.

465   Ibid., 45.

466   Ibid., 43.

467   Oguz, "Hayek on Tacit Knowledge," 159.

468   Michael Polanyi, *The Tacit Dimension* (London: Routledge, 1966), 4.

469   Ibid., 6.

470   Ibid., 20.

or intermediate results of these processes, the subject experiences its perceptions, judgements, decisions, actions as 'intuitive'."[471]

As described above, learning is not necessarily the result of the conscious and systematic acquisition of knowledge, but often the result of unconscious processes. In an experiment, test subjects assumed the role of a factory manager in a computer simulation. They were tasked with maintaining a specific volume of sugar production by making adjustments to factory staffing levels. The system's underlying functional equation was not revealed to the test subjects. During the learning phase they didn't know that they would subsequently be required to take a knowledge test. The test showed that the test subjects were able to regulate production in the sugar factory without being able to explain exactly how they did so.[472]

In another computer game, "Jeans Factory", the correlation between system knowledge and system control was investigated. The experiment involved test subjects who were tasked with maximizing the profits of a company active in a market with just one major competitor by making decisions on retail prices and production volumes. Explicit knowledge was measured via a 'teaching back' procedure, the results of which were used to reconstruct the mental model of the test subjects. The study concluded that "no significant correlations are found between the quality of the mental model of the test persons and the amount of profit they have generated; also the quality of the considerations during their problem solving does not correlate with the amount of profit obtained".[473] Strikingly, business administration students, with a relatively extensive economic knowledge, generated significantly lower profits than students of education or psychology.[474] The researchers found that the broad knowledge base of the business administration students actually hindered their performance.[475] A conclusion that can be drawn from the theoretical model of tacit knowledge and the experiments outlined above is that, in relation to the restricted access to task-relevant knowledge provided by verbal communication, any measurement of performance that employs only questionnaires "cannot convey a real image of a person's competences".[476]

This is, incidentally, also the reason why it is impossible to ascertain the factors involved in entrepreneurial success simply by asking entrepreneurs. Instead, it is the task of scholars to make as explicit as possible the implicit, tacit knowledge. This is a challenging endeavour and will only ever be possible to a certain degree. This subject will be examined in more detail in Chapter 7.

Also of relevance to this book is the term 'informal learning', which – despite a number of overlaps – is not the same as 'implicit learning'. Karen E. Watkins and Victoria J. Marsick draw a particular distinction between the terms 'informal learning' and 'incidental learning'. Their most general definition is this: "Informal and incidental learning is learning from experience that takes place outside formally structured, institutionally sponsored, classroom-based activities." They employ 'informal learning' as an overarching concept that encompasses all of these forms of learning, whereas 'incidental learning' is defined as the by-product of other activities. Informal learning can be planned or unplanned, but it mostly occurs consciously to some extent, as it is, after all, a learning process. In contrast, incidental learning is largely unintentional and is embedded in an individual's belief system.[477]

In a study conducted by the German Federal Ministry of Education and Research, the results of international research indicated that "almost 70% of all human learning processes take place outside educational institutions".[478] Informal learning is defined here as 'instrumental learning' and as 'a means to an end'. The purpose is, in contrast to formal learning, "not the learning itself, but finding better solutions to out-of-school tasks, challenging situations, or a life problem, with the aid of learning".[479]

As the study's findings demonstrate, this could even be perceived as an advantage of informal learning, that it is not rationed or filtered by an authorized pedagogical authority; rather it develops "directly as the product of holistic environmental experiences".[480] The most decisive element of the distinction between formal and informal learning is that, "in informal learning, in general, the primary goal is not to learn something specific, but to achieve a purpose better through learning, that is, that informal learning, typically in connection with other activities and objectives, is usually a useful and necessary aid to coping better in the environment".[481]

Günther Dohmen points to the numerous characteristics that the concepts of informal and implicit learning have in common. These characteristics are:

- "Learning outside formalized learning contexts and educational institutions"
- "Casual learning in other (not primarily learning-related) contexts"
- "More focused on successful action and problem solving than on the analysis of factors and the theories of reasoning"
- "Direct holistic learning from complex environmental experiences".[482]

---

471 Georg Hans Neuweg, *Könnerschaft und implizites Wissen: Zur lehr- und lerntheoretischen Bedeutung der Erkenntnis- und Wissenstheorie Michael Polanyis* (Münster: Waxmann Verlag, 2001), 13.

472 Ibid., 25–26.

473 Ibid., 27–28.

474 Ibid., 28.

475 Ibid., 28.

476 Berry and Broadbent cited in ibid., 28.

477 Karen E. Watkins and Victoria J. Marsick, "Towards a Theory of Informal and Incidental Learning in Organizations," *International Journal of Lifelong Education* 11, no. 4 (1992), 288.

478 Günther Dohmen, *Das informelle Lernen: Die internationale Erschließung einer bisher vernachlässigten Grundform des menschlichen Lernens für das lebenslange Lernen aller, Bundesministerium für Bildung und Forschung* (Bonn: BMBF, 2001), 7.

479 Ibid., 19.

480 Ibid., 21.

481 Ibid., 23.

482 Ibid., 35–36.

However, apart from these commonalities, there are differences in emphasis between the two terms. These primarily relate to the degree of consciousness involved. In the case of informal learning, this is generally higher than is the case for implicit learning.[483]

Wiebken Düx and Erich Sass refer to "learning in informal contexts", as the learning itself is not informal; rather the context in which it takes place is. Here it is important to recognize "that incidental learning also takes place in extremely formalized contexts".[484]

One example of this is sport, which – as is revealed by an evaluation of the interviews – played a central role in the childhoods and teenage years of many of the UHNWIs who are the subject of this study.[485] In the 2010 collection *Informal Learning in Sport*, Nils Neuber emphasized that informal learning plays a crucial role in sport. The feedback that is of such key importance to the learning process was far more direct in the field of sports than in other fields, because children and young people experience the effectiveness of their actions directly and "at first hand". The elementary importance of experiencing a feeling of empowerment has been well documented in the field of early-years movement education – but also applies generally to all informal learning in sports.

Empirical studies have shown that sport involves the informal learning of competences that "are fundamental to the common goal pursuit and the implementation of individual or group-related interests: discipline, perseverance, self-assertion, assumption of responsibility and problem-solving ability (assertiveness)".[486] These are all central competences for entrepreneurial activity. This shows the importance of addressing informal learning experiences – for example, in sports – in the interviews, in addition to the question of formal education requirements.

4.6. FINANCIAL SUCCESS AND FORMAL EDUCATION

The hypothesis that academic qualifications and formal education play a subordinate role in entrepreneurial and financial success is widely and strongly asserted in the United States – both within the field of academic wealth research and in popular self-help literature. In his book *Millionaire Dropouts: Inspiring Stories of the World's Most Successful Failures*, Woody Woodward presented the biographies of 100 well-known individuals without a university degree.[487]

There are a lot of examples of famous people who dropped out of school or university, or decided not to study in the first place, including the Russian billionaire Roman Abramovich, Paul Allen and Steve Ballmer (Microsoft), Roland Baron (Baron Capital), the British billionaire Richard Branson (who left school at the age of 16), the American billionaire Edgar Bronfman, and many more. Even Google founder Sergey Brin and Warren Buffett only graduated from university when they were already wealthy men. However, the widely held belief that a majority of billionaires failed to graduate from university is factually incorrect. A UBS and PwC study[488] shows that 82% of the world's billionaires are university graduates.

Nevertheless, there is an impressive list of wealthy individuals who are not. Michael Ellsberg, author of the book *The Education of Millionaires* (2012), which he based on a series of interviews with millionaires without academic qualifications, firmly states that academic training is not an important factor in the attainment of wealth. "Around 90% of the people I interviewed and feature in this book are literal millionaires, and several are even billionaires ... All of the millionaires and successful people I interviewed for this book said 'no thanks' to the current educational model."[489] The book provocatively argues that what is taught at universities will only ever help a very small number of graduates to achieve financial success, and may actually hinder others. The book has been enthusiastically recommended by renowned investors and entrepreneurs, including the famous investor Peter Thiel and the WordPress founder Matt Mullenweg. "Education is still necessary to learn how to do the great work that gets you paid. But these days, almost all of the education that ends up actually earning your money ends up being self-education in practical intelligence and skills, acquired outside of the bounds of traditional educational institutions."[490]

Another study, published in the United States in 2009, examines the role of academic training on the one hand, and practical management experience on the other, for the success of entrepreneurs. Interviews were carried out with 63 entrepreneurs who ran their own health food stores. Their entrepreneurial success was measured against the number of years of management experience they had amassed and the academic education they had received (on a scale of 1 (for elementary school) to 7 (for a PhD)).[491] The result: while there is a correlation between the 'founder human capital'

---

483 Ibid., 36.

484 Wiebken Düx and Erich Sass, "Lernen in informellen Kontexten: Lernpotenziale in Settings des freiwilligen Engagements," *Zeitschrift für Erziehungswissenschaft* 8, no. 3 (2005), 395.

485 See also Section 9.5 of this book.

486 Marion Golenia and Nils Neuber, "Bildungschancen in der Kinder- und Jugendarbeit: Eine Studie zum informellen Lernen im Sportverein," in *Informelles Lernen im Sport: Beiträge zur allgemeinen Bildungsdebatte*, edited by Nils Neuber (Wiesbaden: VS Verlag für Sozialwissenschaften, 2010), 198.

487 Woody Woodward, *Millionaire Dropouts: Inspiring Stories of the World's Most Successful Failures* (Murrieta: Millionaire Dropouts, 2006).

488 *Billionaires: Master Architects*, 17.

489 Michael Ellsberg, *The Education of Millionaires: Everything You Won't Learn in College about How to Be Successful* (New York: Portfolio / Penguin, 2012), 10.

490 Ibid., 17. Moreover, although statistics show that college graduates in the US earn roughly 65% more than those without college degrees, the author also questioned this correlation: such comparisons omit opportunity costs (i.e. the time and financial contributions required to finish college). If this figure were instead invested in an index fund generating a return of 8%, the economic return would be greater than that generated by studying. See also ibid., 243 et seq.

491 Gerry Segal, Dan Borgia, and Jerry Schoenfeld, "Founder Human Capital and Small Firm Performance: An Empirical Study of Founder-Managed Natural Food Stores," *Journal of Management and Marketing Research* 4 (2009), 3–4.

and entrepreneurial success, it is extremely weak. The correlation between the number of years of management experience and business success is somewhat stronger, while the correlation between entrepreneurship and school education or academic attainment was shown to be weaker.[492]

Another study of 506 Italian high-tech start-ups, published in 2005, found that "the nature of the education in economics and of the prior work experience of founders exerts a key influence on growth. In fact, founders' years of university education in economic and managerial fields and to a lesser extent in scientific and technical fields positively affect growth while education in other fields does not."[493]

What does German academic wealth research say about the role played by academic education in the creation of wealth? The study "Wealth in Germany" shows that wealthy individuals are more likely to have graduated from university-preparatory school or university than members of the middle class. Among the middle class, 19.6% are university-preparatory school graduates and 21.8% are university graduates. In percentage terms, the interviewees who had graduated from university-preparatory school (and, in brackets, those who had attained a university degree) were grouped as follows:[494]

- Wealthy individuals in dependent employment: 50.7% (46.6%)
- Wealthy entrepreneurs: 44.2% (37.5%)
- Wealthy individuals, self-employed freelancers: 52.2% (46.8%)
- Wealthy individuals, others: 32.6% (33.3%).[495]

This shows that, on the one hand, the wealthy are far more likely to have enjoyed a top-rate education than individuals from the middle class. On the other hand, among the entrepreneurs (by far the study's largest and wealthiest group), there were far fewer university-preparatory school and university graduates than there were among the group who had attained their wealth as employees or as self-employed freelancers. Böwing-Schmalenbrock explained this as follows: "Yes, a majority of entrepreneurs were university-preparatory school graduates, and many of them had studied at university. But, in comparison with those in the other employment categories, fewer members of this group had obtained the highest possible academic qualifications or, in particular, the highest professional qualifications. The path to entrepreneurship is far more likely to involve technical and craft-based skills than theoretical knowledge."[496]

This explanation falls short of the mark. Entrepreneurs may well benefit from craft-based skills and technical knowledge, but other factors play a far more substantial role. Two factors are crucial for entrepreneurial success:

1. Certain personality traits
2. 'Tacit knowledge', 'intuition', and 'gut instinct', all of which are the products of implicit learning.

A number of the authors introduced in Chapters 3 and 4 emphasized the importance of personality traits. Other authors highlighted the importance of learned skills, which can be acquired by both trial and error, and imitation. Case studies have shown that a great deal of entrepreneurial learning is the product of experimentation.[497]

However, as shown here, intuition and implicit learning play an essential role. It has already been pointed out that, according to Reber, intuition is an end product of the process of implicit learning.[498] But implicit learning has very little to do with academic intelligence. It is far more important, in the view of Reber, Walkenfeld, and Hernstadt, to distinguish between practical (implicit) intelligence and academic (explicit) intelligence.[499] The results of implicit learning are overwhelmingly – if not completely – unconscious, as has been demonstrated in numerous experiments.[500]

The American psychologist Robert J. Sternberg developed the concept of 'successful intelligence'. According to his model, successful intelligence has an analytic, a creative, and a practical aspect. "The analytical aspect is used to solve problems, the creative aspect to decide what problems to solve, and the practical aspect to make solutions effective."[501] Sternberg argued that individuals who rely too much on their analytical skills will be less effective than individuals who only make use of these skills when required to do so in specific situations.[502] During a research project to investigate practical intelligence, Sternberg surveyed a large number of individuals in management positions. "Many of the executives interviewed during our studies of practical intelligence complained that they could hire a top-level graduate of a business school and get someone who might be good at analysing textbook cases of business problems but was unable to come up with innovative ideas for new business products or services."[503]

Böwing-Schmalenbrock's discovery that a majority of wealthy individuals had changed professions before they became rich (primarily because they entered

---

492   Ibid., 5.

493   Massimo G. Colombo and Luca Grilli, "Founders' Human Capital and the Growth of New Technology-Based Firms: A Competence-Based View," *Research Policy* 34 (2005), 795.

494   Böwing-Schmalenbrock, *Wege zum Reichtum*, 207–209.

495   It is somewhat surprising that this group has more university graduates than university-preparatory school graduates.

496   Böwing-Schmalenbrock, *Wege zum Reichtum*, 209.

497   Deakins and Freel, "Entrepreneurial Learning," 153.

498   Reber, "Implicit Learning," 232.

499   Reber, Walkenfeld, and Hernstadt, "Implicit and Explicit Learning," 894.

500   Reber, "Implicit Learning," 229.

501   Robert J. Sternberg, *Successful Intelligence: How Practical and Creative Intelligence Determine Success in Life* (New York: Penguin Group, 1997), 47.

502   Ibid., 48.

503   Ibid., 130.

self-employment in order to become entrepreneurs) corresponds with the findings of Sternberg's research. "What successfully intelligent people have in common is that they decide what their field is and then they seek to succeed within it. There is no single criterion for success, and people who are gifted in a large sense, are those who can find personal success in a field of their own choosing and, sometimes, their own making."[504]

If entrepreneurship is an essential prerequisite for wealth-building, and entrepreneurial success is, on the one hand, dependent upon specific personality traits and, on the other hand, the product of implicit, unconscious learning processes, which in turn result in the ability to make intuitive decisions, it comes as no surprise that there is a weak correlation among entrepreneurs between academic achievement and financial success.

Existing Attempts to Explain Success: What Role Does Chance Play? 5

Michael Raynor, Mumtaz Ahmed, and Andrew D. Henderson calculated the probability that high-performing companies were successful purely because they had been lucky. Their hypothesis: "The 'great' companies from which these studies draw their conclusions are mostly just lucky." This "reveals the folly of attributing outcomes arising from systemic variation ... to the supposedly unique attributes of a few individuals, who are really just the luckiest coin flippers".[505]

Many wealthy individuals – as well as other successful personalities – frequently mention fate or luck as significant factors in their success. Franz Walter and Stine Marg interviewed 160 entrepreneurs and executive managers of large companies.[506] In particular, the findings contained in the section "The Careers of Germany's Business Leaders", which was written by Roland Hiemann, are of interest. Hiemann reports that, when asked how they had come to occupy their current leadership position, a majority of those interviewed answered along the lines of "You know, that was never really my plan."[507] He adds that "Captain Happenstance" might be an appropriate headline for a majority of the biographies.[508]

He then goes on to qualify his statement: "The admission that one's own career path lacked an exact plan, and that it was determined just as much by luck and serendipity needs to be put into context in two respects: Firstly, this should not be taken as an indication of the absence of ambition or motivation and, secondly, in no way should it be misinterpreted as disorientation or a lack of control over one's professional destiny ... In addition, stressing the role of luck and the favour of one's superiors

---

504   Sternberg, *Successful Intelligence*, 153.

505   Michael Raynor, Mumtaz Ahmed, and Andrew D. Henderson, "Are 'Great' Companies Just Lucky?" *Harvard Business Manager* (April 2009), 2.

506   Franz Walter and Stine Marg (eds.), *Sprachlose Elite? Wie Unternehmer Politik und Gesellschaft sehen* (Reinbek: BP Gesellschaftsstudie, 2015), 19.

507   Roland Hiemann, "'Geplant war das alles nicht': Werdegänge deutscher Wirtschaftsführer," in *Sprachlose Elite? Wie Unternehmer Politik und Gesellschaft sehen,* edited by Franz Walter and Stine Marg (Reinbek: BP Gesellschaftsstudie, 2015), 39–40.

508   Ibid., 41.

does not obscure the entrepreneur's self-determination or self-esteem; it appears much more to be an expression of these qualities."[509]

In 2008 and 2009, Swiss sociologists interviewed 100 individuals, many of whom were millionaires. They quoted one such interviewee as saying, "I have just had a great deal of luck in my life."[510] Other interviewees were equally willing to ascribe much of their success to luck.[511] Despite such proclamations, the sociologists concluded, "Wealthy individuals tend to ascribe their wealth overwhelmingly to personal qualities ... The rich appear to have earned their wealth by personal merit. The rich have – partly because of their material resources – the feeling that they possess extraordinary abilities."[512]

In contrast to these inner convictions of many rich and successful individuals, they repeatedly emphasize the importance of luck and serendipity when they are interviewed. In 1996, the American professor of psychology Mihaly Csikszentmihalyi published a highly regarded study, *Creativity: Flow and the Psychology of Discovery and Invention*. Between 1990 and 1995 he interviewed 91 extraordinary individuals. Each of his interviewees had made a significant contribution in an important field – science, art, economics, or politics. His interviewees included 14 Nobel Prize winners.[513] Scientists, authors, and artists were more heavily represented than representatives from the business sector (only three of the interviewees belonged to this group).[514]

Throughout his study, Csikszentmihalyi considers the role that luck or serendipity had played in the success of his interviewees. According to Csikszentmihalyi, "When we asked creative persons what explains their success, one of the most frequent answers – perhaps the most frequent one – was that they were lucky. Being in the right place at the right time is an almost universal explanation."[515] "Meeting the right people"[516] was also important.

Luck, the author concludes, is undoubtedly a crucial component of creative discovery. Csikszentmihalyi profiles a very successful artist, whose works sold well and ended up on the walls of the best museums. This artist once admitted ruefully that there were at least a thousand artists as good as he is – yet they are unknown and their work is unappreciated. The one difference between him and the others, he said, was that years back he met at a party a man with whom he had a few drinks.[517] He goes on to reveal that this man later provided him with a great deal of support.

Csikszentmihalyi then proceeds to qualify his statement regarding the huge significance of luck and coincidence. Nevertheless, it is still important to stress the limited importance of the role of the individual, as this is frequently overstated. "Yet one can also fall in the opposite error and deny the individual any credit ... But many people never realize that they are standing in a propitious space/ time convergence, and even fewer know what to do when the realization hits them."[518] He acknowledges that the success enjoyed by these individuals does indeed depend to a large extent on luck, but relativizes this by adding, "So beyond these external factors where luck holds sway, what allows certain individuals to make memorable contributions to the culture is a personal resolution to shape their lives to suit their own goals instead of letting external forces rule their destiny. Indeed, it could be said that the most obvious achievement of these people is that they created their own lives. And how they achieved this is something worth knowing, because it can be applied to all our lives."[519]

Csikszentmihalyi thus significantly qualifies his pointedly provocative opening assertion that even if every new idea or new product has its origins in an individual, it does not follow that this innovation is necessarily the direct product of any particular traits possessed by that individual.[520] Elsewhere he even says, "Rather, as they moved along in time, being bombarded by external events, encountering good people and bad, good breaks and bad, they [the individuals interviewed for the study] had to make do with whatever came to hand. Instead of being shaped by events, they shaped events to suit their purposes."[521]

In his book *Outliers: The Story of Success*, the Canadian journalist Malcolm Gladwell sought to identify why extraordinarily successful individuals are so successful. His central hypothesis is that personality traits, intelligence, etc. are of minor importance in explaining the success of exceptional individuals. "I want to convince you that these kinds of personal explanations of success don't work … The people who stand before kings may look like they did it all by themselves. But in fact they are invariably the beneficiaries of hidden advantages and extraordinary opportunities and cultural legacies that allow them to learn and work hard and make sense of the world in ways others cannot."[522]

Gladwell is convinced that extreme success is not the result of superior personality traits or strategies, but of having worked extremely hard and enjoyed a great deal of luck. Gladwell uses the examples of two highly intelligent individuals –

---

509   Ibid., 43–44.

510   Mäder, Aratnam, and Schillinger, *Wie Reiche denken und lenken*, 182.

511   Ibid., 207.

512   Ibid., 310.

513   Mihaly Csikszentmihalyi, *Creativity: Flow and the Psychology of Discovery and Invention* (New York: Harper Collins, 2013), 13.

514   This is shown in the appendix of Csikszentmihalyi's book, which contains short biographies of the individuals he interviewed; see also ibid., 373 et seq.

515   Ibid., 46.

516   Ibid., 186.

517   Ibid., 46.

518   Ibid., 46–47.

519   Ibid., 151–152.

520   Ibid., 45.

521   Ibid., 181.

522   Malcolm Gladwell, *Outliers: The Story of Success* (London: Penguin Books, 2008), 19.

the world-renowned physicist J. Robert Oppenheimer and a largely unknown and unsuccessful genius, Chris Langan (IQ 195) – to demonstrate that intelligence is no guarantee of success. Gladwell claims that research has shown that intelligence is certainly a factor in both success and failure, but that this only applies up to an IQ of somewhere around 130.[523] But having an IQ higher than this does not result in any additional real-world advantage. According to Gladwell, someone with an IQ of 130 is, for example, just as likely to win a Nobel Prize as someone with an IQ of 180. He believes that 'practical intelligence', namely knowing what to say to whom, knowing when to say it, and knowing how to say it for maximum effect, is far more important.[524] However, according to Gladwell, this is a set of skills that is not in a person's genes; they are learned – and children from wealthier families are far more likely to learn these skills than the children of poor parents. Moreover, the fact that the family someone is born into is determined by luck serves the author as proof of his hypothesis that luck is the most crucial factor. Just like Csikszentmihalyi, Gladwell highlights the fact that people like Bill Gates emphasize the role luck has played in their success. "I was very lucky," said Gates at the beginning of the interview in which Gladwell asked him about the reasons for his success.[525]

So why do successful people often cite luck or serendipity when explaining their success? Csikszentmihalyi, Gladwell, and other authors do not ask this question, preferring to accept at face value their interviewees' assertion that they were lucky. There are actually three reasons why successful people cite luck when they are asked to provide an explanation for their success:

- – Their answer contains an element of truth. Strokes of luck are just as important in life as unfortunate coincidences.
- – They may subconsciously be attempting to deflect envy.
- – Their answer is often a result of perplexity, because they do not consciously know why they are or have been successful.

5.1. THE ROLE OF HAPPENSTANCE

Authors such as Csikszentmihalyi and Gladwell always follow a similar line of argument. If a successful person had not happened to be at a specific place at just the right time, or had not known the right people, they never would have become successful. Philosophy and the philosophy of history have dealt extensively with the importance of chance. In his doctoral dissertation "Chance and Contingency in the Theory of History", Arnd Hoffmann defines chance as follows: "Chance is the coincidence of independent chains of action, which, as individual actions, are based on motives and expectations, and result in goals that, in their confluence and impact on events, only become significant for the actors themselves as the unintended, unpredictable, unexpected, improbable or surprising."[526]

There has been a great deal of heated debate within the field of history as to whether it is sensible or even legitimate to explore history by means of counterfactual assumptions. In 2005, Hoffmann stated that over the past 20 years there had been an obvious growth in interest in the question "What would have happened if...?"[527] Some historians even argue that every causal explanation must contain implicit counterfactual observations, even if these are not made explicit. "If such-and-such a cause or combination of causes had not been present, we imply, or if such-and-such an action or series of actions had not been taken, things would have been different. If we do not believe they would have been, we should not give the causes or actions in question the importance we do."[528]

In books such as Gladwell's, counterfactual assumptions are of great significance, even if these are not explicitly developed. The reader is constantly confronted with questions such as: What would have happened if Bill Gates hadn't had the opportunity to work on a large computer for free? It is difficult to pursue such assumptions to any kind of satisfactory endpoint. Would Gates still have enjoyed such incredible success in his field? And, if not, would he have been equally successful in some other field, as a result of specific traits, such as the combination of his extraordinary intelligence and his outstanding entrepreneurial qualities, or the strength of certain personality traits and his application of successful strategies?

Success is not primarily a question of the opportunities that present themselves to an individual, but much more a question of whether an individual, firstly, even recognizes them as opportunities and, secondly, is able to make the most of them. It is likely that other people are presented with similar opportunities but either do not recognize them as such or fail to exploit them sufficiently, if at all. The novelist Max Frisch once said, "Chance shows me what I have an eye for."[529] Whether opportunities are recognized or used depends to some extent on Openness to Experience – one of the categories of the Big Five personality theory. Numerous studies have shown that entrepreneurs and wealthy individuals exhibit a higher-than-average openness to experience.

Also interesting in this regard are the findings of the psychologist Richard Wiseman, who investigated how people perceive the role of chance in their lives and how they react to unexpected opportunities. His observations demonstrate that extroversion correlates with an increased probability that someone will

---

523   Ibid., 79–80.

524   Ibid., 101.

525   Ibid., 55.

526   Arnd Hoffmann, *Zufall und Kontingenz in der Geschichtstheorie: Mit zwei Studien zu Theorie und Praxis der Sozialgeschichte* (Frankfurt-am-Main: Vittorio Klostermann, 2005), 51.

527   Ibid., 143.

528   Hawthorn quoted in ibid., 151.

529   Frisch quoted in ibid., 56.

encounter unexpected opportunities and actively exploit them. "Anyone who claimed that they had 'been lucky' over and over again was usually much more extroverted than others. This high degree of extroversion means that these self-declared 'lucky ones' come into contact with far more people and, because extroverts are typically more open towards others, they more often benefited from information, feedback and other helpful hints that raised their chances in almost every area of their lives."[530]

Wiseman literally placed two opportunities in his subjects' paths: one in the form of a banknote, which he placed on the floor on their route to the research laboratory, and the other in the form of a potential employer, who approached the subject in a café to engage them in conversation. "The 'lucky ones' found the money immediately, and engaged in enthusiastic conversation in the café, where they found out about a hugely interesting job. Almost all of the 'unlucky ones' walked straight past the money and failed to take advantage of the opportunity to engage in conversation in the café."[531] This demonstrates that the identification and exploitation of chance occurrences is also the result of certain personality traits and attitudes.

Books such as Gladwell's, which attribute a large proportion of the success of people such as Bill Gates and Steve Jobs to a chain of happy coincidences, have an inherent suggestive power, because they lead readers to keep asking: If this single event or that one piece of luck hadn't happened, what would have been different? The more fortunate coincidences an author relates, the more likely the reader is to assume that the person they are reading about wouldn't have been anywhere near as successful if they hadn't enjoyed such a series of serendipitous events. This is, of course, possible, but it is impossible to prove. It would not be that difficult to identify a significant number of negative events or unhappy coincidences in the lives of these successful people, which could only be described as bad luck. If, instead of being so successful, these individuals had actually failed, it would be just as easy to construct a suggestive sequence of unlucky events, which would equally have to serve as an explanation for their failure. But this would neglect the fact that it is far more the way in which a person reacts to events, and less the events themselves, that leads to certain results.

The likelihood that someone would only ever experience either good or bad luck during their lifetime is very low. During the course of many years and decades, good and bad luck would be expected, on average, to balance each other out. Hoffmann referred to this way of thinking as a 'compensation theory'. In this way, coincidences are compensated for by other coincidences.[532]

Without a doubt, happenstance and luck do play a role, but this role varies significantly, depending upon the field of activity involved. While emphasizing the role of luck, Michael J. Mauboussin also admits that there are substantial differences between different fields and activities. He proposes a luck/skill continuum and introduces a variety of sports and other activities as examples. He places roulette at the 'pure luck' end of this spectrum, whereas chess is at the 'pure skill' end of his spectrum.[533] In order to decide where on the continuum a certain activity belongs, the following question can be used as a guide: "Ask whether you can lose on purpose. In games of skill, it's clear that you can lose intentionally, but when playing roulette or the lottery you can't lose on purpose." Lawyers acting to legalize online poker in the United States even used this test in support of their legal arguments.[534]

Even if it is true that chance is a factor, a person's reaction to a chance event or encounter is certainly of greater significance. Winning the lottery is one example of unexpected luck. However, people who win major prizes on lotteries often lose their winnings within just a few years.[535] In contrast, there are self-made millionaires and billionaires who have lost everything and, just a few years later, have been able to rebuild their fortunes.

Inheriting a large fortune is an example of a fortunate coincidence in which the individual who inherits plays no part. But there are plenty of examples of heirs who lost their fortunes within two or three generations. Robert Arnott, William Bernstein, and Lillian Wu demonstrated in 2015 that the fortunes of the majority of the super rich are depleted very quickly. They ask, "Where are the current hyper-wealthy descendants of past entrepreneurial dynasties – the Astors, Vanderbilts, Carnegies, Rockefellers, Mellons, and Gettys? … The originators of great wealth are one-in-a-million geniuses … In contrast, the descendants of the hyper-wealthy rarely have that same one-in-a-million genius … Typically, we find that descendants halve their inherited wealth – relative to the growth of per capita GDP – every 20 years or less … Today, the massive fortunes of the 19th century are largely depleted and almost all of the fortunes generated just a half-century ago are also gone."[536]

Nevertheless, there is no denying that luck and chance do actually play a role, although it is no coincidence that people are generally less concerned with this than with the question of identifying the proven strategies for success. After all, what can one deduce from the realization that luck or chance play a role? For one's own actions, not very much, which is why it is understandable that explanations for success tend to relate to factors upon which an individual – to at least some extent – can exert an influence.

---

530   Heiko Ernst, "Glück haben – Wie sehr bestimmen Zufälle unser Leben?" *Psychologie heute* 4 (2012), accessed 27 October 2017, https://www.psychologie-heute.de/archiv/detailansicht/news/glueck_haben_wie_sehr_bestimmen_zufaelle_unser_leben_glueck_haben_wie_sehr_bestimmen_zufael.

531   Ibid.

532   Hoffmann, *Zufall und Kontingenz*, 30.

533   Michael J. Mauboussin, *The Success Equation: Untangling Skill and Luck in Business, Sports, and Investing* (Boston: Harvard Business Review Press, 2012), 90.

534   Ibid., 19.

535   See also Zitelmann, *Reich werden und bleiben*, 13–15.

536   Robert Arnott, William Bernstein, and Lillian Wu, "The Rich Get Poorer: The Myth of Dynastic Wealth," *Cato Journal* 35, no. 3 (2015), 2.

5.2. LUCK AS AN UNCONSCIOUS DEFENCE AGAINST ENVY

In his book, *Envy: A Theory of Social Behaviour*, Helmut Schoeck developed the hypothesis that the terms "good and bad luck, chance and opportunity" play "a crucial part in controlling the problem of envy". As Schoeck points out, "man can come to terms with the evident inequality of the individual human lot, without succumbing to envy that is destructive of both himself and others, only if he can put the responsibility on some impersonal power – blind chance or fortune".[537] When successful people point to luck, this serves as an unconscious defence against envy. "A sportsman, a schoolboy or a businessman who has scored an unusually brilliant success, thus becoming a possible object of envy, will simply shrug his shoulders and say: 'I suppose I was just lucky'. In this way, though usually unconsciously, he seeks to disarm possible envy"[538] by pointing to an "aimless, unpredictable and uncontrollable power which shapes events either favourably or unfavourably".[539]

When an extremely successful person declares, "I was just lucky," their statement makes them far more likeable, human, and pleasant than if they made reference, for example, to their outstanding intellect or exceptional personality. On the other hand, we all recognize the psychologically unburdening effect of interpreting success as the result of skill and failure as the product of unfortunate external circumstances. "My successes belong to me, my failures belong to others"[540] is a familiar explanation. Many studies show that "people who fail to achieve a goal, or are unable to master a task, tend to blame their failures – irrespective of the real reasons – on external causes, such as superior opponents, adverse circumstances or simple bad luck. With success, they do the exact opposite. This is viewed primarily as the result of their own skills and abilities, and hardly ever as the result of a weak opponent or advantageous circumstances."[541]

In the case of extremely successful individuals, however, there is – as demonstrated by the interviewees in the Csikszentmihalyi study – often clear evidence of the opposite pattern, as they credit their success to the result of a great deal of luck, or at least postulate that this may be the case. There is perhaps a degree of coquetry at play here. The unconscious envy defence mentioned by Schoeck definitely could be a key factor, although there is certainly a third reason as to why extremely successful people so often cite luck or coincidence as factors in their success.

5.3. USING LUCK AND COINCIDENCE TO EXPLAIN SUCCESS

When we are unable to explain a successful outcome, we all too often jump to the conclusion that luck must have been the root cause. Mauboussin is among those authors who have strongly emphasized the role of luck. In support of his hypothesis, he introduces the economist Sherwin Rosen's analysis "The Economics of Superstars". "[Rosen] observed that a few superstars – 'performers of first rank' – earn incomes that are vastly larger than performers with only modestly less ability. While fans may prefer the superstars to lesser performers, he argued that the difference in skill is too modest to explain the sizable gap in pay."[542]

This is a prime example of the tendency exhibited by many authors to over-hastily conclude that luck or chance have played a role, while failing to consider other explanations. Mauboussin's definition of luck follows a subtraction or residual method. "In this sense, luck is a residual: it's what is left over after you've subtracted skill from an outcome."[543] He argues, for example, that even if superstars have a level of talent similar to that of the average musician, they still earn so much more that this difference cannot be explained on the basis of their musical skills alone. "There are a variety of ways to assess skill or quality. For example, you might evaluate a song according to its rhythm, tonality, lyrical content, vocal quality, and instrumentation. Different people may have different lists or may weight those qualities in different ways. But no matter how we assess someone's skill, luck will also help to shape our opinion through social influence. So luck is not only behind the inequality of outcomes, it determines what we perceive to be a skill."[544]

Here and elsewhere, the fallacy of the subtraction method described above, whereby luck is the residual once 'skills' have been subtracted from 'outcomes', is a direct consequence of defining the term 'skill' too narrowly. In this case, the mistake is to assume that a superstar's higher earnings can only be the result of their musical skills, which, if these are not possible to categorize or quantify, leaves luck as the only remaining explanation.

This is, however, patently not the case, as can be demonstrated by the example of Madonna, who, at one time, was the highest-paid singer in the world. When asked whether Madonna was gifted, her manager, the woman who had paved the way for Madonna's first musical successes, answered, "She had just enough skill to write a song or play guitar … But more than anything, it was her personality and that she was a great performer."[545] When she won her starring role in the film *Evita*, Madonna had to first undergo three months of professional voice coaching.

---

537   Helmut Schoeck, *Envy: A Theory of Social Behaviour* (Indianapolis: Liberty Fund, 1966), 285.

538   Ibid., 285.

539   Ibid., 285.

540   Louis Schützenhöfer, *Vom Charme des Scheiterns: Krisen für einen Neustart nutzen* (Vienna: Verlag Carl Ueberreuter, 2011), 38.

541   Ibid., 38.

542   Mauboussin, *The Success Equation*, 123.

543   Ibid., 16.

544   Ibid., 125.

545   Quoted in Lucy O'Brien, *Madonna: Like an Icon – The Definitive Biography* (London: Transworld Publishers, 2007), 49.

At the time, she was already one of the most famous and successful singers in the world. Her success, and her high earnings, were not a product of any extra-special musical talent, nor were they the result of luck or coincidence; they were the product of an exceptional ability to position and promote herself.[546]

The same applies to many other entrepreneurs and superstars whose success cannot be explained by any exceptional specialist skills or product features but is the result of outstanding promotion. The billionaires Dietrich Mateschitz (Red Bull) and Richard Branson (Virgin) are perfect examples of this.[547] Even in the case of undoubtedly very capable investors – such as Warren Buffett – at least a small element of their success can be attributed to brilliant self-promotion skills.[548]

It is not only scholars and other authors who hastily turn to arguments founded on luck and chance. In many cases, successful individuals themselves do not know, or at least are unable to articulate, exactly why and how they have become so successful. This is precisely why qualitative social research is necessary to fill this gap. Arnd-Michael Nohl stated, "Although it is true that the interviewees clearly know how to deal with specific problems, it is not to be assumed that they have access to this knowledge, that they can easily explicate it." Nohl refers to Karl Mannheim's 'atheoretical knowledge', which must first be explicated by researchers.[549]

Michael Polanyi coined the term 'tacit knowledge'. In Section 4.5, the importance of implicit learning was emphasized, which can culminate in implicit knowledge or an intuition. Whether one speaks of tacit knowledge, implicit knowledge, or atheoretical knowledge, it is in any case clear that we often know more than we ourselves are aware of or can explicitly explain. Guy Claxton titled his essay on the subject "Knowing Without Knowing Why".[550] And Hayek pointed out that there are a number of things we can do very well, without knowing how. "It is characteristic of these skills that we are usually not able to state explicitly (discursively) the manner of acting which is involved."[551]

As has been shown, successful people are often unable to explain in explicit terms why they are successful. Can a successful author explain exactly 'how' he writes? Can a successful musician explain exactly how she is able to achieve greater success than other musicians? As their actions are often the product of implicit learning and proceed intuitively, this is difficult to explain. Perhaps these people have never thought very carefully about it, or they lack the ability to reflect on such topics at a more abstract or even scientific level. And, even if they had done so, they often lacked the distance and basis for comparison necessary to provide appropriate explanations. When the reasons for a person's current or past successes remain hidden to them, it is no surprise that they turn to explanations such as luck or chance.

When people offer luck or coincidence as explanations for their success, the three above-mentioned factors may combine. Unable to explicitly communicate their tacit knowledge, an interviewee resorts to offering luck as an explanation, a consequence of their embarrassment, which in turn has three concurrent benefits: the explanation contains a sliver of truth, it 'sounds good' to the interviewer, and it functions as an unconscious defence against envy.

546   Zitelmann, *Dare to Be Different and Grow Rich*, 79–84.

547   Ibid., 202–223.

548   Ibid., 222–223.

549   Arnd-Michael Nohl, *Interview und dokumentarische Methode: Anleitungen für die Forschungspraxis*, 4th rev. ed. (Wiesbaden: Springer VS, 2012), 16–17.

550   Claxton, "Knowing Without Knowing Why."

551   Hayek, "Rules, Perception and Intelligibility," in "Studies in Philosophy, Politics and Economics" (London: Routledge & Kegan Paul), 43.

6 Dispositional Personality Traits: The Big Five and Beyond

In psychology, 'personality' is defined as "the totality of all the characteristics that characterize a person in an enduring manner, and make him unmistakable".[552] Personality, according to Pervin, refers "to psychological qualities that contribute to an individual's enduring and distinctive patterns of feeling, thinking and behaving".[553]

'Differential psychology' or 'personality psychology' – the terms are used largely synonymously nowadays[554] – investigates dispositional personality traits. These are the "broad, non-conditional, de-contextualized, and implicitly comparative features that a person expresses repeatedly in different situations and over time. This refers to relatively global (in contrast to very specific) characteristics, which describe typical (i.e. not bound to specific conditions or situations/contexts) experience and behaviour".[555]

These personality traits are relatively stable both over time and in a variety of situations, and can therefore be measured reliably – for example, using self-assessment questionnaires or during interviews by third parties. The subject of personality psychology is therefore the study of "psychological functions and dispositions which 1) vary interindividually between persons, 2) have a stability over time, and finally 3) are consistent across different situations".[556]

Dispositional personality traits are constants that – at least from a certain age – hardly change, whereas adaptions are more transitory and do change over time. These 'adaptions' can also be consciously developed or altered by counselling and learning strategies. "Characteristic adaptations include motives, targets, plans, values, attitudes, self-image, specific skills and talents, learning styles, coping strategies, defence mechanisms, and many other aspects of human personality."[557]

Among the numerous models used to describe various personality types, it is the Big Five model that has largely come to dominate over the past decades, although the model certainly has its critics and those who point to its limitations.[558] "One explanation for the popularity of the Big Five model is that, after decades of controversy, we now have a uniform personality model, into which other models for describing personality can be integrated."[559]

The first personality theories to use between three and five key traits to describe personalities emerged as early as the 1930s, but what is today known as the Big Five model was most systematically developed by Paul T. Costa and Robert R. McCrae. In keeping with other personality theories, the Five Factor model is a product of factor analysis. This involves the measurement of a range of personality variables. Such variables should correlate strongly within an individual factor (e.g. extroversion) and as little as possible between different factors (e.g. extroversion and agreeableness).[560] Costa and McCrae's Five Factor model defines five traits: Neuroticism, Extroversion, Openness to Experience, Agreeableness, and Conscientiousness.

The term 'conscientiousness' comprises the following traits:
- Conscientious (thorough, meticulous) – as opposed to negligent (careless, irresponsible)
- Hardworking (diligent, efficient) – as opposed to lazy (apathetic, sluggish)
- Well organized (methodical, systematic) – as opposed to disorganized (purposeless, haphazard)
- Punctual – as opposed to late
- Ambitious – as opposed to aimless
- Persevering (tenacious, persistent) – as opposed to quitting.

"Conscientious people are rational, informed, and generally think of themselves as being high in *Competence*. Part of their success results from their organization and *Order*, which makes them efficient in work … They are high in *Achievement Striving*, pursuing excellence in everything they do; and they are necessarily high in *Self-Discipline*, to be able to accomplish their goals. Finally, they are characterized by *Deliberation*, making plans in advance and thinking carefully before acting. Theirs is a life clearly directed along the paths they choose to pursue."[561]

Individuals with a high degree of Neuroticism tend towards nervousness and frequently worry about what could go wrong. They find it difficult to deal with stress and are therefore vulnerable. They tend towards impulsive reactions.

---

552   Philipp Yorck Herzberg and Marcus Roth, *Persönlichkeitspsychologie* (Wiesbaden: Springer VS, 2014), 19.

553   Cervone and Pervin, *Personality*, 8.

554   Herzberg and Roth, *Persönlichkeitspsychologie*, 13.

555   Ibid., 5.

556   Ibid., 18.

557   Ibid., 5–6.

558   For examples of this criticism, compare the following two papers: Burghard Andresen, "Risikobereitschaft (R) – der sechste Basisfaktor der Persönlichkeit: Konvergenz multivariater Studien und Konstruktexplikation," *Zeitschrift für Differentielle und Diagnostische Psychologie* 16 (1995); Gerard Saucier and Lewis R. Goldberg, "What Is Beyond the Big Five?" *Journal of Personality* 66, no. 4 (1998).

559   Herzberg and Roth, *Persönlichkeitspsychologie*, 44.

560   Ibid., 25.

561   Robert R. McCrae and Paul T. Costa, *Personality in Adulthood: A Five-Factor Theory Perspective* (New York: The Guilford Press, 2003), 50–51.

Overall, they are not very psychologically stable.[562] Facets of neuroticism include anxiety, irritability, depression, shyness, impulsiveness, and fragility.[563] This does not mean, however, that they are neurotic in the clinical sense. "Psychiatric patients who were traditionally diagnosed as neurotics tend to score very high on this dimension, but many individuals score high without having any psychiatric disorder."[564]

As shown in Chapter 3, previous studies have demonstrated that wealthy individuals and entrepreneurs are characterized by high Conscientiousness but also by low agreeableness. McCrae and Costa associate low agreeableness with words such as 'ruthless', 'suspicious', 'stingy', 'antagonistic', 'critical', and 'irritable'. "Test subjects with very high scores for agreeableness", according to Jürgen Hesse and Hans Christian Schrader, "have a pronounced need for harmony; they can back down too quickly and tend to be too trusting".[565]

The terms Extroversion and Openness to Experience are used in this context in the same way as they would conventionally be used. Individuals with high Extroversion are talkative, determined, enterprising, energetic, and courageous. In contrast, individuals with low Extroversion (i.e. introverts) tend to be taciturn, undecided, unmotivated, and anxious. Individuals with high Openness to Experience are imaginative, creative, and curious.[566]

Personality traits are more than mere habits. On the contrary, many habits have nothing at all to do with personality traits. McCrae and Costa point out that 'traits' are closer to motivations than they are to habits. "In many respects traits resemble motives rather than habits, and it is often unclear whether a disposition such as excitement seeking should be called a trait or a motive. Trait appears to be the broader term, indicating motivational, stylistic, and other aspects of human consistency."[567]

Personality traits can be measured via observation, either by an assessment carried out by a third party or by a self-assessment. Which of the two methods is more accurate? Are third parties or self-assessments more reliable? In support of self-assessment, McCrae and Costa report the following: "Individuals have spent a lifetime getting to know themselves, and they alone can draw on the subjective experience that tells them whether they truly enjoy an activity or, deep down, harbor vague doubts or anxieties. Provided that respondents are honest with themselves and with the researchers, self-report is probably the best way to measure personality."[568] Numerous studies have examined the correlation between the results of self- and third-party assessment and have reported high levels of consistency. There are strong correlations in both directions, in particular between self-assessments and assessments carried out by husbands and wives, who understand their partner's personality better than an outsider.[569]

The questionnaire used for this study has much in common with McCrae and Costa's Big Five model. It comprises 50 questions, each of which has five elements. The questionnaire is modelled on the NEO Five Factor Personality Inventory (NEO-FFI), created by Costa and McCrae, which was first translated into German by Peter Borkenau and Fritz Ostendorf.[570] Although a number of the questions were initially somewhat inelegantly translated into German (e.g. use of double negatives), the test subjects generally had no problem completing the questionnaire in the allotted 15 minutes. The answers were then evaluated in relation to the personality traits Neuroticism, Extroversion, Openness to Experience, Agreeableness, and Conscientiousness.[571] The findings are presented in Chapter 17.

As a clear majority of the interviewees were over the age of 50, this raised the question of whether it actually made sense to measure their personality traits at all. If an individual's personality traits proved to be highly mutable – that is, if a person's personality was very different at the age of 30 in comparison with the age of 60 – then questions in relation to personality would only have a limited epistemological value, or it would be necessary to make greater efforts to explore the interviewee's personality in their younger years.

But if personality is a constant, undergoing only minimal change over time, then it would certainly make sense to measure personality as it is today, and assume that the differences in relation to an interviewee's more youthful personality are less important than the commonalities. A large number of studies have confirmed what McCrae and Costa so compellingly presented, namely that the major personality traits undergo little change once an individual has reached the age of 30.[572] Admittedly, numerous studies have demonstrated that a number of Agreeableness traits become stronger with age, while a number of Extroversion traits weaken as the years pass,[573] but these changes are far outweighed by the totality of immutable personality traits.

Although the Five Factor model dominates contemporary scholarship, there have also been critics of the model.[574] Some researchers have called for the factor Openness to Experience to be replaced by the factor Conventionality.[575]

---

562 Ibid., 47–48.

563 Herzberg and Roth, *Persönlichkeitspsychologie*, 43.

564 McCrae and Costa, *Personality in Adulthood*, 46.

565 Jürgen Hesse and Hans Christian Schrader, *Persönlichkeitstest: Verstehen – Durchschauen – Trainieren* (Munich: Stark Verlagsgesellschaft, 2014), 95.

566 Cervone and Pervin, *Personality*, 265–266.

567 McCrae and Costa, *Personality in Adulthood*, 28.

568 Ibid., 40.

569 Ibid., 42–43.

570 Hesse and Schrader, *Persönlichkeitstest*, 88 et seq.; reprinted in the appendix of this book.

571 Ibid., 94.

572 McCrae and Costa, *Personality in Adulthood*, 81.

573 Ibid., 62.

574 See also Herzberg and Roth, *Persönlichkeitspsychologie*, 46 et seq.

575 See also Saucier and Goldberg, "What Is Beyond the Big Five?"

In relation to this study, the most relevant approach is the one adopted by Burghard Andresen, who sought to prove that Risk-Taking Propensity should be considered as a sixth underlying personality trait.

Andresen points out that, time and time again, studies have indicated a sixth, distinctive higher-order dimension of personality. "On this, scales for risk and competition seeking are particularly important in the physical challenge and threat area, along with measures of activity, energy, achievement motivation and dominance, as well as scientific, technical and sporting interests."[576]

He describes the complexity of the 'R' factor (Risk-Taking Propensity) as follows: "The central aspect is surely the risk-taking propensity, with high proportions of leadership, achievement and competition motivation. Other aspects include civil courage, assumption of responsibility in crises and disaster situations and heroic personal actions."[577] Empirical research has shown that propensities demonstrated by individuals with a high R factor include the following:[578]

- Preference for economically oriented risk-taking and expansive entrepreneurial behaviour
- Preference for higher, more dynamic, and more flexible work demands
- Interactive–dynamic leadership style, social dominance
- Creative–dynamic professional and success motivation, innovative tendencies.

Among the key concepts underpinning the 'R' factor, Andresen listed:[579]

– Willpower	– Leadership ambitions
– Assertiveness	– Sense of defiance
– Commitment	– Motivation
– Determination	– Willingness to experiment
– Independence	– Awareness of power
– Fighting spirit	– Autonomy
– Ambition	– Pursuit of profit
– Athleticism	– Entrepreneurial mentality.
– Competitive attitude	

The common denominators of this construct are the "offensive, risky and, at the same time, strong 'moral' values oriented to challenging, dangerous or difficult environmental situations".[580]

The studies on entrepreneurial personality cited in Chapters 3 and 4 of this book also found that the Five Factor model on its own cannot sufficiently explain the specific traits of a successful entrepreneur. For this reason, the interviewees featured in Part B were asked to assess their own risk-taking propensity. As demonstrated in Chapters 3 and 4, this aspect of the entrepreneurial personality is of great relevance and correlates strongly with an individual's tendency towards optimism.

Lastly, a further fundamental aspect addressed during the interviews was the degree to which an interviewee tended towards conformism or nonconformism in their behaviour. There are, after all, a number of theories on the entrepreneurial personality (such as Schumpeter's) that find that a disposition towards nonconformism (even though this is not always the term the researchers employ) is characteristic of the entrepreneurial personality.

Personality traits, as measured by the Big Five or other models, can only provide a partial explanation of our behaviour. In addition to these traits there are – as already mentioned – so-called 'adaptions', which are influenced on the one hand by personality traits and on the other by the environment, and which can therefore be altered. These include 'motives' (although, in this case, there is a large degree of overlap with personality traits), 'interests', 'values', and 'attitudes'.[581] While numerous studies have been carried out to investigate the stability of the Big Five traits over a person's lifetime, there is a shortage of appropriate studies on these characteristic adaptions.[582]

In this book, the term 'personality' is defined in fairly broad terms to encompass personality traits, which remain relatively constant and can be measured, for example using the Big Five model, as well as characteristic adaptions, namely motivations, values, attitudes, and action strategies.

In this context, it is also worth considering the utility of measuring the correlation between personality traits and the genesis of wealth with regard to an individual who has specifically set themselves the goal of becoming rich. One would assume that the number of people who have the personality traits required to become rich is far greater than the number of people who actually become rich. The identification of such personality traits can, therefore, only really serve as an aid to individuals as they develop self-awareness and reflect upon untapped potentials. The action strategies, attitudes, and beliefs that, in combination with the dispositional personality traits, actually shape the personality are mutable to a far greater extent. To this extent, the analysis of the characteristic attitudes and action strategies of individuals who have, as a result of their own efforts, become rich, can certainly make a valuable contribution to the development of action patterns and learning goals for individuals who have set themselves the goal of becoming rich.

---

576   Andresen, "Risikobereitschaft," 213.
577   Ibid., 223.
578   Ibid., 224.
579   Ibid., 229.
580   Ibid., 210.
581   See also Herzberg and Roth, *Persönlichkeitspsychologie*, 75–100.
582   Ibid., 132.

7 | Methodology

7.1. THE LIMITS OF QUANTITATIVE METHODS IN ACADEMIC WEALTH RESEARCH

Quantitative and qualitative approaches in social research have their justification and can meaningfully complement one another.[583] In this book, which takes people with a net worth in the tens to hundreds of millions as its subject, qualitative methods were employed. There are several reasons for this.

There is no random sampling that provides a sufficient number of individuals worth tens to hundreds of millions for a quantitative investigation.[584] The decision to adopt a qualitative approach to this study of UHNWIs is therefore a result of the fact that, firstly, suitable data are not available for a quantitative analysis and, secondly, it is unclear how this data could be gathered. This does not, of course, rule out the possibility of solving this problem someday, and of creating a sufficiently robust data set that would permit the use of quantitative methods for research into the wealth elite.

Jochen Gläser and Grit Laudel argue that the justification for a qualitative investigation on the grounds that quantitative methods cannot be used is too defensive. "This justification is hardly applicable today. It may well, indirectly, declare the relation-oriented explanation strategy to be the better strategy, which, unfortunately, simply could not be used due to unfavourable conditions. Today, we can argue more offensively, and write that the social mechanisms that interest us are usually only identifiable via qualitative methods."[585] Nevertheless, it can be argued that if it were possible to use quantitative methods to generate a robust data set for the group of UHNWIs, then this should and, indeed, must be done. The argument that qualitative methods have to be used because, due to the absence of such a data set and the fact that the development of such a data set cannot be achieved in the foreseeable future, however, in no way implies that the results would be necessarily inferior. These are simply the only suitable methods for the subjects of this investigation, which, therefore, makes them the correct methods to employ.

The greatest challenge in researching UHNWIs is the difficulty of gaining access to this group. Firstly, the group is extremely small. Secondly, for a number of reasons, this group shields itself more intensely than average members of the population. Most of these individuals have a team of employees tasked with, among other things, blocking outside contact (in particular, but not only, from strangers). This is designed to enable these individuals to pursue their commercial activities without disturbance or distraction. As these wealthy individuals worry about the envy of other groups, a strong desire for privacy is also to be expected. After all, time is the scarcest resource for this group. The greater the value an individual can create in a productive hour, the less willing they will be to devote time to things that neither are economically productive nor serve to relieve the stresses of their working lives. In contrast to other professional groups, appointments with members of the wealth elite often have to be arranged several months in advance.

"In qualitative studies", according to Hans Merkens, "the incentive for empirical surveys often rests in the fact that accessibility to a certain case, group or institution has already been assured. Once this has been achieved, selection procedures are not the most important consideration, and selection can proceed according to accessibility."[586] This is equally true of this investigation. "For the actual selection", says Merkens, "in many cases, where no fixed sampling plan is available at the outset of the investigation, the snowball method is an apt procedure ... The interviewer asks each interviewee to recommend further suitable interviewees."[587]

So how did the author gain access to the UHNWIs whose interviews form the basis of this book? The author started by creating a list of 30 to 40 entrepreneurs and investors that he assumed possessed net assets worth at least tens or hundreds of millions. These were individuals he already knew personally, most only in passing, but a number of them as closer acquaintances. These people were contacted either personally or in writing and asked if they would be available for an anonymous, personal interview lasting one to two hours. Within this initial group, individuals who had built their wealth via real estate (e.g. as developers, fund initiators, or investors) were overrepresented. They ultimately represent about half of the interviewees. The reason for this high degree of personal access is that the author has been active, first, as a journalist since 1996 and then, since 2000, as a consultant and investor in the real estate industry.

583 See also Udo Kelle and Christian Erzberger, "Qualitative und quantitative Methoden: Kein Gegensatz," in *Qualitative Forschung: Ein Handbuch*, 10th ed., edited by Uwe Flick, Ernst von Kardorff, and Ines Steinke (Hamburg: Rowohlt, 2013), 299 et seq.

584 Grabka, "Verteilung und Struktur," 31.

585 Jochen Gläser and Grit Laudel, *Experteninterviews und qualitative Inhaltsanalyse als Instrumente rekonstruierender Untersuchungen*, 4th ed. (Wiesbaden: VS Verlag für Sozialwissenschaften, 2010), 71.

586 Hans Merkens, "Auswahlverfahren, Sampling, Fallkonstruktion," in *Qualitative Forschung: Ein Handbuch*, 10th ed., edited by Uwe Flick, Ernst von Kardorff, and Ines Steinke (Hamburg: Rowohlt, 2013), 288.

587 Ibid., 293.

PROFESSIONS OF THE 45 INTERVIEWEES
Real estate developers: 14
Finance sector (funds, leasing, financial services, financing, stocks, etc.): 9
Other real estate (fund initiators, investors, construction, etc.): 6
Real estate brokers or sales: 4
Food industry and wholesale: 4
Medical technology or IT: 3
Consulting and service companies: 2
Manufacturing (steel, consumer goods, etc.): 2
Other: 1

In light of the high proportion of individuals from the real estate industry, the group could appear to be more homogenous than it actually is. About half of the individuals may be involved in the real estate sector, but the activities of a developer, a contractor, a fund initiator, and a broker are extremely different and require very different qualifications, which means that the group is actually much more heterogenous than first appearances would perhaps suggest.

Most of the interviewees are self-made millionaires, which is advantageous, because it makes it easier for this group to answer the question "How did you get rich?" than for individuals who inherited a part of their wealth to answer the same question. For inheritors, it is always important to ask whether they have substantially grown the wealth they inherited, or whether they have merely maintained it at a similar level, or even depleted their initial fortune. Only in the first case can conclusions be drawn that are relevant for the questions set out in this book. The criteria for selecting a person for this study was that they had either built their wealth on their own or had significantly grown an inheritance. Simply put: anyone who had turned EUR 100 million into EUR 10 million was obviously not relevant to this research; anyone who had transformed EUR 10 million into EUR 100 million was. After the interviews, the interviewees were asked whether they could recommend any other interviewees who would fit these criteria. Plus, some interviewees were suggested, or even recruited, by one of the professors who supervised this work. In total, the author conducted 45 personal interviews from October 2015 to March 2016. Each interview lasted between one and two hours, as is reflected in the 1,740 pages of transcription that resulted. With four exceptions, all of the interviews were conducted in Germany. Four of the interviewees are no longer resident in Germany (three of them live in Switzerland); however, they are all still German citizens.

The advantage of the qualitative approach to the topic was mostly "to describe spheres of life 'from the inside out,' namely from the perspective of the individuals involved". This is generally the claim of qualitative research, because "it wants to help develop a better understanding of social realities, and call attention to processes, interpretive patterns and structural characteristics. These remain concealed from non-members, and even the actors caught up in the routines of the everyday may not be conscious of them themselves."[588]

Qualitative approaches are particularly suitable for marginal and minority social groups, whose ways of life are largely unknown and foreign to most people. Uwe Flick, Ernst von Kardorff, and Ines Steinke's postulations on the value of qualitative research apply in particular when considering this group. Qualitative research uses "the foreign, that which deviates from the norm, and the unexpected as a source of knowledge and as a mirror, which, in its reflection, makes the unknown know and the known unknown and thus opens further possibilities for (self-)knowledge".[589] According to Flick, Kardorff, and Steinke, "Qualitative research is always to be recommended where the exploration is focused on fields that have not been subject to a great deal of exploration, and is supported by the use of 'sensitizing concepts.'"[590]

The strength of qualitative research lies more in describing social groups and developing questions than in providing causal explanations as delivered by standardized procedures. In this study, the self-conception of UHNWIs is reconstructed. This reconstruction includes their personal explanations of their own success. Differences and similarities in personality traits and their biographies are also presented in extensive detail. However, as there was no control group consisting of non-wealthy individuals, a causal explanation of the particular economic success of UHNWIs cannot be provided. This methodological restriction is discussed in more detail in the final chapter, which sets out the limits of this study.

7.2. DEFINITION AND COMPOSITION OF THE TARGET INTERVIEWEE GROUP

Any survey of a wealthy target group first has to address the fundamental question, how can the worth of the individuals' assets be estimated? For the study Wealth in Germany, the following approach was selected: the sampling first assessed "freely available capital assets", which the researchers believed represented approximately one quarter of a household's total assets.[591] The advantage of this approach is that those surveyed were easily able to provide a relatively accurate assessment

---

588 Uwe Flick, Ernst von Kardorff, and Ines Steinke, "Was ist qualitative Forschung? Einleitung und Überblick," in *Qualitative Forschung: Ein Handbuch*, 10th ed., edited by Uwe Flick, Ernst von Kardorff, and Ines Steinke (Hamburg: Rowohlt, 2013), 14.

589 Ibid., 14.

590 Ibid., 25.

591 For a methodological comparison, see Lauterbach, Hartmann, and Ströing, *Reichtum, Philanthropie und Zivilgesellschaft*, 47 et seq.

of their freely available capital assets.[592] The disadvantage, however, is that it is not certain that these assets actually represent roughly 25% of a household's total assets. For the individuals interviewed in this book, this was naturally not the case, as a large portion of their wealth is in illiquid assets (companies, shareholdings, real estate), which are not regularly valued. Almost no one with, for instance, assets of EUR 300 million would ever keep EUR 75 million liquid for any length of time. For this reason, the approach adopted by the study Wealth in Germany (which interviewed individuals with a median wealth of just EUR 1.4 million) was deemed to be inappropriate.

A single criterion was used to determine whether an individual should be regarded as a potential interviewee for this book: Do they have a net fortune, i.e. after the deduction of all outstanding liabilities (such as mortgage loans), of at least EUR 10 million? In assessing this criterion, the interviewees provided self-assessments. The question as to whether someone belonged to the target group or not was easy to answer, because, if they did belong, their net wealth was significantly higher than the minimum EUR 10 million.

Before the interview process began, one concern was that it could be difficult to obtain accurate information from the interviewees regarding their net wealth. The reasons for this concern were:

1. Even within the context of a confidential interview, not everyone is willing to disclose their financial circumstances. As a solution to this problem, it was decided to create a range of categories to which the interviewees could assign themselves. The following categories were used: EUR 10–30 million, EUR 30–100 million, EUR 100–300 million, EUR 300 million to 1 billion, EUR 1–2 billion, and more than EUR 2 billion.

2. There are objective difficulties in determining net wealth. It was necessary to make a fundamental decision as to whether the value of owner-occupied real estate and/or company assets should be included or not. A number of studies exclude the value of owner-occupied real estate, which is, however, simply a result of the fact that the parties who commissioned the studies were primarily interested in the investment or allocation of liquid wealth. In contrast, Knight Frank's regularly published The Wealth Report does include both investment and owner-occupied properties. Among the UHNWIs (i.e. those with net assets of more than USD 30 million) who appeared in The Wealth Report in 2014, owner-occupied real estate (which averaged 2.4 properties per UHNWI) represented 30% of their assets.[593] Regarding the question as to whether company assets should be included or not, there are arguments both for and against. For many UNHWIs, their companies' assets represent the lion's share of their wealth. In the case of listed companies, it is relatively easy to quantify the value of these assets. The company's market capitalization on a specific date can be used, together with

the public details of the number of stocks held by an individual; it is then fairly straightforward to calculate the value of the individual's assets. In the case of unlisted companies, it is much more difficult to determine or even estimate the value of their assets. Ever since the wealth tax was suspended in Germany, no ongoing valuations have been carried out. And, due to significant variance in company valuations, it is very difficult to arrive at a reliable estimate. A majority of the individuals interviewed for this book are entrepreneurs who hold shares in unlisted companies and tend to know the exact value of their companies only if they have recently been assessed for a specific reason (e.g. a planned sale).

The value of liquid assets (bonds, stocks, demand deposits, etc.) is the easiest to determine because they are usually known to the individual. In the case of owner-occupied property, it is not quite so straightforward. After all, an individual is not normally aware of the property's current market value. For investment properties (i.e. those that are rented out), it is possible to provide an estimate of fair market value. The fair market value is, in simple terms, the product of multiplying a property's net annual rental income by a mathematical factor, which is known as a 'multiplier'. The interviewees knew the net annual rental income they received from a property – this is, after all, entered in their annual tax returns. A number of factors and assumptions need to be considered in relation to determining the correct multiplier, including the location, quality, and utilization of the property. Once the market value has been determined, the value of any outstanding mortgage loans is subtracted. The end result is an estimate of the value of an individual's net assets.

These considerations show that it is not easy to accurately determine an individual's wealth, especially given the fact that these individuals have often not had the assets of the companies they own, or their real estate assets, valued recently, and therefore cannot say for themselves how much they are actually worth. This problem is avoided by using broad categories, rather than attempting to determine an individual's exact wealth. This approach has the advantage that it is more likely the interviewees will be prepared to assign themselves to a broad category than to state their exact net wealth (which, as outlined above, is anyway difficult to determine and often not known to the individual). In addition, the above-mentioned difficulties do not usually have a significant impact on wealth assessments based on broad categories. Even if a person cannot place an exact value on their assets, or is unwilling to do so, they are likely to be able to estimate whether this value, for example, lies between EUR 30 million and 100 million or between EUR 100 million and 300 million.

---

592   Ibid., 50.

593   *The Wealth Report* (London: Knight Frank Research, 2014), 11.

Before the interviews took place, a preparatory telephone conversation was used to determine beyond doubt whether the potential interviewees belonged to the target interview group, namely whether they had net assets of at least EUR 10 million. It was only necessary to ask this question in a very small number of cases. The interviewees were asked to assign themselves to one of the categories at the very end of their interview. Petersen observed that statistical information and "sensitive investigations, which can be expected to cause irritation, perhaps even resistance, among some respondents" should be dealt with at the end of an interview. On the same subject, he explicitly observed: "The question that elicits the greatest resistance among interviewees is that of income. For pragmatic reasons it should therefore be the very last that is asked: Any misgivings that may occur will not subsequently interfere with the flow of the interview. If an interviewee refuses further information, this, of course, remains without consequence, as the interview is finished anyway."[594]

The interviewees were therefore assigned to categories on the basis of their own self-reported assessments, which were checked, where possible, against publicly available information, such as the details that have appeared in the lists of wealthy people that regularly appear in *Manager Magazin*. Based on their wealth, many of the individuals who should appear in these lists are actually omitted (which was a source of relief to these interviewees). Only two individuals refused to make a self-assessment of their wealth, and neither appeared in the lists published by *Manager Magazin*. Nevertheless, in both cases industry estimates were available, although the author decided to place both individuals in a category one level below these industry estimates.

WEALTH CATEGORIES OF THE 45 INTERVIEWEES (IN EUROS)
10–30 million: 11
30–100 million: 20
100–300 million: 3
300 million–1 billion: 8
1–2 billion: 1
More than 2 billion: 2

SOURCE OF THEIR WEALTH
Self-made entrepreneurs: 36
Family entrepreneurs: 5
Entrepreneurs who inherited a small business and grew it substantially: 4

AGES OF THE 45 INTERVIEWEES (IN YEARS)
30–39 = 2
40–49 = 7
50–59 = 12
60–69 = 7
70–79 = 17

GENDER
44 male
1 female

The study's lowest wealth quartile comprises those individuals with net assets worth between EUR 10 million and 30 million, and the upper quartile comprises those with assets worth at least EUR 300 million. In total, 36 of the interviewees were self-made entrepreneurs. In most cases, they had either inherited nothing or only very small amounts. Four interviewees had inherited very small businesses, which they had then substantially expanded – for instance transforming a business with two stores into one with many hundreds, or taking a small core business and turning it into a pan-European enterprise. Five interviewees were family entrepreneurs, and four of these had vastly increased the value of their family's assets. In the case of a single interviewee this could not be confirmed with absolute certainty – there were indications that this interviewee had maintained the family fortune rather than substantially increasing it.

That the interviewees tended to belong to higher age groups was natural, as it often requires a number of decades for self-made entrepreneurs to build this degree of wealth. More than half of the interviewees were over the age of 60, and only two were below the age of 40. Among the interviewees, 44 of the 45 were men. An analysis of the lists of the wealthiest individuals in the world, such as those that appear in *Forbes* (among others), clearly shows that a majority of the richest women have inherited their wealth. Individuals who inherited the vast majority of their wealth were, however, explicitly excluded from this research.

---

594   Thomas Petersen, *Der Fragebogen in der Sozialforschung* (Munich: UVK Verlagsgesellschaft, 2014), 71.

7.3. REASONS FOR SELECTING THE GUIDED INTERVIEW METHOD

A variety of methods for qualitative research have become established in the social sciences. Even with regard to the question of how an interview should be conducted, a number of approaches have been put forwards. "Unfortunately", say Gläser and Laudel, "there are countless names for interviews, a majority of which lack any systematic foundation. In the literature there are 'focused', 'biographical', 'narrative', 'qualitative', 'problem-centered', 'standardized', 'semi-standardized', 'non-standardized', 'guided', 'open', 'free', 'themed' and other interviews."[595]

Cornelia Helfferich distinguishes between 13 interview variants, including 'narrative interviews', 'guided interviews', and 'problem-centred interviews'.[596] These types of interviews differ in how much interviewers intervene in the interview process.[597] For example, during a narrative interview, the interviewer should play a more reserved role, whereas during a problem-centred interview, the interviewer plays a much more active role, introducing prior knowledge and developing content in a mutual dialogue.[598]

For this study, the narrative interview approach was ruled out because the topics involved are too complex and demand that the interviewer play a more active role. It was not expected that the interviewees would address the specific questions known to be relevant for this work unless explicitly requested to do so.

Ralf Bohnsack distinguishes between 'reconstructive' and 'standardized' procedures. In the case of standardized procedures, the aim is to eliminate the influence of the interviewer, as fully as possible, by providing very strict guidelines on how to behave during the interview. Such restrictive guidelines are necessary as these methods require that the results are determined largely independently of the researcher or the interviewer, and, ideally, that identical results would be achieved by another researcher or interviewer.

This is not possible with qualitative interviews. "In an open interview", explains Bohnsack, "as in all open procedures, the main concern is to allow the interviewees to develop a theme in their own language, in their own symbolic system and within their framework of relevance; this is the only way that interviewer(s) or observer(s) can avoid projecting meaning onto the individual expression, meaning which would be unwarranted".[599]

Qualitative research is dominated by non-standardized interview forms in which neither the interviewer's questions nor the interviewee's responses are standardized.[600] In non-standardized interviews, a distinction is made between guided interviews, open interviews, and narrative interviews. Guided interviews were used for this research. From the research presented in Chapters 1 to 6, epistemological questions, topics, and hypotheses were formulated that structured the course of the interview and the subsequent evaluation. In the case of a narrative interview method without such guided questions, it would not have been possible to be certain that these topics would be addressed by the interviewee.

In a guided interview, the pre-formulated questions create a structure, ensuring that essential aspects of the research question are not overlooked during the interview. This does not mean, however, that the interview will proceed in the exact order set out in the interview guide.[601] Andreas Witzel views this guide mainly as a "memory support for interviewers", and Michael Meuser and Ulrike Nagel emphasize that this is not "to be treated as a standardized sequence schema".[602] The guided interview method was also selected because, on the one hand, the interview process can be structured, but on the other hand, this method is open and flexible enough to set different priorities – depending on the interviewee – or to change the sequence of the topics depending on the course of the conversation.

A fundamental question in deciding on the appropriate interview form is: Do the interviewees actually 'know' why they became successful? Here we first have to define what is meant by 'know'. Hayek pointed out that "the knowledge which any individual mind consciously manipulates is only a small part of the knowledge which at any one time contributes to the success of his action".[603] Hayek showed that explicit knowledge plays a subordinate role to implicit or tacit knowledge – especially in the case of entrepreneurs. Section 4.5 shows how important implicit learning and implicit knowledge are for the target group.

Arnd-Michael Nohl repeatedly emphasizes – using the terminology established by Karl Mannheim – that an interviewee's knowledge, especially at the moment at which it is acted upon, is often atheoretical knowledge, which must first be explicated by the researchers.[604] The anecdotes and descriptions in the interviews served to explicate this atheoretical and conjunctive knowledge.[605]

When you ask wealthy people how and why they have become rich, you will often be met with useless answers, or a series of generalized platitudes.

---

595   Gläser and Laudel, *Experteninterviews und qualitative Inhaltsanalyse*, 40.

596   Cornelia Helfferich, *Die Qualität qualitativer Daten: Manual für die Durchführung qualitativer Interviews*, 4th ed. (Wiesbaden: Springer VS, 2011), 36–37.

597   Ibid., 41.

598   See also ibid., 45.

599   Ralf Bohnsack, *Rekonstruktive Sozialforschung: Einführung in qualitative Methoden*, 9th ed. (Opladen: Verlag Barbara Budrich, 2014), 22–23.

600   Gläser and Laudel, *Experteninterviews und qualitative Inhaltsanalyse*, 41.

601   Horst Otto Mayer, *Interview und schriftliche Befragung: Grundlagen und Methoden empirischer Sozialforschung*, 6th ed. (Munich: Oldenburg Wissenschaftsverlag, 2013), 37.

602   Witzel, and Meuser and Nagel quoted in Nohl, *Interview und dokumentarische Methode*, 15.

603   Friedrich August von Hayek, *The Constitution of Liberty: The Definitive Edition* (Chicago: University of Chicago Press, 2011), 75.

604   Nohl, *Interview und dokumentarische Methode*, 17.

605   Ibid., 43.

In a survey of 61 top German managers (all DAX executives and managing directors from the most successful family businesses), the answers given to questions relating to the sources of their individual success included self-motivation, enthusiasm, fun at work, optimism, and communication skills.[606] Of course, it is possible to ask direct questions about the sources of someone's success, but no interviewer should expect this approach to generate any particularly interesting results. Therefore, such general questions were avoided in the interviews for this book. Respondents may 'know' why they have been successful, but this knowledge is often hidden because they themselves can rarely reflect, abstract, and formulate their knowledge. This is the task of the social scientist.

Interpretive social scientists do not therefore assume "that they know more than the actors, but that the latter themselves do not know what they really know, having an implicit knowledge that is not easily accessible to them by reflection".[607] Nohl emphasizes that this is precisely why it is so important to distinguish between argument, evaluation, description, and narrative. It is crucial for interviewers "to take account of the actors' experiences without being taken in by their subjective ascriptions of meaning".[608]

Thus, the so-called 'question of truth' is addressed. Is what the interviewee reports actually true? This can, of course, be verified when simple facts are concerned. However, if it is not a matter of verifiable facts, but self-perceptions, justifications, etc., then a degree of restraint on the part of the interviewer may be advisable. According to Helfferich, the attitude of interviewers who fancy themselves to be in possession of the truth, a truth that they believe to be superior to the truth of the interviewee, is problematic. For: "Believing that one possesses superior knowledge leads to the expectation during the interview situation – of which we are speaking here – that the narrator must necessarily articulate himself in accordance with this knowledge. The more explicit the interviewer's expectations of what and how much a narrator is to tell, the more the principle of openness is violated."[609]

The principle of openness is subject to particular emphasis in qualitative social research. This principle requires "that the empirical research process must be open to unexpected information. What is particularly important in this context is information relating to essential aspects of the subject, which are not covered by the understanding developed in advance of the study, or even contradicted by it. The principle of openness requires researchers to avoid rashly ascribing observed facts to known categories."[610] What is meant by openness is best explained by describing its opposite, namely "an interviewer's tendency to introduce a preconceived opinion or theoretical knowledge into the interview situation and only to recognize and understand those interviewee utterances that correspond to this prior knowledge".[611]

This was of particular relevance to this study when it came to reconstructing the self-images of the wealth elite. However, this openness should never be allowed to lead to a situation in which interviewees' statements are reproduced absent of criticism – and without questioning. For these reasons, narrative interviews were deemed to be unsuitable for this research. A dialogue approach allows an interviewee to be asked whether certain interpretations might not be little more than self-stylization or self-justification. However, such an approach is akin to a tightrope walk. On the one hand, the interviewer needs to ensure that the communicative atmosphere is not poisoned by such challenges. On the other hand, it is important that the interviewer fully exploits every opportunity to make inquiries – and that a critical approach to certain interviewees' self-stylized portrayals is not left to the post-interview evaluation stage.

For example, Chapter 5 has already pointed out how to interpret situations in which wealthy people dismiss their success as the product of luck or coincidence. In a narrative interview, the statement that one had simply been lucky would not be met with follow-up questions and may even escape further scrutiny altogether. In a problem-centred interview, the interviewer would inquire several times about the business decisions where luck played a decisive role, inquiring as to how much of a contributing factor – from the interviewee's perspective – luck had been in comparison to other factors, and ascertaining the extent of unfortunate events or conditions in comparison to fortunate coincidences.

There is also the problem that respondents – even in anonymous interviews – tend to give socially desirable and compliant answers. For example, the pursuit of money and wealth as a central motive of action has distinctly negative overtones in Germany. Anyone who says that 'making as much money as possible' is their main motive will feel immediate pressure to justify their stance, because this motivation is seen as superficial and materialistic. There is far more acceptance when wealth is shown to be a by-product or even an unintended consequence of other socially accepted motivations (see Section 7.4). Conversely, it also appears possible that motivations may be reinterpreted – for example, a goal-oriented approach might be suggested at a later date by the interviewee ("At the age of 20, I had already made plans to become a millionaire"). This cannot be really be examined and might, depending upon the case, be nothing more than an attempt at self-stylization or self-mythologizing.

This means that, in a problem-centred interview, an interviewer faces the dual challenges of not simply taking all statements at face value and not imposing

---

606 Eugen Buß, *Die deutschen Spitzenmanager: Wie sie wurden, was sie sind – Herkunft, Wertvorstellungen, Erfolgsregeln* (Munich: R. Oldenbourg Verlag, 2007), 129.

607 Bohnsack quoted in Nohl, *Interview und dokumentarische Methode*, 45.

608 Nohl, *Interview und dokumentarische Methode*, 45.

609 Helfferich, *Die Qualität qualitativer Daten*, 98.

610 Gläser and Laudel, *Experteninterviews und qualitative Inhaltsanalyse*, 30.

611 Helfferich, *Die Qualität qualitativer Daten*, 114.

their own values and explanatory patterns in such a way that it is longer possible to express, reconstruct, and understand the interviewee's self-perception.

In an overview of the admissibility of questions in specific interview formats, Helfferich illustrates what is 'allowed' in the different variations and what is not. In the narrative interview, the interviewer provides narrative stimulus, but no new topics are introduced, there is no confrontation with contradictions, details are not required, etc. – whereas this is all possible and important in 'dialogical' interview formats, such as in a problem-centred interview.[612]

7.4. ISSUES OF SOCIAL DESIRABILITY BIAS IN INTERVIEWS WITH ELITES

A particular problem with interviews is the tendency of interviewees to respond with socially desirable answers. The term 'socially desirable' refers to personal characteristics that will be viewed favourably by the members of a society.[613] 'Social desirability bias' is a term used in social science "when answers are systematically skewed in a socially desirable direction".[614] This arises because of the "need for interviewees to gain recognition via their culturally appropriate and acceptable responses" or because of the desire of survey respondents to present themselves in a positive light.[615] This owes far more to a respondent's attempts to defend an idealized view of themselves during the interview than to any desire to consciously or deliberately make false statements.[616]

It is therefore necessary to differentiate between whether an opinion, attitude, or preference is regarded as socially desirable within society as a whole, or in only a subpopulation. "Behaviours and other traits of persons, such as opinions and attitudes, may correspond to general social norms or norms of a particular subpopulation. The extent to which a feature corresponds to existing conceptions, i.e. to which it is socially desirable, may vary from group to group." It is relatively easy to imagine situations in which a respondent attributes a characteristic to themselves that is generally regarded as socially undesirable but positively assessed within the respondent's narrower social environment.[617]

This tendency to provide socially desirable responses could certainly arise during the interviews with the UHNWIs. These individuals differ from many of the other groups that are questioned in the context of social science research. "Members of an elite are more accustomed to presenting themselves or their organization in public. They have more contact with journalists, and tend to view the interviewer as a journalist. Accordingly, they ... seek to present the facts which are important for their external image."[618] They also have a tendency, born out of habit, to "provide official statements",[619] which, as a general rule, introduces a bias towards social desirability in their response behaviour. Whereas the research has primarily concentrated on addressing the extent to which the interview situation itself, or the expectations of the interviewee themselves, created or promoted this bias towards socially desirable responses, another aspect, which arises in particular in interviews with members of an elite, has been given far too little attention: Could it be that this bias towards socially desirable responses is nothing more than a habitual strategy, employed so often and over such a lengthy period of time that it has become ingrained?

It is certainly possible that motivations such as defending against envy or strategies of justification could play a role, particularly as the wealthy are often forced to adopt defensive positions during societal and media debate. In addition, money and its related topics are to some extent regarded as taboo ("You don't discuss money"), and attitudes and behaviours that prioritize the pursuit of wealth are often viewed critically. All of this could certainly lead wealthy individuals to provide socially desirable responses.

Even John D. Rockefeller, in his day the richest man in the world, was subjected to immense social and political pressure as a consequence of his success and his wealth. He never tired of asserting that wealth was not his prime motive; rather it was the chance by-product of his "humble desire to serve God and humanity". Rockefeller, as revealed by his biographer, "preferred to portray his fortune as a pleasant accident, the unsought by-product of hard work".[620] The biographer, however, believes that this presentation is less than credible. According to reports, Rockefeller's father had "a passion for money that amounted almost to a craze". This was an aspect of his father's personality that Rockefeller admired and, according to unanimous reports from a range of sources, even as a child he dreamed of riches and set himself ambitious monetary goals.[621]

In the book *How to be a Billionaire: Proven Strategies from the Titans of Wealth,* Martin S. Fridson states that billionaires "tend to downplay their interest in wealth altogether" and that "the businessman is the only sort of person who,

---

612   Ibid., 107.

613   Petra Hartmann, *Wunsch und Wirklichkeit: Theorie und Empirie sozialer Erwünschtheit* (Wiesbaden: Springer Fachmedien, 1991), 43.

614   Ibid., 52.

615   Marlowe and Crowne quoted in ibid., 68.

616   Hartmann, *Wunsch und Wirklichkeit*, 69–70.

617   Ibid., 217.

618   Gläser and Laudel, *Experteninterviews und qualitative Inhaltsanalyse*, 181.

619   Ibid., 181.

620   Chernow, *Titan*, 33.

621   Ibid., 29–33. It is important to treat such reports with a degree of scepticism as later stylizations are often incorporated – to correspond with the individual's ultimate achievements – and statements or circumstances may be exaggerated or even invented.

when he obtains the object of his labours, namely, making a lot of money, tries to make it appear that it was not the object of his labours".[622]

In a collection of essays containing excerpts from interviews with multi-million-aires that was published in Switzerland in 2010, money was only really mentioned – if at all – with the assurance that it had not been a significant motivating factor. Money as a motivating factor is something we often like to ascribe to others but are unwilling to see in ourselves. In response to a question regarding whether he had the impression that "money is not the main motivating force for many entrepreneurs", one of the respondents replied, "I never thought that I would make money from my business. In fact, the opposite was true, it was a huge risk … But there has been a shift in the culture of entrepreneurship. Today, profit is the most important thing. But we live in an age in which we have all become piranhas, whether we are conscious of that fact or not."[623]

Another interviewee, when asked what money and wealth mean to him, responded, "Money is always just a means to an end. The accumulation of material wealth per se is dangerous if it is not accompanied by the necessary modesty and humanity."[624] A third interviewee admitted defensively that "possessions and wealth are not, inherently, bad things" and explained his views as follows: "Anyone with money also has the opportunity to take it upon themselves to do good. They can share, support, help."[625]

For his book *The Entrepreneurial Code*, Rainer Nahrendorf carried out 14 interviews with entrepreneurs. To the extent that money is ever thematized as a motive for entrepreneurship, it is done so in a negative context, namely with the assurance that it played no role whatsoever: "The opportunity, as an entrepreneur, to earn large sums of money for private consumption does not excite him."[626] "Money", said another entrepreneur, "can never be a motive to decide to become self-employed. It is created as a by-product, when a business idea works well."[627] And a third interviewee emphasized that, "We are creatives. You can't measure us in euros."[628] The mentor of one of the interviewees said, "you have to view entrepreneurship as an obligation and not primarily as the source of personal wealth".[629]

Instead, when discussing the motivations for their actions, the interviewees stated that it was the "preservation, the growth of their businesses and the jobs that depended on them"[630] that were always their chief concerns. One entrepreneur explained his success thus: "We retained our humanity at all times."[631] Another entrepreneur mentioned "ensuring sustainable growth and transferring a healthy business to the next generation"[632] as an over-riding motive. He quoted Frederick the Great: "It is the duty of every good citizen to serve his fatherland, to consider that he is not on this earth for his benefit alone but that he must work for the common good of the society in which nature has placed him."[633]

This is a clear example of just how strong the bias among entrepreneurs towards official and socially desirable statements is: it is more desirable to talk about the obligation to create jobs, or to speak of 'sustainability' and the 'responsibility towards society', instead of even once admitting that material motivations, namely the pursuit of wealth, could also have played a role in the decision to become an entrepreneur.

The fact that entrepreneurs are in the habit of offering polished PR statements was a major factor in the decision not to allow them to authorize the texts of the interviews. Whenever possible, journalists also avoid doing this, because they know that their interviewees will often use the authorization process to smooth the rough edges off their statements to such a degree that all that remains are empty and boring soundbites. The Swiss sociologists Ueli Mäder, Ganga Jey Aratnam, and Sarah Schillinger, who published the above-mentioned collection of interviews, gave their respondents the opportunity to authorize the final texts of the interviews. The researchers reported that, during the course of the authorization process, a number of crucial statements were either substantially reformulated or entirely deleted.[634] The final interviews included a number of empty statements, such as the following: "In my view, the key to my success in working to promote the interests of all stakeholders is a lived value system, transparent 'rules of engagement', a functioning, mutually respectful collaboration between the governing body and the CEO, and between group management and the Board of Directors ... Within this context, I try to influence interests through various discussions. Transparent argument and the credible evaluation of company interests, economic and social interests are of paramount importance."[635]

We don't know whether such sanitized statements are the product of PR Department editing during the authorization process or whether they are a product of the interviewees' habitual rhetorical rituals, but this is not important. Whichever is the case, this was certainly another argument against allowing the interviewees to retrospectively authorize the texts of the interviews conducted for this study.

---

622   Fridson, *How to Be a Billionaire*, 4.

623   Mäder, Aratnam, and Schillinger, *Wie Reiche denken und lenken*, 198.

624   Ibid., 251.

625   Ibid., 242.

626   Rainer Nahrendorf, *Der Unternehmer-Code: Was Gründer und Familienunternehmer erfolgreich macht* (Wiesbaden: Gabler Verlag, 2008), 96.

627   Ibid., 110.

628   Ibid., 143.

629   Ibid., 178.

630   Ibid., 118.

631   Ibid., 90.

632   Ibid., 183.

633   Nahrendorf, *Der Unternehmer-Code*, 182.

634   Mäder, Aratnam, and Schillinger, *Wie Reiche denken und lenken*, 169.

635   Ibid., 207–208.

This was, in any case, unnecessary as, in contrast to the Swiss study, the anonymity of the interviewees here was guaranteed. Prior to the actual interview, an agreement was signed by both parties in which the interviewer guaranteed that the name of the interviewee would not be disclosed at any point and the interviewee agreed that, under this condition, the author would be permitted to reproduce excerpts from their interview.

After the interviews, each interviewee was sent a summary of their interview, along with a number of key quotations from the interview, in order to ensure that no specific contexts had been misunderstood, at which point it was made explicitly clear that the interviewee was not being asked to provide authorization of the text. Only one of the interviewees made more extensive corrections, although, even in this case, the core content of the interview remained unchanged.

In formulating the questions, great care was taken to minimize stimuli or incentives that might potentially encourage socially desirable responses or lead to generalized platitudes. After all, there are a large number of interviews with elites that clearly demonstrate that this bias towards socially desirable responses is frequently underestimated:

In a 2007 survey of major German businesses involving interviews with 61 top managers (managing directors and CEOs of major family businesses and DAX-listed stock corporations), the author succinctly states that "It is impossible to determine to what extent the interviewed managers provided socially desirable answers. At the same time, there are no indications of such tendencies."[636] But what does the author mean, there were 'no indications'? The interviewees were asked to rank the importance of 18 different factors and, in the final ranking, honesty, driving progress, imagination and creativity, independence, and professional competence were ranked highest, whereas power, in stark contrast, was ranked at the lowest point on the scale.[637] The findings of the researcher, that power plays no role in the conception of the self today, would appear to be somewhat premature. The researchers believe that the motive of power has been supplanted by "cooperative values oriented towards public spirit and service to the community", such as "one has to have time for other people, otherwise one becomes cold".[638] In explaining their *own* success, 34% of the top managers named values such as "a willingness to work in a team", whereas just 7% admitted to "ambition".[639] In clear contrast to their own answers, when asked to list the qualities they valued most highly in the next generation of managers, the CEOs and managing directors ranked a combination of 'ambition' and 'commitment' most highly, and by some distance to the next highest qualities.[640]

Leon Festinger's theory of cognitive dissonance can also play a role in explaining the social desirability bias described above. The concept that underpins his theory is that an individual strives to establish "internal harmony, consistency, or congruity among his opinions, attitudes, knowledge and values. That is, there is a drive toward consonance among cognitions."[641] One derivation from the theory of cognitive dissonance is of particular relevance to the "discrepancy that can arise between an individual's self-conception and their actual behaviour". Should an individual's expectations of themselves prove wrong, this results in cognitive dissonance.[642] According to Festinger, dissonance can also arise because of an inconsistency between "what is considered appropriate or usual" and an individual's actual behaviour.[643]

The pursuit of money for its own sake and, in general, holding money in high esteem clearly do not correspond to the self-images held by many people, or to what is socially regarded as "appropriate or customary". This can lead to cognitive dissonance, which may be more or less pronounced, depending on the individual concerned. "For some people, dissonance is an extremely painful and intolerable thing, while there are others who seem to be able to tolerate a large amount of dissonance ... Persons with low tolerance for dissonance should show more discomfort in the presence of dissonance and should manifest greater efforts to reduce dissonance than persons who have high tolerance."[644] This could explain why a number of wealthy individuals are more readily willing than other people to admit a material orientation, namely the motive to build wealth.

The responses outlined above suggest that more attention needs to be paid to the topic of socially desirable answers, particularly in the case of elite interviews. The interviewer, therefore, has to use the opportunities presented "by the formulation of the questions and design of the interview to reduce the bias towards socially desirable responses, to further 'neutralize' the questions".[645]

In the research, a multitude of methods have been developed, to the extent that it is nearly impossible to keep track of all the methods used to 'neutralize' this problem. It can be accepted that a number of people are more likely, and others less likely, to exhibit this social desirability bias in the responses they provide.[646] In her doctoral dissertation, Petra Hartmann addressed the issue of social desirability in extensive detail and, in particular, investigated strategies by which an individual's bias towards social desirability could be ascertained. The most common method is the use of so-called SD (social desirability) scales.

---

636 Buß, *Die deutschen Spitzenmanager*, 10.

637 Ibid., 116.

638 Ibid., 117.

639 Ibid., 129.

640 Ibid., 196.

641 Leon Festinger, *A Theory of Cognitive Dissonance* (Stanford: Stanford University Press, 1957), 260.

642 Martin Irle and Volker Möntmann, "Die Theorie der kognitiven Dissonanz: Ein Resümee ihrer theoretischen Entwicklung und empirischen Ergebnisse 1957–1976," in *Festinger, Leon: Theorie der kognitiven Dissonanz*, edited by Martin Irle and Volker Möntmann (Bern: Verlag Hans Huber, 2012), 357.

643 Festinger, *A Theory of Cognitive Dissonance*, 13.

644 Ibid., 266-267.

645 Gläser and Laudel, *Experteninterviews und qualitative Inhaltsanalyse*, 138.

646 Hartmann, *Wunsch und Wirklichkeit*, 60.

The sobering findings of an analysis of a range of SD scales, all of which were subjected to comprehensive testing, was, however, that it is "doubtful to what extent it is at all possible to construct an instrument for the subsequent elimination or control of response bias".[647]

SD scales serve, in simple terms, to ascertain whether, and to what extent, an interviewee exhibits a bias towards social desirability in their responses. This involves asking an interviewee additional questions designed exclusively to determine the extent to which the interviewee's responses are shaped by a desire to provide socially desirable answers. These additional questions are not related to the actual research questions.

The extra time involved in the use of such additional questions was one consideration against their employment during the interviews. Even if the number of additional questions was restricted, the time spent answering them would reduce the amount of time available for the important questions of direct relevance to the research. Furthermore, this may have created a situation in which the intention of the additional questions would be revealed, therefore rendering the instrument immediately ineffective, which Hartmann states is often the case. Or, when faced with a range of bewildering questions, the sense of which they do not understand, an interviewee may be confused, and the interview itself could be disrupted.

All of this would be justifiable, so long as the SD scales delivered what they promised – that is, if they actually made it possible to answer the question of whether and to what extent a person exhibits a bias towards socially desirable responses. As the analyses and tests of such SD scales have led to the conclusion that they are hardly able to answer this question, no such instruments were used for the interviews for this book. Other instruments were also ruled out, including the 'Bogus Pipeline Technique', by which an interviewee is systematically deceived.[648]

In the case of oral interviews – and in contrast to the written surveys upon which Hartmann primarily focuses – there is another method that can be used to ascertain to what extent an interviewee tends towards social desirability, and it is a method that can be employed at the time of the interview rather than retroactively: namely, the use of specific instructions and cues to counteract this bias.

Gläser and Laudel recommend that the first strategy the interviewer should employ is to point out to the interviewee that there are a range of public opinions on the topic at hand. This could involve reference to disparate reporting in the media, or reference to anonymous public statements ("many people say").[649] Or, the interviewer may include in their question an acknowledgement that other interviewees have already provided answers that were socially less desirable. "With such a strategy, one attempts to make it clear to the interviewee that he or she is not alone in their experiences and opinions, but that they belong to a group and that it is common to speak uncomfortable truths during such an interview."[650]

A further option rests in the – otherwise to be avoided at all costs – technique of suggestive questioning, "in order to build up a counter-pressure to the bias towards socially desirable answers".[651] When a certain socially undesirable answer is formulated by an interviewer in a careful and agreeable manner, the interviewer is signalling that such answers are certainly 'allowed'. As Petersen repeatedly pointed out, it is "not only absurd, but also methodologically wrong" to declare certain questioning techniques generally impermissible. Under certain circumstances, "even massively suggestive questions are justified in the research, in fact, they can even be quite necessary. The only decisive point is that the use of such questions serves the pursuit of knowledge, rather than manipulation."[652] Petersen argues that this approach could be particularly necessary in order to overcome response barriers and to counteract the tendency of interviewees to shape their answers in accordance with some image of the "idealized self".[653]

Research carried out to determine whether a particular 'wording' can be used to minimize social desirability bias has delivered contradictory findings. Here is an example of a question formulated using 'forgiving wording': "Social scientists have discovered that an increasing number of people have affairs while being in a relationship. Have you cheated on your last/recent partner?" Or: "Many people do not have the time to vote anymore. Did you participate in the last national election?"[654] The principle behind forgiving wording is always the same. "On one side, it is useful to choose an 'everybody-does-it' approach when formulating sensitive questions. Another possibility is to use wordings which convey the impression that the behaviour in question is (1) appreciated by authorities, (2) has been carried out for comprehensible reasons or (3) is already presumed by the interviewer."[655]

The findings of an analysis of whether forgiving wording actually achieved what it was deigned to achieve were published in 2012 but the authors came to the conclusion that the results were unclear.[656] A doctoral dissertation was also published on this topic in 2012 and found that, in general, in relation to wording

---

647   Ibid., 247.

648   In this experiment an apparatus is employed: the interviewee is told that this apparatus can precisely measure the intensity and direction of opinions and attitudes, which is, of course, not the case. For comparison, see Hartmann, *Wunsch und Wirklichkeit*, 93 et seq.; Hans Dieter Mummendey and Ina Grau, *Die Fragebogen-Methode: Grundlagen und Anwendung in Persönlichkeits-, Einstellungs- und Selbstkonzeptforschung*, 6th ed. (Göttingen: Hogrefe Verlag, 2014), 187 et seq.

649   Gläser and Laudel, *Experteninterviews und qualitative Inhaltsanalyse*, 138.

650   Ibid., 139.

651   Ibid., 137.

652   Petersen, *Der Fragebogen in der Sozialforschung*, 210–211.

653   Ibid., 212.

654   Anatol-Fiete Näher and Ivar Krumpal, "Asking Sensitive Questions: The Impact of Forgiving Wording and Question Context on Social Desirability Bias," *Quality & Quantity* 46, no. 5 (2012), 1613.

655   Ibid., 1602.

656   Ibid., 1612.

and related techniques, there is "a clear imbalance between the claims made about of the importance of these methods in textbooks … and the empirical effects that can actually be demonstrated".[657]

In formulating the questions that inherently possessed the greatest tendency to elicit socially desirable responses, an interviewer could address this matter directly and ask the interviewees to be careful to formulate their responses irrespective of the degree of social desirability involved. Hans Dieter Mummendey and Ina Grau highlight the significant effect of instruction on interviewees: instructions are able to "move mountains".[658] "In general, one can assume that instructions exert such a significant influence on the reactions of test subjects that even minor variations to the questionnaire's instructions are sufficient to generate substantially modified responses. In countless empirical studies, the systematic variation of instructions led to changes in behaviour without it ever being necessary to check the effectiveness of such experimental or quasi-experimental variations of condition variables (manipulation verifications) in advance."[659]

To the author, the problem of socially desirable responses arising during the actual guided interviews appeared to be less of an issue than at first was feared. Generalized, well-meaning phrases, of the kind usually contained in official PR statements (see the examples from other interviews of elites above), were almost never expressed. The same was true of the tendency to qualify, or completely dismiss, the pursuit of wealth or material goods as a motive, or to ascribe one's own economic success to luck, all of which were much less pronounced than in the other interviews with wealthy individuals cited in this chapter. On the other hand, there were a number of answers that the interviewees themselves must have known could not easily be interpreted as socially desirable. For example, one interviewee explained that he likes it when others are envious of him. Another interviewee said that money is important to him because it increases his chances with women.

It is likely that the near absence of the issue of socially desirable responses is largely the direct result of the author's sensitivity to the topic. Firstly, it became evident that it was crucial that no general questions were asked about the reasons for an individual's success; rather, facts were elicited or stimuli for anecdotes were provided. Secondly, it was decided not to ask the interviewees to authorize the final transcriptions of the interviews. That the author himself is also wealthy may well also have contributed to the fact that self-justification played a lesser role than if the interviewees had not been aware of this.

7.5. METHODS OF TRANSCRIPTION

The interviews were recorded with a recording device and transcribed by a third party. There are several methods of transcription. "The aim of a transcript is to represent the word sequences (verbal features) produced during the interview, often in combination with phonetic features, e.g. pitch and loudness (prosodic features) and coverbal, non-linguistic behaviour (whether vocal, as laughter or throat clearing – paralinguistic features – or non-vocal, as gestures or visual behaviours – external features) on paper as accurately as possible so that the particulars of a unique dialogue become apparent."[660]

Whether information other than verbal features is recorded is a decision that depends on whether the considerable additional effort involved is proportionate to an added yield in the evaluation. A decision about the transcription method should be made beforehand so that only those aspects of the interview intended for analysis are actually transcribed.[661] The author decided to have the transcripts produced in the literary style and without special transcription rules. In order to answer the research questions, it is not necessary to use transcriptional characters or to record paralinguistic or extralinguistic features. The effort to produce such a transcription would be much greater, readability would be impaired, and the possible added value for the evaluation of the content would bear no relation to the extra effort involved.

However, one requirement for the transcription was that the name of the interviewee, all other personal and company names, and city names should be replaced with 'xxx' so that no conclusions can be drawn about the identity of the individual interviewees. If any products were mentioned by which it might be possible to identify an interviewee, the word '[product]' and similar general formulations have been used in square brackets. The same procedure has been used, for example, for location data. For some particularly sensitive topics, even the reference number of the interviewee has been omitted in the discussions in Part B, or replaced by 'A', 'B', 'C', etc. All of this serves to protect the data and to ensure anonymity.

Several decisions also needed to be made in relation to how the interviews should be evaluated:

1. Should they be coded or not?
2. What aids should be used? Should the analysis involve computer-based qualitative data analysis or not?

---

657   Felix Wolter, *Heikle Fragen in Interviews: Eine Validierung der Randomized Response-Technik* (Wiesbaden: Springer VS, 2012), 72.

658   Mummendey and Grau, *Die Fragebogen-Methode*, 182.

659   Ibid., 87.

660   Sabine Kowal and Daniel C. O'Connell, "Zur Transkription von Gesprächen," in *Qualitative Forschung: Ein Handbuch*, 10th ed., edited by Uwe Flick, Ernst von Kardorff, and Ines Steinke (Hamburg: Rowohlt, 2013), 438.

661   Ibid., 444.

Philipp Mayring recommends an elaborate system in which the text is segmented and coded into small units.[662] Mayring, who is a proponent of very strict and consistent rules for interpreting texts to ensure that they are understandable and inter-subjectively verifiable,[663] adds, however, that these procedures "[should] not be understood as techniques that can be blindly transferred from one object to another". Qualitative content analysis is "not an established technique", and "contextual arguments should always be awarded priority over procedural arguments in qualitative content analysis".[664]

Gläser and Laudel criticize Mayring's procedure, which "ultimately analyses frequencies rather than extracting information".[665] They recommend an alternative evaluation system, which they call 'extraction'. The author decided not to carry out computer-aided content analysis but to work with traditional methods, as, in his view, the additional effort would not have been proportionate to any additional gain in knowledge.

7.6. NATURE OF THE HYPOTHESES

A further methodological question, which, despite the fact that it has already been addressed, will be explicitly discussed here: Is it necessary to form hypotheses for an investigation, and, if so, on what basis? And what characteristics do hypotheses have in qualitative social research?

While it is indisputable that the formation of hypotheses prior to the start of an investigation is of central importance in quantitatively oriented methodology, this has been the subject of some controversy in the field of qualitative research. "Precisely because one is aware of the fact that knowledge affects perception and action, one wishes to avoid a situation in which the researcher is 'committed' to certain aspects on the basis of distinct hypotheses, which he 'draws' only from his own (scientific and everyday) field of relevance, but whose 'suitability' in relation to the interpretive patterns of the persons examined by him is not guaranteed from the outset."[666]

In a view long held by various scholars, hypotheses could have a tendency to impair the openness of the researcher, which is a necessary condition of qualitative research, and thus they should be avoided altogether from the outset. Some researchers have even gone so far as to say that researchers should be free from all previous knowledge and should even have to forgo the study of theoretical and empirical work on their subject, lest this impair their openness.[667]

However, such a strict rejection of ex-ante hypotheses has been disputed, in particular, by researchers led by Christel Hopf. They argue that hypotheses are also significant in qualitative research. The central issue is, as Werner Meinefeld postulates, fulfilling two seemingly contradictory expectations: "On the one hand, to satisfy the epistemological requirement for incorporating prior knowledge into the methodological control, and, on the other hand, not to abandon the interpretative a priori, to allow the sociological analysis to take its origin from genuine meaning, and not to impose the categories of the researcher in the act of interpretation."[668] It is not that the formation of hypotheses in and of itself is inherently biased, but the lack of willingness to revise ex-ante hypotheses at any time and to substitute more plausible hypotheses during the research process.

Gläser and Laudel also point out that testing hypotheses via empirical investigation is merely "a special variant". "Not all research hypotheses are actually tested. In some cases, hypotheses only serve to explicate and fix the researcher's preconception so that they can be systematically integrated into the investigation."[669] Hypotheses should be tested in qualitative social research "only in exceptional cases" – i.e. when they are confirmed or rebutted. "They can, however, guide the empirical survey and the evaluation, because they provide a focus for the knowledge being sought (the research question). They also explicate the researcher's presumptions, which have an influence on the investigation, an influence which should never be underestimated."[670]

For qualitative research, Gläser and Laudel recommend developing so-called guided questions, which correspond to the hypotheses of quantitative or "relationship-oriented" research. Guided questions are not theoretical questions and also not to be confused with interview questions, but they specify the information that needs to be gathered. These are a "few, complex, pointed questions, whose answers will yield the necessary, empirical material".[671]

---

662   Philipp Mayring, *Qualitative Inhaltsanalyse: Grundlagen und Techniken*, 12th rev. ed. (Weinheim: Beltz Verlag, 2015).

663   Ibid., 61.

664   Ibid., 52–53.

665   Gläser and Laudel, *Experteninterviews und qualitative Inhaltsanalyse*, 199.

666   Werner Meinefeld, "Hypothesen und Vorwissen in der qualitativen Sozialforschung," in *Qualitative Forschung: Ein Handbuch*, 10th ed., edited by Uwe Flick, Ernst von Kardorff, and Ines Steinke (Hamburg: Rowohlt, 2013), 266.

667   Ibid., 268.

668   Ibid., 271.

669   Gläser and Laudel, *Experteninterviews und qualitative Inhaltsanalyse*, 31.

670   Ibid., 77.

671   Ibid., 91.

PART B

Interviews with
45 ultra-high-net-worth
individuals

8 Structure and Topics of the Interviews

Part A presented the status of wealth and entrepreneurship research, as well as theories of behavioural economics and learning theories, as far as these were significant for the formulation of hypotheses and guiding questions. The resulting guiding questions, which became the basis for the interviews, are reproduced in the appendix, as is the questionnaire containing the Big Five personality test.

This resulted in a total of 12 thematic complexes for the evaluation of the 45 interviews. These were examined for statements on the following topics:

1. Special features of the interviewees' youth (time at school and university, informal learning experiences in sports, and early entrepreneurial activity)
2. Motivations for setting up a business
3. The role of goal-setting
4. The importance of the concept of 'money' to the interviewees
5. The importance of sales skills for financial success
6. The role of optimism and self-efficacy
7. Risk propensity
8. The relationship between analytical and intuitive ('gut') decisions
9. The personality traits of the Big Five theory: Neuroticism, Extroversion, Openness to Experience, Conscientiousness, and Agreeableness
10. Willingness to engage in confrontation
11. Nonconformism and willingness to "swim against the current"
12. Dealing with crises and setbacks.

The most important task was to systematize these statements, to identify similarities and differences, and to look for patterns that are characteristic of the interviewees as a group. These questions also define the structure of the evaluation and presentation of the interviews in this part of the book.

During the evaluation of the interviews, the expectation was confirmed that, in addition to the similarities, there were also differences between the interviewees, which made it possible, in many cases, to classify individual groups or types. For example, there was a large group in which gut decisions dominated analytical decisions, but there was also a group of interviewees for whom the exact opposite was the case. Another example: in some interviews, a type of entrepreneur emerged who had set up their own business because they could not fit into prescribed structures and hierarchies because of their personalities as employees. But there was also a group of interviewees for whom this was not the case. They had made a successful career as an employee, but they were too impatient to wait for many years to get to the top of an existing company, so they went into business for themselves. In many areas, it was possible to identify patterns that were characteristic of (almost) all interviewees, but there were often characteristic differences that allowed different types to be distinguished by their behaviour.

ABOUT THE STRUCTURE

Chapter 9 deals with the formative, early years of the UHNWIs, their social origins, and their relationships with their parents, school, and university. Two aspects have emerged as particularly significant: the young person's commitment to sports and early entrepreneurial activities. The question of how significant formal education qualifications were compared to informal and implicit learning is also examined here.

Chapter 10 discusses what motivated these UHNWIs – almost all of whom have their own businesses – to establish independent businesses at some point in their lives. Is the hypothesis that entrepreneurs are 'misfits' who could not fit into the prescribed structures of existing companies as employees and therefore decided to become self-employed really true? Or would these people have been able to make a successful career in existing companies?

Chapter 11 examines whether the interviewees have set (financial) goals or whether they describe their wealth as a by-product of their activity, which they had not intentionally planned and aimed for as a goal.

Chapter 12 more closely examines the motivations of the UHNWIs, who were asked what they associate with the concept of 'money'. In particular, questions were asked about the motivations of security, freedom and independence, the possibility of investing in new things, self-affirmation, and recognition by others. It becomes clear how different the motivations of the UHNWIs were – factors that played a big role in one case were meaningless in another.

Chapter 13 focuses on the importance of sales skills and abilities for the professional and financial success of these UHNWIs. This topic, which has so far been underestimated in the research, turned out to be particularly important in the interviews. From the interviewee's perspective, what traits and abilities are most important for sales success?

Chapter 14 discusses the relationship between optimism and self-efficacy. How optimistic are the UHNWIs, what do they mean by optimism, and have they considered the risks of excessive optimism?

Chapter 15 investigates the risk propensity of UHNWIs, which is related to the degree of optimism previously discussed. How open to risk do they estimate themselves to be? Are there discrepancies between self-perception and external perception? And has the propensity for risk remained constant throughout their lives, or have they taken less risk in later life than in the early stages of their entrepreneurial activity?

Chapter 16 looks at how these UHNWIs make decisions. Is intuition or analysis the key factor? And what do people mean when they say they make decisions based on gut feeling?

Chapter 17 examines the results of the Big Five personality test that the interviewees took. How strong are the personality traits Neuroticism, Extroversion, Openness to Experience, Agreeability, and Conscientiousness?

Chapter 18 examines how compatible or confrontation-prone UHNWIs are. The results of the Big Five test are linked with an evaluation of the interviews.

Chapter 19 examines the role of 'swimming against the current' and a contrarian approach to investing in the financial success of these UHNWIs.

Chapter 20 deals with how these UHNWIs handle crises and setbacks. How have they dealt with psychological setbacks, and what strategies have they developed to cope with major difficulties in their entrepreneurial life?

At the beginning of each chapter, the theses and questions from the literature in Part A are restated for each respective topic.

Formative years 9

9.1. SOCIAL BACKGROUND

The study based on the survey Wealth in Germany, which surveyed individuals with an average net wealth of EUR 2.3 million, found that a substantial majority (64%) of these individuals came from middle-class households. A further 21% grew up in low-status parental homes, while 15% were raised in high-status households. The key findings of Böwing-Schmalenbrock's study in relation to social origins were:

1. "An intergenerational comparison reveals that the 'lower classes' are massively underrepresented as recruits to the ranks of the wealthy"
2. "Secondly, and more frequently than would conform with the socio-economic stratification of contemporary German society, they typically come from the middle classes"
3. "In relation to the social structure, the wealthy are far more likely to have grown up in high-status parental homes".[672]

In contrast, research into the social background of members of the *economic elite* finds that "the higher an individual's economic position, the greater the significance of their social background. Access to the economic elite, in its strictest sense, is largely reserved for the scions of the upper middle class and (even more so) the upper class."[673]

The academic wealth-research findings cited above apply to the "millionaire next door", a group that was not the subject of the research carried out and presented in this book. Hartmann's findings, however, relate to the economic elite, although, as demonstrated in Section 2.1, Hartmann's definition of the economic elite largely focuses on the ranks of the executive management of large companies.

---

672   Böwing-Schmalenbrock, *Wege zum Reichtum,* 210–211.
673   Hartmann, *Der Mythos,* 87.

The German wealth elite, which is the subject of this book, is restricted to individuals possessing assets worth tens to hundreds of millions of euros and is a group that has so far not been the subject of scholarly research.

During the course of the interviews, each interviewee was asked about their father's profession. It was initially striking that:

1. Very few were the product of blue-collar households or lower social strata. Equally few were the offspring of wealthy families. A clear majority grew up in middle-class households.
2. The number of self-employed parents was above average in comparison with the population at large. Of the 45 interviewees, 27 had fathers who did not primarily work as employees. More than half were entrepreneurs, self-employed, or farmers.

> ## PROFESSIONS OF THE INTERVIEWEES' FATHERS
> Entrepreneur: 14
> Self-employed: 4   Civil servant: 7
> Employee: 9   Blue collar: 2
> Farmer: 7   Freelance professional: 2

ENTREPRENEURS

A total of 14 of the interviewees had fathers who were entrepreneurs, some of whom belonged to the economic middle class, others to the economic upper class. It was not always obvious which classification was applicable. The individual professions of the fathers were:

- Father was the owner of a medium-sized steel company; the son took over the family business.
- Father was a member of the management board of a watchmaking company (family business) with 3,500 employees, and owned 11% of the company. The company went bankrupt and the father was subsequently a member of the economic middle class.
- Father and mother were joint owners of a medium-sized garden supply business that had been founded by the interviewee's grandfather.
- Father owned a butcher's business with one main store and two additional stores.
- Father owned a chemical works, which became insolvent when the son was ten years old. In subsequent years, the father no longer owned his own business and belonged to the economic middle class.
- Father had a large company, which he sold when the son was 12 years old. The family was wealthy.

- Father owned a large, internationally active company (family business), which the next generation took over in an extremely difficult economic situation.
- Father and mother owned a medium-to-large-sized company, which the son transformed into a global corporation.
- Father owned a medium-sized medical technologies company, which had fewer than 100 employees at the time. The son expanded the company into an international business with 2,000 employees.
- Father owned a large company in the ports sector, which had been in family ownership for several generations.
- Father started out as an employed, middle-class engineer. He subsequently took over the company in which he worked and became wealthy.
- Father owned a cigar factory and belonged to the economic middle class. The interviewee emphasized the fact that he was the product of three different entrepreneurial families (biological father, stepfather, mother).
- Father took over distressed companies from banks and belonged to the economic middle class.
- Father was initially an employed member of the management board of a company, before becoming self-employed, buying and turning around distressed companies.

SELF-EMPLOYED

The fathers of four of the interviewees had their own small businesses and belonged to the economic middle class.
- Father was a salesman and sold fire-safety equipment.
- Parents owned a small furniture store.
- Father was a master butcher and later owned a small restaurant.
- Father was a merchant trader and photographer – i.e. a small businessman.

EMPLOYEES

In the case of nine interviewees, the fathers (and in one case the mother) were employees and economically belonged to the middle class.
- Father was a director of a music publisher.
- Father was a surveyor.
- Father was a ventilation systems engineer.
- Father was an employed architect.
- Father was a director of a chemical factory.
- Father was a paralegal in a lawyer's office.
- Father was a deputy managing director of a music publisher.

- Father was a technical employee.
- Son grew up with his mother, who served as a financial director of a large company but nevertheless belonged to the economic middle class.

FARMERS

Seven of the interviewees had parents who were farmers, five with small operations and two with medium to large ones.

- Farmer (medium to large).
- Wealthy farmer (also owned companies in other sectors).
- Small-scale farmer.
- Father and mother were farmers with a small operation.
- Farmer and pig breeder, economically unsuccessful.
- Farmer with small operation.
- Farmer with small operation, impoverished.

CIVIL SERVANTS

The fathers of seven interviewees were civil servants, five of them teachers.

- Mid-ranking civil servant.
- Teacher (previously entrepreneur).
- Teacher.
- Father and mother were both teachers.
- Teacher.
- Father and mother were both teachers.
- Senior civil servant (senior government official).

BLUE COLLAR

- Father was a production controller.
- Father was a warehouse clerk.

FREELANCE PROFESSIONAL

- Father was a lawyer but died in the Second World War when the son was four years old.
- Father was a surgeon and owner of one of the largest accident and emergency practices. He enjoyed great economic success and wealth.

9.2. EARLY INFLUENCES AND CAREER PLANS

Did their parents raise the interviewees to strive for money and wealth? Was this a topic that was discussed at home? The interviewees said it was not. Money was either not discussed at all or only in a negative sense. Not infrequently, the interviewees reported that the pursuit of money had been strictly frowned upon in their parental homes. Many of the interviewees described their parents as belonging to the educated middle class:

Interviewee 4: Money was more of a taboo. Moralized, tabooed and it was rather like, anyone who talks about money has surrendered to the evil of money. [...]
Interviewer: That's strange, especially as he [the father] was an entrepreneur and making money should have been completely legitimate for him.
Interviewee 4: Yes, but my mother's influence was more dominant and her ideas prevailed.
Interviewer: Did your mother grow up as a Protestant?
Interviewee 4: Yes, in a Protestant environment.

Interviewee 17: I am different from my parents. It wasn't about being a rebel, but I have a very distanced relationship to my parents, because they think completely differently from me. For my parents, earning money is unethical. My parents were basically of a type that doesn't really exist nowadays, the archetypal educated middle class. [...] Money is not important. [...] Yes, that's something that does not exist nowadays. You could ask him anything. He had answers to questions on any topic, any subject, because of his comprehensive, humanistic education. But he didn't know a single thing about business. [...] So a firm grasp of the Bible, although he was never at church. So you could ask him anything about the Jewish faith, or Buddhism. He is also someone who travelled a lot in his time. He had foreign, Korean composers. At a time when no one travelled, he was in Asia and looked after them. But he was never interested in money.

Interviewee 25: I had no role model for entrepreneurial activity in my family. My family was out of touch with the real world, they were in their own little academic world. The real world was totally alien and strange to them. [...] They lived in their own educated, bourgeois world. And there were absolutely no entrepreneurs in our family. They were all primarily either doctors or teachers. But actually no entrepreneurs. So no entrepreneur role models, no guides, from whom I could learn. So, I would say, I somehow decided to become an entrepreneur for myself, in a roundabout sort of way.

Interviewee 34: No, my father lived according to the principle ora et labora [pray and work]. So he was a very Christian person, it was a very Christian family. Money was of no importance at all. Rather the goal was to emigrate to Israel one day and to be on Mount Zion for the rapture, so it was a pietistic background. Farming served to feed us and to raise the children. I have eight siblings, so nine children, and there were no discos, no newspapers, no television, nothing. There was only the Bible, mass, the youth choir, classical music. That is my background. [...]
Interviewer: [...] So money was probably viewed rather negatively at home?
Interviewee 34: That's how it was. The vile mammon. You definitely shouldn't strive for money and things that you don't really need.

Interviewee 35: No, [...] I was raised to believe that one should keep money at arm's length. [...] So money is really something rather negative.

However, children and young people are not only shaped by their parents but also by their broader social environment. Did the UHNWIs have role models in their youth? Were they influenced by the example of other people or families as well as by their parents? Some reported that as children and adolescents they were attracted by the lifestyles of other relatives or acquaintances, especially in contrast to the middle-class narrow-mindedness they experienced in their parental homes. For one of the interviewees, this influence was the grandmother:

Interviewee 3: I wasn't interested in money as such, but of course, I always thought it was great when a person could live in pleasant surroundings. I hated my parents' pettiness and I always thought it was nice, for example, at my grandmother's, they had a hunting lodge in Brandenburg, I was often there and she always told stories. With her lifestyle, she was what you would now call a grand dame. She had always lived well and thought life was wonderful. My paternal grandmother was a very fun-loving woman. My maternal grandmother was the daughter of a shipowner. They had a shipping company here in Berlin, near Berlin. Her husband was an officer and well, that was exactly the opposite, it was an extremely strict environment, they also lived here in Berlin, in the style of a Prussian officer's family.[674] And my other grandmother was much more the fun-loving, easy-going, Bavarian family.
Interviewer: And that attracted you more?
Interviewee 3: Yes, they were great, that was a good thing.

Another interviewee, whose parents were teachers, spoke about the family of a friend whose parents were entrepreneurs. He found their lifestyle very attractive:

Interviewee 6: I didn't have any explicit professional ambitions, but I always wanted more than just survival, even if we weren't exactly poor. Let's say, I hoped for more than the rather modest life of a civil servant. I always wanted to have more. I had a friend at school whose parents were entrepreneurs. I found this extremely desirable, their flair, where they were always working hard, but also a different standard of living dominated.
Interviewer: Did you spend much time at their house?
Interviewee 6: Yes.
Interviewer: And what was it that appealed to you, that made you say "Wow, I think this is actually better than at my place"?
Interviewee 6: I guess it was their more bourgeois behaviour and attitude to life in general. So, it wasn't just about having a bigger car. They didn't read only one newspaper, there were always three in the rack. They didn't save money in the wrong places. And this Protestant work ethic, which we had at home, I thought that was, how to put it, very self-restricting, petty almost. At my friend's house, I found the somewhat more generous way of thinking that shaped an entrepreneur's household to be very attractive, and that was very inspiring to me.

Another interviewee spoke about his cousin, who married the daughter of the richest construction company owner in his city. The elegant lifestyle of this family impressed him:

Interviewee 10: My cousin married the daughter of the richest construction company owner. And then I thought that maybe having a construction company wouldn't be the worst thing. That's where the idea came from.
Interviewer: What attracted you to it? Was it so different from the petty bourgeois conditions at home?
Interviewee 10: Yes, they lived in an elegant world. They had an elegant lifestyle. [...] That was the thing, I was always impressed by beauty and elegance.

---

674   The interviewee is contrasting his father's family (the traditional Prussian way: disciplined, strict, serious) with the open, joyous approach to life exhibited by his mother's family.

The parents of another entrepreneur were simple butchers and saved every penny they had in order to send their son to the Salem elite boarding school.[675] There he was introduced to another world, as so many classmates came from rich families. Incidentally, a surprising number of the interviewees attended private schools, including those who – like this one – came from humble backgrounds or the middle class:

> **Interviewee 13**: When you were still so young, around 10, 14 or 15, it was certainly not always easy for me as a young boy, knowing that the other children came from all over the world and belonged to the richest families in the world. My advantage was that I am not envious, or at least not much. So, actually I never had a problem with it. I never begrudged people their wealth and such, but it did motivate me. All these different kinds of people, whether in terms of economics, creditworthiness or power, and, all these types together, from all over the world, gathered there together. And that was more the motivation for my life, you want to find a way to achieve your goals and be satisfied. [...] I was often at friends' for holidays, in the fifth, sixth, seventh grades, and you then automatically become a part of that world. [...] So I basically grew up among friends and that's how I came to know the world, without experiencing envy.

The parents of the next two interviewees were not rich but still lived in neighbourhoods among many well-to-do people. Here, they experienced the lives of the rich every day – and this impressed them and aroused their desire to one day be one of them. This son of a teacher put it like this:

> **Interviewee 16**: Maybe you just want to escape, you know, escape your parents' misery and do everything better. So I have to say, you can hardly imagine it today, but we only went to a restaurant every four or six weeks because we were always so short of money. With three children, as a civil servant, you had to drink at home before you went out, so you only drank a coke in the restaurant and, as I said, a restaurant visit was exceptional. We often had stew at home so that we could use up the week's leftovers. And if I accidentally asked for 2,000 instead of 200 grams of ham, I was sent back to the butcher's to return it because it was too expensive. [...] And of course, what impressed me all my life, we were very, I don't want to say poor, but we were a family with limited means in the midst of so many well-situated rich families. We lived in [upscale suburb of a city in Baden-Württemberg]. And we had an old VW Variant.[676] The newest car we ever bought was a ten-year-old, second-hand Passat, and we still had a black-and-white

television until 1982, because we couldn't afford a colour TV. So we didn't live in poverty, but we lived a very, very thrifty life. And when we went on holiday, my father did not drive at full speed, because he wanted to save on fuel. We had everything that everybody else had, just not the newest or best. I would press my nose up to the glass of the shop windows as we walked past and wish I could have what was on display. My friends were all sons of district attorneys, great merchants, and the like. They got a Golf GTI as a high school graduation present, while I had to work for my Passat Diesel AA.

Interviewee 18: [...] We lived in Starnberg, you shouldn't ignore that. At that time Starnberg was the place to be; many of the nouveau riche lived there. All of the glitterati of Munich showed up on the weekend.
Interviewer: Did that impress you to some extent, did it make you think, "Hm, this type of life wouldn't be so bad"?
Interviewee 18: Yes, that life, that lifestyle. I bought my first bicycle for DM 5 with my own money. And I had friends who were around 16 years old at the time, who had special drivers' licences and drove to school in a Porsche or a Jaguar E-Type. Or in summer they came on a motorcycle. Yes, the [unintelligible] children, for example, they all went to school with me. And when they turned 16, they all got a Porsche. That really turned me on, of course.

An interviewee who now works in the real estate sector got to know a wealthy property developer through one of his father's colleagues, who impressed him enormously with his personal lifestyle. He reported that this inspired him early on to become a property developer, so that he could also live such a life:

Interviewee 36: My father had a colleague, his best friend, Professor xxx, and he had a son, xxx. Xxx was a property developer. He developed supermarkets for xxx in Frankfurt. Maybe you know him?
Interviewer: No. And what did you like about that?
Interviewee 36: Yes, I can tell you. You're going to laugh. He always had the best-looking girls. Always models, but really nice ones. Like James Bond, Moonraker, the leading actress. And he always drove great cars and was always jolly. He was always fun-loving and I was impressed by the lovely girls and the hot cars. That's what I wanted and I thought, that's a great profession.

---

675   Schloss Salem is Germany's most prestigious international boarding and day school.
676   The VW Variant was a station wagon typically driven by lower-middle-class owners.

This interviewee, however, was an exception in that he aspired very early on to the profession in which he would later work. The professional aspirations of the other interviewees were not very spectacular. Nobody reported that they had wanted to become a multimillionaire as a child, and very few had wanted to become entrepreneurs. The professional aspirations of these UHNWIs during their childhoods hardly differed from those of other children. Even though they had, to some extent, craved the more affluent lifestyles that they had been exposed to, this was not necessarily reflected in unusual professions. When asked what career ambitions they had in childhood and youth, they answered:

> **Veterinarian**. Of course, on the farm, I always had a lot to do with animals, but I was certainly influenced by my family and teachers, who thought early on that I should be steered in the direction of law or business, and they decided that I should become a lawyer or a businessman.

> When I was very young, of course I wanted to be a **train driver** or an **astronomer** or something like that...

> I wanted to be a **film director and then a journalist** [...] Maybe the reason I wanted to be a journalist was because there was a competition at the *Süddeutsche Zeitung* [one of the leading daily newspapers in Germany] for the best school newspaper article, which I won.

> I wanted to be a **pastor**. Or a researcher, or a doctor or psychologist.

> For a long time I wanted to be a **forest ranger**. [...] When I was a child, I used to spend a lot of time in the forest when I was at my aunt's. And I really liked that and wanted to be a forest ranger for a long time, but then ... I can't remember having any other career ambitions when I was a child. Not a race car driver or anything else.

> I wanted to be a **geologist**, because I was interested in fossils. That was my biggest career ambition.

> I had two career ambitions. One was to be a **gardener**. And the other was always to be a **banker**. I thought that would be easy, to be a branch manager at a credit union or a savings bank, they were in every village, I thought that would be an interesting job. It has to do with money, with people, they always wore suits. And they had nice offices and earned good money – as I saw it at the time.

When I was young, I thought about becoming an **engineer**. I seriously considered studying at the university in Darmstadt, at the Technical College, but then I gave up on that idea, because I was told that the chances of becoming a self-employed engineer were slim and that's why I decided to study law instead. I never wanted to be an employee, you know? But the desire to be self-employed was always very strong.

If I'm honest, I had **no idea** what I wanted to be.

Well, no, I **really didn't have any specific ambitions**. I was always sure that I could do anything in principle and that it really didn't matter what I did, somehow I would be successful. That was my attitude and when I left school, I kind of slipped into my profession by accident.

When I was very young, I thought of becoming an **officer**. Not necessarily because of the whole military aspect, but because it's just one of those positions where you have complete authority. And then, at some point, I thought of going into tourism. Something like a **tour operator**.

I wanted to be a **pilot**, but I couldn't do that for health reasons. [...] Early on it became clear that I couldn't do it because I can't hear anything in one ear.

To make cheese. **Master cheese maker**.

My grandfather was a mechanical engineer, a qualified industrial engineer, my father and grandfather thought that I should also be a mechanical engineer, to be a qualified **engineer**, which is what I did.

No, no career ambition. **No career ambition.**

I wanted to be an **architect**.

The main thing for me was **to make money. No matter how**. It had to be legal but effective.

For me, my **career ambition or goal** was actually **sports**. Sports were important for me. I was involved in competitive sports.

When I was a child, all I wanted was to be a good father for my family. And I wanted a lot of freedom, nothing more. **I didn't know anything about a career.** I started out logging and driving a timber lorry.

No, I always thought like an entrepreneur and **wanted to do something entrepreneurial.**

I had many ideas. Then, when I was a teenager, I wanted to be a **race car driver**, or a **musician**. But ultimately, reality stepped in and I have always made reasonable decisions.

When I was a child, I had the typical dreams. The last big one that I can remember was **forest ranger**. I love nature.

No, I didn't have **any particular career ambitions**, if I'm being honest. No, I really didn't have any. But then I studied **theology** after I graduated from secondary school.

My dream was, I didn't have a clear vision of exactly what I wanted to do. There were two people who I always used as reference points, who I found very fascinating. That was Josef Neckermann, who was an extremely successful **equestrian and entrepreneur**. And Paul Schockemöhle is another example.

I wanted to be a **hotelier**. I wanted to run a hotel.

I never **had any idea of what I wanted to do.**

Yes, **train driver** of course, like all boys at some point. Nothing serious though.

I wanted to be a **lawyer**.

No, nothing out of the ordinary. So, when things became clearer, one possibility was **psychology**. Then, for a long time, also architect and businessman, then salesman came later.

Engineer.

Architect.

Geneticist.

Doctor.

Excavator driver.

9.3. RELATIONSHIPS WITH PARENTS

Many biographies of wealthy individuals detail the massive conflicts that arose with figures of authority during their subjects' childhoods and adolescent years – above all with their parents and teachers.[677] For this reason, one of the interview questions focused on the interviewees' relationships with their parents during their formative years – and whether there were conflicts beyond those normally associated with the tempestuousness of puberty. Most of the interviewees, however, reported relatively harmonious relationships. Those who reported significant conflicts were in the minority. Typical responses included:

Interviewee A: I never had [conflicts]. We were quite different, and I am the youngest of five children. My father came back from the war, out of captivity, which meant he didn't want any more conflict, didn't really go looking for conflict. Yes, there were, of course, political disagreements, which was normal for that generation, and is probably also true for our generation. We blamed our parents. We asked them how any of that [the Nazi dictatorship] could ever have been allowed to happen. That's something that everyone had to deal with. But we never pushed things to their limits, there was never a total breakdown in relationships.

Interviewee B: I never had serious disagreements with him [the father]. I never rebelled against the way he did things. It's more like, from the very beginning, I made allowances and tended to go along with the way he did things.

Interviewee C: I always had a good relationship with my parents. They were actually very tolerant and lived contentedly together and were very modest. My father, as I've already said, was a civil servant and we didn't really have that much money. My family's other money, which had come from my mother's family, was slowly being eaten away, but my father had never really been so impressed by that anyway.

Interviewee D: Conflict-free home life, a good home life. Conflict-free, apart from what you'd normally find in any family.

Interviewee E: I was never rebellious, but I had a quite distant relationship with my parents, because they had a very different way of thinking about things.

---

677 Zitelmann, *Dare to Be Different and Grow Rich*, 105–114.

For my parents, earning money is unethical. My parents were basically of a type that doesn't really exist nowadays, the archetypal educated middle class. [...] But I didn't spend much time with my parents, from about the age of 14, because my journey to school took an hour, so I spent more time in the company of friends. I cut the apron strings quite early on and moved in with my wife when I was 18. Conflict [with the parents] was minimal, I think, though there were intellectual disagreements. When I look back on it, I think I was quite well-behaved. No, no, it wasn't so extreme. I went my own way, as I moved out of my parents' home so quickly.

In contrast, a minority of interviewees reported massive confrontations, in particular with their fathers. Here are three examples:

Interviewee F: Basically, I did everything that you weren't supposed to do. My father said I was looking for punishment. [...] I did things that no one else would ever think of doing. I was at my worst until I was through puberty. That's when things were really difficult. At some point after that, I started to be more sensible. That was when my father said, "Look at that, he's finally getting his act together." That was when I started to get involved in sports.

Interviewee G: I had nothing but confrontations.
Interviewer: And were they serious?
Interviewee G: Totally.
Interviewer: So what typically triggered the confrontations?
Interviewee G: My father was extremely authoritarian. A really brutal man who beat me a lot.
Interviewer: At what age was the situation most extreme?
Interviewee G: It lasted until I was 16 or 17. That was the period when we clashed the most. After that, things got easier, I just stopped talking to my father and he stopped talking to me. I didn't like him, and he didn't like me either. I had long hair and supported the left-wingers and greens, you know, the environmentalists. More the greens, I was never really that left-wing. But I was definitely green. [...] He thought that it was delusional. And it was, he was right. It was a form of opposition. Then I met a teacher with the same political leanings, who, in a way, brainwashed me.

Interviewee H: Let's put it this way, I fell out with my father after he exerted his influence to make me do military service even though I didn't want to and wouldn't actually have had to. As a child, despite my involvement with competitive sports, I had something wrong with my heart, which would have given me the chance to say that I was physically unfit for the military. But my father put a stop to that and, for that reason, I had to do military service after all. That created a huge chasm between us. The second source of conflict was that my father was a very dominant person. He was successful, but then he experienced a massive failure, which caused lots of conflicts with my mother because he dragged her down with him. My mother had built up her own business, but she lost it because she had put it up as collateral for my father. And that created a situation that had an impact on me, too. When it got to the point that I wanted to go to university, I couldn't get any support, any student grants or loans, because my father hadn't always been completely broke, so I had to pay my own way through university.

But all in all, the hypothesis that UHNWIs experienced massive conflicts with their parents during their formative years, as is reported in the biographies of many billionaires, was not confirmed by these interviews.

9.4. SCHOOL AND UNIVERSITY[678]

There is a common assumption that high-level educational qualifications are an essential prerequisite for social advancement. In Section 4.6 it was shown that there are good reasons to question the validity of the assumption that educational attainment plays a key role in whether an individual will achieve great wealth. On the one hand, the formal educational qualifications of the interviewees were indeed superior to those of the same age group across the entire population. Of the 45 interviewees, 29 were university graduates and 38 had completed secondary school with a university-entrance certificate. Eleven – almost a quarter – had actually received doctorates, the highest possible academic qualification. Bearing in mind that just 2% of the German population hold doctorates, it is evident that the level of academic attainment within this UHNWI group is significantly higher than that of the population at large.

---

678   The German secondary school system comprises three types of school, roughly equivalent to junior high, high school, and university-preparatory schools. Grades are awarded on a scale of 1 to 6, with 1 being outstanding, 2 very good, 3 satisfactory, and 4, 5, and 6 representing unsatisfactory to totally unacceptable. Grades in all subjects are combined and averaged, which can result in a final score that includes a decimal place (e.g. 1.5 or 2.7).

> **INTERVIEWEES' HIGHEST ACADEMIC QUALIFICATIONS**
> Completed compulsory education: 7
> University-entrance certificate but did not study
> at university (or dropped out): 9
> University graduate: 18
> Doctorate: 11

On the other hand, there are no indications that as academic attainment increases, there is a corresponding increase in wealth. This becomes clear when the lowest quartile of the 45 interviewees is compared with the highest quartile. After all, in the lowest quartile, namely those individuals with net assets worth between EUR 10 and 30 million, three had been awarded doctorates and seven were university graduates. Only one had graduated from secondary school without going on to study at university. In the highest quartile, which includes all individuals with assets worth EUR 300 million or more, one person held a doctorate and five were university graduates. Three either had graduated from secondary school but not gone on to university or had started a degree course and subsequently dropped out. And two had not graduated from secondary school with a university-entrance certificate but had completed compulsory education.

> **COMPARISON OF EDUCATIONAL ATTAINMENT:**
> **LOWER AND UPPER QUARTILES**
> **In the lowest category (EUR 10–30 million): 11 cases**
> Completed compulsory education: 0
> University-entrance certificate, but did not study at university: 1
> University graduate: 7
> Doctorate: 3
>
> **In the category of more than EUR 300 million: 11 cases**
> Completed compulsory education: 2
> University-entrance certificate, but did not study
> at university or dropped out: 3
> University graduate: 5
> Doctorate: 1

In a majority of cases, the interviewees did not perform exceptionally well at school or university. Most reported that they achieved no more than average results at school. Here is an overview of the interviewees' performance at school and university:

- Interviewee was among the top 5% at university-preparatory school, studying law; awarded a doctorate in law with satisfactory grades.
- Interviewee attended Salem, the most prestigious boarding school in Germany; studied metallurgy; graduated with honours.
- School: very good grades in German and history, very bad at mathematics and chemistry; studied business administration; awarded a doctorate (with a 'pass' grade).
- School: German, art, and music very good; other subjects not so good. Studied biology to become a teacher but dropped out.
- School: mediocre; sports were more important. University: law, first state examination, and doctorate.
- School, initially good, then not so good because earning money outside school became more important. Studied sociology and political science (distance learning).
- Best in class at technical high school (didn't graduate with a university-entrance certificate), then did an apprenticeship as an industrial clerk.
- Very good grades in secondary school; studied law and graduated with honours, then did an MBA. Doctorate in law.
- Did badly at school and at university. Studied agricultural economics, but sports were far more important; dropped out of university.
- "One of the best five" at school (monastery school), followed by business administration at university.
- Very good at school; top grade for a master's in industrial engineering; awarded a doctorate summa cum laude.
- University-entrance certificate with just about satisfactory grades (2.9); didn't study.
- Satisfactory grades in university-entrance certificate (2.7); studied business administration (graduated with mediocre grades).
- University-entrance certificate; didn't study.
- Middle school; didn't study.
- Studied mechanical engineering; dropped out.
- Studied to become a teacher; studied business administration (best master's grade of the past ten years = 0.7[679]); trained as an auditor/tax consultant.
- Dropped out of school; didn't graduate from school.
- Poor grades at high school, then studied to become a surveyor and graduated with good grades.

---

679   In extremely rare cases in certain German states, it is possible to achieve a grade that is better than a 1, as in this exceptional case.

- Graduated middle school; apprenticeship as an assistant pharmaceutical technician.
- Finished middle school, but with poor grades.
- Decent university-entrance certificate grades (2.1); studied business administration with acceptable grades (2.0).
- Poor secondary school grades, then an apprenticeship as a hearing aid acoustician; became a master craftsman.
- Average grades at secondary school; studied industrial engineering, graduating with good grades (1.8); doctorate with satisfactory grades (2.0).
- Very good university-entrance certificate grades (1.6); studied theology ("best exam result in my year group": 2.0).
- Average at secondary school; graduated with excellent grades in law, studied business administration, then awarded doctorate in law.
- Mediocre university-entrance certificate grade (2.9); graduated in business administration with satisfactory grades (2.0).
- Attended boarding school; an average pupil; studied business administration at St. Gallen.
- Mediocre university-entrance certificate grades (2.9); studied economics; good grades at university.
- Poor performance at technical secondary school; studied engineering and was ultimately very good.
- Attended boarding school; average performance; later studied business administration and awarded a doctorate.
- School; university-entrance certificate ("in the top third"); did an apprenticeship while studying law; awarded a doctorate magna cum laude.
- School; University-entrance certificate grades (3.0); mediocre business administration degree (2.7); joinery apprenticeship.
- Average university-entrance certificate grades (adult education) (2.0); carpentry apprenticeship and policeman; graduated in business administration with satisfactory grades (2.3).
- Average at school; studied economics with good grades; awarded a doctorate in economics.
- Average university-entrance certificate grades (2.5); studied economics with satisfactory grades (2.0); doctorate cum laude.
- Average university-entrance certificate grades (2.2); studied mechanical engineering; graduated with very good grades (1.3).
- Mediocre university-entrance certificate grades (2.9); studied business administration with mediocre grades (3.0).
- University-entrance certificate with average grades, then studied economics but dropped out.

- Very good university-entrance certificate grades (1.3); didn't study; went straight into business for himself.
- University-entrance certificate; studied industrial engineering.
- Average university-entrance certificate grades (2.1); studied mathematics and biology; dropped out.
- Excellent university-entrance certificate grades (1.0); studied business administration and had very good grades ("best in my year group") (1.3).
- Good university-entrance certificate grades (1.9); studied medicine but dropped out.
- Poor university-entrance certificate grades; didn't study.

Only nine of the interviewees reported that their secondary school or university grades were excellent and that they were among the best in their year groups. Of these nine individuals, six belonged to the lowest wealth category (EUR 10 to 30 million), two belonged to the next highest wealth category (EUR 30 to 100 million), and only one belonged to the group with a fortune worth more than EUR 300 million. Two in particular had distinguished themselves with outstanding academic performances – one gained his university-entrance certificate with almost perfect grades (1.0) and went on to be the best or second best in his year group at university. The other was awarded the highest grades (0.7) in the past decade for his master's degree. Both belonged to the lowest of the wealth categories.

Among the 11 who had achieved the highest level of academic attainment (doctorate), the picture was entirely heterogenous. Three were in the lowest wealth category (EUR 10 to 30 million), five were in the next highest category (EUR 30 to 100 million), two were in the category of EUR 100 to 300 million, and one was a multi-billionaire. The individual with the highest academic qualifications, who had both been excellent at school and received an almost perfect grade for his master's degree, going on to receive his doctorate with the award summa cum laude, found himself in the lowest of the wealth categories. Of the three billionaires, one had a doctorate, one had dropped out of university, and the third had only graduated middle school. Despite the fact that the interviewees, on the whole, had higher academic qualifications than the population at large, the overall picture was extremely heterogenous and no clear pattern emerged that would conclusively indicate that superior performance at school or university should be viewed as a prerequisite for achieving a very high level of wealth.

A second hypothesis, developed in Part A of this book and tested during the interviews, was that individuals who go on to become very rich more frequently and more intensely engage in confrontations with authority figures in their youth. As has already been demonstrated, this hypothesis was not confirmed by the interviewees' reports of their parental homes. So were things different at school?

As far as their performances at school were concerned, a majority of the interviewees were decidedly average. Many were 'rebellious' or regularly engaged in confrontations with their teachers. Here follow a few examples.

One interviewee reported that he was in constant conflict with his teachers, in part for political reasons:

> **Interviewee 6**: I was often hauled before the headmaster to explain myself because I had orchestrated demonstrations against the Conference of Education Ministers. [...] And we organized school strikes, and I hung banners on the outside wall of our school to protest against the Conference. I guess I was generally quite a troublemaker in my class. I sat at the back of the classroom and secretly read *Der Spiegel* magazine[680] and drank beer under my desk. That was clearly intended to provoke. Despite all that, I still did well at school, but I was certainly provocative during my last four years of secondary school.

The next interviewee, who went on to set up a large medical technology company, was also very politically active at school, which became a source of constant conflict with his teachers. In terms of school grades, he was among the top third of his year group, so this was not the source of the conflicts:

> **Interviewee 32**: Let me put it this way – at school, I was very involved. I was class president, school representative, state school representative, and all that kind of stuff. [...] And then, in my home state of North Rhine-Westphalia, I was the representative for all the secondary schools in the state. [...]
> **Interviewer**: That's interesting. I was just about to move on to your time at school. Were you more of a good, average, or poor pupil at school, when it came to your final grades?
> **Interviewee 32**: I was always in the top third.
> **Interviewer**: And were you something of a rebel?
> **Interviewee 32**: Yes, definitely. Definitely. [...] I was always rebellious, defiant. And I'm not really sure why, looking back on it now. For example, I had to give the speech at our secondary school graduation ceremony and I included a quote from Hitler's *Mein Kampf*. But I had to hand in my speech in advance and the school council wanted to stop me from giving it. [....]
> **Interviewer**: And so, while you were at school, what form did your rebellion take?
> **Interviewee 32**: It was largely because I just wouldn't conform. Another example: We published critical articles in the school newspaper, and then, at a state-wide school open day, I was going to attack the whole system of pupils' joint responsibility that the state of North Rhine-Westphalia

had put in place, and the head of the school board said, "If you're going to do that, I won't come," or words to that effect.

In contrast, the following interviewee, who went on to build a successful IT company, performed poorly at school. He also reported political activism, which led to confrontations with his teachers at his conservative, Latin-and-Greek-dominated university-preparatory school:

> **Interviewee 33**: So I was quite rebellious and worked just hard enough at school, following the motto, "a good horse only jumps high enough to clear the fence". I never really received anything more than mediocre grades (3.0) and, when school got more serious in the last couple of years, I was always in danger of having to repeat a year.
> **Interviewer**: Okay, so you didn't do well at school. And you were rebellious. What did that relate to? Was it rebellion against discipline, or was it more political?
> **Interviewee 33**: A combination of the two, really. But maybe a bit more on the political front. A typical issue at the time was the NATO Double Track Decision, things like that. Those were the kinds of things 16- and 17-year-olds were tackling back then. And then the anti-nuclear movement got started and I was always deeply involved, and conscientious objection, you know, refusing military service, was another really big topic for me. Back then, everyone was required to do military service, but you still had to take a really tough test to prove your pacifism, your conscience. [...]
> **Interviewer**: And that also led to conflicts at school?
> **Interviewee 33**: That led to conflicts, confrontations, arguments. I was at a very conservative, humanist, Latin-and-Greek-dominated university-prep school.

A number of interviewees admitted that they engaged in constant power struggles with their teachers in order to ascertain who would emerge the stronger from such confrontations. The next interviewee, who went on to enjoy success in investment banking and real estate investment, reported that he had "always been rebellious":

> **Interviewee 42**: In seventh and eighth grade my teacher gave me demerit points for bad behaviour 30 times. [...] At 14 and 15 I tended towards rebellion, and then, I took that seed of rebellion and pushed things even further.
> **Interviewer**: In your case, was it more a question of just causing trouble

---

680   *Der Spiegel* is one of the leading liberal news magazines published in Germany.

to rebel against discipline, or was it, as is the case with other interviewees, more of a political nature? Or simply, screw this, I'll do what I want.

Interviewee 42: It wasn't just a question of being against something. There were a number of teachers where I recognized that they just weren't able to lead a class, or in terms of their subjects, I thought that some of them just didn't know their subjects well enough. So I played little games with them. Just games. I provoked the teachers to the point where they lost their temper. Or I deliberately caused chaos, just to see what would happen. That's how I got my kicks.

A number of interviewees reported that they had to change schools, or were frequently suspended or expelled from school, often as a result of the confrontations they had with their teachers. One interviewee describes his own behaviour as "a disaster":

Interviewee 9: The result of my feeling that "I'm no good in my class, no good at school" was that I became disruptive and was repeatedly expelled from school, because of what I had done, and then my parents kept on getting calls from the school, along the lines of "Your son has broken the school's rules and we would suggest that you remove him."

The next interviewee also experienced severe disciplinary problems at school. He was kicked out of five schools, repeated three school grades, but still achieved very good results when he graduated from secondary school (1.3):

Interviewee 40: And when it came to my final years at school, I always managed to find a way to scrape through. Right at the end there was just one school in our area that would take me, and they said, "We'll still take you on but you have to hit the ground running and major in mathematics from day one if things are going to work out."

Interviewer: I understand. And why exactly were you kicked out of school?

Interviewee 40: Oh, a variety of reasons. [...] Disciplinary issues. I skipped school or was stubborn over some things. Always really idiotic things. That's still a tendency I have today. [...] I have always been difficult, rubbed people up the wrong way.

One interviewee reported that he had constant disciplinary problems throughout his school career. He said that he had "changed schools more frequently than other people change their shoes":

Interviewee 45: I was terribly bored at school. That was definitely one aspect of it. But there were also huge distractions. There were plenty of things I would rather have been doing.
Interviewer: So it would be true to say that you had considerable disciplinary problems at school.
Interviewee 45: Yes.

The next interviewee, who went on to become very rich, left school without any formal qualifications. His class teacher told him that he would never amount to anything anyway:

Interviewee 18: It was like this, I went to secondary school in [city]. And my father died when I was 17. And I was a bit of a miscreant. I would only study when it was fun. And if it wasn't fun, then I simply didn't study. I also just stopped going to school. And my parents, my mother, couldn't cope with the situation...
Interviewer: So then you simply dropped out of school?
Interviewee 18: Yes... there were one or two teachers I got on with, but there were lots of teachers I couldn't stand. You have to understand, back then there were still a lot of teachers around from the Nazi time. And they still acted that way. And I can still remember when my class teacher – she also taught Latin and German – said to me, "xx, you'll never amount to anything." I can still remember that vividly today.

Another wealthy interviewee reported that he constantly skipped school, before dropping out completely. Later on, the penny dropped and he eventually completed technical high school. He studied engineering and was ultimately one of the best in his subject:

Interviewer: So, turning to your time at school, would you say your performance was good, average, or poor?
Interviewee 30: I was a poor pupil, more of a bad pupil. Because I was always interested in completely different things. I often skipped school. Instead of going to secondary school, I would spend time with another pigeon breeder. That was much more interesting to me.
Interviewer: And how did you do in your university-entrance exam?
Interviewee 30: I eventually went back to school and ended up graduating from technical high school.[681] And that was when I drew a line under school.

---

681   This is a lower form of graduation, after only 12 years of secondary education, and does not entitle the graduate to study at university.

I got into trouble. Lots of trouble, you know? [...] I had problems with teachers because I kept skipping school. I'm sure my mother worried a lot. [...] And then I decided to quit school, because I just didn't want to be there anymore. I just kept on getting into trouble and my mother wasn't happy. [...] I dropped out at some point in eighth grade. Then I basically worked on building sites and as a carpenter and joiner. [...] And then, all of a sudden, something inside me clicked and I said to myself, "Right then, now you've got to do it!" And that's when I went back and studied for my technical high school exams.

Many of the interviews reported that school did not interest them in the slightest. This was also true for the next interviewee, who, alongside school, was engaged in a number of business ventures; he earned a great deal of money and said that he "wasn't interested in the slightest" in school. He didn't do very well at school, and explained during the interview, not without a certain arrogance, that he simply had not been prepared to "lower himself to the intellectual level [of his teachers]":

Interviewee 19: I had too many things going on outside school and my performance at school suffered because I wasn't interested in the slightest. That's why I started working, alongside school, at the age of 15. And that's why my final school grades (3.4) were so poor. [...] I just had problems with my teachers. I was only on the same wavelength with one or two teachers, the rest I hated. And they hated me because I was so disinterested and wasn't prepared to lower myself to their intellectual level. That was too stupid for me. That was maybe the main reason, but there was a second reason. I always had an overpowering ambition to become independent.

One interviewee, who later set up a very successful real estate company with several hundred employees, finished middle school with mediocre grades. He reported constant conflicts with his teachers and described himself as a "troublemaker":

Interviewee 20: Yes, I was something of a troublemaker, both at junior high and then at university-prep school. I had to quit at fairly short notice because I wasn't doing well, my grades weren't good enough and I had trouble with my teachers. And it didn't end there. [...] Ultimately, school was more or less a secondary concern for me. And as far as the trouble I had with teachers is concerned, I always had the feeling they treated me unfairly. And that was a feeling that ran all the way through my time at school. So I went to middle school and just about scraped through, mainly because I was so good at sports. [...] But there were plenty of confrontations at school.

The next interviewee, who later built a successful construction company, described how school caused him actual physical pain and how he constantly battled with his teachers and was regarded as one of the "top three troublemakers" in his school:

> **Interviewee 27**: I graduated secondary school with a "wonderful" grade of 2.9, which wasn't at all great, I have to admit. But I couldn't have been lazier. [...] I just found it impossible to enjoy school. And, at that moment in time, I didn't want to be pigeon-holed in that way. For some reason, I always had a bit of physical pain when I was at school. I was great at making friends, but engaging fully with the subjects at school just wasn't for me. [...] But at school, I was really, extremely antagonistic. I was always viewed as one of the top three troublemakers.

One of the wealthiest interviewees is dyslexic and admits that he is still unable to read fluently today. When asked about his final middle school grades, he responded, "My final grades were poor, naturally":

> **Interviewee**: I am dyslexic. That means that I can't read fluently. Over there, they're currently reading a contract, and I'm miles behind them. And running a company means being able to read a huge amount every day. With the letters that I receive, if you send me a letter, I read the first couple and the last couple of sentences. If they match up with what I was expecting, then I'm happy, I feel good. If they don't match up, then my secretary reads the letter aloud to me. I have roughly 200 pages to read every day.

Striking though the number of reported conflicts with teachers may be, this is by no means a trait that is shared by all of the interviewees. Many reported a relatively conflict-free time at school. A number were actively involved as school representatives or in other official bodies, and assumed responsibility at an early age. The next interviewee attended a sister school of the Salem international boarding school:

> **Interviewee 2**: I was never an outstanding pupil at school. We had a school parliament or student council, which had an important role within the school. The council decided, for example, whether a pupil should be expelled or not. The student representatives always had a say in such cases; the headmaster could not make that sort of decision alone. At the age of 17 or 18, the school assembly elected me to the highest representative position within the school, as their direct representative and first point of contact for the teaching staff. I held that position for a year, so you could say that they believed that

it was something I was capable of. In the mornings I read the morning prayer, and I said grace before meals, led the daily assembly. Lunch would start, and I would stand up at the front and read out the notices or announcements, news from the sports teams and clubs, organizational matters, everyday things. [...] I wasn't generally a rebellious sort. Not at all. I was reliable, dependable. At least, I always tried to be dependable.

Another interviewee, despite his family's very modest background, attended Salem boarding school, and held a number of prestigious positions:

Interviewee 13: At school I held a number of senior offices. I was the spokesperson for services and sports clubs. We were at boarding school, at Salem [...] And the school always had a student spokesperson. The two highest offices were student spokesperson and just below that was the parliamentary spokesperson. Then came the offices that I held. As spokesperson for services, I was completely responsible for the fire and first-aid services. Then I was the sports spokesperson because I was already engaged in competitive sports. Those were the two high offices that I held at the time.

9.5. SPORTS

Of the 45 interviewees, 23 were competitive athletes or, at least, recreational athletes with above-average ambitions.

SPORTS THE INTERVIEWEES PURSUED INTENSIVELY IN YOUTH
- Rowing until shortly before secondary school graduation.
- Tennis with daily training, still playing in the men's league as an adult.
- From the ages of 8 to 18, track and field athlete; trained five times a week; competed in national championship at 1,000 metres.
- From the ages of 16 to 34, a competitive athlete; Hessian champion in downhill and combination skiing; also table tennis at district level; handball for five years intensively, including championships.
- Sports spokesperson at Schloss Salem; a competitive athlete from the ages of 13 to 20; daily decathlon training; champion of Baden-Württemberg; among the top ten in Germany.
- Basketball from the ages of 8 to 18; played in the second national league.

- Football from the ages of 15 to 23, training four times a week; played at Berlin in the highest league; studied sports.
- Four years of artistic gymnastics; participation in Baden-Württemberg state championships.
- Chess master in his age group in Cologne; also played against adults in the top division.
- Show jumping (competitive).
- Eventing rider (10 years in the German national team; seventh place at the Olympic Games).
- In the German military's dedicated sailing sports group, which consisted of ten people; sailed in regattas.
- Ski racer for four years; Baden-Württemberg championship.
- 1,500 metres, middle-distance, participated in state championships.
- Competitive swimmer from ages 13 to 17; Westphalian champion.
- Intensive horse rider from ages 10 to 14; participated in children's tournaments.
- Tennis from ages 6 to 16, four years competitively.
- Volleyball from the ages of 6 to 19, of which six years competitively; the team was often district champion and achieved third place in the state championships.
- Rowing from the ages of 12 to 18, competitively; won several regattas.
- Competitive judo from the ages of 6 to 16; was in the North Rhine-Westphalia (NRW) squad and won the NRW state championship with his team.
- Ten years in track and field, middle-distances (800 metres, 3,000 metres); among the top three state-wide.
- Track and field from the ages of 15 to 20; state champion at 1,000 metres.

Most of these were *not* team sports, but individual disciplines such as track and field, gymnastics, tennis, skiing, horse riding, table tennis, chess, judo, and swimming. However, there were also true team sports, such as handball, football, volleyball, and basketball. Some interviewees expressed their views on how they were shaped by competitive sports and on the skills that they acquired and used later in their professional lives. One interviewee, who rowed competitively, stated:

Interviewee 1: Also in professional life [...] the ambition to want to be the best is crucial. You learn to approach your limits and transcend them and you must also be able to cope with them psychologically. As an officer, this was one of the most important criteria for me when I selected other people. Do you lose your nerves or keep a "clear head" despite the precarious situation?

Plus, success in competitive sports requires sacrificing many pleasant aspects of life. And athletic performance increases self-confidence and acceptance in society.

Many interviewees emphasized that they later, as entrepreneurs, preferred to recruit competitive athletes because they considered them most likely to be top achievers in their chosen profession:

Interviewee 5: I hired a lot of competitive athletes as employees. Because I've always said performance athletes are also likely to be top achievers at work. I have a tennis player who is now the managing director of xxx. I always told him when it got tough, "Now you have to go all out," and he knew exactly what I was talking about. So I think, when you... most good athletes have a clear idea even at a young age. And clear goals. And have tried to achieve them with a great deal of commitment and ambition [...] Basically I enjoy competition. I think competitions are also exciting. It's got to be fair and reasonable, and I liked doing it when I was a child. I didn't like to lose, but I also found people terrible who were sore losers for three days when they hadn't won. At work, you're sometimes a bit more relaxed, but I still have my bite, you know? And when I want to achieve something, it doesn't matter at what age, then I go all out.

One interviewee was involved in track and field for ten years as a competitive sport and competed in the German championships over 1,000 metres. He came from a very humble background and was a millionaire by his early 20s. Sports showed him that, even with unfavourable conditions, it is possible to achieve great goals:

Interviewee 7: I was a middling athlete, but I noticed early on that through rigorous and hard training you can be among the best. That's what I did, and I became a state champion in middle-distance running and qualified for the German championship. The same was also true for other disciplines. I learned that with consistent training you can also break into the top from difficult initial situations and with moderate talent. Sports have shown me that it is possible and you can win.

The next interviewee, who now owns eight companies in the food industry, reported that he had no real talent for volleyball. But he spent six years playing this sport competitively, and with his team often won the district championships and even came in the top three at the state championships. Sports had shown him how to overcome "the limits of talent" through tireless training. Above all, sports had given him a lot of self-confidence:

> **Interviewee 37**: I was not at all gifted, but I learned to go beyond the limits of talent through really tireless training. That took me very far in this sport, which I wasn't really made for. Alongside chess, which we haven't spoken about, volleyball was the stabilizing factor in my life when I was young. I played chess during lessons – actually always – the teachers were glad I was busy and did not bother others too much, which I otherwise always did. Volleyball then took up four of five afternoons a week, and most weekends from September to March. At the age of 16, I started as an assistant coach and then, at 17 I was responsible for the entire youth team 12–16. That was a lot of responsibility and that allowed me to mature. I think volleyball also inspired me because all the interesting and intelligent girls were playing volleyball; unfortunately most of them were unattainable. In addition to internalizing the value of "practice", I also learned that every game can be turned around, and that there is always a "good five minutes", but that's something I didn't learn until later. [...] Sports stabilized my life and kept me away from many of the things that were very popular in the area, i.e. getting stoned, smoking, drinking, etc. I realized that I could never be the spectacular match winner, but in my position I was the intelligent conductor of the entire game, which was totally satisfying [...] I tanked up a lot of self-confidence playing sports.

Another interviewee participated intensively in competitive sports from his early youth until his mid-30s, neglecting school, university, and his career to do so. He described himself as a teenager who was extremely undisciplined and difficult, and had numerous conflicts in school. He learned discipline through competitive sports. Sports taught him that with his – limited – talents, he could achieve the best for himself and live up to his potential within his possibilities:

> **Interviewee 9**: At some point I started to be more sensible. That was when my father said, "At last, he's getting his act together." That was when I started playing sports.
> **Interviewer**: Yes, how old were you then?
> **Interviewee 9**: 16.
> **Interviewer**: OK. Did you then take up really competitive sports?
> **Interviewee 9**: That's right. Two things: skiing and track and field, just running, middle-distances. Actually, I ran at least five to six times a week when I was 18 or 19. If I wasn't running, I would break into a sweat. [...]

Interviewer: Did you also participate in championships?

Interviewee 9: Yes, German championships and so forth. I participated everywhere. Just to be clear, I was never anywhere near to the levels of European or world championships. [...]

Interviewer: Do you see an analogy to what you did in sports and what you later did in the business and financial sector? Do you see analogies there, or, let's say, parallels?

Interviewee 9: Yes. You know, when you are so completely disorganized as a child, you're not good at anything, and sports really gave me a great sense of discipline. And taught me to set clear goals. Just to make it all clear. But, and this was almost more important, I gave my best. I was very happy when I came sixth or eighth in a run against much better competitors, when I knew that they could actually run 30 seconds faster than me. [...] What that showed me, and I've often discussed it since, is just how unrealistic people frequently are when it comes to their own abilities. And that, I think, is one of the most important things in sports, that you recognize and have a realistic notion of exactly what you can accomplish. I was sure that I was never talented enough to become German champion, but I tried to the full extent of my abilities, where I knew I could keep up, I tried to achieve the best I could.

The next interviewee was a successful decathlete – he was state champion, ranked 15th in Germany, and participated in international competitions. Sports taught him "[to] have insane determination and [to] box your way through". That's what he learned for later life. "You are wired this way for some ten years and, of course, you automatically take this with you into later life." He added that he had realized at some point that he didn't have the genetic potential to make it to the very top. When he recognized this, he retired from competitive athletics:

Interviewee 13: So when you do decathlon, then you have to be tough, right? Decathlon is not for everybody, and not everybody is up to it. [...] So you do a decathlon and you have to get through two days of competitions and beforehand, you always have to train for each discipline for months on end, of course you have to be tough, of course you have to have endurance, of course you have to fight until you collapse and despite all that, you still have team spirit among the decathletes. Decathletes are different from sprinters. Sprinters are purely focused on themselves and ignore everything else around them. During the decathlon, there is always a team spirit, even with the others. And still you have to have insane determination and box your way through. So, of course, that stays with you. You are wired this way for some ten years and, of course, you automatically take this with you into later life.

The next interviewee was a successful equestrian who even took part in the Olympic Games. He reported that he had always been driven to improve and not to be satisfied with what he had already achieved. When, however, he realized that missing out on qualifying for the next Olympic Games was not affecting him as much as it had in the past, he felt he had simply "had enough":

Interviewee 27: I'm always amazed at how many different types of motivation there are for something like this. I'm somewhat surprised, and sports is a good illustration, but riding is one of those sports that you have to do every day because you have the animal. There are people who simply do not want to get better and who don't have sufficient attention to detail, who are not focused on the individual details that make up the whole. There is a lot of management involved, even there. In this case, the horse. It is the same thing here. So a bit of restlessness, always wanting to get better and then to say, "What's the next step?" And not to be satisfied. I'm never happy with things the way they are. That's not an option. Simply to say, "This is great as it is." I've only ever done that once. That was in 2000, during the Olympic year in Sydney, I prepared myself in the winter so meticulously for something in a way I've never done before, with a personal trainer, with a dressage trainer, and I was on the horse every day for three or four hours, alongside my studies and I worked really, really intensively with two horses. For the first time, I had two horses, which were supposed to go to the Olympic Games. In the end, I didn't even make it to the first showing, because both horses had gone lame. [...] And that was the turning point for me because when I realized I hadn't qualified, there would have been times in the past when I would have cried my eyes out for a whole week. If that had happened when I was 16, it would have killed me. But it didn't bother me at all. When I didn't qualify, I said, "Well, it could happen to anyone, it's just your turn, that's all." In principle that's not a bad attitude towards dealing with failures, saying to yourself, "Well, you'll just have to do better next time." For me it was the time when I thought, "You've simply had enough." Somehow, I was just lacking the final drive, the one you need in sports to carry on, although I was still at the beginning of my riding career in terms of age. And, looking back on it now, I'm sure I would have had the best chances. But at that moment, I had had enough; that was a moment when I thought that I didn't need it anymore because, actually, I was quite satisfied with the way it turned out. And then I said, "That's just bad luck."

One successful investor, who is today in the top wealth quartile among the group of interviewees, is still an enthusiastic sportsman. For him, the motivation in sports, as in business, is the need to measure himself against others, to compete with them, and to beat them:

> **Interviewee 41**: I rowed. That was my competitive sport. I even rowed internationally, also for the German team, even on the men's team although I was still a teenager, still in school. And once, I participated in the university championship, in single sculls, I made it to the final race. That was my main sport [...] Yes, I won some regattas in an eight, as well as in a four. [...] I was also in a regatta on a canal, I can't remember what it was called. And I was in the team in an eight and in a four and I also trained in singles.
>
> **Interviewer**: Do you think that you unconsciously learned something while playing sports during this important, formative time that you used later in life? Did you gain experience for yourself or how would you summarize it in terms of abilities or qualities?
>
> **Interviewee 41**: I think the main thing I learned about myself was that I am simply a fighter when it comes to sports. That is still the case today. I don't want to say that I'm a bad loser, but I don't like to lose that much. I like to win. Today, I like to play golf. Look here, there's a really great trophy that I won and I have a lot, maybe 20 of them at home. So I love the challenge and to measure myself against others. It's always been that way with me, even as a child, in everything, in all sports. When I was in the military, I trained the volleyball team and I also played football during my time in the armed forces and, of course, track and field too. My best discipline was the high jump.

The next interviewee, who became wealthy in the financial and real estate sectors, spent ten years as a competitive judoka and was in the judo squad of North Rhine-Westphalia. He described something psychologists call the experience of self-efficacy, i.e. self-realization: "I can control it, it's entirely in my hands":

> **Interviewee 42**: You learn focus, teamwork and also how to assert yourself, of course. Discipline. I will never be good in anything if I let myself go. You have to develop a passion for something.
>
> **Interviewer**: What else would you say? So these were important keywords that you have taken from your sporting days into later life.
>
> **Interviewee 42**: Fairness. Fairness in the end, that effort pays off. Yes, when I train a lot, then I'll be successful. In the sense of vanquishing my opponent. I do something and that has consequences, a result and I can control it. Recognizing that I can control it, it's entirely in my hands. I don't have to accept

any God-given environment, I can determine my own opportunities, I can determine my own future, my development.

The next two interviewees were track and field athletes, and both emphasized how important it was to learn that they were able and willing to "torture themselves" and not least that they understood the inner logic "more training, better results." They later applied this to their professional lives:

Interviewee 43: Well, I would say on the one hand, the routine that is involved in training, and the self-discipline that you need. And having to overcome your own lack of will power, when it's two degrees and sleeting outside, but you go running anyway. You could say that this is the ability or the willingness to torture yourself. I think that's what is important.

Interviewee 44: Of course, the most basic logic for a runner: more training, better results. That's the maxim. And, for me personally, as an endurance runner, you always have to train. It doesn't matter if it's a good day or not, whether someone plays you a good ball or not. And so I learned that whether it's freezing cold or sweltering hot, your birthday or Christmas, you have to train. The consistency of training, the endurance, keep going, for competitions as well as in training, but also a very high degree of self-motivation. A runner is always a bit lonesome. Always driving yourself on. This self-motivation. And I learned to persevere, even with light injuries or very swollen knees.

The interviewees were successful in sports, but not so successful that they could have earned their living from sports. Some retired from competitive sports due to injuries or because they realized that they would never rise to the absolute top of their sports due to their genetic makeup. One interviewee, who did not compete in sports but played the violin with the same intensity and was very successful, explained, "At the exact moment that I realized I would never be a world star with my violin, I put it to one side" (interviewee 4).

9.6. EARLY ENTREPRENEURSHIP

As shown in Section 3.2.i, there are a number of studies that suggest that entrepreneurial talent is already evident in early youth. For this reason, the interviewees were also asked whether and by what methods they had earned money as young people. Many of the interviewees began earning money while they were at school or university. But, and this is striking, a majority didn't have typical student jobs (bar staff, taxi drivers, temporary workers in factories). They had their own ideas and approaches. They tended to sell and distribute things rather than working for an hourly wage. They learned how to organize, manage, and run projects. Some of them even founded their first companies when they were still teenagers.

The range of things the interviewees sold, produced, or organized alongside their time at school or university is nothing short of incredible. Some of them may only have earned relatively small amounts from their enterprises, but many frequently earned a few thousand Deutschmarks per month and, in certain cases, as much as hundreds of thousands of Deutschmarks per year.

- Sold cosmetics products via structured distribution
- Sold private winter gardens
- Sold insurance products
- Sold used car radios
- Sold used cars
- Sold leather handbags door to door
- Sold second-choice wheel rims
- Organized homework supervision that was delivered by others
- Stripped down old motorcycles and sold the parts
- Organized a bicycle-repair service
- Refurbished old motorcycles and sold them
- Sold old egg cartons as noise insulation
- Sold car-wash systems to gas stations
- Tuned mopeds for money
- Built and sold his own radios
- Sold costume jewellery to retailers
- Sold real estate investment funds
- Sold stocks in companies
- Raised, slaughtered, and sold animals
- Bred and sold pigeons
- Traded in stocks, warrants, and other derivatives
- Sold construction services
- Bought and sold real estate
- Rented out apartments
- Wrote and sold a book on tuning mopeds
- Sold furniture via direct sales
- Set up a film club and used the income to finance the renovation of an old train station
- Redeveloped an old factory building into a communication centre for political work.

Here follow a number of examples of the interviewees' early entrepreneurial activities. One interviewee traded stocks at the age of 17:

Interviewee 1: I got involved with stocks early on. It's not something I picked up from my father, it's something I did for myself.
Interviewer: How old were you?
Interviewee 1: I was 17 or 18. I used the small amount of money that I had at the time, it wasn't much, we didn't have a lot. After I finished my schooling, I spent two years in the military, as an officer, and I got a really decent severance payment, which I saved. That was my nest egg; it saw me through university and I made some money with stocks.

Another earned a lot of money with his own ring business while at university:

Interviewee 3: While I was at university, my first taste of entrepreneurship was a ring business. The parents of one of my friends had their own jewellery businesses and had contacts to jewellery manufacturers, one of whom had silver enamel jewellery to sell, which was fashionable in the 1970s. So, my friend and I, we bought these rings direct from a manufacturer and each of us had 12 or so shops that we sold the rings to. Not jewellery shops, jeans shops. There was no costume jewellery at the time, no costume jewellery firms like Bijou Brigitte and the like, not like today. So, I had 12 shops, and he had 12, and every two weeks, on a Thursday evening, we would call them and ask them what they had sold. [...] Then we set up vending machines; they were white and dispensed blue plastic eggs that we could put the rings inside. We rang the shops every second Thursday evening to ask what they had sold during the week, and they would tell us, two red ones, two green, four blue, and so on, and, early on Friday morning, we would drive over to the manufacturer and collect new rings and then, on Friday afternoon, we would restock the vending machines and collect our earnings. We bought the rings for about DM 8.50 and the jeans shops paid us DM 19.50, but only when they sold a ring, which they did for between DM 38 and 50. We did that for quite some time and it worked well. It was never a really big business, but enough for each of us to earn between DM 3,000 and 4,000 per month. That was a lot of money for a student, and especially given the fact that we only spent one morning every two weeks hanging out with the owners of the jeans shops, drinking a glass of prosecco while we refilled the vending machines [...] That was definitely a lot of money back then. I can still remember, my parents used to give me DM 1,000 per month, and that was a lot. But to have DM 3,000 or more, wow!

The next interviewee earned up to DM 20,000 per month as a radio presenter while at school and university:

> **Interviewee 6**: Ever since I was 10 or 11, I pretty much always had little jobs that started small and became a bit bigger. I started by helping out in grocery stores and earned a few Deutschmarks. Then I worked on the cash registers and started earning decent money at a fairly young age, which meant that, even when I was at school, I always had a few hundred Deutschmarks in my pocket. That was certainly a lot of money for a school kid [...] and I earned it because I always worked really hard; while the others were off spending their afternoons and evenings kicking a football around, I was working. But I enjoyed it, it wasn't that demanding. I basically worked all the way through secondary school. I pretty much always had one or two jobs alongside school. [...] At the time, I was working in radio as the Morning Man. That was the first time I started to earn real money, while I was still at school. Which is why I only ever turned up for the third lesson of the day. [...] [He continued working in radio while he was at university.] I didn't put my radio career on hold until after university; I did it parallel to my studies. It was actually quite easy to combine the two. I didn't actually work that many hours, but when you are earning DM 150 per hour and a show lasts four or five hours, you don't need to. So, working 30 days a month resulted in an incredibly high wage. Sometimes I worked for two stations, one show in the morning and one in the afternoon, and in a good month I would earn DM 15,000 to 20,000. That was two or three times higher than my father's salary as a teacher. And that was more or less parallel to my studies.

Another interviewee worked in structured finance sales while at university and earned up to DM 10,000 per month:

> **Interviewee 9**: And I set up a sales team in Stuttgart, where I was living at the time, followed by a second in Heidelberg. I travelled back and forth between the two cities and earned my first money. [...] So, that was officially parallel to university. [...] I either requested time off, or muddled through, or didn't complete all of my courses. [...] And then I worked for xxx, and even at the time, with plenty of ups and downs, there were months when I earned DM 10,000. Back then as a trainee or as a management trainee, people were maybe earning around DM 1,800 per month. That was good money, highly paid. That's when I lost the urge to really want to study and graduate. I said to myself, "Why do you need to study, you can already earn more with what you're doing right now."

At the age of 22, and parallel to university, the next interviewee became "Germany's most successful salesperson":

Interviewee 10: I was always involved in lots of things at the same time, one of which was a revision course, which helped me a lot. That was for three hours, from 6 to 9pm every Thursday, for students who were struggling at university and wanted extra support. That's where I learned the most. Then I sold investment products for xxx on a commission basis. I was the most successful salesperson in Germany. [...] What they said about me was, "Actually, the man can't sell, but he succeeds on the basis of his personality and product knowledge." Before I had always thought to myself, "I can't sell." And there I was at 22, the most successful investment salesperson in Germany.

From his bedroom in his parental home, another interviewee earned EUR 40,000 in six months trading stocks – and used the money to buy his first apartment:

Interviewee 12: I don't remember exactly when, but... For as long as I've been able to think, I have been earning money. I basically started with selling plums that I picked from the plum tree. Then, a bit later on, I started selling things and set up a little shop in my parents' front garden. Then I wanted to open a restaurant in the front garden, but my parents didn't think that was such a great idea. When I got a bit older, I started to work in promotions, travelling from bar to bar selling things. I would say, "Look here, we're running a competition and, in return for entering the competition, I get your addresses." The addresses I collected were used for a follow-up approach. Then I worked for a while in a call centre, making appointments and acquiring customers for a wine dealer. Then I did gardening work, chopped down trees, and got my friends involved, as quasi-subcontractors, to chop down trees for my grandfather or neighbours. I was always working, even distributing flyers, but the things that interested me most were the things that not just any idiot could do. Things that I could have some degree of influence or control over, things I could do quickly and efficiently to earn the same or even more in a shorter space of time [...]
Interviewer: And what was the first thing that you did after you graduated from secondary school?
Interviewee 12: I started to work at the stock market. I traded with my own money. It was the crash that taught my brother and me that the markets could fluctuate wildly. And then, as soon as I finished school, I did my mandatory community service, but I kept on getting myself signed off sick, because of my oversized tonsils. I told them that I always suffered from a sore throat and, while I was signed off sick, I traded on the stock market.

Then, after about four months, I went to the community service office and asked, "So, what do I earn per hour while I'm here?" And they said, "Around about EUR 5 per hour." So I replied, "I'll give you EUR 15 just so that I don't have to come anymore." So I went to the doctor and got myself signed off sick again because they wouldn't accept my proposal. So I started to trade warrants, certificates, and derivatives on the stock market and earned my first money that way. Basically, six months after I finished secondary school, I was in a position to buy my first apartment.

Interviewer: With your stock market profits?

Interviewee 12: In six months I had earned roughly EUR 40,000. Because I literally worked from early in the morning all the way through to late in the evening. Every day. And I saved every cent I had earned from my community service. Then I sold everything that I owned. Altogether I had EUR 40,000 and was still living at my parents. I used that money to buy my first condo in Berlin-Tegel.

At 19, before starting university, this interviewee set up a construction company:

Interviewee 16: I worked for everything during my youth and, sure, my father gave me DM 500 a month while I was at university, but that was nowhere near enough. So, I had to earn the other DM 500 that I needed to live on. I've basically been working since I was 16, and it was completely normal for me to work while I was at school. [...] I became self-employed while I was at university, at the age of 19 and a half or 20. That's when I set up my business, xxx. The business still exists, under the name xxx. That's the registered merchant, where everything started, the motor, the foundation of everything since. [...] After my community service, I officially registered the company. I did my community service straight after school and there was always the problem that, between the end of community service and the first day at university, there was a gap of approximately six months with nothing to do. People were more or less forced to register themselves as unemployed. But I didn't want to do that and set up my own business instead, because I didn't want to be unemployed. [...] So I demolished and rebuilt the partition walls in basements, making them look good. And I chipped plaster off walls and re-plastered them. I removed debris and rubbish. I laid cables and was a bricklayer and renovated small apartments. And that was xxx. I wasn't a registered master craftsman, and back then things were a little stricter as, technically, no one was allowed to have a building company unless they were a master craftsman. But I slipped under the radar by renovating bathrooms and apartments, anything I could, and calling it a construction assistance service.

At 15, another interviewee earned money from a booklet on tuning mopeds, and at 19 he concluded his first real estate deal:

> **Interviewee 19**: [He never asked his parents for money.] That's why I started to tune mofas [motorized bicycles] when I was 15, to earn money. I learned quickly and used the time that I had, while I was repeating a year at school, to write a booklet on tuning mofas, which I sold via a motorcycle magazine. I ran black-framed adverts: "For sale, manual for tuning mofas," for mofas and mopeds, which I sold for DM 20 cash. That was a lot of money at the time. And I thought to myself, "The advert cost DM 80, you're bound to get more than four orders." I ended up getting 600 orders. So then I thought to myself, "Three more adverts and you'll be able to take over xxx." Although it didn't quite turn out that way.
>
> [While at university:] I lived off my booklet for a while, from my royalties. I carried on selling it. I was still earning, let's say, DM 400 to 500 per month. And this was in about 1980 or '81. So that was DM 500, and you could rent an apartment for that. From my own earnings I bought myself a motorbike for my 18th birthday and went on to do my first real estate deal when I was 19. My uncle lived next door to a burned-out bungalow. He was a successful drinks wholesaler and I never understood how he could stand to live next door to a burned-out bungalow. It also smelled of smoke. So, one day, I asked him, "Why don't you buy it?" And he said, "You know what, the whole thing would just be too complicated, too difficult. It's going to be auctioned by xxx and no one dares to touch it, I'm not even sure what the risks are." So I asked him how much the land with the burned-out bungalow was supposed to cost, and he told me that it cost DM 50,000. And I asked him, "So what does that other piece of land over the road cost, the one where there's no burned-out bungalow?" And he said, "That costs DM 100,000." And then I said, "Right then, I've got to go." So I went straight to the bank. I had a bank account there at the time and there was at least DM 400 in it. I told them that I wanted to buy the lot next to my uncle's. I could see that all around the offices heads were popping out of cubicles because they all thought that the proverbial fool had walked in. That's when I found out that if you wanted to buy property, you needed collateral, securities. I didn't know that before. So, to cut a long story short, I mortgaged my motorbike on Tuesday and signed a contract on Friday. In the evening I headed over to my club, we had our own club, and started to tell people what I'd done, that I'd just bought some property. And they asked me which notary was involved. And I said, "I didn't see a notary." And they said, "Then you haven't bought any property." And I said, "Yes I have. Two clerks at the local savings and loan bank signed the contract for the property, I don't think you need a notary for that."

The upshot was that they had just sold me the debt; I had bought a non-performing loan. I then had to organize the auction myself, but it all worked out well. I ended up buying the bungalow myself and asked a friend, who had been kicked out of school and worked for a building company, how much it would cost to demolish the bungalow. And he said, "I'll do it for you for DM 1,000." And I said, "No that's not what we'll do. You'll do it for DM 2,000, but only when I sell the property." I bought the property on a Thursday and the bungalow was demolished by Saturday. I was standing in the garden and there was my uncle, standing next door, staring at me in disbelief. I hadn't told him anything, you see, because I thought he might be jealous. I waved to him and called over, "Thanks for the tip. I've just bought it." Two months later, I sold it for DM 100,000. I went to xxx and said, "First off, I'd like my motorbike back. And secondly, do you have any other properties like that?" And I did that on the side, travelling backwards and forwards between Karlsruhe and the Saarland. Sometimes it took me six months to sell a property on.

From the age of 15, the next interviewee was involved in selling things, and at 19 he bought his first property:

Interviewee 20: I sold things, and, of course, I was able to make a bit of money from sports. For example, when mofas and mopeds were all the rage, we tuned them, nothing too fancy. We'd use lubricating gel to tighten the cylinder head and then we'd fit a higher-tamping screw.
Interviewer: And you earned money doing that?
Interviewee 20: Sure, I earned DM 20 or 50 each time. And then, later on, with a friend of mine, xxx, we sold furniture for xxx. That was direct sales. We went into the areas where new houses had been built.
Interviewer: How old were you when you did that?
Interviewee 20: 17.
Interviewer: And that was basically cold sales, going door to door and selling furniture?
Interviewee 20: Yes, we'd ring the doorbell and ask, "You're building?" There were a lot of single-family homes being built in the less desirable suburbs, where families were building their own homes, or at least parts of their own homes, and we were there on a Saturday afternoon. And we'd sometimes help out, organizing for a carpet to be laid, acting as agents for the people who fitted the carpet. Or we bought leather handbags, and sold them on commission. We bought them for DM 5 or 10 and sold them for about DM 30. [...]
Interviewer: So you were basically always selling.

Interviewee 20: Always selling. [...] I'd say that my sales skills are about 80% of what I am. The most important thing for me is definitely my sales talent. [...] I was then working in a pharmacy, I'd met my wife by that time and my parents had died. We were living in what had been my parents' apartment. The building belonged to a construction company and we basically renovated the apartment, did a wonderful job with it, and in return the owner gave us either a rent-free period or a guarantee that the rent wouldn't increase. And then the owner went bankrupt and the building transferred to the bank, which wanted to sell the apartments individually. As ours was by far the best apartment, everyone wanted it. That was what made me find out about property and real estate financing. So I said, "Okay, I'll buy the building." And that was a crazy idea and my wife started to panic, "You work at a pharmacy and now you want to buy the building?" My bank turned me down and I could understand why they turned me down [...] Too little equity. So we went to a different bank, and the first rejection had shown me that I needed to prepare things differently. So the second bank, xxx, they approved the financing.

Another interviewee set up an amateur film club while he was still at school, attracted members from 40 schools, and used the proceeds to finance the renovation of an old train station:

Interviewee 22: I always thought like an entrepreneur and wanted to do something entrepreneurial. I started while I was still at school, organizing things, approaching it like a business. I really enjoyed that. [...] I was in a group for young Catholic students at the time, and we'd been more or less given an old station by the German Railway. It was in a horrendous condition. Of course, the youth group didn't have any money to renovate it. Which is when I had the idea of setting up a film club here in Cologne. To advertise via schools and organize a film screening once a month. We ended up showing films to up to 1,000 people from 40 schools around Cologne each month, selling tickets to the film club. With the proceeds we were able to finance the renovation of the train station.
Interviewer: So that was a business enterprise, but not one from which you made money personally?
Interviewee 22: That was never my intention, to make money for myself. My personal benefit was the fact that we raised the money we needed to renovate the train station.
Interviewer: Do you have any other examples? A number of other interviewees have told me about their business activities during their youths.

Interviewee 22: Okay, as a student I wanted to earn a little extra, so, rather than working for an hourly wage, I organized a homework service. I was the organizer and also got involved myself, but most of the homework tutoring was done by others.

As a student, another interviewee leased and redeveloped a vacant factory building, bought it, and rented it out as a centre for political work:

Interviewee 25: That's when I started with real estate. By chance, while I was a student, I was in [city] and in the old industrial district I came across a vacant factory, which I initially leased and then bought. I rented it out as a centre for political work. We transformed it into a warehouse and distribution centre for products from the Third World. We delivered the goods to other retailers, and basically built it up as a real business, which also created jobs. And then, via a sponsor organization, I involved a number of other charitable organizations, political organizations. We got together and rented this factory space, which was about 4,000 square metres, not at all small. And I very quickly took on the role of managing director. I was responsible for organizing everything and created a paid position out of my role, which I took up immediately after my first university exams. [...] The charitable organization then set up a limited company, as a business enterprise, to manage the property, and I was managing director of the limited company. That was my first major real estate project. [...] It lasted about four years [...] In parallel I ran two other real estate projects, in addition to redeveloping the factory.

At 18, the next interviewee started to sell insurance products part time, and at 19 he got involved in the structured sales of cosmetic articles:

Interviewee 29: Just after turning 18 I got involved in structured sales, selling insurance products. That was a pretty brutal learning process. I had to cope with lots of rejection and a fair amount of envy. [...]
Interviewer: And how long did you do that for?
Interviewee 29: For two years, until I joined the military. And then at sales conferences, those organized events for salespeople, for those who have closed lots of deals, you get invited to the events for the best salespeople. For that day and age, it was possible to earn good money. [...]
Interviewee 29: And then I realized that maybe insurance wasn't exactly the best thing for me, so I switched over and joined a structured sales team for cosmetic products. [...]

Interviewee 29: I started off by selling to friends, family, acquaintances, which is what everyone does at the very beginning, isn't it? I was really good at convincing women, at showing them that they could look better with a bit of makeup. And then I asked a couple of my female friends to sell cosmetics for me. That's how I started my little sales team.

Interviewer: How old were you at the time?

Interviewee 29: I must have been 19. I had just graduated from secondary school. I was still at school and just about to graduate.

Interviewer: And then you joined the military.

Interviewee 29: Yes, but I carried on with the sales.

Interviewer: While you were in the military?

Interviewee 29: While I was in the army. There were tanning creams, I can remember it well, I took a whole crate of tanning cream with me when I joined up and sold it all to my fellow soldiers so that they could look good. Or a spray for shoes so that they would shine and you wouldn't need to clean them. Things like that, that's what I sold.

At 17 or 18, another interviewee started to trade cars and car radios, and then he became involved in selling home winter gardens:

Interviewee 34: I started by buying cars in the newspaper. I would buy a car and then run an advert in the newspaper the following week and resell it. It wasn't long before my friends heard what I was doing. It got to the point that as soon as someone I knew decided they needed a car, they would come to me and say, "I need such and such a car, can you get one for me?" So I would go and buy the car for them. I didn't charge my friends the full price. Or if someone I knew wanted to sell their car, they'd come to me and ask, "Can you sell my car for me?" The same happened with the car radios. If someone needed a radio, they would also ask me if I could get one for them.

Interviewer: And how many years did you do that, with the cars?

Interviewee 34: It must have been three or four years in total.

Interviewer: And what would you say, how much did you earn each month from buying and selling cars? Was it very different each month?

Interviewee 34: Yes, but it was quite a lot of money for that day and age. I made sure that I earned DM 1,000 per car.

Interviewer: And how many did you sell?

Interviewee 34: Two or three per month. I was making between DM 2,000 and 3,000 on the side. [...]

Interviewee 34: And then a friend came to me and said that he had set up a company in Stuttgart. The company xxx already existed back then. They were uniquely positioned selling home conservatories and winter gardens. My friend asked me if I'd like to be a sales representative and I said yes, naturally. So I started doing that and I expanded my operation very quickly. I was selling real extensions and organizing planning and construction permits, offering to have the foundations constructed, everything. And I was very successful. I was soon earning DM 100,000 or 110,000 a year. Just from my commission as a sales representative.

This interviewee earned money parallel to school and university, selling egg cartons and stripping and fixing up motorbikes:

Interviewee 37: We got the egg cartons for free because my friend's father was a manager at an egg processing business and they always had mountains of these cartons. I had often asked myself what could be done with all of those egg cartons. And then I realized that there are school bands, young people who practice their music indoors and make a lot of noise. If they covered their rooms in egg cartons, the noise problem was solved. So we started marketing our solution, that was one thing. Then, starting from the age of 18, I began to maintain motorbikes for all my friends. I ended up with a huge motorbike shop, almost 1,000 square metres of space. It was an old stable or forge. There were lots of used motorbikes standing around, so we took them apart and sold the parts. With the money I made, I was able to finance myself all the way through university. I was really happy until my father died.
Interviewer: Let me get this straight, you didn't repair the motorbikes, you stripped them down and sold the parts?
Interviewee 37: Stripped them down, or sometimes fixed them up.
Interviewer: So basically old motorbikes?
Interviewee 37: Sometimes taking old parts to build new motorbikes, that kind of thing. Whatever worked best at the time. I also spent a lot of time working on cars, welding cars together for friends, adjusting the steering, or replacing axle stubs, that kind of thing. I spent every weekend in overalls, working. Every weekend.
Interviewer: How old were you when you were doing that?
Interviewee 37: That was the time from 18 to 23. I was really happy. I had a number of motorbikes and cars.
Interviewer: Is it possible to say, on average, how much you earned?
Interviewee 37: DM 5,000. [...] And that was just working weekends.

Another interviewee sold car washes to gas stations to earn money parallel to university. At the age of 20, he began his sales career while still at university:

> **Interviewer**: So what did you do to earn money while you were at university?
> **Interviewee 38**: Basically, as I've told you, we were in sales. A friend of mine had a company that made car washes for gas stations. The company still exists today. So we sold this equipment to filling stations. [...] Those were the days when automated car washes were just starting. So that's what we sold and I always made enough money from that [...]
> **Interviewer**: And can you still remember how much you earned on average, each month?
> **Interviewee 38**: Let's see. There was the normal student grant, that was about DM 300 or 350 a month, and there I was, averaging DM 1,500 to 2,000 each month, easy. [...]
> **Interviewer**: And did you sell anything else?
> **Interviewee 38**: Yes, I went on to trade property, organize lettings, that kind of thing.
> **Interviewer**: And how old were you then?
> **Interviewee 38**: That was while I was at university. I must have been 20.
> **Interviewer**: And what exactly did you do in real estate? Were you a realtor?
> **Interviewee 38**: Yes, I was a realtor. I wasn't officially a realtor, but I heard things, put people together. For example, I would hear that some retail space was available and I would speak to a few people.

At 16, another interviewee was selling wheel rims and, parallel to school, he began to work for a real estate company:

> **Interviewee 40**: There was a large wheel rim manufacturer near where I lived. I don't know if anyone in Berlin nowadays would know the name. I was able to get hold of second-choice wheel rims; the paintwork was damaged. We sold them on commission, which meant we could take them for nothing and only had to pay for them when we sold some. We sold them to garages and auto stores. In Essen, in the market outside the drive-in cinema, places like that.
> **Interviewer**: How old would you have been then?
> **Interviewee 40**: I must have been 16 or 17. It was a real wheel rim business. Second-choice wheel rims, just with scratches on. A set of rims cost about DM 2,000 in a shop and we were getting them for DM 600 or 700, by the pallet load. [...] Selling them for around DM 1,300. [...]
> **Interviewer**: How long did you sell wheel rims for?

Interviewee 40: Until I finished secondary school.

Interviewer: I guess it varied, but what would you say you earned each month, on average?

Interviewee 40: I can remember very well. I was earning the same as someone working full time. While I was still at school, I was earning between DM 2,500 and 3,000 per month.

This interviewee studied industrial engineering. While he was studying, he worked in financial sales and was extremely successful, earning a few hundred thousand Deutschmarks in sales:

Interviewee 41: I worked in sales and, although I was by far the youngest, I generated the highest sales revenues.

Interviewer: What did you sell?

Interviewee 41: I sold shares in companies, for example. And because I spoke English, I was sent over to America, because the company was having trouble raising enough equity from investors here in Germany. They sent me over to conduct the negotiations. [...] I generated more business than they did and had a deeper understanding of the business. I was the unofficial spokesman for the group and basically negotiated the conditions for the entire group. And I demanded changes to the product, to improve it so that it was easier to sell. I got things done on both sides.

Interviewer: And while you were at university, can you remember how much you were earning? It must have varied from month to month, but on average? We still had the Deutschmark then.

Interviewee 41: Even as a student I was earning six figures, high six figures. I bought and sold property, even buying some for myself. [...] It wasn't just DM 100,000, it was a lot more, even as a student.

Interviewer: So about DM 100,000 per year? [...]

Interviewee 41: No, it wasn't a hundred thousand, it was a few. A few hundred thousand.

Interviewer: There would be many who would say, "Now I'm earning so much, why do I need to study, why don't I drop out?"

Interviewee 41: Yes, but I'm ambitious and wanted to achieve something in life. I've always been like that, always ambitious. But it's not as if I ever told anyone, not my fellow students. I never told them, "Look, I've got a big fat bank account." Of course, I bought myself some nice things, I had a nice car and nice apartment, things like that, but on the whole it was ambition that drove me. I was also motivated by the fact that I had to help my mother out.

Another interviewee began his entrepreneurial activity working in animal breeding between the ages of 10 and 18:

> **Interviewee 43**: I've been working since I was six. Working for money. Yes, in the field. I basically ran a small farming business. I bred animals, fed them, slaughtered them, and sold them. It was admittedly fairly small scale, but that's what I always did.
>
> **Interviewer**: And how old were you when you started to do this as a business, if I can call it that?
>
> **Interviewee 43**: I was – let me just think for a moment – I was in third or fourth grade, so I must have been ten or eleven.
>
> **Interviewer**: And how old were you when you stopped?
>
> **Interviewee 43**: I did it until I was 18.
>
> **Interviewer**: So that was breeding animals and selling them?
>
> **Interviewee 43**: Exactly. On a very, very small scale, but it meant that whenever I wanted to buy something for myself, I could.

What all of these activities have in common is that the interviewees did not work for an hourly wage in their youths; rather their earnings depended on their sales skills or organizational talents. At an early age, these UHNWIs learned that it is not time that is money; on the contrary, it is inventiveness, sales skills, networking, and organizational powers that determine how much you earn.

INTERIM FINDINGS

A majority of the interviewees came from middle-class families. They were not predestined from the cradle to become rich. It is, however, striking that the parents of 60% of the interviewees were self-employed – a figure that is ten times higher than in the German population at large. The parents were frequently entrepreneurs, small business owners, or farmers – most of them were not rich, but neither were they in somebody else's employment. This shaped the way the children viewed self-employment, and it was therefore almost a foregone conclusion that they would go into business for themselves when they were older. The remaining 40% of the parents were either employees or civil servants, and only two were blue-collar workers.

It is important not to underestimate the importance of role models outside the parental home. In their youths, some of the UHNWIs were impressed by the lifestyles of wealthy parents of friends, rich relatives, fellow boarding-school pupils, or rich neighbours. Nevertheless, very few set themselves the specific goal of one day becoming multi-millionaires. The early career aspirations of those who would go on to become very wealthy were not all that different from those of other children or young people.

The recruitment of the wealth elite differs substantially from that of the 'economic elite', as revealed by earlier research. Whereas the parents of the top business managers who work for large companies tend to come from the grand bourgeoisie, and habitus plays a key role throughout their careers, the selection processes for joining the ranks of the wealth elite are very different. It is also true to say that school and university education did not play a decisive role for these UHNWIs.

Although a majority of the interviewees received a high-quality school and university education, in this respect they were no different from many of their peers. Their performance during their formal education tended to be average. There is no correlation between their performance at school or university and the level of wealth these individuals went on to achieve. Those who achieved the most at school or university did not proceed to join the highest ranks of the wealthy. A third of those who went on to accumulate substantial wealth did not study at university, and one seventh did not even complete their secondary school education.

The theory of informal learning claims that around 70% of all human learning takes place outside formal educational institutions.[682] And the theory of implicit learning states that learning processes are often unconscious and not consciously directed. This learning can, of course, still take place within formal contexts. Many of those who went on to become very wealthy were rebellious. While they were at school, they learned how to engage in confrontation, how to stand up to dominant norms and behavioural standards, and how to assert themselves against authority figures. This benefited them in later life, and was an early indication of their non-conformity and their ability to swim against the current, which has been highlighted as a characteristic of many who go on to become entrepreneurs (see Chapter 19 for further details). Or they learned to take responsibility. The interviewees frequently related that they had been class presidents or student representatives, that they had published school newspapers or organized political initiatives.

Of greater importance, however, were their extracurricular activities. With very few exceptions, all of the interviewees pursued either competitive sports or they earned money in an atypical, entrepreneurial manner. Of the 45 UHNWIs, there were only six to whom neither of these applied. More than half of the interviewees were involved in competitive sports while they were at school. In many cases, sports were actually far more important to them than school. As athletes they learned how to handle victories and defeats and how to beat their opponents; they learned to tolerate frustration and developed self-confidence in their own abilities. Those involved in team sports also developed team-working skills. But a majority of the interviewees were not involved in team sports; they were individual competitors.

They were track and field athletes, skiers, equestrians, swimmers, tennis players, or judoka. They achieved impressive athletic performances, won district and state titles, and even competed in national championships. But at some point they acknowledged that they were lacking the genes that would enable them to compete at the very highest level. Others were forced to abandon their athletic careers as a result of injury.

It is also striking to learn how these UHNWIs earned money alongside school or university. Typical jobs for teenagers or students, i.e. those paid by the hour, were the exception. A look at their varied ideas and initiatives reveals a tremendous amount of creativity. They sold everything, from cosmetic products to home winter gardens, from second-choice wheel rims to automated car washes, from used cars and motorbikes to insurance products and closed-end funds, from animals they had bred themselves to jewellery, from handmade radios to second-hand car radios. There can be no doubt that these experiences shaped the young people who would later become entrepreneurs. They learned to organize, to sell, to think like entrepreneurs. They learned – often unconsciously – and acquired the implicit knowledge that is of such great importance for any entrepreneur or investor. And their early entrepreneurial experiences were the ideal preparation for setting up their own businesses later in life.

---

682 Dohmen, *Das informelle Lernen*, 7.

10 Motivations for Self-employment

At the beginning of their path to wealth, the interviewees faced the decision of setting up their own businesses. Among these UHNWIs, 40 of 45 had been self-employed all their lives or almost all their lives. The five interviewees for whom this was not the case, and who were board members or managing directors of companies, either owned stock in these companies or were successful as investors alongside their main occupation. However, three of these five were in the lowest wealth category (EUR 10 million to 30 million) and two in the category above (EUR 30 million to 100 million).

Academic wealth research has shown that most rich people are entrepreneurs. This is even more true of UHNWIs, because it is not easy to amass net assets worth tens or hundreds of millions as an employed executive in Germany; this is only possible for a small group of DAX or MDAX board members, or board members of companies of comparable size. On the one hand, self-employment is the prerequisite for becoming rich; on the other hand, most self-employed people never become rich – quite the opposite. The probability of failure is so high that, as described in Section 3.2.b, researchers have invested a lot of effort in explaining why people choose self-employment even though they are faced with an unfavourable risk–reward ratio.

One explanation for this is that "many entrepreneurs are misfits, difficult employees who start their own firm because they are unwilling to submit to authority and find it difficult to work in a prestructured environment".[683] It was their "inability to submit to authority and accept organizational rules that drove them to become entrepreneurs".[684]

Is it possible to confirm this misfit theory for UHNWIs? The interviewees were asked about their motivation for choosing self-employment. In particular, entrepreneurs who had previously worked as employees were asked whether they could have imagined prospering in an existing company – or not. The answers varied. The first section of this chapter presents UHNWIs who could never have imagined themselves working or prospering as employees, and who in fact often said that they would have found it difficult to fit into the structures of an existing large company.

However, it turns out that there is another group to which none of this applies. These people, who are quoted in the second section of this chapter, started out as employees, quickly climbed the career ladder, and would probably have advanced further. However, they quit at some point because rising up the career ladder would have taken too long for them, or because they realized that their earning potential as employees was too limited.

Finally, there is a third group, for whom the question of whether they should be employed or self-employed never arose. Often their parents were already self-employed and they earned money outside of school or university, so that the idea of working as an employee was never something they seriously considered. Or they were children of entrepreneurs who knew that they would eventually enter the family business without ever seriously considering an alternative. This group is discussed in the third section of this chapter.

10.1. THE 'MISFITS': "I COULD NEVER HAVE WORKED AS AN EMPLOYEE"

The misfit hypothesis, which identifies entrepreneurs as outsiders unable to find their place within prescribed structures and hierarchies, held true for this interviewee, who is today the chairman of the board of a company of which he is also the majority stockholder. He became self-employed immediately after completing secondary school. He reported that he never had the option of working as an employee and explained that this was due to the fact that he is a difficult person, someone you would have had "to give pills" to in order for him to function as an employee. He was simply far too rebellious and too much of a know-it-all:

> **Interviewee 16**: I think I am a difficult person and I was even more difficult when I was younger. You could say that it took me 27 years to become an employee. I have never had an income tax card or pay slip. Now I am the chairman of the board of a stock market company, so I am now technically an employee. You can imagine what would have happened 27 years ago, if I had become an employee back then. I was simply not ready, not mature enough. [...] I had to cut my teeth. I first had to gain the experience that I have since gathered. I would never have achieved success if anyone had tried to turn me into an employee. You would have had to give me pills.
> **Interviewer**: I suppose that was because you were so rebellious.

---

683 Hisrich, Langan-Fox, and Grant, "Entrepreneurship Research and Practice," 582.
684 Kets de Vries, "The Dark Side of Entrepreneurship."

Interviewee 16: Too rebellious and I always knew better than everyone else. Right or wrong, I was always up front and if the front was wrong, then I was wrong up front.

Another interviewee spent several years as an employee, ultimately as the managing director of a municipal company. Although he was successful, he recognized that, in the long term, he was not suited to such a position. He went "crazy" there, and would not have survived "that" for an extended period of time. "I would have ended up in the loony bin." He then went on to set up his own company:

Interviewee 25: So then I quit because trying to work like a businessman within a municipal authority can drive you crazy. You can't survive that for long. I would have ended up in the loony bin. There was no support for anyone. You have to fight for every inch within a municipal company, every inch of freedom. That is exhausting, especially when you are just a small mini-company, as we were then. [...] And then there was a totally absurd, borderline hysterical political debate. I was constantly at City Hall to see Mr xxx and test the waters, to see what he was thinking that day. But it was a funny period for me. I met everyone, the whole crowd. That was certainly very interesting for me. [...] And then I said, "Right, I've had enough of this, I'm never going to make a business of this." I negotiated a severance package, which they were happy to give me. It was a bit of a golden parachute, let's put it like that. They didn't really need to do that, but they were happy and said, "You have always done everything so well, building everything up, super." So we agreed a severance package and I used the money to start my own business. They paid me DM 120,000. [...] Then I founded my own company.

This first group also includes the following interviewee, who worked for himself while he was at university and earned a great amount of money. For this reason he never even considered applying for regular jobs when he graduated from university. "That was never an option." The decisive factor was his desire for independence. Above all, he was repelled by the idea of potentially working for a boss to whom he felt superior. He did not want to have to "kowtow" and parrot his boss's words. The possibility of making more money was never a primary factor, he said:

Interviewee 3: The financial side of things was purely theoretical. It was important to me that I could make my own decisions, that I didn't have to wake up every morning and go somewhere to do a job where someone else would say, "This is what you have to do now." I wanted to decide things for myself. That was always important to me.

Interviewer: I know that you never did it, but do you think that you have the personality structure to work as an employee, to be told what to do every day? Or would that have caused too much conflict?

Interviewee 3: No, I never would have been able to work as an employee. I never could have made a career of it, of that I'm quite sure.

Interviewer: And why not?

Interviewee 3: It's only in an ideal world that your managers are great and wonderful people, the kind of people you can look up to. And when there are people there, and you have to ask yourself, what kind of an idiot is this, and kowtow to them, and say things like, "That's another great idea you've had, Mr Smith ..."

Another interviewee, one of the wealthiest to participate in this research, spent two years after university working as an employee. Although his boss was a tremendous salesman, in other respects he was "a disaster". As a result, this interviewee presented his boss with two alternatives: either he would continue to work for the company on a freelance basis (and at the same time be able to work for other companies) or they would have to go their separate ways:

Interviewee 22: It became clear to me relatively quickly that I never wanted to make a career for myself at xxx or xxx, but that I should do something for myself. But it wasn't connected to any financial goals of the type you have just mentioned.

Interviewer: But you never thought about working as an employee in the long term, even though you worked for a few years as an assistant?

Interviewee 22: Yes, that was the first few years. But after the first two years it was already clear that that wasn't going to last.

Interviewer: What were you like as an employee? Let's put it this way, there are some people who will never make good employees because they are too headstrong or have other character traits that make them difficult. Is that how it was for you, or were you basically a good employee? Or were there conflicts?

Interviewee 22: The question is, how do you measure that?

Interviewer: Well, according to the degree of conflict potential. Did you have to deal with frequent conflicts with your boss, or anything like that?

Interviewee 22: Definitely, and my boss wasn't used to it, but maybe it did him good. But I have to be clear here, this was the time immediately after university. I joined them as soon as I was finished with my exams and after two years, I told him, "Now I either want to become self-employed, for you and others, or we go our separate ways."

Interviewer: And what was it that motivated you to become self-employed?

Interviewee 22: I wanted to accomplish what I believed I could, without anyone else ordering me not to do it. [...] In many ways my boss, Mr xxx, was a genius. He was an incredible salesperson and I learned a huge amount from him. At the same time, he was a disaster in many respects. In the end I went to him and told him that this combination was something I didn't want to deal with in the long run. The combination of genius and disaster is not a strong enough basis.

Because his father wanted him to, the next interviewee started his career with a large company and attended an executive training programme there. After just four weeks he left the company and the training programme. He had previously established his own real estate brokerage and quickly realized that he did not fit in at a large company. He views himself as an "alpha type" and had the feeling that the company wanted to start out by "knocking him down a peg or two":

Interviewee 40: I joined them in November. I had promised my father that I would. It was difficult. [...] It goes without saying, but when you join an executive training programme and you are an alpha type, then they start off by trying to knock you down a peg or two. They want to break you, because no big company wants alpha types. So, after exactly four weeks I went to my roommate, who is now one of my best friends, we were sharing a small apartment at the time, it was just before Christmas, and I told him, "Right, I'm packing my clothes. I'm out of here." I can remember it well.

Interviewer: [...] So, let me just recap. You'd already had problems at school and you would probably never have been able to make a career for yourself at a large company.

Interviewee 40: Exactly. That's exactly right.

Interviewer: Because you were too headstrong and obstinate.

Interviewee 40: Absolutely. [...] That's right. And then, after just under six weeks, I was gone.

Interviewer: What was it that triggered your decision? How were things there?

Interviewee 40: I didn't enjoy it at all. The fire in my belly was for completely different things. I didn't enjoy it at all, including the way they were bringing psychologists in. Every presentation was filmed and analysed for rhetoric, body language, gestures. That was extreme, wasn't it? So I packed my suitcases and went to xxx. The parent company was in xxx, so I headed over to the head of HR, and spoke to the lady there, who is 78 today and with whom I still have a great relationship. [...] I went in and she said, "You can't just quit. When you signed your employment contract, you agreed that you would have to buy yourself out of your contract if you wanted to leave early, because we can't just fill the position with anyone else." And I told her, "I don't have any money, but I'll pay as soon as I do have the money, but I'm going to quit now." And she told me to sit down for a moment. We recently laughed about the whole thing. She asked me what I wanted to do after I left and I told her that I wanted to set up a real estate company. She told me that it would be great if I could keep her informed of how my business developed and I wouldn't have to worry about the damages clause in my contract.

A number of interviewees started out as employees but began to establish their own businesses parallel to their regular jobs. This was the case for the next interviewee, who worked as a radio presenter and, at the same time, worked independently as a real estate broker. He used the money he earned to buy himself a Jaguar, which he parked demonstratively outside the radio station in order to flaunt his financial independence. A few years later he abandoned his – very well paid – job at the radio station and has been extraordinarily successful as a real estate broker ever since:

> **Interviewee 6**: I never wanted to be dependent on [my boss] and, from my first big sale, I bought myself a Jaguar. Not because I especially needed a Jaguar, but because I wanted to stand outside the radio station and show my boss, "I don't need you at all." And he had thrown almost everyone out by then and his assistant went to him and asked him if he had seen that I was driving a Jaguar. So he came to me and asked me if I was earning too much working on the radio. And I told him, "No, but as you know, I have another job on the side." I felt as if he couldn't touch me, I felt invincible. Of course, I needed a job somewhere. I even wanted the job too, but I wanted independence. I wanted to show everyone, "I don't need you at all."

The next interviewee reports that he worked 'pro forma' as an employee for a short period of time, simply because that was a condition of becoming a tax consultant. Nevertheless, he hardly ever turned up for work and basically did what he wanted. He acquired lucrative business for the company and was soon earning more than his bosses:

> **Interviewer**: So that means you were basically never an employee, at no point in your entire life? You started straight out as an entrepreneur [...]

Interviewee 10: That's right, I never worked as an employee. I had a pro forma job, because I had to in order to become a tax consultant. I could never be an employee. Even when I had the pro forma job, I was only ever there for half a day a week; I basically did what I wanted.

Some of the interviewees spoke in very derisory terms about the tasks that regular employees have to contend with. The next interviewee had not spent a single day in his life as an employee, and admitted that he could never imagine doing so. The entire concept of being paid by the hour was unattractive to him. As soon as he left school, he began to work as a stock trader:

Interviewee 12: The things that interested me most were the things that not just any idiot could do. Things that I could have some degree of influence or control over, things I could do quickly and efficiently to earn the same or even more in a shorter space of time.

The next interviewee spent some time as an employee with a public sector company. Because he was handling the company's real estate business, he negotiated a contract that included a lucrative profit participation. After just 12 months, he explained proudly, he was earning three times as much as Germany's Chancellor. His next role was with a real estate brokerage company, and 80% of his wage was performance based; in the worst year, this amounted to DM 1.1 million. But even this didn't satisfy his financial ambitions. Half a year later he set up his own company on the side – formally in his wife's name – in the field of property development and rental apartment privatization:

Interviewer: At that time [when he was working for a public sector company] you didn't earn so much. You just had a regular employee's salary, didn't you?
Interviewee 19: At that time I was earning incredibly well, because I had helped set the whole thing up. There were seven or eight of us and we were earning so much from our real estate business, and then I managed to negotiate a profit participation. [...] And then, after 12 months, and I can remember this well, I earned three times as much as the Federal Chancellor. I thought to myself, "You negotiated that well, didn't you?" I was having a great time.
Interviewer: So, even as an employee? In that regard, you weren't really an employee, were you? It was more like you were self-employed.
Interviewee 19: Then I found out about [real estate company] and they made me an offer, the kind of offer I just couldn't turn down. And then

I spent five years as the managing director of xxx. Even in the worst year, which was 1995, I reckon I earned DM 1.1 million.

A number of the entrepreneurs seized the opportunities life presented them with and sold their companies for a great deal of money. As a rule, they did so under the condition that their companies' new owners would continue to employ them for a number of years, now as employees as part of a far larger structure. For many, this turned out to be a traumatic experience, as was the case for the following interviewee, who was self-employed both before and afterwards, and realized in these few short years that he is unsuited to the life of an employee in a large company. As he himself explains, he "always had problems" and was engaged in constant confrontations with the supervisory board and others:

> **Interviewee 20**: Actually, I felt quite uncomfortable while I was there. That was one of the problems while I was at xxx. Even when I had a strong gut feeling, I first had to fill out hundreds of forms and submit all of my proposals to the board for approval. And the deals that I wanted, they had all disappeared by the time I was authorized to go after them. The deals that involved quick gut reactions and decisions, that was really good. And the deals that involved hundreds of forms and describing things over and over again, that mostly ended in nothing.
> **Interviewer**: And that's when you realized that it was driving you mad.
> **Interviewee 20**: Yes that was it. It was a good experience to have. The first two or three years were fine, but then, at some point, you realize that you don't quite fit in the system.

The next interviewee reported that he was always getting into trouble at school and drove his teachers up the wall. Once he graduated from secondary school he did a banking apprenticeship and then went on to study in the United States. He studied mathematics and biology, but dropped out after six terms and worked in the United States as an investment banker. He was certainly successful, but reveals that even there he still had many "problems":

> **Interviewer**: How long did you work for the bank, how many years?
> **Interviewee 42**: Two and a half years.
> **Interviewer**: And did you have problems while you were working for the bank, like you did at school? Or were things...
> **Interviewee 42**: I always had problems with discipline. [...]

Interviewer: So how much of your life have you spent as an employee? You spent two and a half years as an employee there.

Interviewee 42: It was those two and a half years. Afterwards I moved to the United States to study, but I dropped out. [...]

Interviewer: Let's take one step back: Do you think you could have made a career for yourself, working as an employee at the bank, or would there have been too many problems? Or did things get better in the States, as time went by? [...]

Interviewee 42: I had a certain degree of freedom, but I caused trouble from time to time, of course I did. As an employee working inside a large company, that was never a big enough stage for me.

10.2. "THINGS MOVE TOO SLOWLY FOR ME IN SUCH COMPANIES"

A number of interviewees reported that they certainly could have made a career as employees. This applies to the following UHNWIs, all of whom began their careers (as did many in this group of interviewees) working in the banking sector, before they at some point decided to strike out for themselves.

The first interviewee began by working as a bank employee for four years. He could probably have made a career for himself there. The fact that he set up his own business was primarily driven by financial considerations. He came to the conclusion that life as an employee was simply "financially unacceptable". He recalled sharing a night-time drive with a colleague, with whom he would shortly set up a business, and remembered confessing to the colleague, "You know what? Such a large structure, where you have no real control over your own destiny, that's nothing for me in the long term. Very soon, I'll be doing my own thing." When asked about his motivations for taking such a decision, he replied:

Interviewee 5: I think that I'm basically not the type of person to settle for that kind of life. I was in a small department at xxx bank and could certainly have carved out a career for myself, but I had a very strong and fundamental economic argument. And that's what I told the bank's advisory board chairman, Mr xxx, I told him: "Mr xxx, it is financially unacceptable for me to remain here because my salary is x today and in ten years, when I'm married with two or three children, I won't be in a position to provide for them in the manner to which I am accustomed. I need to take another path."

Interviewer: So it was clear to you that you just couldn't earn enough as an employee, as is often the case.

Interviewee 5: Financially, no, there was no chance of that.

The next interviewee spent four years as a bank employee. But it wasn't long before he was earning three times as much from his part-time entrepreneurial activities as he was from his full-time regular job. This was a common experience among this group of UHNWIs. They didn't always have the courage to go into business for themselves from the very beginning, but gained in self-confidence through working for themselves on the side and realized that this gave them the opportunity to quickly earn far more. Taking the plunge and resigning from a regular job in order to embark on full-time self-employment was certainly the right thing to do:

> **Interviewee 13**: While I was working at the bank, and with the approval of the bank's directors, I spent my evenings with a friend buying, renovating, and reselling apartments. We worked every evening. I didn't have any money at the time, but my friend did. I had the know-how and he had the money and we split everything 50/50. I'd finish at the bank at 6pm and then head off to renovate the apartments, to organize everything, and to sell them on.
> **Interviewer**: And how long did it take you before you were earning more from that than from your main job?
> **Interviewee 13**: Less than a year. [...] After a year and a half I was earning three times as much as I earned at the bank, just working evenings. I realized that I couldn't carry on as I was for much longer, so I soon started to look around for a new project, a bigger project, and I found one in Munich. After four years at the bank, I resigned and went and bought the property in Munich. [...]
> **Interviewer**: Okay, and then you were quickly earning a lot more. Let's focus on the time you spent as an employee [...] There are people who go on to become entrepreneurs, and they say that they found it difficult to work in a bank, as one of a large group of employees, that there are too many conflicts and the like. Or were you more of an easy-going employee?
> **Interviewee 13**: The entrepreneurial gene was always in me; after all, I grew up in an entrepreneurial family. And many of my friends, and their parents, they were nearly all entrepreneurs. I spent most of my time surrounded by entrepreneurs and businesspeople, whether at home or at friends' houses. And, when I'd been at the bank for about two years and my boss received a medal for ten years' service to the bank, I went to him and said, "I'm really sorry, Mr. xxx, but I will never get that medal." He didn't take it badly, he told me that he pretty much thought the same. I have the entrepreneurial gene and it was always clear to me that I would do something for myself one day.
> **Interviewer**: And was that your main motive for becoming self-employed?
> **Interviewee 13**: My motive was a mixture of freedom, self-determination, and, quite possibly, having the chance to earn more money. I was spurred by a mixture of those three motivations, I think.

Like the previous two interviewees, the following interviewee also started out by working for a number of banks, for a total of 14 years. He climbed the career ladder quickly and, by the age of 36, was chairman of a bank. But a future that involved "being reconfirmed as the chairman of the bank every five years" was not something that set his heart racing. He made the decision to become a freelance asset manager:

> **Interviewee 31**: And at that time I realized that the perspective of doing that for the next 25 years was not what I wanted. So I said to myself, be true to yourself and go into business for yourself. Which is what I did in 1981. [...] And no, it was more the urge to get the most out of myself. I wanted more than just being reconfirmed as the chairman of the bank every five years. I mean, I had made it to the position of chairman by the age of 36 and wouldn't be pensioned off until I was 65. That was something I simply couldn't imagine. So the logical consequence was to take the plunge, which I did. It was the best decision I've ever made in my life.

The next interviewee spent three years working for a bank, where he was also very successful. But the career path to the top positions would have taken too long for him. "I could never have made a career for myself at the bank, no. That would have taken far too long":

> **Interviewee 36**: I think the route to the top would have taken too long for me. In principle, I wouldn't have had anything against becoming chairman of the board of xxx bank. That would have been very elegant, with a chauffeur, tailored suits, always looking so elegant. I certainly would have liked that.
> **Interviewer**: And what would you say was your motive for going into business for yourself?
> **Interviewee 36**: It was really clear: the urge to achieve more. If you are a CEO who can do anything, sure, that would be fine. But not with committee-based decisions, paperwork in triplicate, sign here, left and right. No, all the organization and time in the office, I didn't want any more of that.

The next interviewee ran his own successful business parallel to his studies at university, but initially started working for a bank subsidiary after he graduated. From the very beginning he always had the goal of going into business for himself and viewed his position at the bank simply as "the apprenticeship you need to get into business":

Interviewee 38: After university I started working for xxx. As an employee in sales and distribution. The starting salary was DM 1,700 per month. [...] So, I was there for two and a half or three years. And then I set up my own business.

Interviewer: So that means, if I have this right, you've only spent two and a half years as an employee in your entire life.

Interviewee 38: Yes, that's right.

Interviewer: And then you had your own business.

Interviewee 38: But that was basically the apprenticeship that you need to get into business. And I got involved in leasing because that was the only way, as a new graduate, to get involved with negotiating at board and management level. Because financing decisions of that magnitude for real estate leasing are only ever handled by the board or senior management.

Interviewer: So that was sales. And why did you set up your own business? After all, I assume you were earning a fairly decent salary in sales.

Interviewee 38: When I left xxx, we were on a minimal fixed salary and the rest was based on sales and results. I was earning over DM 200,000 at the time.

Interviewer: That was a huge salary in that day and age.

Interviewee 38: Yes, that was a massive salary at the time. And then I went into business for myself, together with my former partner from xxx. We set up xxx, you know? My argument for leaving the bank was this: I went to my boss and he asked me, "Why are you leaving? You're earning a good salary, you have so many opportunities here." I replied, "The only job I want here is yours, and I'm not going to get it." To which he replied, "No, you're certainly not." And that was it, so I told him I was going into business for myself.

The next interviewee completed an internship with an investment bank and stayed at the bank for ten years. He climbed the career ladder, but at some point had the feeling that too much of his work involved tasks that were neither intellectually challenging nor particularly profitable for the bank:

Interviewee 43: Yes, I progressed from a basic analyst to team leader and then ultimately to chief strategist. I could have continued with my career at the bank. I left while I was still quickly advancing up the career ladder. There wasn't really a single major reason, it's not that I was a difficult character or definitely had to go into business for myself. It was just that I'd had enough. [...]

Interviewer: And what was it that prompted you, what was your motivation to say "I'm going off to set up my own business"?

> **Interviewee 43**: On the one hand I was worried about the banking system and, on the other hand, and this was probably the key factor, there were just too many things in investment banking that I had to do simply because they had to be done. There was too much compliance, too much red tape, and too many clients who weren't intellectually stimulating and didn't really deliver profits for the bank either. The system was essentially totally vague. I wanted to be more involved, so I left and went into business for myself.

One of the other interviewees enjoyed extraordinary success as an employee and even managed to convince the management of the company he worked for to suspend an investment prohibition for his department because he had developed such a convincing concept. At some point he realized that he could do everything himself, so he set up his own business, and took over and optimized the business concept of his former employer:

> **Interviewer**: What was it that prompted you to say, "Now I'm going into business for myself"?
> **Interviewee 18**: So, I was working for xxx at the time and, judged according to the standards at the time, was very successful. [...] There was a total ban on investment and the entire senior management had been sacked. I developed an attractive concept, which was also attractive for the board [...] [so I] managed to get them to loosen their investment ban.
> **Interviewer**: So, in this case, they made an exception.
> **Interviewee 18**: Yes, that's right.
> **Interviewer**: And then, at some point, you said, "I could basically do all of this for myself."
> **Interviewee 18**: And then I saw [that he had all the skills necessary to run his own business].

The next interviewee was successful as an employee of a very large company and worked on a self-employed basis for another company parallel to his main job. He eventually left his main job and bought 10% of the other company he was working for. In addition to financial motivations, he was also motivated by the fact that the prescribed structures within a major international company got on his nerves. "All of this committee nonsense", as he puts it, "rubbed me totally up the wrong way":

> **Interviewee 11**: I had decided, because there was really no other option, to stop working for xxx at some point so that I could concentrate on making

a career for myself with xxx, which I definitely could have done, but I couldn't do both in the long run.

Interviewer: Of course, you couldn't do both. But that is certainly a decision. Looking back on it now, what would you say triggered your decision, apart from your relationship, your friendship with xxx, which couldn't have been your only reason for making such a decision? What led you to say, "I'm leaving now, I can't continue on this path"?

Interviewee 11: I'd spent eight, almost ten years with xxx. The time was right for me to do something completely new and that's what I really wanted. I'd always done things because I enjoyed doing them and I had wanted to be involved with xxx and it was certainly interesting. You could achieve things there, develop things, be in the thick of things. And that's what I enjoyed, so I did it.

Interviewer: The opportunity, in the long run, to earn far more than you would have earned as an employee.

Interviewee 11: That was also a factor. [...] But it wasn't really the most decisive factor. I'm sure I could have earned a lot of money with xxx. It's always the case that you have to differentiate, but if you're in a senior position with a company like xxx or like xxx, it's not as if anyone normally has to worry about poverty. I just wouldn't have enjoyed it. Incidentally, and this is perhaps another very important aspect, I didn't really enjoy the whole institutionalism at xxx, you know? Everything was decided by committees, submissions to the board, resolutions of the board, the supervisory board, all of this committee nonsense. That really got on my nerves and rubbed me totally up the wrong way. The entrepreneurial element was missing, the enjoyment and fun. You never had the chance; everything had to be approved by the board.

The following interviewee is atypical in many respects, switching between roles as an independent sales representative, entrepreneur, investor, bank chairman, and senior manager, which means he has the qualifications of both a senior manager and a self-employed entrepreneur. He started his career as a sales representative selling financial products:

Interviewer: You were an independent sales representative...

Interviewee 7: Yes, I was. That was the courage to get out from the security as an employee, where I had been taken on by the municipal utility company, and to strike out for myself as a sales representative.

Interviewer: So you could have stayed with the municipal utility company?

Interviewee 7: Yes, yes, I could have.

Interviewer: So why didn't you do that?

Interviewee 7: Well, the pace was just too slow for me, working as an accounts receivables clerk, which I was at the time. At the municipal utility company in xxx, your career for the next 40 years is mapped out for you.
[...]
Interviewee 7: [...] and then someone asked me, which fits quite well here, they asked, "So, are you an entrepreneur or are you a manager?" I think it might even have been you who asked me that. [...] And I told them: "I'm actually an entrepreneurial manager." Basically that's the best way to define it. An entrepreneurial manager is someone with a management role within a company, but who doesn't act in the same way a traditional manager does, someone who is not so penned in by structures. Of course, I accommodate myself with the structures, integrate myself, but I decide. I take an entrepreneurial approach, I do my job in the bank to the best of my knowledge and belief, I do my job in the same way that I would if the bank belonged to me.

In exactly the same way, the following interviewee also found that climbing the career ladder within a large company took too long. He received a great deal of support and was promoted quickly. But the path to the CEO position was "very long" and he wasn't prepared to "wait in line for ten years". So he quit and founded his own company with a friend:

Interviewer: You spent five years as an employee, if I have got that right. There are employees who set up their own companies because they realize that the role isn't something they want or are suited to, that they have constant problems and want to strike their own path. Was it like that for you? Or, there are others who could have imagined making a career for themselves within a major company. Which type are you? [...]
Interviewee 27: I think I could definitely have made a career for myself. From day one I rose through the ranks and was promoted again and again. There were about 7,000 employees working for the company. I think I'd be right to say that I was a bit of a favourite of xxx. I started off as his assistant. But he very quickly promoted me, after only about three months as his assistant, he sent me out into the world and let me make a career for myself. I definitely could have made a career for myself there. I was always the youngest. [...] The head of personnel always told me, and I think it would be right to say, that I had a good future there. I was always the one that they had confidence in, maybe to one day even run the business. And I really enjoyed myself, right from the start. [...] Making my mark on history with xxx, being driven around by a chauffeur, attending supervisory board meetings, all of that. It's more or less the big wide world that you dream about as a student.

There were lots of positive discussions and it's always good when you are promoted like that. I think I had the qualities you need in a major company. I had a sense for politics, and when the five directors had a problem position that they needed to fill and they couldn't agree, there were basically only two people who could do the job, and I was one of those two, I was the compromise that they could all agree on. So they always said, "Mr xxx, he can do it." In the end I didn't take advantage of it. After two or three years, once the initial excitement had passed and the work became a little boring, with lots of things repeating themselves, I realized that I wasn't driving things forwards as much or as quickly as I could have. At that point, my relationship to the company took a turn for the worse and I was very unhappy. But I have always been able to differentiate between the company, which hadn't really changed, and myself, who had changed. It wasn't the company's fault; I had just changed too much. **Interviewer**: And that was why you went into business for yourself? This dissatisfaction that such a major company isn't right for you and you'd be better off in the business world by yourself? Or did you take the view that you would never be able to achieve your financial ambitions within such a company? What were your motivations?

Interviewee 27: No, it was definitely the dissatisfaction. The financial side of things never really interested me. That's not my main or primary goal. I think that is ultimately a by-product. Of course, it's also fun, the liberty and freedom that it brings, but my goal was independence, to be able to set things up for myself and to achieve things for myself. And the route to becoming CEO in such a big company, especially when you start out at the age of 20, would have honestly been too long and my life would have been too short. I didn't want to wait in line for ten years [...] Things move too slow for me in such companies, and it takes too long to rise to a position of responsibility. That's mostly why I was so personally dissatisfied at the end, sitting in so many meetings but not actually achieving much, I wasn't prepared to settle for that. I want a life, wanted to live in freedom.

10.3. "I NEVER THOUGHT ABOUT WORKING SOMEWHERE AS AN EMPLOYEE"

Many of the interviewees were surprised when asked why they had become entrepreneurs rather than applying for positions as employees, because they had never seriously considered this as a realistic alternative. This was often linked to the fact that they had already earned considerable sums while studying at university, as was the case for the following interviewee, who earned up to DM 200,000 per year parallel to his university studies:

Interviewee 29: I've never been an employee.

Interviewer: What, never in your life?

Interviewee 29: Never.

Interviewer: And why is that, why was that never an option for you, working as an employee?

Interviewee 29: It was an alien concept to me, because, let me tell you, I had set up a business for myself while I was a student. Prior to that, there were just jobs. But when you earn DM 100,000 or 200,000 in a year, and that's what I did as a student, I earned DM 200,000 in a year, that's a huge amount of money, relatively speaking, isn't it?

[His father then pressured him to complete an internship with a bank.]

Interviewee 29: And then, in the university holidays, he forced me to do an internship at xxx in Vienna. But I was already in business for myself by then, while I was studying. Just imagine, while I was still a student, I flew to Vienna on a Sunday, stayed there for the internship from Monday to Wednesday, at xxx in their mergers and acquisitions division, all to keep my father happy. And then on Thursday I flew home and worked on my real estate business on Thursday, Friday, and Saturday.

Interviewer: And how long was the internship?

Interviewee 29: That was three months. [...] It should actually have been longer, but after three months I said, "Right, I've seen enough now." Three months was just about right, because my father was so highly regarded there. [...]

Interviewer: So, because of the financial aspects, the option of working as an employee was never a realistic one for you.

Interviewee 29: I wanted to be independent. I wanted to be financially independent, but I also wanted, as an individual, to be independent in what I did. And it was never an option to work as an employee.

The next interviewee described three branches of his family, all of which were entrepreneurs. This provided him with a kind of "permanent vaccination" – not in an ideological sense, but in the sense that meant it would never have occurred to him to work as an employee:

Interviewee 39: Yes, three branches of my family and all three were entrepreneurs. I only ever thought about business and entrepreneurship, even if my parents didn't involve me directly. [...] That was, if I can put it this way, a kind of vaccination. I wouldn't say it was in my DNA, but it was a type of permanent vaccination. It was never something I thought about, working somewhere as an employee. But it's not as if I ever rejected the idea ideologically.

The following interviewee had also not spent a single day in his life working as an employee. Parallel to university he worked in sales, and earned a few hundred thousand Deutschmarks per year. He reported that it never crossed his mind to work as an employee. After the positive experience of earning such large sums while he was a student – selling financial products – it was clear to him that he should continue working for himself:

> **Interviewer**: After you graduated, what was your first professional job? Have you ever worked as an employee?
> **Interviewee 41**: No, never.
> **Interviewer**: Did you ever consider it, or was it never really an option, working as an employee?
> **Interviewee 41**: It was never an option for me.
> **Interviewer**: You were already earning so much.
> **Interviewee 41**: I was already earning so much, had set up my company and then I was able to win xxx as a client, and they generated high revenues and I never looked back.
> **Interviewer**: So, the idea of working as an employee never occurred to you.
> **Interviewee 41**: No, it's not something I ever considered.

A number of interviewees joined their family's business. For them this was an entirely natural step to take. It was clear at an early stage – even if it wasn't something that was always spoken about – that they would take over the business at some point in the future:

> **Interviewer**: You have already said that you took the decision to join the family business at a fairly early stage. What were the reasons for your decision?
> **Interviewee 2**: There were no real reasons. My father's business was already a very important business. [...] It was a very important business and I never really questioned whether that was the right option or not. If I questioned anything, or had any doubts, they were more related to whether I would actually be successful. But whether I actually wanted to or not, that was never something I debated. I always had the feeling that my father believed I could do it. That was something I felt from the very beginning, sort of a crown prince role. Not in the sense that I was elevated above any criticism, but I had every opportunity and his belief, his support. He did everything he could to make sure that I could take on the role.

The next interviewee said that it was clear from the outset that he and his two brothers would take over their family's business. This wealthy interviewee reported how this preordained step was self-evident to him as he was growing up:

> **Interviewee 24**: From the outset, from the age of 12, 13, 14, it was clear that my father would involve his three sons in the business, and I was the middle son. He viewed all three of us as his successors and that was a thread through our education, our upbringing. Not so explicit, but it was certainly something that came across to us. We'd all poked our noses into the business, seen how things worked, what happened there. My father took us, I was eight or nine, and we had a look at everything. So, from my father's perspective, it was always clear that we would be his successors. I practically grew up with that expectation.

The father of one of the other wealthy interviewees was himself an entrepreneur, but stopped at the age of 60 and handed his business interests over to his son. The business had 17 branches at the time. When the interviewee retired 50 years later, the number had risen to 600. The workforce had expanded from fewer than 100 to more than 2,000. That he would one day assume control of the business was never in doubt; the question never even arose:

> **Interviewer**: At what point did you know that you would take over the family business? When was that?
> **Interviewee 32**: That was basically never in doubt; the question was never asked.
> **Interviewer**: So it was self-evident, never explicitly discussed?
> **Interviewee 32**: No one ever even thought about it.

The following interviewee was very successful with an international company, which he subsequently left in order to join the family business. He grew the company into a global corporation and is now one of the 1,000 richest men in the world:

> **Interviewer**: During your time as an employee, would you say you were a difficult employee, someone who had frequent conflicts with their boss? Or were you more easy-going?
> **Interviewee 26**: No, no. I started out as assistant to the managing director and eight weeks later I was the managing director, you know? [...] Later on I became managing director of xxx [business division] and finally I was managing director of xxx [business division] [...]

Interviewer: I have met a number of entrepreneurs who say that they would never have been able to climb the career ladder because they were difficult individuals. Was it like that for you?

Interviewee 26: No, no. If the family business hadn't been there for me, I wouldn't have left. I took home a share of the profits [...] and I was earning so much that, when I came home, my father just couldn't believe it when he saw my payslips.

The following interviewee didn't join his family's business immediately after university; he initially set up his own company. It was only later on that he joined the family business because he felt a responsibility to continue the business:

Interviewee 28: My great-grandfather founded xxx, which used to be a very big mechanical engineering company, for mills. And the way I was raised was not to say, out of necessity, I'll change everything and earn lots of money, or to change what I could change and get away from this type of business. For me it was much more a case that when you inherit a family business, or parts of a family business, that you have to work and view them as something you hold on to for a while, build into something successful and then pass on. When you're in the sixth generation, you haven't been brought up and you don't join the company to say, "Right I'm taking over from the fifth generation and as the sixth, I'm the one who gets to live it up and spend it all."

Another entrepreneur, who is one of the 100 richest Germans, joined his family business at a young age. He originally wanted to attend a university-preparatory school because he had received good grades at junior high school but, looking back, he is happy that he chose a different path because he went on to transform his family's business into a major global company. Had he gone to university-preparatory school and not joined the business when he did, he now believes he would have ended up as a "senior local government officer":

Interviewee 15: I was 16 and a half and it was a really interesting time. Based on what my parents and I knew at the time, and could have known at the time, without knowing what was going to happen later, it would have been natural to send me to university-prep school so that I could go on and study. No one would ever have said that I should stay on the farm and do my apprenticeship. If I'd gone to university, I would have been finished in 1963. Anyone who studied back then was set up for life. [...] Pretty much 90% of the people who did that, they weren't really set up for life, maybe that was the wrong way to put it, but they certainly had the best chances, didn't they?

Interviewer: But who can say, maybe you would have been less successful had you done that?

Interviewee 15: Now comes the funny part, right? I probably would have ended up as a senior local government officer.

INTERIM FINDINGS

The hypothesis that entrepreneurs are misfits, who were difficult and rebellious employees who would therefore have been unable to make careers for themselves in existing companies, was confirmed by a number of interviewees. They view themselves as difficult people, individuals who are too unorthodox to integrate themselves into prescribed structures or subordinate themselves to others.

In part, they expressed this in drastic terms – one believed that he would have had to have been given pills to function as an employee. He was too rebellious and too much of a know-it-all. Another said that he would have been driven crazy working in a publicly owned company and that he would not have been able to bear that in the long run: "I would have ended up in the loony bin." Another reported that the idea of potentially working for a boss to whom he felt superior, and to whom he would have been forced to 'kowtow to' or parrot the words of, was repugnant to him. Yet another quit the company he was working for after just four weeks. He sees himself as an 'alpha type' and had the feeling that the company wanted to start out by "knocking him down a peg or two".

But alongside this group, there are a number of UHNWIs to whom this does not apply. Before they founded their own businesses, they initially worked for large companies – often in banks – and made careers for themselves. For them, either things progressed too slowly or they perceived their earning potentials as too limited. One succinctly observed that, given his extremely high financial demands, he simply could not "economically allow" himself to continue working as a bank employee. Another had already risen to become chairman of the bank at the age of 36. But the idea of "being reconfirmed as the chairman of the bank every five years" did not appeal to him. The next interviewee worked for a bank for three years and was also very successful. But the career path to the top would have taken too long for him. "I could never have made a career for myself at the bank, no. That would have taken far too long." Another reported that it would have simply taken far too long for him to rise through the ranks of a major company. He received a great deal of support and was promoted quickly, but the career ladder to the position of CEO was "very long" and he didn't want "to wait in line for ten years".

A third group never even had to choose between self-employment and a career as an employee. For them it was always clear that they would only ever go into business for themselves. One interviewee, who had never spent a single day as an employee in his entire life, earned hundreds of thousands of Deutschmarks a year from sales, parallel to his university courses. He reported, as did a number of other interviewees, that he had never once considered working as an employee. The same applies to many of the interviewees who joined their families' businesses. This generational succession was clear for most of this group from their early childhoods onwards, unspoken but self-evident, so that there would never have been any other option.

The misfits theory is true for some of the interviewees, but it does not hold true for all of them, only for a subgroup. There are certainly a large number of UHNWIs who have carved out careers for themselves in large companies, or could have, but then decided to quit because it would have taken too long to make it to the top and they viewed the potential earnings as unattractive.

Wealth as a Goal
11 in Life?

What role does goal-setting play for the very wealthy? Beginning with Napoleon Hill's classic *Think and Grow Rich*, popular wealth literature is dominated by the notion that writing down quantitatively exact financial goals and setting deadlines for achieving them is the essential prerequisite for becoming rich. Goal-setting theory, originally developed by Edwin A. Locke and Gary P. Latham, and since confirmed in hundreds of empirical studies (see Section 3.2.e), also finds that challenging and specifically formulated goals lead to better results than vague notions of goals, and that individuals who set themselves specific goals are more successful than those who set themselves either vague goals or no goals at all. J. Robert Baum demonstrated that the expectations of goal-setting theory, whereby more challenging and specific goals lead to better performance, have also been empirically proven in entrepreneurship research.[685]

In contrast, there are, for example, the results of the study published by Franz Walter and Stine Marg, for which 160 entrepreneurs and the board members of major German companies were interviewed.[686] The tenor of their answers to the question of how they had secured their senior executive positions was often that they had not carefully planned their careers.[687]

For this reason, one of the questions raised in the interviews conducted for this book was whether these wealthy interviewees had set themselves specific goals, in particular financial goals. If their answers were affirmative, they were asked whether they had written these goals down, how often they had done this, and whether they had used techniques to visualize their goals.

The findings were ambiguous. The hypothesis put forwards by popular wealth literature that *only* those who write down specifically formulated financial goals can achieve great wealth was not confirmed. A number of interviewees firmly rejected such methods and stated categorically that goal-setting had never played a role in their lives, and there were others for whom this was never relevant – for more on this, see the second section of this chapter. On the other hand, over 40% of the interviewees strongly asserted that they regularly set themselves goals in various areas of their lives – overwhelmingly in writing.

11.1. "IF IT'S WRITTEN DOWN, IT CAN BE VERIFIED"

One interviewee reported that, for the past 30 years, he has written down his goals every January. He has developed a ritual for this and spends a week fasting. During this week he contemplates his goals, writes them down, and visualizes them.

> **Interviewee 5**: Very early on we came into contact with a person who taught us a lot about self-awareness and sensitivity training. One of the first things he taught us was that you have to formulate your goals in exact terms, and you have to visualize them if possible. And set them down in very specific terms. From then on, which must be over the last 30 years, I have always written down my goals for the year in January, always writing a lot. [...] For many years now I have been going on a fasting retreat every January; that's where I formulate and write out my goals.

For one of the youngest interviewees, the specific and written formulation of goals, and their visualization, also plays a crucial role. He reported that he started out at a young age setting himself the goal of being financially independent by the age of 30. Later on, he set himself the goal of having EUR 100 million, which he has not quite achieved yet. As he is still very young and is well on his way to reaching this goal, he has raised the bar once again. In his office, above the door ("where I can see it from my desk"), he has put up the number "1,000,000,000":

> **Interviewee 12**: Yes, and the number is written out in big fat figures. And I show it to everyone, but I don't just tell them that it is my goal, I tell them that is what I am definitely going to achieve. I have no doubts about that. So, that is just another interim goal. That's how I approach everything. I think the term "goal" is wrong, you know? When you have a goal, you reach it and that's it, finished. Goals are okay, but that is what I am going to achieve in any case. Which is why, once I reach my interim goal, I'll set myself a new goal [...]

In particular, visualization plays a key role for him:

> **Interviewee 12**: Yes, that is something I'm totally into. Taking the big things, the small things, the medium-sized things and always visualizing them.

---

685   Baum, "Goals and Entrepreneurship," 463.

686   Walter and Marg, *Sprachlose Elite?*, 19.

687   Hiemann, "'Geplant war das alles nicht,'" 39–40.

I would say that I am a master of visualization. Yes, I can immerse myself so deeply into things that I totally burn them into my brain, so that they physically appear before my eyes.

During the interview he showed me the lists and spreadsheets on his computer, which he opens, updates, and reviews every day to see how much closer he is to his interim goals and major goals:

> **Interviewee 12**: Every day, every single day. I have a table, a spreadsheet, here, I can show you [...] Everything is written out in lists, I have different versions, because this list is essential to me. It's an Excel table and, building on that, there are other lists, that's what's loading right now. Everything is written down, everything visualized, down to even the smallest goals. As soon as I set myself a goal, I write it down. "What is my goal for this year? What is my goal for this month? What is my overall goal?" And so on, everything is written down.

Visualization was also a crucial tool for the next interviewee. He started by setting himself the goal of becoming a millionaire, but didn't put this down in writing. Once he had reached this first goal, he began to write his subsequent goals down on paper. He developed a number of rituals for this process and commissioned a feng shui consultant to create a 'wealth corner' in his house, where he prayed every day that he would achieve his financial goals:

> **Interviewee 19**: Once I had achieved my initial goal, I sat down and wrote out my next goal, that I wanted to be worth 10 million, that would have been Deutschmarks back then, by the age of 40. And I reached my goal. Almost to the day, what you might call a precision landing.
> **Interviewer**: That's really interesting. So did you have a notebook, or did you stick your goals up on the wall?
> **Interviewee 19**: I asked a feng shui consultant to redesign my house. I have to say, that helped me a lot. There were so many obstacles in my way, where things weren't working out, and after the feng shui, suddenly they started working out. Of course, you can call it a self-fulfilling prophecy. [...] But I couldn't care less. It's the results that count and it all worked out. The consultant created a "wealth corner" for me, where I spent a minute or two praying every day. There is a picture in the wealth corner and I stuck my written goal behind the picture. And I achieved my goal, with what you might almost call deadly precision.

The next interviewee diligently followed the instructions provided by popular wealth literature. He took his cue from classics such as Napoleon Hill's *Think and Grow Rich* and Joseph Murphy's *The Power of Your Subconscious Mind*, which he consumed with great enthusiasm. He started reading these books and setting himself goals at the age of 17. He has always been fascinated by the question of why some people are successful while others are not:

> **Interviewee 29**: Those are the typical laws of success. Consistently believe in a goal, and at some point, maybe in a different form, your goal will be realized. That's how it is.
> **Interviewer**: So you regularly set yourself goals, including financial goals.
> **Interviewee 29**: Absolutely, yes. [...] Well, I often like to think in terms of images. I got myself a copy of the Ferrari catalogue, you know? I cut the pictures out of it and looked at them every day. And that reminded me what I was working so hard towards, as an example. [...]
> **Interviewer**: So that was the Ferrari. What about after the Ferrari? What was the next thing you cut out?
> **Interviewee 29**: At some point it was the house. Owning my own home. Those were quite large sums, I wanted to be financially independent. That was my greatest goal, to be financially independent.
> **Interviewer**: And did you link that goal with a specific amount of money?
> **Interviewee 29**: Absolutely. Naturally, you want to earn your first million at some point. That's a big number. That seems unachievable, but then you say to yourself, "Of course, I want to reach that million."

Setting goals out in writing and visualizing their achievement is not limited to the financial sphere. The following interviewee, a very successful businessman in the field of medical technologies, reported that he started to write his goals down when he was just 16. Five years before their actual engagement and wedding, he wrote both dates on stones and gave them to his future wife. He proudly related that he did get engaged and married on those exact dates. For two decades, until he was in his mid-30s, he consistently wrote down all of his goals. By that point, however, it was no longer necessary for him to do so. The goals fed through from his conscious mind into his subconscious:

> **Interviewee 32**: I was very focused on writing down my goals.
> **Interviewer**: And for how many years did you write down your goals?
> **Interviewee 32**: Let's say until I was in my mid-30s.
> **Interviewer**: And then, why did you stop?

Interviewee 32: Basically because I didn't need to write them down any more, you know?

Interviewer: But you did it until you were in your mid-30s.

Interviewee 32: Yes, I planned all of my life goals, my whole life with a final goal. [...] I asked myself, where do you want to be by the time you are 70? And then I broke it down into blocks of seven years. And then I even planned everything year by year. I was very focused on my planning, even daily planning. [...] Setting myself daily goals and especially asking myself, "Are you satisfied with yourself?" There are people who say, "I'm not doing well, things aren't working out." And that's either because they don't know what they have achieved or, in relation to their expectations, they have no sense of when they are doing well and when they are doing badly. But if they set themselves daily goals that they could look at every evening, they would have a positive sense of what they had achieved. They could say, "You did that," and that would give them a boost for their next goal. I planned my time meticulously. [...]

Interviewer: And these goals, did they always apply to a range of areas? You probably broke them down into company, family, health and fitness, things like that.

Interviewee 32: Yes, in every area of my life. That's absolutely right [...]

Interviewer: And you always wrote them down. I'm just wondering why, at the age of 35, with most of your life still ahead of you, you stopped.

Interviewee 32: Well, you get into a routine. Things feed through from your conscious mind into your subconscious. Everything that we have to learn, you don't need to explicitly read the instruction booklet any more. Once you've learned to drive a car, you don't need to keep on consulting the operating manual.

Interviewer: Okay, but you still had the goals.

Interviewee 32: Of course I did. I knew exactly what I wanted and what goals I wanted to achieve.

Many interviewees reported that they write down specific and wide-ranging goals, as did the following interviewee, who became rich from an IT business. He adopted this approach in 1990, and wrote out a life plan while he was on vacation. This became so extensive that he filled a "thick folder" with his plans. In addition to this life plan, he also wrote out seven-year plans and annual plans:

Interviewer: And what kinds of things did you incorporate into your seven-year plan?

Interviewee 33: Everything, I even included private things like building a house, and wishes, which can be very effective, the kinds of things you would like to treat yourself to. But I also included revenue figures, client groups, profit targets, the size of the workforce.
Interviewer: So things from both your professional and personal lives?
Interviewee 33: Yes, professional and personal – not in Excel spreadsheets, but in prose, in complete sentences. I painted a picture with words of how it would feel to achieve my goals.

Not all of the interviewees who set their goals down in writing did so from the very beginning. The next interviewee said that he always formulated goals but that he only began to write them down systematically when he was between 35 and 40:

Interviewee 36: I am very precise nowadays. That's what I learned, and that's what I do. But one thing I always had was an image, a vision, from very early on. Some of the friends I had as a teenager say to me now, "You were always beaming and telling us that you were going to drive a Jaguar and have a beautiful home." I have always had a good life, a luxurious life with lots of women and a lot of fun. That's the picture I always had in my mind's eye, I even knew roughly what my house would look like. [...] So, what I want to say about goals is that I always said that I wanted to be rich and I had that as a goal from the age of about 18 or 20. [Since age 35 to 40] I really wrote it all out properly and looked at how much I was earning. Today I make a great deal more. I also write out weekly goals; I set goals in every area of life.

An entrepreneur from the food industry started to set systematic goals at the age of 43 and developed a written plan for the following 30 years. One of the goals he set was that his fortune should grow by at least 10% every year. But even in his case, the goals are not limited purely to the financial realm. He constantly checks his written goals against the reality of what he has actually achieved in each area of life. In addition, he works his way through a written catalogue of questions once every three or four months:

Interviewer: And these goals, you wrote them down somewhere?
Interviewee 37: Exactly, and I always check the goals against what I have really achieved. [...] I do that all the time. I'm not one of those people who makes resolutions at the start of the year; I'm always checking, always fine-tuning. Then I have a catalogue of 200 questions that I answer anew all the time.

Interviewer: What kinds of questions?

Interviewee 37: About things that are important to me. Whether my attitude to life has changed, what I want to achieve for my children, what I want to achieve for my wife. Just things that keep me focused.

Interviewer: And you have all of this written down?

Interviewee 37: Yes, I have collected them over many, many years. I also picked up a few questions from other questionnaires.

Interviewer: And how often do you go over the questions?

Interviewee 37: Every three or four months.

Interviewer: And how long does it take you to answer all of the questions?

Interviewee 37: Half a day. [...] I don't work through every single question. I pick an area, say "Money and Assets", and I go through the relevant questions and that makes me aware of a number of things again. Or I take the topic "Wife and Family", or I have one called "Friends". And under each heading I have questions, things like, "Who do you not want to have anything to do with in the near future?" Or, "Who do you want to see a lot of?" And then I try to structure it all for myself.

One interviewee, who is over the age of 70, emphasized the fact that she only started to write down her goals roughly 15 or 20 years ago. These goals are formulated every year, covering every area of life, and as new goals are set, existing goals are reviewed to see whether they have been achieved or not:

Interviewee 14: I always set goals. I set myself goals every single year.

Interviewer: Let's focus on goals then. When do you set your goals, in the new year?

Interviewee 14: I start some time before New Year's Eve, before the end of the year.

Interviewer: And do you write your goals down on paper?

Interviewee 14: Yes, I write them all down on paper.

[...]

Interviewer: And what types of goals do you set for yourself? They probably cover various aspects of your life.

Interviewee 14: Yes, they cover lots of different areas of my life. They cover business, but they also cover some private areas.

Interviewer: And when did you start writing your goals down?

Interviewee 14: I've been doing it for 15 or 20 years, I can't say exactly.

Interviewer: That long?

Interviewee 14: Yes, I've been doing it that long.

Interviewer: And how did you come up with the idea of writing down your goals?

Interviewee 14: I'm not sure, I picked it up myself somewhere and after all, I do it for my employees, too; they are given revenue targets, a variety of targets.

Interviewer: And the goals, do you quantify them, specify them with figures?

Interviewee 14: Yes, that's exactly what I do.

Interviewer: That's the only way to measure what you have actually achieved.

Interviewee 14: Yes, otherwise you can't measure them and you might as well not bother setting any goals at all.

Interviewer: [...] So you do that once a year. And do you ever look at your goals again during the year, to remind yourself, or do you keep them all in mind?

Interviewee 14: No, I certainly need to look at them again to remind myself. I do that probably once or twice during the year, but not more often than that. And when I set myself new goals, then I always look again and see what I have once again failed to achieve.

Interviewer: That is certainly interesting. So that means that your goal-setting is related to different areas of your life; do your goals include financial goals?

Interviewee 14: I set myself the target of achieving everything that I really wanted to achieve by the age of 40. In terms of my private life, that included having a family, having children. And it was important for me to be financially independent by the time I turned 40.

Interviewer: And did you have an idea of what financial independence meant to you, a figure?

Interviewee 14: Yes, naturally...

Another interviewee, who is also over the age of 70, set himself a written financial goal for the first time when he was in his mid-40s. He stressed just how important it is to set goals down in writing. He strongly believes that every goal needs to be documented, otherwise it will be too vague and impossible to verify:

Interviewee 26: I set myself one really specific goal. I was in Puerto Rico when Hurricane Hugo struck. I'm no longer sure exactly what year that was, but it must have been in the early 1990s. And I said to myself, "You have to have 20 million in cash in the bank, to make sure you are financially independent." And I wrote that goal down.

Interviewer: Approximately how old were you then?

Interviewee 26: It was the early [19]90s, so I must have been almost 45, around 40.

Interviewer: And you wrote that goal down?

Interviewee 26: Yes, I always write my goals out on paper. Every five years I set out my goals by writing them down.

Interviewer: How long have you been doing that, writing out your goals?

> **Interviewee 26**: It's something I've always done. Always.
> **Interviewer**: Throughout your life?
> **Interviewee 26**: Yes, all through my life.
> **Interviewer**: Even when you were younger, as a teenager?
> [...]
> **Interviewee 26**: [...] No, only since I started working.
> **Interviewer**: So, since you were 30.
> **Interviewee 26**: Yes, ever since I started working I have been writing down my goals, the things I want to achieve. It's no different to the targets we have in business, is it? We have quarterly targets, annual targets, three-year targets.
> **Interviewer**: But you also did it for yourself, your personal goals?
> **Interviewee 26**: Yes, that's clear. When something's written down it can be checked, it can be verified, otherwise it's just too vague. Every goal needs to be documented.

The following interviewee reported that he had always set himself goals, but only started to formally write them down later on. All of his early goals were related to a specific portfolio of property, but later he extended his goal-setting to include wealth targets:

> **Interviewee 6:** I didn't always write the goals down on paper. I only really started to do that when I realized that, as a businessman, I needed to work more systematically and that it was necessary to set myself formal revenue targets. I started by writing out my revenue targets.
> **Interviewer**: And when was that? How old would you say you were?
> **Interviewee 6**: In my early to mid-30s. I am now 45, so it must have been 10 or 15 years ago. [...] And then at some point I wrote out how big my real estate portfolio should be.
> **Interviewer**: So, you specified a number of apartments?
> **Interviewee 6**: I did that at the age of 35. I always measured the portfolio in terms of apartment buildings and then I assigned a value to the apartment buildings and that's how I arrived at my goal; I said, "That's how much I want to be worth."

Many of the interviewees make regular use of written notes to keep track of whether they are on the right path. Like a number of other interviewees, the following interviewee writes out and reflects upon his goals in January each year:

Interviewee 20: Yes, basically every January is when I ask myself, "So, what do you want?" It is primarily a thought process that I begin in November or December. I look back and reflect: "Am I doing the right things?" And then, in January, I write it all out: "How do you want to shape the coming year for yourself?" That's always in January; that's when this process happens for me.

Interviewer: So you don't just set goals for yourself, you also ask yourself questions: "Am I even on the right path"?

Interviewee 20: Yes, because I believe that you always channel your power, your energy, in a single direction, and then you struggle with yourself. Then you have to go into yourself and say to yourself, I'll exaggerate a little here, but you say to yourself, "Do I want 120 employees at xxx, or just 60? No, let's turn it into a boutique." You have to question what you do in that time. You have to ask yourself whether you've achieved something good or not. That's what I ask myself.

Interviewer: And you set yourself qualitative goals, or do you set down numbers and figures to specify what you want to achieve in different fields?

Interviewee 20: Yes, of course. All of my employees know that I set targets, for example that xxx needs to generate certain sales revenues, certain profits, or what new employees we need to recruit. So I give the whole business shape. For example, we've started doing a New Year event in addition to our Christmas party. We use that to give us fresh impetus in the new year.

Interviewer: And do you only write down goals for the company, or do you do the same for yourself?

Interviewee 20: That's something I also do for myself personally.

Not all of the interviewees write out their goals as extensively or systematically as those cited above. The next interviewee, a real estate entrepreneur, decided to become a millionaire by the age of 40, to have a fortune in the tens of millions by the time he was 50, and to have a fortune in the hundreds of millions by the time he reached 60. He is now in his mid-50s:

Interviewee 34: My goal isn't chiselled out in stone and it's not as if I'm working like crazy to achieve it. Rather, I said to myself, you should be a millionaire by the age of 40, a double-digit millionaire at 50, and a triple-digit millionaire at 60. Those are my goals.

Interviewer: And when did you come up with those goals?

Interviewee 34: I set them after I graduated from university, when I first got involved with real estate. I said to myself, "You should be a millionaire by the time you are 40. If you're not, then it's not working out."

The following interviewee did set himself specific goals but didn't initially tie these to a specific amount of money that he one day wanted to own. Ten years ago, he specified a sum of money that would allow him to live an "opulent lifestyle" from the interest payments alone:

> **Interviewee 13**: In my mid-30s, I worked it all out, how much I would need without having to touch the capital. My parents' financial worries have always had an impact on me, so I wanted to be able to live an opulent lifestyle from the interest payments alone, without touching the capital.
> **Interviewer**: Although the interest rates looked a lot different ten years ago.
> **Interviewee 13**: Yes, interest rates were much higher then, which is why I increased the amount at some point.
> **Interviewer**: That's right, it depends on how you have invested the money, but even if you are working with the assumption of 3%, even that's not so easy to earn nowadays, is it? [...]
> **Interviewee 13**: So, I raised the amount to EUR 20 million, roughly ten years ago. And that's cash assets, capital assets. Not my private house, which actually consumes money, but real capital assets, you know?

In the case of the next interviewee, the goals were not to be taken literally, but were symbolic of the fact that he wanted to achieve unlimited wealth. Perhaps this is similar to the technique used by Arnold Schwarzenegger, who, during training, pictured his biceps as mountains,[688] in full knowledge of the fact that they would never really reach the dimensions of actual mountains:

> **Interviewee 4**: Yes, at some point I set myself a very, very high target. You could call it a visionary goal, or even a crazy goal.
> **Interviewer**: When was that?
> **Interviewee 4**: That was when I was here in [city], I was always thinking in terms of extremely large figures. Millions, billions, trillions, sextillions. And I was just enamoured by the word "sextillion" and said to myself, "There's an endless amount of money in the world; I'll work towards a sextillion."
> [...]
> **Interviewer**: And did you also write that goal down anywhere?
> **Interviewee 4**: I thought about my goal on an hourly basis. Every day, x times, I thought about it, immersed myself in it.

11.2. "IT JUST HAPPENED"

The large number of interviewees who reported that they had consciously planned their futures, in writing and in extensive detail, suggests that this has indeed been an important instrument and an aid to wealth-building for many. In contrast, there were other interviewees who categorically denied that they ever set themselves financial goals. When asked whether he had ever set himself the goal of becoming a millionaire, the following UHNWI responded:

> **Interviewee 7**: In all honesty, the goal of becoming a millionaire? No, never.
> **Interviewer**: Never?
> **Interviewee 7**: Never.
> **Interviewer**: So, it just happened?
> **Interviewee 7**: No, I always wanted to be independent, that was my driving motive. I'll tell you now, this is anonymous, isn't it? It was never about becoming a millionaire. For me it was always a question of independence. Freedom and independence.

The following interviewee, who is one of the richest people in Germany, is quite sceptical with regard to everything related to goals, planning, and strategies. He is "100% certain" that he never set himself the goal of achieving what he has subsequently achieved. On the contrary, it just happened:

> **Interviewer**: Did you ever have the vision, "So, I want to turn it into something much bigger"? Or did that happen without you having set a specific goal?
> **Interviewee 15**: I am 100% certain that was never a goal.
> **Interviewer**: So it just came about.
> **Interviewee 15**: It just happened. Everybody talks about strategies today, every year when they are making more new plans for the coming year. I didn't have a strategy. I always look at things in terms of three choices. There's a good strategy, a bad one, or no strategy at all. The bad one is catastrophic, you go bankrupt. The good one is of course the ideal one. Although I often joke that you can only know which strategies were the good ones with hindsight.

---

688 Bill Dobbins and Arnold Schwarzenegger, *The New Encyclopedia of Modern Bodybuilding* (New York: Simon & Schuster, 1999), 402.

The following interviewee made a similar point. When asked whether he had ever set himself financial goals, he answered in the negative and stated that real life "always worked out differently". He even fears that setting goals has the potential to "easily lead you into a dead end":

Interviewee 35: No, no, no. I read about that in your book, but it's not something I have ever done. I have never written down goals, never set out that "I want to achieve this thing or that thing." As I have said, I think things always work out differently. If you set yourself goals, that can very easily lead you into a dead end. At least, it's not something I have ever done. I know from my own life that I have never written down any of my major decisions. On the occasions when I have set goals for myself, life always worked out differently.

These UHNWIs emphasized that money wasn't the motivating force behind their actions:

Interviewee 17: I don't believe money was ever a driving force. I was driven by the fact that I wanted to run my own business at some point. For me, it was about self-determination. In all honesty, money was never a driving factor, never. I always said, once you've got your own business, that's the freedom to shape things and the money will follow later.

The next interviewee stressed that he had never made an entrepreneurial decision based solely on how much he could earn from it:

Interviewer: Some of the people I have spoken to have told me that they have set themselves a financial goal at some point in their lives. One told me that he wanted to be a millionaire by the time he was 30. There are others who have never done anything like that. How was it for you? Some even wrote down the very specific goals they had set for themselves.
Interviewee 18: No.
Interviewer: So that is just how it turned out for you, without setting goals.
Interviewee 18: I can honestly say that I have never made an entrepreneurial decision based on the fact that I could earn this much or that much. Never.
Interviewer: And for yourself? Have you ever said, "Later in life I want to..."?
Interviewee 18: No, never. Never.

Naturally, many entrepreneurs set out written goals for their companies, but this does not necessarily mean that they do the same in relation to their own personal lives or finances:

> **Interviewer**: Have you ever set goals for yourself? A number of the people I have spoken to, they sit down in January, for example, and write down their goals for the year.
> **Interviewee 24**: No.
> **Interviewer**: Not financially or professionally?
> **Interviewee 24**: No, no.
> **Interviewer**: Haven't you ever set goals?
> **Interviewee 24**: We have our planning.
> **Interviewer**: For the company, but not personally.
> **Interviewee 24**: But I don't have any personal goals, not in the sense of, "Next year I'm going to do this or that." That's not something I have ever done.

Success, greatness, and recognition are far more important for many entrepreneurs than achieving financial goals. The next interviewee, who has achieved success as an entrepreneur and investor in the finance industry, also sets sales targets, but admits that his motivation to beat and be better than others is so dominant that he would have even sacrificed higher earnings if it meant being placed higher in sales rankings:

> **Interviewee 44**: I didn't set myself any financial goals, I set myself sales targets. Of course, at the very beginning, you set the goal of being able to rent a bigger apartment or buy a bigger car. Those were my material goals, but I never set financial goals. And then there are my sales targets. I really just always wanted to be better than the guy in the office next door. I wanted to be better than everyone in the city, everyone in the country. I wanted to be better. I wanted to be successful, and success is often rewarded with money, isn't it? But it was the sales success itself that was far more important to me. If they had ever come to me and said, "If you bring in higher sales revenues, you'll climb to the top of the sales rankings, but we can't pay you any extra commission for those additional sales," I still would have chased the sales.
> **Interviewer**: I understand. And these sales targets, you probably wrote them down somewhere?.
> **Interviewee 44**: Yes.
> **Interviewer**: Regularly, at specific intervals, or once a year? How did you do it?
> **Interviewee 44**: On a monthly basis.

INTERIM FINDINGS

For many of the interviewees, the written formulation of goals played an important role. Some of these wealthy individuals followed the advice given in popular wealth literature to the letter. They set themselves specific financial goals and exact deadlines for achieving them. An astonishing number of interviewees described a process of detailed goal-setting, which they carried out once a year. They took the time to define milestones for the next year, while also reviewing the goals they had set for the previous year in order to assess what they had achieved.

A number of interviewees carried out this review at shorter, more regular intervals – every month and, in some cases, even on a daily basis. Such planning needs to be done in writing, as many emphasized. Only written and quantifiable goals are ultimately verifiable. A number of interviewees extensively document the goals they set. They develop life plans, seven-year plans, five-year plans, monthly plans, which in extreme cases fill thick folders or are saved in Excel documents on their computers.

Many described the detailed visualization techniques or other rituals that they are convinced help them to reach their goals. One interviewee had worked with a feng shui consultant to create a 'wealth corner' in his house, where he prayed every day for the achievement of his financial goals, and one had fixed his aspirational '1,000,000,000' in large figures above his office door. Another detailed the 200 questions he has formulated and regularly answers in writing. Yet another spends one week at the beginning of each year fasting and setting his goals for the year ahead.

For many interviewees, this process of goal-setting is not only restricted to defining financial objectives. One interviewee, for example, also sets goals for his body weight. Another wrote the precise dates of his future engagement and marriage on stones and gave them to his future wife. One reported that he had set down in writing exactly how he wanted his next girlfriend to look. "If you define your goals as precisely as you can, then you have the greatest chance of working instinctively towards them, in order to actually achieve them," emphasized one interviewee who, incidentally, was one of those who didn't set themselves financial goals, but later regretted not having done so. "I really should have done that; it would have made things a lot easier."

The finding that formulating more challenging and specifically defined goals is a valuable aid is consistent with the goal-setting theory described in Section 3.2.e – a psychological theory, confirmed in numerous studies, that claims that challenging and specifically formulated goals lead to better results than vague notions or ideas, and that individuals who set specific goals will be more successful than those who either set vague goals or fail to set any goals at all.

Nevertheless, not all of the interviewees employed such goal-setting techniques. A number explained that, although they set revenue targets for their companies, they do not formulate any personal financial goals. Others expressed general scepticism and questioned whether it is at all possible or makes any sense to set life goals. The hypothesis of popular wealth literature, that it is 'only' possible to achieve great wealth by setting down specific, quantifiable financial goals in writing and constantly visualizing these goals, could not be confirmed. This *can* be a path to wealth, but it is by no means the only one. It would also appear to be less than likely that everyone whom Napoleon Hill spoke to as he was writing his book *Think and Grow Rich* formulated all of their goals in writing and consistently followed the methods he described. Even though Hill claimed to have spoken to large numbers of people who either were wealthy or had been very successful in other areas of life, it is impossible to verify exactly what methods they used, and one must not forget that Hill's book was not a scholarly work.

On the other hand, studies that claim that the lives of the wealth elite are largely not planned, but rather the result of a series of chance circumstances, should also be viewed with some scepticism. As has been shown in Chapter 5, and in Chapter 7 on methodology, in socio-psychological terms, subjects who attempt to play down their success by attributing it to a series of lucky coincidences may be subconsciously employing envy-defence strategies, or may be providing answers during the interview that they believe will be deemed as socially desirable by their interviewer.

12 What Does Money Mean to You?

As an analysis of the biographies and autobiographies of extremely rich individuals shows, there are many different reasons for people to aspire to wealth. Thus, there are examples of wealthy people who live exceptionally modestly in relation to their material possibilities (Warren Buffett is a prominent example), while there are others for whom the exact opposite is true.[689] During the course of these interviews, it also became clear that the interviewees ranked the benefits of being very rich very differently.

In order to better understand their motivations, the interviewees were asked to explain what they associate with the concept of 'money'. This was formulated as a more open question, in order to reduce the problem of socially desirable responses described in Section 7.4. As each of the interviewees owns considerable assets, this question, which proceeded from the inarguable assumption of the interviewees' extreme wealth, enabled additional information regarding the motivation for their actions to be obtained indirectly, without the need for direct questioning.

On a scale of 0 to 10, the interviewees were asked to rank the things they associate with money. On the basis of preliminary conversations, six potential answers were identified, although, at the end of the interview, each interviewee was specifically asked whether the interviewer had forgotten anything and whether there was another aspect that they associated with money that had not been included in any of these categories. A majority of the interviewees said that this was not the case. There were, however, a number of additions, which will be addressed later. For each of the possible answers, the interviewees were able to use a full sliding scale from 0 (completely unimportant to me) to 10 (extremely important to me):

- A: Security, namely that "I won't have any financial problems unless I make a massive mistake"
- B: Freedom and independence
- C: The opportunity to use the money for new things, to invest
- D: Being able to afford the finer things in life
- E: Having money is personal confirmation that you got a lot of things right
- F: With a large amount of money, and despite the envy the wealthy are sometimes confronted with, you receive greater recognition and have the opportunity to meet interesting people.

The following table shows the scores the 45 interviewees gave for each of these six statements.

A	B	C	D	E	F
–	10	3.5	9.5	–	0
Question not asked					
Question not asked					
1.5	9	8	7	3	6
10	10	6	8	6	5
1.5	9	1	9	1	0
Question not asked					
8	–	4.5	3.5	5	2
Question not asked					
"I'm a gambler"					
8	8	9	2	4.5	2
10	10	10	10	10	10
7.5	5	8	7	6	6
2.5	8	10	3	3	0
7	8	10	2	10	5.5
0	10	10	5	0	0
6	10	10	3	7	4
5	8	–	6.5	–	5
8	10	10	10	8	10
2	8	10	4	8	8
3	10	–	–	–	–
8	10	5	2	0	4
7	6.5	7	1	9	8
7.5	10	8.5	6	9	4.5
0	10	10	2.5	0	0
10	10	7	5	–	–
8	10	8	3	5	2
10	–	–	8	–	–
8	10	4	4	5	3
6	9	10	9	8	8
4	7	9	3	4	8
10	8	3	8	3	3
9	10	5	7	4	5
2	6	6	5	3	3

---

689   Zitelmann, *Dare to Be Different and Grow Rich*, 273 et seq.

A	B	C	D	E	F
8	8	6	2	4	–
10	9	4.5	8	6	8.5
10	10	7	4	10	9
10	10	5	5	7	10
8.5	10	–	–	–	–
8	10	9.5	5	3.5	3
10	10	8	6.5	8	9
3 (earlier)	10	8	6.5	7.5	7
3	10	10	3	5	5
8	10	6	7	6	7
10	10	8	9	5	0
A	**B**	**C**	**D**	**E**	**F**

Numbers with decimal points are used where an interviewee suggested a value such as '6 to 7', which is rendered as 6.5. '–' or 'Question not asked' means that, for a variety of reasons, this aspect was not addressed.

The following summary details the number of interviewees who rated a specific aspect as unimportant (0–3) and the number who rated the same aspect as important to them (7–10).

	0–3	7–10
A – Security	9	23
B – Freedom and independence	2	34
C – Creating something new	1	23
D – Finer things	10	13
E – Self-affirmation	8	12
F – Recognition	12	11

In first place, and by a wide margin, the interviewees rated freedom and independence as the aspect they most strongly associate with money. Only five interviewees selected a value below 7 for this aspect. This aspect was awarded the highest value, 10, by 23 of the interviewees, whereas only nine did so for security, and the category 'being able to afford the finer things in life' was only given the maximum score by two. There were only two interviewees who didn't associate money with 'freedom and independence'; they answered:

Interviewee 8: Strangely enough, I wouldn't really associate that with money. Intellectual independence is much more important to me, and I don't need money for that.

Interviewee 28: Freedom and independence, to me, would mean freeing oneself from all appointments, meetings, time pressures, and the like. That's not something I can do in my life. I'm always bound by appointments and it doesn't matter how much money I have; my commitments would never allow me this kind of freedom.

The balance of the interviewees who rated an aspect as important (7–10) or unimportant (0–3) is shown in the following chart:

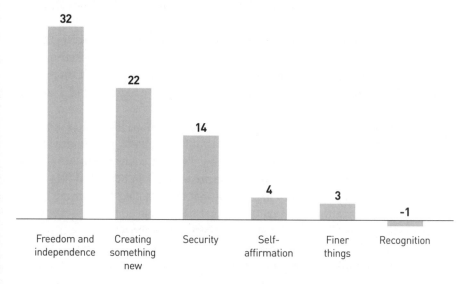

This shows that perceiving themselves as being free and independent is important for the self-image of these wealthy interviewees. Almost all of the interviewees, including those over the age of 70, regularly work and devote a significant amount of time to their professional activities. This is despite the fact that none of them has to work for financial reasons. When asked about the importance of freedom and independence, one interviewee responded:

Interviewee 25: That's how it is for me. [...] That's the key. I even joked about it once to a group of people, that the only superiors I ever want to answer to are the bank I do business with, and God.

Not all of the interviewees, on the other hand, shared an appreciation of being able to afford the finer things in life. For 13 of the interviewees, though, this was a very important factor. They placed great value on cars, houses, and holidays.

In contrast, there were ten interviewees for whom this had either played no role or was not a significant motivation. One of the richest of the interviewees, who is well known for his ascetic lifestyle, provided a very short response to the category 'being able to afford the finer things in life'. He answered succinctly, "Move on, doesn't apply to me." For this wealthy interviewee, money is simply a tool he needs to perform certain entrepreneurial tasks. "I always only saw tasks and what I wanted to create, and I needed money to perform those tasks and create those things." Another answered curtly when asked what role money plays for him and whether it had enabled him to buy the finer things in life: "Holds no interest for me." And one simply said, "I don't do that," awarding the category a single point.

There were, however, others who were equally emphatic in answering in the affirmative. One of the interviewees answered "100% a 10" when asked to rank the importance of being able to buy the finer things in life as a motivation for him on the scale of 0 to 10. Another, who awarded this aspect a high score of 8, added:

> **Interviewee 36**: There's no question that I've got more than enough to live on. But money means having a happy, beautiful life, being able to travel, you know? Let's say you meet somebody new. I've lost count of the number of people I've taken to Capri or Venice and so on. You can't do all of that if you haven't got any money, can you? It's not that I'm boasting or showing off, or that I had to have the hotel suite; it's just being able to travel somewhere whenever you feel like it. You just head off with someone new that you've met, or you go skiing, when the weather's great. Being able to do lovely things, that's what I think is really important.

A similar picture emerges in relation to the following aspect: "With a large amount of money, and despite the envy the wealthy are sometimes confronted with, you receive greater recognition and have the opportunity to meet interesting people." While 11 interviewees agreed that – despite the envy they sometimes encounter – they enjoy greater recognition because of their wealth, 12 stressed that, in their opinion, this plays no role whatsoever. They emphasized the fact that they also enjoy recognition within society independent of their wealth.

In all, 12 of the interviewees regard money, and the extent to which they have increased their fortunes as a result of their entrepreneurial decisions and investments, as a confirmation that they have done many things right in their lives. But eight of the interviewees said that this aspect did not play any role for them. One, who places great emphasis on ethical conduct and his commitment to the investors who have entrusted him with their money, explained why he does not view wealth as a confirmation of doing many things right in life:

Interviewee 22: I know too many people who have made a great deal of money off the backs of others to believe that. It's not as if they have done things the right way. I don't believe that at all.

All of the interviewees were asked whether there were other important associations they had with money that had not been covered by one of the six specified categories. They mentioned the broadest possible range of aspects. Some emphasized philanthropy or the opportunity to help others financially or to act as patrons. While these individuals also admitted that this was never their initial motivation for becoming wealthy, this aspect plays an important role for them now that they are wealthy:

Interviewee 43: Yes, it's also important to me that I can use the money for good causes or to act as a patron or do something good in the fields that interest me, the things that are important to me. I can give something back to society or shape things in society, things that are close to my heart. That is important to me. It was never my motivation to become wealthy, but it is very important to me today.

Interviewee 5: Let's put it this way, what I like about having money is that you can also pass some on to people who don't have any. I would give that an 8. It definitely plays a role for me.

Interviewee 8: The chance to help other people, not necessarily with money. It might sound funny, but you can't help most people with money, can you? But if you don't have to count every penny, you can certainly help other people. As I said, not by giving them money, but because you can afford the luxury of immersing yourself in their problems and looking to see if there are any solutions. When they are just busy trying to make ends meet, they don't have that freedom, do they?

Interviewee 14: Yes, that [the chance to help others] would be a 10. And of course, at my age, I've just returned from [another country]. And over there I've got this cardiac catheter laboratory, which now has a charitable foundation for heart problems. That's a wonderful thing, and I have to say that I now want to do more things like that. That involved a large donation, of course, but I was recently there and had the privilege of observing four operations. [...] There were seven or eight doctors who operated all day and were incredibly committed, and things like that are definitely a priority for me. That's what I can do with money.

A number of interviewees also added that they associate money with the chance to pass their wealth on to the next generation:

> **Interviewee 17**: Okay, so if you take security and think of it in general terms, not just for yourself, but also for the family. [...] Maybe what's missing here is the desire to be able to pass something on. Then you come onto the inheritance tax debate. [...] That's a very important aspect, whether it's right or wrong, that's definitely a philosophical problem. And so, in spite of the fact that I've done well enough without inheriting any wealth myself, I certainly have a good feeling that the next generations are well provided for. That's how I like to put it, even though I'm sure that they will do well for themselves on their own. [...] So that's a clear focus. For example, when I sell some real estate, I don't want to spend the money, I want to reinvest it, multiply it, and pass it on. [...] That's a very important aspect that is maybe missing here.

Several interviewees mentioned motivations that may well have played a role for others as well, but which those other interviewees may have perceived as not socially desirable and therefore refrained from mentioning (for further details on social desirability bias, see Section 7.4). For example, two of the interviewees specifically mentioned that they were motivated by the fact that money made them more attractive to women:

> **Interviewee**: For me, money was always also important in relation to women. I mean, for my girlfriend. I don't believe that I would have been totally hopeless with women without my money. I was always totally generous when it came to my girlfriends. I really thought that I had better chances with women if I had something to offer. That was always far more important to me than having a big car, for example. And that whole confirmation aspect, I never needed that. That's why I've given that category a low score, but if by being able to afford the finer things in life you also mean in terms of girlfriends [...] that was really important to me. That was a major motivating factor, for sure.

> **Interviewee**: When someone talks to me about beautiful girls, I imagine a bus driver. He'd have to be the most charming man in the world to be successful with beautiful girls, wouldn't he?

It is hardly surprising that some interviewees only identified motivations that are deemed to be socially desirable and easier to talk about (such as freedom and independence), while others identified motivations of an entirely different nature. Even though only a small number of interviewees openly addressed such motivations, it can be assumed that they are not the only ones for whom these are important factors. In one case, an interviewee admitted that he likes it when other people are jealous of his wealth:

> **Interviewee**: Pity you get for free, envy you have to earn. I'm more proud of the fact that some people envy me. That I can deal with. And I actually want it, too. I don't want people to feel sorry for me. I want them to envy me.

Two interviewees confessed that their fear of poverty had been a key motivating factor in their lives. "You had money, and then it's gone." This fear, "to end up in poverty one day", was a very important motivation for them:

> **Interviewee 34**: If you had asked me how important the motivation was to avoid ending my days in poverty, or the fear of ending my life in poverty, you know? How important it is for me to do everything I can to make sure that I don't end up in poverty? That's how important it is to me, to do everything possible to make sure that I don't fall into poverty. You had money, and then it's gone. If you'd asked me, I would have rated that a 9 or a 10 on your scale of motivations. [...] The more money people have, the more they worry about losing it all.

Had this question been explicitly raised, it is likely that a greater number of interviewees would have identified it as a motivation. One of the interviewees even admitted that this was his "main driving force":

> **Interviewer**: I always thought that this was a complete list, but somebody told me recently that there was a point that I had missed, and I think he was probably right. He mentioned the fear that you could become poor again. Does that play a role for you?
> **Interviewee 37**: Yes, a really big one.
> **Interviewer**: And if you had to give it a score? I never would have thought of it, but he was right, wasn't he?
> **Interviewee 37**: That's my main driving force.

And another of the UHNWIs described a dream that had been extremely important to him, namely the vision of someday ending his life homeless on the streets:

> **Interviewee 42**: At the age of 17 or 18 I had a dream. I woke up dripping with sweat. I saw myself somewhere, under a bridge. It's an image that has always stayed with me, that made me realize that I had two choices, either I would be very successful or I would end up homeless, on the streets, living under a bridge. It was totally obvious to me, there were only those two extremes.

For another interviewee, money is simply the "most important regulator for many decisions". Having money forces one, in both private and business spheres, to act reasonably. If one does not do so, it will decrease, whereas acting reasonably will ensure that it increases:

> **Interviewee 23**: Money is an extremely difficult product. Money requires that you act responsibly and take decisions sensibly. That notion has always dominated my actions, the notion of not destroying money. [...] Money is the most important regulator for decisions – privately and in business.

And another interviewee considered money to be a unit by which to measure his personal development:

> **Interviewee 4**: So, for me there's another point. I have a somewhat critical view of this today, but I used to see a magic in money, you know? A magic that allows me to fulfil myself.
> **Interviewer**: What do you mean by that exactly?
> **Interviewee 4**: I basically mean, if you wanted to put it negatively, using money to establish a position of power. [...] And if you wanted to put it more positively, and focus on the positive aspect, then I mean that it holds a potential for self-development. Yes, you could say that with the instrument of money, inherent in the instrument of money, I can measure my personal development. [...] What I mean by that is making the greatest challenges verifiable and measurable, using money to make them measurable.
> **Interviewer**: Like an athlete? He knows how many seconds it takes him to run a certain distance, doesn't he?
> **Interviewee 4**: Exactly.
> **Interviewer**: And you say, now I have this amount of money and that is my way of measuring that I have overcome certain challenges.
> **Interviewee 4**: That's right, exactly right.

Interviewer: And in sports, which also applies to some of the people I've interviewed, there's often a competitive element. One of my other interviewees told me, "I always wanted to be No. 1, just like in sports, and that having more money than the others is my way of measuring that." Has that also been a factor for you?

Interviewee 4: Yes, a major factor. I have music, which I love and has been a major theme throughout my life. And that continues today. And then I am really, really interested in money, music, concerts, and the like. But at the exact moment that I realized I would never be a world star with my violin, I put it to one side.

The following interviewee described money as "the motor to live your life to the full":

Interviewee 12: Then, yes, it is absolute personal fulfilment. To me, it is obvious, and it's what a lot of people say over and over again without actually living their lives accordingly, but you really do only have one life. And once you have recognized that fact, once you really have that realization embedded in your mind, then money is the motor to live your life to the full. In our world, money is the motor.

An unusual response was provided by the following UHNWI, who had the categories A to F read aloud to him:

Interviewee: I can tell you, they are all good questions, the right questions, but they're just not my thing, you know?

Interviewer: All of these things?

Interviewee: None of them apply to me. I'm a gambler.

Interviewer: And what do you mean by that? Please explain it to me, what exactly do you mean? That's really interesting.

Interviewee: Yes, I'm a gambler. I bet on a card and fight to make sure that I win. [...] For example, when someone asks me, and they often do, "Do you want to go to the casino?" Then I say, "No, I never go to the casino." My job is the game, you know? I place my bets and can never know how it will end, but I fight for it.

INTERIM FINDINGS

The interviewees associate money, namely possessing a substantial fortune, with a range of different advantages in life. In order to better understand their motivations, each of the interviewees was presented with six aspects that can be associated with money. They were asked, based on the importance of these factors to them, to rate each aspect on a scale of 0 (totally unimportant) to 10 (very important).

The wide variety of responses reflects the broad spectrum of motivations. Being able to afford the finer things in life (namely expensive cars, houses, or holidays) was of major importance to 13 of the interviewees, whereas ten asserted that this plays no role whatsoever for them. For the remaining interviewees, this aspect was neither very important nor totally unimportant. Security was rated as especially important by roughly half of the interviewees, but there were also nine interviewees who said that this was of no importance to them whatsoever.

There was only one motivation about which almost all of the interviewees agreed. They associate wealth with freedom and independence. The notion of being financially free united almost all of the interviewees. No other motivation was so frequently rated so highly. Only five of the interviewees rated this aspect with a grade that was not in the highest category of between 7 and 10. Of the interviewees, a total of 23 even went as far as to rate this aspect with the highest possible score, a 10.

In second place was the opportunity to use the money for new things, to invest. This aspect was rated as extremely important by 23 of the interviewees and only one ranked this aspect as of lesser importance.

When asked to comment on the importance of money and their motivations for wealth, it is important to consider the possibility that individuals will provide answers that are perceived as socially desirable. It is to be assumed that other motivations exist, in addition to those disclosed in the interview situation. Nevertheless, a number of interviewees did mention other associations, such as the fact that money improves your chances with women. One interviewee openly confessed that he likes it when other people envy his wealth. Three of the interviewees admitted that they fear becoming poor and that this has been a key driver of their actions.

Some emphasized the importance of philanthropy or the opportunity to help others with money or to be active as patrons, although they did admit that this was not their initial motivation. "That wasn't a motivation for becoming wealthy, but it is very important to me today."

The Importance
of Sales Skills 13

Werner Sombart was among the first to identify sales skills as one of the defining traits of the entrepreneur. An entrepreneur needed to "confer with another, and, by making the best of [his] own case and demonstrating the weakness of his, get him to adopt what you propose. Negotiation is but an intellectual sparring match."[690] These skills are required at all times, irrespective of whether an entrepreneur is engaged in attracting the best employees, selling products, or a major corporate acquisition. In essence, it is always a question of the entrepreneur being able to convince their counterpart of the advantages of agreeing to the contract.[691] To achieve this, according to Sombart, the entrepreneur has to arouse interest, build trust, and inspire a desire to buy. It is irrelevant how this is achieved. However, it is never a question of employing coercive means, as the aim is always for the counterpart to enter into a contract of their own volition.[692]

Recent entrepreneurship research has accorded less attention to this skill, which is commonly referred to as 'salespersonship' or 'sales talent'. And yet the American wealth researcher Thomas J. Stanley reports that 47% of the millionaires he surveyed assess their sales skills, namely their ability to sell their ideas and products, as a key factor in their financial success.[693] The ability to sell is a characteristic shared by a majority of the interviewees.

Each interviewee was asked whether they would be described by others as a good salesperson. And, if this was the case, the following supplementary questions were asked: To what extent did these skills contribute to your financial success? In your own view, what are the most important skills and strategies that have made you a good salesperson?

In Section 9.6, it was shown that many UHNWIs began to sell products or services during their youths, from which they earned their first money.

---

690 Sombart, *The Quintessence of Capitalism*, 54.

691 Ibid., 54–55.

692 Ibid., 55.

693 Stanley, *The Millionaire Mind*, 45.

During the interviews, two in three of the interviewees explained that their talents as salespeople had been a significant factor in their financial success. More than one in three even went as far as to claim that they owed between 70% and 100% of their success to their talents in sales.

ROLE OF SALES SKILLS IN ENTREPRENEURIAL/FINANCIAL SUCCESS, BASED ON SELF-ASSESSMENT

- "I was always first and foremost a salesman, and I love it, still do today."
- Sales skills played an extremely important role.
- Owes 80% of his success to his sales talent.
- Sales talent contributed 70% to his financial success.
- Sales fascinated him from a very young age and was "one of the decisive factors" in his success. He has an "insane amount of fun selling".
- At the age of 22, he was already the most successful salesman in Germany in his field.
- "No one who wants to be successful can make it without a talent for sales."
- Sales talent contributed 70% to his financial success.
- "Selling is probably the magic word," and 80% of her success is definitely down to her sales skills.
- Claims he owes 50% of his success to his sales skills. "I have always been a good salesman."
- "I'm a salesman through and through" – sales talent contributed 80% to his success.
- His success is 100% due to his sales talent.
- His success is 80% due to his sales skills.
- Sales skills rated very highly. Responsible for 40% of his success.
- "70% of my success is definitely down to my sales skills."
- On a scale of 1 to 10, he would rate the importance of his sales skills 10+.
- 80–90% of his success is a direct result of his sales abilities.
- 70% of his success is due to sales skills.
- 70% of his success is due to sales skills.
- "Everything is sales." 80% of his success is due to sales.
- 80% of his success is due to sales.
- At least 80% of his success is determined by sales. "No matter what we do, we are always selling."
- 80% of his success is determined by sales.
- "I am an excellent self-marketer."
- 50% of his success is a direct result of his sales abilities.

- Not a good salesperson.
- Sales skills contributed 98% to his success.
- "A very important element in my success."
- Sales skills contributed 70–90% to his success.
- Sales skills contributed 50% to his success.
- Views himself as a very good salesman because he is not the stereo-typical salesman.

13.1. "NO MATTER WHAT WE DO, WE ARE ALWAYS SELLING"

For many people, the term 'salesperson' has negative associations. It is immediately striking that this is not the case for a clear majority of the interviewees. They have a positive view of the term 'salesperson' and offer wide-ranging definitions of the role. They do not just associate sales with selling products and services. Rather, they assign a far more comprehensive meaning to the term – analogously to Sombart's understanding of the concept of the trader.

Sales talent, related one interviewee, contributed 50% to his success. As he sees it, "being good" is nowhere near enough; your "presentation" is also important:

Interviewee 26: Otherwise, you can forget it. If the presentation isn't right, you might as well stay at home. That is a clear insight. Nowadays, being good is nowhere near enough. Whatever it is you are doing, you've got to be able to sell it. And for me, the path my life has taken is maybe different, but I was always good at sales.

Another interviewee sometimes earned DM 10,000 per month, parallel to university, from selling financial products. "So I said to myself, 'I can earn so much more doing that, why do I need to study?' Anyway, it fascinated me. I enjoyed selling so much." The ability to sell was "one of the key factors" for his success. "I enjoyed it enormously… The success, clinching the deal, the feeling of success afterwards when I could say, 'I closed another deal.'" He once won a competition run by the sales company's general agency, because he had made the most sales, "but I was prepared to be out and about all day and all night". Being singled out, asked up onto the stage, and receiving a gold watch for his sales success motivated him – not least because he had triumphed against salesmen who were twice his age. He compares sales success with athletic ambition. "So you say, 'I clinched 39 deals' and that is basically the same ambition as in sports, just in business."

The interviewees' great appreciation of sales skills is independent of the sectors in which they were themselves in business. "I don't believe that anyone who wants to be successful can do so without a talent for sales," explained one interviewee, who became rich with a research company. When asked about the foundations of her success, one interviewee, who became wealthy in the food industry, explained that she owed 80% of her success to her sales talents. Ultimately, in her opinion, everything depends on sales, as she also had to sell her ideas and visions:

> **Interviewee 14**: I love selling. Selling is probably the magic word. I think, I mean, I've always thought that I am good at selling, that I am a good salesperson. I started out working in the shops and learned the ropes myself.

When asked what percentage of her success she would credit to her sales talent, she replied:

> **Interviewee 14**: Yes, sales is definitely important ... very important. That's got to be 80%, because, you know, I have to be able to sell my ideas. I had to be able to explain my visions and my ideas to other people and impress them, win them over, so that they could make even more out of them.

An auditor, who made a fortune as an investor, describes himself – even though others largely know him for his expertise as an auditor and tax adviser – as a "salesman through and through". He regards his success not primarily as being due to his professional expertise but rather as a product of his ability to establish and build networks:

> **Interviewer**: If you were asked, would you say that other people would describe you as a good salesman, as someone who is skilled at winning new clients?
> **Interviewee 17**: I'm a salesman through and through.
> **Interviewer**: And how about in relation to your professional success, leaving your investments to one side for now, what percentage of your success would you say is a result of your sales skills?
> **Interviewee 17**: Yes, networking. Purely networking. Building up a network.
> **Interviewer**: So, would you say, I don't know, 80%?
> **Interviewee 17**: Yes, certainly. [...] It's not from my professional knowledge. [...] That's exactly why, to work seriously in our business, you have to reach a certain size. Because the salespeople have to recognize that they're not quite so brilliant at the day-to-day auditing work, so you need to work together with real expert auditors. And that's the balancing act in our profession,

you need a combination of both talents, winning clients and auditing. You get the auditor, who has never been involved in winning clients, and he needs a salesman. And the sales guy needs a real expert auditor – there are very few geniuses around who can do both. You could count them on the fingers of one hand.

An entrepreneur who built his fortune in the field of medical technologies stressed: "Everything is sales" – every idea, every successful negotiation, it all boils down to sales. He credited 80% of his success to his sales skills:

Interviewee 32: Everything is sales. Everything is sales. I even started taking rhetoric classes when I was 16, you know? And selling was my strength. You have to sell everything, ideas, products, everything needs to be sold, doesn't it? You need to be able to judge your partners and your clients correctly, and convince them.
Interviewer: And if you had to take a percentage and say, "Sales talent contributed so much to my success as an entrepreneur," what would you say?
Interviewee 32: A lot. 80%. Every idea, every successful negotiation, it all boils down to sales. [...] Convincing people is sales. [...] Yes, every negotiation is selling an idea. Every single negotiation. You have to be able to convince other people to do something. And when you sit there with ten other people, you need to convince all ten of them. That is nothing but sales.

A property developer's business is extremely complex. They need to acquire land, convince planning authorities and banks, and ultimately sell projects to private buyers or institutional investors. A highly successful property developer put it in a nutshell: "No matter what we do, we are always selling":

Interviewer: And if you had to pick a percentage, how much would you say your talents in sales – and you started selling at a very young age – how much would you say your talents in sales contributed to your success as an entrepreneur?
Interviewee 34: A minimum of 80%. No matter what we do, we are always selling. When I arrange a loan, I am selling my product. When I buy land, I am selling my company as the perfect partner. When I hire someone, I am selling my company as the right place for them. It's all sales, in one form or another. It always involves making it clear to someone else that this is right for them. If I want planning permission, I have to convince some moron to grant permission in exactly the way I want it, not some other way.

Another interviewee, the owner of eight companies in the food industry, also thinks it is important to understand sales in far broader terms. When asked to assess the degree to which sales skills had contributed to his success, he responded:

> **Interviewee 37**: Yes, I am an excellent self-marketer, you know?
> **Interviewer**: So, if you had to say, x percent...
> **Interviewee 37**: 50%. Yes. Of course, selling doesn't just mean that I sell my products. [...] It means that I sell my company during a job interview. It means that I sometimes sell people a solution that they maybe don't even really need. So at least 50%. It's all about drawing people in, convincing them, and somehow being authentic and true to yourself.

One interviewee, who had been successful in investment banking and the real estate sector, emphasized the importance of sales, pointing out that, in the final analysis, you are always selling yourself:

> **Interviewer**: So what proportion of your business and financial success would you say you owe to your sales talents? If you spontaneously had to name a percentage?
> **Interviewee 42**: 70 or 80%. At the end of the day, we are always selling ourselves, with every act of communication. I have certain intentions, and I am always trying to convince others to adopt my ideas.

The interviewees are not salespeople in the sense of the traditional negative stereotypes. It is because they do not come across as 'typical' sellers, who bombard their customers with torrents of words, that these interviewees have enjoyed such success in sales. One interviewee, who, even as a student, enjoyed massive success selling tax-efficient financial products, explained: "At the age of 22 I was the most successful salesman [in the tax-efficiency industry] in Germany [...] I was able to answer every question, always professionally, always objectively." The recipe for his success in sales was a combination of superior knowledge, a rational approach to sales, and absolute conviction in what he was selling. In his opinion, the crucial factor was one he learned as a tutor, namely "to explain things simply" and "hold rational conversations". "I was the most successful [commission-based broker] in Germany [...] What they said about me was, 'Actually, the man can't sell, but he succeeds on the basis of his conviction and product knowledge.' So I had always thought to myself, 'I can't sell.' And there I was at 22, the most successful salesperson in Germany."

The following interviewee was also of the opinion that a good salesperson is not always recognized as such by others:

Interviewee 22: When it comes to being good, I don't think that they would say we're full of hot air, which would be the equivalent for many people of "They are good salesmen." Rather they would say, "The product is persuasive" or "The plan they have brought us, that's persuasive."

Another interviewee, who has enjoyed success in the real estate industry, began by explaining that he is not a sales talent, but then subsequently corrected his self-assessment. He clarified that he was referring to the "typical sales traits that most people talk about", which do not apply to him:

Interviewer: Would other people describe you as a good salesman?
Interviewee 45: That's an interesting question. I certainly wouldn't describe myself in that way, but maybe I have a wrong self-image. Others have said that I am always very credible in getting my point across, which is, incidentally, also true.
Interviewer: Why would you never describe yourself as a good salesman?
Interviewee 45: Because the qualities I would use to describe a good salesman are not qualities I see in myself, e.g. being able to woo others. [...] If you were to send me to one of those sales training courses, they'd take one look at me and say, "My God, he's got a lot to learn." That may be true, but still everyone comes, and anyone who has sat across the table from me buys, because they believe me.
Interviewer: But couldn't it actually be that someone whom others describe as a good salesman isn't actually a good salesman at all? You know, there's a hypothesis that says the best salesperson is someone whom others don't even perceive as a salesperson. They say, "He's credible, convincing, I trust him. I'll buy from him." [...]
Interviewee 45: That's all well and good. But you assume that these others, the ones you talk about, know that the salesman who comes across as a good salesman, possibly isn't such a good salesman after all. The typical sales traits that most people talk about don't apply to me. But on the other hand, I believe that I am good at sales. [...] That's because I go into sales conservations without expecting them to buy. The final result of the meeting doesn't matter. That's really important. So, I go in and I say, the customer is going to get all of the information he can get out of me, along with my opinions. And he is also going to sense from me that I'm indifferent about whether he buys from me or not. [...] Of course, you should always have a goal in mind, that's right, but if your goal at the start of a meeting is, "He has to buy something from me," the customer will sense that. An especially cultivated and educated person will sense that from a mile away.

13.2. "NO REALLY DOESN'T MEAN NO"

Sombart described the sales process, which he viewed as crucially important to the entrepreneur, as "an intellectual sparring match". The real sales process begins when the salesperson is met with a "no" that they need to turn into a "yes". Several interviewees reported that this is the specific process that they enjoy the most. One interviewee from the real estate sector explained that "no really doesn't mean no"; rather it should be understood as "yes, but show me". He described how he probes clients' objections and skilfully deflects any doubts before they are explicitly raised or discussed:

> **Interviewee 4**: Yes, at the very start of my career it didn't take me very long to recognize and probe that "no". This wasn't just a sales technique. Modern salespeople are taught that "no" is how any sale begins, but I have always treated it as a request: "Dear salesman, please spend more of your time with me, make more of an effort for me." All the customer is really saying is, "I want to enter into a better relationship with you, a deeper, more open and stronger relationship." "No" really doesn't mean "no". What it really means is, "Yes, but show me." At least, that's how I've always understood it, and still do today.
>
> **Interviewer**: Could you give me an example of how you've dealt with a situation, so that I have a better picture of what you are saying? Something you have in mind, maybe an image or a situation?
>
> **Interviewee 4**: [...] You have to understand your customer's objections in advance. And you need to take the sting out of his objections, deal with them before he is even consciously aware of the objection. You really need to address that during your discussions. I can give you an example from my sales experience. You know, for instance, that an apartment would be right for a prospective buyer. You know that it matches their search criteria, but you also know what the objections are. You know what the biggest objections will be.
>
> **Interviewer**: And you dispel them before the customer has a chance to even verbalize them.
>
> **Interviewee 4**: Yes, you deal with them upfront. Before you even offer him something, you deal with those objections. But how do you deal with them, that's the question, isn't it? Never on a rational level. Let me give you an example: There's a property development and close by there's a brothel, within view of the development. Of course, 80% of customers turn you down for that very reason, you know? So, you have to discuss this with your customers at the outset, but, naturally, you can't talk about brothels, you can't talk about difficult locations and the way they will develop. You have

to speak about it on a personal level. What does that mean personally, how can you translate that onto a person's personal or psychological level? To recognize that there are things around us, even in us, that are not always right, not good, that aren't acceptable, that don't fit in our idealized world, but are nevertheless part of our world? You need to address that and ask the customer, "How is it in your life, are there any things that irritate you, that you'd rather get rid of, but that you accept? And are there things around you, people or situations, that are basically not good, but that you live with, or have learned to live with?"

Interviewer: That you have come to terms with.

Interviewee 4: You come to terms with it. "Or even things that you could change, things that you have somehow become involved in, but could later change?" When I start by loosening him up on this subject, I can naturally build on that and have a deeper conversation. And then, later on, I can say, "You know, there are a number of irritating factors in our environments and in our lives. Let me tell you about myself…" Then I can explain things from my point of view: "It will change, I have even analysed it in terms of this specific lease contract, which runs for another five years. Once the lease is up, we'll make sure that they are out of there." There are simply some things that you have to face up to, to deal with, and then they change, just like you have told me once yourself. Isn't that right?

The interviewees often reported a special, emotional sense of achievement about when they had managed to turn a "no" into a "yes". One described this as "wonderful. The greatest thing for me":

Interviewer: Does it give you a great deal of pleasure when someone confronts you with a "no" and you are able to turn that around into a "yes"?

Interviewee 5: That's wonderful. The greatest thing for me.

The next interviewee reported how he is able to "turn decisions around", even against majority opinion. He even uses the term "manipulation" to describe this process:

Interviewee 16: I can make a room of ten high-class, well-educated people suddenly think differently, abandon the opinions they previously held, turn decisions around. It might sound a bit funny, but you can really manipulate anything. Anything. It's all a huge illusion and, as an entrepreneur, you decide which illusion people will accept.

The following passage quotes extensively from one interviewee who very clearly described situations in which he was able to transform a potential buyer's emphatic "no" into a "yes":

> **Interviewee 29**: I believe that if you want to be successful you simply have to be prepared to accept a "no" or an objection and then, at some point, you realize that the "no" is not a "no" and that's when it starts to get exciting, doesn't it? That's when you ask yourself, "What have I done wrong, or what has my potential buyer not properly understood?"
>
> **Interviewer**: And can you think of a particular example, a specific situation, where you can say: "I really enjoyed that, someone started with a clear 'no' and I was able to turn that around"?
>
> **Interviewee 29**: Yes, absolutely. I can remember two clear situations, but they might take quite a while to explain.
>
> **Interviewer**: That's fine. Take your time.
>
> **Interviewee 29**: The first one was back when I had just started out with my very first property developments. That was typical residential property development work, on multi-family housing. And then, of course, you need to sell them, don't you? That is always what the banks want, that you have sold a certain number of units. So it really was important. And I had a buyer who wanted a really big unit, we're talking about a lot of money. Everything was sorted out and then one day he came to my office and, rather unfortunately, as sometimes happens, he had to wait for about five minutes. I didn't even know that he was there. He arrived and sat down in my office and my secretary wasn't paying attention. And he was so annoyed at having to wait that he just got up and walked out, saying that he wasn't going to buy from me. So my secretary told me, "He was here, but he left." So I called him and he said, "No, no, Mr. xxx, the subject is closed. I don't want to buy from you anymore. You left me sitting there." He clearly felt that his honour had been offended. I said to myself, "What do I do now?" Then I told him, "You're right, but give me one chance, I need to talk to you." "No, there's no need for you to come to see me." But I still went to see him. I still drove over there anyway, you know? [...] We had already fixed a meeting with a notary. We had wanted to drive over to the notary that evening, and all of this was happening on the same day, in the afternoon. Everything was already set up and agreed. The contracts had already been finalized and everything. And now everything was up in the air again. To cut a long story short, I went over there to him and apologized. I started off by apologizing. [...] And then I asked him lots of questions. I said, "What would you say your problem is, or what have I done wrong?" – questions like that. And he told me that it is unacceptable to make someone wait like that. And I became more and more certain that

it was more of a personality problem with him, that it wasn't really anything to do with the property. The root of the problem was that he felt that he hadn't been taken seriously enough. It was something that he had experienced so often in his life, and now, here I was, doing the same. So it was up to me to convince him that I wasn't like that at all.

Interviewer: And how did you manage to do that?

Interviewee 29: I did it by showing him that I understood him. I can't say exactly how, but I touched a nerve, something in his heart or in his gut, something that made him then say, "Let's see," which then turned into a "Yes, okay, let's do this, let's get going." And then we drove over to the notary together. The drive took us about 30 minutes and we continued to talk the whole way there and the mood became steadily more positive and he did sign the contracts.

This interviewee's second example of how a "no" was transformed into a "yes" was as follows:

Interviewee 29: And the second example relates to a hotel I bought in Heidelberg from the family of a hotelier. [...] We were sitting together in the notary's offices. The appointment with the notary lasted three hours – it was a long contract, a large building. We reached the point of signing the contracts. And he stood up and said, "No." [...] Just stood up and left. What did I do next? As I've said, "no" never really means "no". I sat with the tax adviser and tried to analyse the situation. I wanted to understand what the hotelier's problem could be. And I was able to understand his problem, that it was more to do with his family and a number of other things, but not really with the decision itself, as is so often the case. And again I was able to turn things around, and two months later we were again at the notary's offices and signed the contracts, and the terms were even better for me than they had been originally, because my position had strengthened. So, as you see, "no" never really means "no". And many people, probably a majority, wouldn't be able to deal with that and the "no" would be the end of the matter.

13.3. SUCCESSFUL SELLING WITH EMPATHY, DIDACTICS, EXPERT KNOWLEDGE, AND NETWORKING

When asked to reveal the secrets of their success in sales, the interviewees primarily identified the following qualities in addition to the necessity of hard work and commitment:
- Empathy
- Didactics
- Expert knowledge
- Networking.

Many interviewees spoke about the role of empathy. When asked whether he would describe himself as a very good salesperson, the following interviewee said:

> **Interviewee 4**: Absolutely, yes. And not in the sense of sales skills that can be learned. Of course, you always have to try to develop yourself further, but it's more a question of the quality of empathy, using empathy to assess the situation, you know? Knowing exactly who the person sitting opposite you is. Having an intuition and being sure that you understand what he is thinking and what he is feeling, and adjust your approach accordingly.

A UHNWI from the food industry emphasized the importance of his sensitivity towards his interlocutors and negotiating partners. He described himself as a "totally sensitive guy":

> **Interviewer**: Is there a specific quality you see in yourself that makes you say, "That's basically a sales talent that I have and it has proved to be very important?"
> **Interviewee 37**: I can tell you exactly. I am able to immediately understand what is important to the other person, including what his problem is, and I can always come up with a solution. And they appreciate that. They feel that they have been consulted and advised. They feel that they got totally competent advice. And, of course, I'm a totally sensitive guy, aren't I? Very perceptive and also sensitive, and those two qualities are both connected. But I also believe, and others have said this about me many times, that I can very quickly put myself in the position of others, can see problems from their perspectives, irrespective of whether those are personal problems, or business problems, or technical problems, whatever. It's just something I am good at. I am a problem solver.

The next interviewee, who is from the real estate industry, stressed that his most important skill is "that I am good at reading the other person". He believes you need to overcome "blockades" and find "creative approaches" to convincing others:

> **Interviewee 41**: That's another example of my psychology or my analytical skills, that I am good at reading the other person. And that means that I have a chance to overcome blockades and to find creative approaches to convince others.
> **Interviewer**: And how exactly would you describe this reading of others?

Interviewee 41: I believe that I am very, very good at gauging other people. Where that ability comes from, I'm not sure. It's not something that I have consciously learned.

In many cases it is a matter of recognizing an interlocutor's fears, probing them, and finding the right approach to dealing with them, as the following interviewee emphasizes:

Interviewee 5: I basically try to put myself in their shoes. Fear often plays a significant role, so I need to understand their fears, address them, and dispel any doubts. Those are the basic rules. The basic rule is to put yourself in your partner's position, isn't it? Gauging them correctly. And body language is really important. How is my partner sitting, what does his posture tell me, and even how am I acting myself?

Another interviewee went as far as to state that understanding a client's problems is even more important than being able to offer ready-made solutions to their problems:

Interviewee 8: I think that in the service sector it is extremely important, for the following reason – you have to win your client's trust, don't you? And winning their trust means understanding your client and understanding their problems. And if you can offer your client a solution, well, that's just fantastic, isn't it? But I would say that you are already 60% of the way if you can say, "Let's see if we can't find a solution for you." That, I think, is extremely important and gives the client the feeling that you understand him, you understand his problems, and you are committed to finding a solution.

One of the greatest challenges for property developers is dealing with planning authorities, whose permits are essential for their work. This requires a great deal of empathy, which developers can find psychologically draining. This developer emphasizes how important it is to truly understand your negotiating partner's "different way of thinking":

Interviewee 25: Because of how I was socialized, I would say everything comes under the heading of "empathy". Empathy for the person sitting across the table from you. Understanding his interests, fears, and the things that are important to him. That means really putting yourself in his shoes, seeing things from his perspective. "What is he thinking right now, what is his motivation?" Or, for example, why is he objecting to the plans to build something next door to his property? Sometimes there is just no chance of finding a mutually acceptable solution because you are talking about totally divergent interests. But sometimes it is more a question of vague fears or preconceptions, or an argument that hasn't really been thought all the way through. And, in many cases, you can bring them onside and manage to defuse it to some extent.

Especially in dealings with officials, he stressed that it is crucial to understand their perspectives and working methods – although he added that he now often sends employees to deal with the authorities first because they cope with it better:

Interviewee 25: Many of my industry colleagues have no feeling for how the public sector is organized. They think that everything is organized in the same way as within their own companies. But that is not the case at all, public authorities work very differently. They administer laws and regulations. They have a fundamentally different way of thinking. And once you understand that, then you can find a way to bring them onside. Still, there are a number of officials who are, let's say, stubborn and stuck in their ways, and you have to really think about how best to approach them.
Interviewer: There is a saying, "Understanding everything means forgiving everything." To a certain extent you are saying, "Once I can understand, then..." But what do you do when you are confronted by someone you can't understand, where you would say, "What kind of an idiot have I got here?" [...]
Interviewee 25: I have come to recognize my personal limits in such cases. Almost masochistically I used to accept everything. To the extent that I almost developed a stomach ulcer. I don't do that anymore. I know my limits.
Interviewer: Do you ask someone else to take care of it for you?
Interviewee 25: In some cases, once I realize what kind of person I am dealing with, I delegate the job to one of my employees. Otherwise I would end up blowing my top. I would just come out with it and say, "Hey, you total idiot, I've had enough now." Of course, you can't do that.

As some interviewees stressed, in many cases the objective level is only the surface of the sales process. This investment banker explained how he was able to land a contract worth USD 150 million because he had spoken with his client about one of his hobbies, building trust and creating a sense of shared interests:

Interviewee 42: There is one point. When you have a project, a stock, or a company that someone wants to sell, in my experience every person you are dealing with has a point, a button, that you need to push in order to close the deal. And you have to work out what that button is. You can't do that by talking a lot; you have to listen a lot. That is fundamentally the crucial point. It is only once I am able to find out more about my counterpart that I can start to imagine what that button might be. I can remember, when I was in New York, there was a big IPO that we were involved in. It concerned a Real Estate Investment Trust, shares in a massive shopping centre. And we had this fund manager in Luxembourg and I spent a lot of time talking with him, inviting him to roadshows, but he was always so closed off, like a firmly closed clam shell. And then, during one telephone call, we started to talk about World War II airplanes. Now, I had been very close to my grandparents, spent a lot of time with them when I was younger, and my grandfather had flown planes during the war. So I knew all about the planes, Messerschmitts, Heinkels, all the different models. Anyway, during the telephone call it became obvious that my counterpart was also really interested in World War II planes and we ended up talking about planes for more than an hour. The very next day, if I remember correctly, he placed an order for USD 150 million worth of stocks for the IPO. That was the point at which he knew, "I'm dealing with someone special here, I enjoy talking with him and I trust him." Because we shared a passion. It was actually quite mundane. We were suddenly on the same wavelength, and he was convinced and bought the stocks. [...] Ultimately it is all about the fact that we want recognition or harmony, particularly in the things that are important to us and to the people we are dealing with. Having these shared interests or commonalities and developing them, that's what creates mutual sympathy and is an important factor in getting certain points across to whoever you are dealing with.

Alongside empathy, many interviewees also mentioned didactic skills as having a significant importance. One extremely successful entrepreneur from the financial services sector stresses that, in addition to empathy, he is also "good at explaining" and is able to speak using simple images:

Interviewee 44: So, first of all, that I am good at seeing things from another person's perspective, understanding their motivations and goals. That I am extremely polite and courteous. That I spend a great deal of time listening and that I am able to explain things in simple terms, in simple images. I am good at explaining things illustratively, relating things to everyday situations that everyone can understand immediately. Negotiations have never failed because my counterpart hasn't been able to understand something that I have explained to them. I always describe and translate things in vivid terms, and it has always worked. I am good at explaining.

Another interviewee reported how, with his talent for getting to the crux of the matter and explaining things clearly, it only took him three minutes to convince a manager of one of the largest investment funds in London to invest EUR 50 million in his stocks:

Interviewer: So spontaneously, if you had to say what percentage of your financial success is due to your sales skills, what would you say?
Interviewee 31: I would say that 70% is due to my ability to convince other people of the value of my ideas.
Interviewer: And how do you do that? What is it in particular that makes you so persuasive? After all, everyone has their own approach.
Interviewee 31: [...] When people ask me that, I always tell them the story of when I was at one of the largest investment funds in London. I was incredibly well prepared, I had a 30-page prospectus all ready. You know how it is. A man came in, he was young enough to be my son, and he said to me, "Right, you've got three minutes to explain to me why I should buy your stocks." So, spontaneously, I had to abandon my 30-page presentation and decide in a matter of seconds, what do I say to him? And, once the three minutes were up, he said, "Thank you. We're going to invest EUR 50 million." I think that shows that I have marketing skills, if that's what you'd call it nowadays. I would just say that I used my powers of persuasion to convince him, to make it clear to him, that in this specific situation it would be a good idea to buy these stocks.

The interviewees differ in their opinions on the importance of expert knowledge in sales success. One entrepreneur insists that specialist knowledge merely plays a subordinate role, while emotional factors are far more important:

Interviewee 27: Of course, it's impossible to assess my own sales skills with 100% certainty, but I would say that, given the way deals are made in my industry, the fact that I am a good salesman is one of the most important aspects. [...] Someone once said to me, and I have heard this a lot, that I am the kind of person that people want to do business with.

When you are enthusiastic about what you are doing, and can communicate that enthusiasm because you completely believe in what you are doing and the way you are doing it. If you can break away from what everyone else in the industry is doing, do things that your clients do not expect, and if that comes across as authentic, then you can say that you are a good salesman.

Nevertheless, a majority of interviewees made it clear that, particularly in relation to complex products and services, expert knowledge is indispensable. One of the richest interviewees explained that, on a scale of 0 to 10, he would rate the importance of his sales skills for his success with a 10. In contrast to a number of other interviewees, he attributes the greatest importance to expert knowledge. Superior specialized knowledge is one advantage that family business entrepreneurs have over managers of stock market corporations:

Interviewer: So you are saying that sales skills play the key role?
Interviewee 26: Yes, that's right.
Interviewer: Okay, so could you expand on that a little for me? What does that mean to you personally?
Interviewee 26: First you have to understand that we had a broad range of products. Sometimes, when I was visiting a major customer, I didn't know what I was going to sell him, but I always left having sold something. That means you have to have a deep understanding of your products and what you have to offer. So, when you have a high-flyer, someone who switches industries every two years, there's no way they can have that deep understanding.
Interviewer: So you would say that specialized knowledge is important in sales?
Interviewee 26: Very, very important. Why are family businesses better than major corporations? Because the owners of family businesses possess all of the specialized knowledge. And the others? They jump ship, switch companies. I always say that when it comes to major corporations you can be sure that after two years you won't be dealing with the same person. If he's good, he will have been promoted. If he isn't, he will have been fired. In either case, he's not there anymore, is he?

Successful sales processes begin with the successful acquisition of clients. The decisive factor in client acquisition is networking, a point made by several interviewees. The following interviewee credits his professional success to the network he was able to establish. He reported that, between the ages of 30 and 45, he was out and about every single night, building and expanding his network:

Interviewee 17: And then it comes down to an incredible amount of hard work and commitment. As I tell my young partners, when I look back at my own situation, coming as I did from a large family that placed a high value on education, but had no form of entrepreneurial network, I had to work incredibly hard to create an extensive network for myself. And that meant that between the ages of 30 and 45 I was out and about every single night.
Interviewer: And where did you go?
Interviewee 17: Anywhere and everywhere. To whatever event happened to be on. I remember myself as a young man, hardly knowing anyone, going to these boring events where there were 300 people and I only knew two of them. And five years later you go to the same event and you know 50 people there. At some point the network functions on its own and you don't really need to do anything and people contact you automatically. It takes a lot of hard work and effort, that's what I tell younger people. Anyway, there are lots of different ways to acquire customers. It could be at some industry event, or it could be at the Rotary Club, it could be in a jogging group, playing golf or tennis. Wherever. [...] The only place you can't acquire customers is at home. And of course, going to Sylt or Saint Tropez on holiday is much better than going camping in Mecklenburg-Western Pomerania.[694] You're not likely to find many clients there. No, but what I always say is this: it doesn't matter what you do, the main thing is that you do something relevant. And the bowling club in [downmarket area] won't be as good as the golf club in [upmarket area].

Knowing the right people is certainly a crucial factor in achieving financial success, but the interviewees worked very hard and single-mindedly to build the necessary networks. One interviewee, who believes that he owes 70% of his success to his sales skills, explained his approach to networking:

Interviewer: Personally, what would you say is the secret of networking, the most important aspect? Or maybe you could provide a specific example of how you made a business contact, one that might have been quite difficult to make?
Interviewee 12: Networking: of course, it is important that you actually have something to offer. Then it's important to find a way to approach people as an equal. I know that, as a student, it's difficult to say, "Okay, I'm going to invite xxx out to dinner." But for people to be interested in what you have to say, and for you to be interested in what they have to say...
Interviewer: So do you plan what you are going to say, think about what you have to offer?

Interviewee 12: Exactly, that's exactly what I do. Think about appropriate topics for conversation, things that interest both parties. One thing that I personally can't stand is when someone meets me and immediately wants to pick my brains, when they start off by saying, "Give me a real estate tip, give me this or that." After a minute or two I say, "Why are we actually meeting here?" And he says, "Because I want to learn about real estate from you." But, as I have said, what do I get out of that?

Interviewer: It can't be a one-way street.

Interviewee 12: And that's how you have to approach networking. That is, in my opinion, extremely important, that you always play the ball back, you know?

Interviewer: Can you give me an example of how you won someone over, where you would say, "You know what, I really got a kick out of that, that wasn't at all easy, or it was a particularly good contact"?

Interviewee 12: Of course, the contact I established with the chairman of the xxx bank. That was really important for me because they finance a lot of my projects.

Interviewer: And how did you gain him as a contact?

Interviewee 12: I initially got to know several people from the bank's middle management. And then, at other events I got to know xxx bank's spokesperson. And I put it to him plainly: "So, I have big plans and want to involve xxx bank." It was important to me that I talked to people at the highest level. So there was another situation where I had to be able to communicate with people as their equal. I know the path I want to take, the amount I want to invest, and I want to discuss that at the highest levels, you know? And that worked out. Of course, it created an uproar among the middle management. They knew that I was dealing directly with the chairman of the bank.

Interviewer: So you had achieved a different standing, hadn't you?

Interviewee 12: Yes, yes I had. And not just with them. With banks, it is always important, and the same goes for business contacts. I think that I would describe myself as canny and street smart. I am a very quick learner.

Interviewer: And can you maybe give me an example, a situation where that was very clear?

Interviewee 12: Yes, I was attending an event. And I realized, "Okay, there is the secretary from the company," so I went over to them and spoke to them,

---

694 The interviewee is contrasting the wealth and glamour of St Tropez or the German island of Sylt with Mecklenburg-Western Pomerania, a relatively deprived and sparsely populated region in eastern Germany, which has become popular among campers and lower-income holidaymakers.

and I looked to make sure that the boss of the company was getting the feeling that I was on familiar terms with his company, and then the secretary introduced me to him. So I'm always observing everything that is going on around me. And I always think a great deal about the steps that I am taking. It's never as if I stand there and say to myself, "Let's see. Maybe you'll be lucky." No, I always hold my luck in my own two hands.

When asked whether he enjoyed networking, an interviewee from the real estate industry responded that what he most enjoyed was shaking 5,000 hands at the real estate trade fair Expo Real. "Above all, you have to enjoy people, enjoy meeting them, finding out about them and somehow win them over":

> **Interviewee 5**: Expo Real is absolutely massive. Shaking 5,000 hands and then spending the evenings at three cocktail parties. I could spend five more days at Expo Real if I were physically up to it and didn't have to catch up with all of my work afterwards. It's incredible, the best.
> **Interviewer**: And what is your secret? Can you tell me about the secret of successful networking, how you make contact with the really big figures, the ones you can talk about really big things with?
> **Interviewee 5**: You need the right techniques, you have to be able to present yourself reasonably well. I would say that the first basic principle is that you have to like people, you know? Only someone who likes people is able to lead people, although, of course I don't lead my acquisition partners. Above all, you have to enjoy people, enjoy meeting them, finding out about them and somehow win them over. That has to be something you really enjoy and then you can make it to the top.

The network is just the first step towards success in sales. To refer back to the point made at the beginning of this chapter, as a salesperson is usually met with an excess of people saying "no", it is important to recognize that the "law of large numbers" is the foundation of successful sales. The next interviewee, who credits 100% of his financial success to his sales talents, illustrates this fact as follows:

> **Interviewee 19**: There's something Casanova said about the law of big numbers, at least I believe it comes from him. Like this, "I don't know what it is with you and women, why you don't have girlfriends, but I have a good success rate. If I approach ten women on the street, I end up in bed with one of them the next day, and that's good enough for me."

The following interviewee, who ascribed 98% of his success to his abilities as a salesman, has always kept statistics on his sales success rates:

Interviewee 40: That's something that, as a good salesman, I have always done. Every day I looked back at the ten doors I made it through and tallied that against my results. [...]
Interviewer: Do you still keep your own statistics?
Interviewee 40: Yes, but just for me. I can print out all of the sales appointments I had. After all, we are always selling. Even now, I'm always selling the company. I always keep statistics, keep track of all my appointments, am always selling. But there are people that I don't want to do business with, so I don't sell to them, don't even want them to be impressed by me. But that's a decision I make for myself. But with everyone else, I'm successful at closing deals. When I look back through my diary, I see that they are all coming back to me. As soon as they get back from our meetings, they always write, "It was great, we've got to do something together."

INTERIM FINDINGS

The ability to sell, which Werner Sombart defines as an attribute of the 'trader' and as one of the most important entrepreneurial skills, has been underestimated as a success factor in recent entrepreneurial and academic wealth research. Few other points elicited as unanimous a response from the interviewees – irrespective of the industries they are involved in – as this, that the ability to sell has made a key contribution to their financial success. As shown in Section 9.6, many of them started gaining extensive sales experience at an early age.

Two thirds of the interviewees stated that the ability to sell successfully had made a decisive contribution to their success. More than 30% even credited between 70% and 100% of their success to their talents as salespeople. And this is despite the fact that, at least at first glance, many of the interviewees do not fit the stereotype of salespeople – which is actually one of the secrets of their success in sales. The negative traits that have come to be widely associated with the terms 'sales' and 'salespeople' were not among the associations provided by the interviewees. To the interviewees, sales is about much more than simply marketing a process, product, or service. They define sales far more extensively as just the process of convincing other people – i.e. convincing a public official to grant approval for a real estate development, or convincing a top applicant to join the company, or convincing one's employees to share one's vision, or convincing a banker to approve a loan. "Everything is sales," explained one interviewee.

The "no" that is often encountered at the beginning of a sales process is in no way regarded as a negative by these interviewees. Many explained that turning this "no" into a "yes" gives them their greatest pleasure. To do so, a great deal of empathy is required, a fact that was emphasized by many of the interviewees. They stressed the importance of the ability to "read" people, to gain an intuitive understanding of their fears, blockades, and objections in order to dispel them. Several interviewees described themselves as particularly sensitive or as good psychologists.

In addition to empathy, specialized knowledge is also of great importance, although this needs to be combined with a healthy dose of didactic skills. Interviewees frequently mentioned "being able to explain things clearly" as a crucial ability in successful sales. The importance of networking was also repeatedly emphasized. Interviewees described how, with diligence, commitment, perseverance, and single-mindedness, they established the networks that would create the basis for their financial success.

Optimism and
Self-efficacy   14

Optimism has been the subject of intensive research in both entrepreneurship research and behavioural economics. Optimism and over-optimism are widespread phenomena, and Daniel Kahneman even rates them as the most significant cognitive bias.[695] If they were not optimistic by nature, it is likely that a majority of entrepreneurs would never have gone into business for themselves in the first place. Mathew L. A. Hayward, Dean A. Shepherd, and Dale Griffin proposed that over-optimism helps us to understand why people start companies despite the high likelihood of failure.[696]

For this reason, optimism and over-optimism played an important role during the interviews. Interviewees were asked: "If you had to rate yourself on a pessimism–optimism scale (-5 = extreme pessimist and +5 = extreme optimist), where would you place yourself, and what is your personal understanding of optimism?" Respondents who rated themselves as being extremely optimistic were then asked the following supplementary question: "Optimism is an important characteristic for entrepreneurs and investors, but some would suggest that too much optimism, particularly in the midst of difficult circumstances, can be a dangerous thing. Looking back on your own life and career, have there been any situations where you would now say that your optimism was not necessarily helpful?"

The interviewees' self-assessments revealed a high degree of optimism. Of 40 interviewees, 35 placed themselves in the extremely optimistic range (from +3 to +5).

---

695   Kahneman, *Thinking*, 315.
696   Hayward, Shepherd, and Griffin, "A Hubris Theory of Entrepreneurship," 169.

INTERVIEWEES' SELF-RANKINGS ON A SCALE FROM −5 (EXTREMELY PESSIMISTIC) TO +5 (EXTREMELY OPTIMISTIC)

1: A total optimist	24: +4
2: –	25: +3
3: –	26: +3
4: –	27: +5
5: +3	28: Used to be +4, today −1
6: +4.5	29: +5
7: +4.5	30: +4.5
8: +1	31: +5
9: +3.5	32: +5
10: –	33: +3
11: +3 or +5 (others' perceptions)	34: +3
12: Investment 0, private +5	35: +4
13: +3.5	36: +3.5
14: +5	37: +5
15: +5	38: +3
16: +3	39: −1
17: +4	40: +5
18: +3	41: (Negative range according to
19: +5	Big Five Test)
20: +4	42: +4
21: –	43: +2.5
22: +2.5	44: +5
23: "At least +4"	45: +4

Positive range (+1 to +5): 37 of 40 interviewees
+3 to +5 (very optimistic): 35 of 40 interviewees
Neutral range (= 0): 0 of 40 interviewees
Negative range (−1 to −5): 2 of 40 interviewees

It could be argued that high levels of optimism are not a preserve of the wealthy and that there are, generally, far more optimists than pessimists. Surveys carried out by the Allensbach Institute for Public Opinion Research (AIPOR) between 1992 and 2007 do report that between 51% and 57% of Germans describe themselves as optimists.[697] Nevertheless, among the UHNWIs interviewed for this book, the proportion of optimists was far higher, namely 95%. More striking still is the fact that more than 87% of the interviewees placed themselves in the range of extreme optimism (+3 to +5).

The results of the Big Five personality test also reveal a clear dominance of high optimism. None of the other 50 questions were answered with the same degree of unanimity as those relating to optimism/pessimism. The statement "I see myself as someone who tends towards pessimism" was categorically rejected by 38 of the 43 interviewees – i.e. they see themselves as optimists. A further three rejected the statement with certain qualifications, which means they are also optimists. Only two registered partial agreement and saw themselves as more pessimistic. As such personality traits remain relatively constant, it is likely that these wealthy individuals have not become optimists as a consequence of their success, but that they have possessed this characteristic since they were young.

It is important to point out that, for these interviewees, optimism has nothing to do with a general cheerful demeanour. This was made clear in their responses to the statement "Others would certainly describe me as a cheerful person." Only 10 of 43 interviewees agreed unreservedly with this statement, and a further 12 agreed with some reservations. The number of interviewees who either were undecided or disagreed roughly equalled the number of those who expressed agreement.

Many of the interviewees asserted that being an entrepreneur and a pessimist are mutually exclusive. When asked to rate his own levels of optimism, and to comment on the ratings others would give him, one stock and real estate investor answered thus:

Interviewer: The absolute pessimist is –5. And the extreme optimist is +5. How would you assess yourself?

Interviewee 31: Well, if you were to ask my friends, then I'd be at +5, because they view me as the archetypal professional optimist. But I have always felt that you can only be an entrepreneur if you are an optimist. I mean, being a pessimist and an entrepreneur just won't work.

14.1. "AS A RESULT OF YOUR OWN ABILITIES, YOU ARE ALWAYS ABLE TO IDENTIFY SOLUTIONS"

During the interviews it soon became apparent that what UHNWIs mean when they use the term 'optimism' is identical to what psychologists refer to as 'self-efficacy'. Self-efficacy describes the extent or strength of a person's belief in their own abilities to master certain, even extremely challenging, situations. The spectrum is bookmarked by the beliefs "We're confident that we can do it" (high self-efficacy) and "We perceive ourselves as incapable of doing it" (low self-efficacy).[698]

---

697   Institut für Demoskopie, Allensbach, Germany, AIPOR surveys 4070, 5062, 6042, 6052, 7092, 7098, and 10002.

698   Cervone and Pervin, *Personality*, 438.

The concept of self-efficacy possesses a far greater explanatory power than other previously tested and researched personality traits. Numerous empirical studies demonstrate, as has been outlined in Section 3.2.c, that successful entrepreneurs register higher scores for self-efficacy than other people.

An interviewee from the finance sector, who rated himself with a "strong 4" on the optimism scale, explained what he meant by optimism. For him, optimism means believing that "as a result of your own abilities, or the network you have built, or your intellect, you are always able to identify solutions and to overcome any challenge." This is exactly what is defined as self-efficacy:

> **Interviewee 42**: Ultimately, what I mean by optimism is that you always believe that the glass is half full, and that you always find a way to face forwards, even in negative situations. So, with an awareness of risk, believing in the positive things. And, basically, that as a result of your own abilities, or the network you have built, or your intellect, you are always able to identify solutions and to overcome any challenge.

A highly successful real estate investor, who rated himself at +2 to +3 on the optimism scale, stressed that optimism in no way means seeing everything positively; rather it is far more a question of believing in your own ability to overcome problems. He sees optimism as "self-confidence in one's own actions", again a textbook description of self-efficacy:

> **Interviewee 22**: No, optimism is basically the feeling that you will always emerge positively from whatever situation you have got yourself involved in. That you will always come up with an idea, a solution, that will enable you to master a specific situation. When I think of optimism, I don't mean that the sun will always shine on me, you know? I also mean that I will somehow be able to provide my own warmth from within. So optimism is also related to self-confidence in one's own actions, isn't it? And not just believing that all good things will come to me, that there will be no obstacles, that the wind will always be in my sails. That's not what I would describe as optimism.

Another investment banker and real estate investor defined optimism as the belief in your own "ability to shape things" and problem-solving competence. He is convinced that he can always solve between six and eight of any ten problems – and it is this fundamental conviction that he calls optimism. He places himself between +2 and +3 on the optimism scale:

Interviewee 43: Yes, optimism [is believing] in my own ability to shape things. I always have options, so when I am confronted by ten problems, I know I can solve eight of them. I know that I will never be able to solve all ten, but that I will be able to solve seven or eight. And if I have ten negotiations, where I'm not so sure of the end results, I know that we will be able to steer six or seven of them in the right direction. That, to me, is optimism.

One of the interviewees admitted that, in his industry, he is perceived as "sceptical and in some ways less than optimistic" in relation to general developments across the market. But "for me personally, I am always optimistic because I always have the feeling that there will be a way" (Interviewee 6). He assessed himself as being between a +4 and a +5 on the optimism scale. As he sees it, optimism does not mean viewing the world around him through rose-tinted spectacles; it means having the confidence to believe that, even in difficult market conditions, he will find a way through. A different interviewee expressed the same thoughts as follows:

Interviewee 4: Yes, I see positive opportunities in every situation. Even if everything is collapsing and breaking down, I can relatively quickly learn from the situation. Yes, I recognize opportunities immediately.

An entrepreneur from the IT industry admitted that it may not always be rational to view things positively or optimistically, but that this "confidence in yourself" is a fundamental prerequisite for entrepreneurialism:

Interviewee 33: It might not be rational, but this confidence in yourself, I do believe that it is a fundamental requirement. [...] I suppose that, ultimately, it is also an element of entrepreneurship, that you approach things with a positive attitude.

14.2. "I NEVER COMPLAIN ABOUT PROBLEMS, I LOOK FOR SOLUTIONS"

In the opinion of the interviewees, optimism is required as a corrective to what they see as widespread pessimism. One entrepreneur, who rated himself as +5 on the optimism scale, explained that there are always so many "naysayers" around that you do not stand a chance unless you adopt a fundamentally optimistic attitude to counteract their cynicism:

Interviewee 29: You need optimism as an entrepreneur, and the more you have, the better, because you will always encounter people who say, "No, there's no way that will work." People who are always trying to stop you from doing something. And then you add the market conditions to the mix, the general market situation. There are so many factors that basically make an investment or business idea inadvisable. And if you are not optimistic, in your own personal nirvana, then I don't think you can be so successful as an entrepreneur. [...] That, unfortunately, is one of the greatest obstacles we have in our society, that we have so many naysayers all around us, who just want to bludgeon us into submission, so that we have no chance, you know? If you don't approach things with a certain degree of optimism, you don't stand a chance. I'm not talking about investments where you can clearly say, this would be a mistake, those you should steer clear of. But if you made a mistake, you need to have the optimism to say, "Okay, this is where I get out. I might have lost 50% of my stake, but I've learned a valuable lesson, and that is a good thing."

An entrepreneur who has enjoyed substantial success in the field of medical technology also views optimism as a necessary corrective against "all these blabbermouths who keep going on about what doesn't work". He believes that optimists devote their time to finding solutions to problems, as opposed to wasting time complaining about them:

Interviewee 23: I am an optimist.
Interviewer: So a pessimist is –5, an optimist is +5.
Interviewee 23: Okay, then I would say I am at least a +4. [...] And I love dealing with opportunities and challenges. I never complain about problems, I look for solutions, and always positive solutions. I simply cannot stand it, all these blabbermouths who keep going on about what doesn't work. They should just get on with the job they're paid to do, which is finding solutions to problems, trying to develop fresh perspectives. No, I am fundamentally positive. I don't complain about anything.

Another entrepreneur, who also rated himself at +4 on the optimism scale, believes that pessimists place obstacles in their own way. To him, optimism means concentrating on what is "doable" rather than devoting time to every factor that may make something "impossible". When asked how he would define optimism, he replied:

Interviewee 45: That in every situation I concentrate on what is doable rather than focusing on the factors that might make something impossible. The classic pessimist places obstacles in his own way.

Interviewer: How so?

Interviewee 45: With the basic attitude that something will never work. My approach, I analyse the whole situation and, when I think that it could work, then it does work. It has to work.

The interviewees associate optimism with a forwards-looking attitude, which means focusing on the opportunities of tomorrow rather than looking back at past problems. This is how an UHNWI from the finance industry, who rated himself as a "full 5.5 with an extra star on top" on the optimism scale, put it:

Interviewee 44: No, my optimism has always been "carry on, it will all work out somehow".

Interviewer: And where does this conviction come from, your belief that it will all work out in the end?

Interviewee 44: It's because I never look backwards. I have never spent long being annoyed by mistakes. I just say, "Fine. Then we're here instead of there, but where do we go from here?" I always look forwards. My optimism is looking forwards and thinking about the opportunities that will come, rather than focusing on yesterday's problems.

Other interviewees stressed the importance of another aspect. Optimism is required if you are to inspire your employees. In a difficult situation, a leader needs to be able to project self-confidence and infect others with a positive perspective, which is another reason why optimism is rated as such an important quality. On the scale from −5 to +5, the next interviewee jokingly rated his optimism with a "+8":

Interviewee 37: It's important to want to inspire people. Others only want to talk people into the ground, talk them down. No one is successful unless they really get behind the things they are doing. And that means that you have to believe in what you are doing. You know what? We all have problems.

Another interviewee, who awarded herself +5 on the optimism scale ("I am an optimist. A total optimist."), explained that optimism is important in order to "motivate employees. I have to infect them with my optimism."

14.3. "HE'S DRUNK ON HIS OWN SUCCESS"

As detailed in Section 4.2, entrepreneurship research and behavioural economics have strongly cautioned against the consequences of optimism and over-optimism. The interviewees were confronted with these warnings and asked whether they shared the opinion that optimism can, at times, be dangerous. As a majority of the interviewees – as demonstrated above – do not understand optimism in the sense of always seeing the positive in every situation, but rather in the sense of having confidence in their own problem-solving abilities, they tended not to recognize the potentially negative consequences of over-optimism.

An interviewee from the finance industry classed himself as "an optimist through and through", but also acknowledged that this was his weakness, explaining that it had been a mistake to assume the economic upswings of the 1970s, 1980s, and 1990s would continue indefinitely:

> **Interviewer**: I have seen that optimism can be damaging for some...
> **Interviewee 1**: It can do that to all of us, because you overestimate yourself, expand too quickly. But when I was younger, I never thought that things could go downhill, I thought there were only ever upsides. I'm an optimist through and through. That's my weakness.
> **Interviewer**: In what way is that a weakness?
> **Interviewee 1**: Well, because economic upswings can't go on forever [...] In our generation there was almost always only growth. You need to remember that between 1973 and, let's say, 2003, things only ever got better, or at least until 2000. After German reunification everything picked up again. Until the end of the 1990s, there was constant growth, all the way through to 2000 or 2002. Then we had the crises.

Another interviewee, who has also been extremely successful in the finance industry, rated himself a +4 on the optimism scale, but also admitted that too much optimism can be a dangerous thing if it leads to someone over-estimating themselves:

> **Interviewee 7**: There are those sayings, "He's drunk on his own success" and "He thinks he can walk on water." There was that Mr. Flowers, who bought banks left right and centre, do you remember? And then everything turned sour and he was wiped out. There are situations where you start to make mistakes because you think you are invincible and indestructible, and that's when you start to make mistakes.

A number of the interviewees, who are very optimistic, have developed methods to suppress their optimism when they need to, especially when they are involved in making decisions with partners who are less optimistic by nature. A property developer, who makes all of his business decisions in collaboration with a partner, said:

> **Interviewee 3**: I am basically much more positive than my business partner, who is always far more cautious and tends to see the glass as half empty, never as half full.
>
> **Interviewer**: But isn't it a good thing if one partner wants to go full throttle and the other partner wants to step on the brake?
>
> **Interviewee 3**: Yes, of course. [...] Although I always approach things with sound judgement; I'm not reckless. I'm not someone who says, "Right, I don't care. I want to see how the chips fall." No, it's always very, very carefully planned and we are always trying to do only the best with our products. But I guess every entrepreneur would probably say that.
>
> **Interviewer**: Isn't it still a good thing that your partner is a bit of a corrective influence?
>
> **Interviewee 3:** Of course. There was something that the boss of xxx said that I thought was really good. He was once asked, "Why is xxx so successful?" And he said, "Because we say 'no' more often than our competitors."

Another interviewee, who awarded himself a +3 on the optimism scale, believes in talking with others in order to "have a corrective influence":

> **Interviewee 5**: I am basically a team player. Always in partnerships, as a rule. There are a huge range of subjects I talk to other people about, even if I have to make a decision by myself; I always have someone at my side who I can explain things to, to have a corrective influence. I don't really like making decisions on my own. I'll make the decision for myself, but I like to hear other opinions.

One interviewee, who also rated his optimism with a +3, reported how, as a result of negative experiences, he has created an environment around himself that protects him from the negative consequences of over-optimism:

> **Interviewee 16**: Anyone [who is around 50] years of age and is in a position where he has not yet understood, who has not already lost a great deal as a result of it. [...] But I have created an environment that keeps me from over-optimism. So, for example, I set up structures with the supervisory board

and with chairmen and joint chairmen and voting rights, where I consciously say, "I'm here at the front. Where are you?" And where I even acquiesce and say, "So you don't think we should? Fine, then we won't. I would have, but you don't want to." It's a case of deliberately setting up mechanisms around yourself. My wife, let me tell you, is one of the most important anti-risk influences; she just says, "No, as your wife I don't want to be involved in that. I'm not prepared to accept that risk." And then I allow myself to be deterred by my wife, even though I, personally, would have gone ahead.

The dangers associated with optimism are lower within very large enterprises, as decisions are not generally made by single individuals. The co-owner of a very large, multi-national family business, who rated himself with a +4 on the optimism scale, gave the following response to the question of whether optimism could also be damaging:

> **Interviewee 24**: Optimism certainly needs to be kept in check, you're absolutely right.
> **Interviewer**: Yes, kept in check. But how can you keep it in check?
> **Interviewee 24**: Well, first of all, the brothers are quite different. This makes for a range of different opinions. [...] But the most important element is that we set a ground rule, that any really important decision has to be incredibly well prepared, as well prepared as possible. And we have some truly great people around us, including sales and marketing experts, and other departments, to help us prepare for any big decisions... [...] And what is the final step? The final step, the last 10% you need to make a decision, that's the tendency towards optimism, or away from optimism. But we have always been incredibly well prepared before we've made any major decisions. That doesn't mean that we were reluctant to take responsibility. No, we just always said, let's gather as much information as we can, prepare as well as we can, objectively. And let's not take five years to prepare; let's get it all done in the next eight weeks.

Very few of the interviewees were not generally optimistic. A successful investor from the private equity sector explained that he has become more pessimistic in response to a number of disappointments and negative experiences. On the scale from −5 to +5 for pessimism–optimism, he assessed himself thus: "Used to be +4, today −1."

Interviewee 28: Nowadays, I'm a −1; I've become more of a pessimist. And ten years ago, I would say I was probably a +4. Over the last few years, my optimism has decreased.

Interviewer: Interesting. How did that happen? That's really interesting.

Interviewee 28: It's a result of the disappointments I've experienced, in people, in partnerships, in collaborations. I've become very sceptical in everything. I'm no longer immediately enthusiastic for something, no longer chase straight after something. I've become very analytical. I start by asking myself ten questions to find out why something might not work or find out where the catch might be. I used to be less cautious and more optimistic.

Interviewer: Ah, okay. And if you had to compare the success that you've had as an entrepreneur over the years, let's take this as a thought experiment, if you had started out as a −1, would you have been so successful?

Interviewee 28: No. Pessimism ruins many opportunities, doesn't it?

Interviewer: But optimism can ruin many things too.

Interviewee 28: You're right, you have to find the right balance. And for me, I think that on a purely cognitive level so many negative experiences have stayed with me, and they outbalance the good experiences, even though there were fewer negative ones. I don't repress the negative experiences and tell myself that everything will work out perfectly. No, I know exactly what went wrong, that I didn't do enough research before I got involved in something. I try to compensate for my pessimistic attitude by doing research and asking questions, and by using my experience. But now, in my mid-60s, I'm just not willing to accept the same risks that I may have been willing to accept in my 30s.

The next example shows that even a high level of pessimism can contribute to long-term success. Property developers are among the companies with the most extreme risk–reward profiles within the real estate industry. Very few companies in the field have existed as long as this interviewee's company. Clearly, pessimism prevented this interviewee from exposing himself and his company to excessive risk. He assessed himself as a −1 on the pessimism–optimism scale:

Interviewer: I just have two more questions to finish off with. Let's take another scale, optimism–pessimism. On this scale, pessimism is −5. That's the total pessimist. The total optimist is +5.

Interviewee 39: I'll answer your question in a slightly different way. Put half a glass of water on the table and I admit I will normally see that glass as half empty, not half full.

Interviewer: So, does that mean you tend more to the pessimistic end of the scale?

Interviewee 39: Yes.

Interviewer: I guess it has really helped you to survive so long.

Interviewee 39: That could well be. [...] When someone asks me, "Are things going well?", I always have a problem claiming that things are going well.

Interviewer: And this –5 to +5 scale, if you were to place yourself on the scale.

Interviewee 39: Then I'd probably say that I am a –1.

Interviewer: –1? I'd probably agree. I also believe that it's benefited you. That's probably what has helped you survive so long. That's my perspective, as an outsider.

Interviewee 39: Yes, yes. Definitely.

INTERIM FINDINGS

Entrepreneurship researchers and behavioural economists have both focused intensively on the subject of optimism and over-optimism. The interviews with wealthy entrepreneurs and investors provided clear confirmation of the hypothesis that entrepreneurs are overwhelmingly optimistic. Among the interview questions, there was no other characteristic that united almost all of the interviewees to the same extent as the self-assessments that revealed that they are especially optimistic. On a scale from −5 (extreme pessimist) to +5 (extreme optimist), 38 of 40 interviewees placed themselves in the positive range, classifying themselves as optimists. Of these, 35 went as far as to place themselves in the very optimistic range (from +3 to +5). The Big Five personality test also revealed high levels of optimism. Again, none of the 50 questions prompted such unified responses as the question on optimism and pessimism. The statement "I see myself as more of a pessimist" was strongly rejected by 38 of the 43 interviewees.

During the interviews it became clear that the way in which the UHNWIs were using the word 'optimism' corresponded exactly with what psychologists have termed "self-efficacy". The term describes the extent or strength of a person's belief in their own abilities to master certain, even extremely challenging, situations. The interviewees defined optimism in their own words as the belief that "as a result of your own abilities or the network you have built, or your intellect, you are always able to identify solutions and to overcome anything". For them, optimism is "self-confidence in one's own actions" as well as "confidence in yourself" and in your own "organizational capabilities" and problem-solving competence. This confirms the findings of entrepreneurship and academic wealth research – namely, that high levels of self-efficacy are a significant characteristic of the personalities of entrepreneurs and the rich.

The interviewees also viewed optimism as an important corrective against "naysayers" who complain about problems instead of solving them. Optimism helps, particularly in difficult situations, to inspire employees and get them to buy into a shared vision.

Only a small number of the interviewees reflected on the problematic flipside of over-optimism. They recognized that an overly optimistic attitude can potentially lead to taking excessive risks. In this regard, a number of interviewees mentioned that they had established decision-making mechanisms to function as counterbalances – such as a partner who was generally less optimistic.

15 | Risk Propensity

Is an increased appetite for risk a precondition for above-average financial success? Academic research has adopted a number of different hypotheses in relation to the risk orientation and risk propensity of entrepreneurs and wealthy individuals:

- **Hypothesis No. 1: Entrepreneurs have a higher propensity for risk.** The Chicago School, represented by social scientists such as Frank H. Knight, defined the entrepreneur as primarily a risk taker.[699] The advocates of this school understand entrepreneurial thinking and action primarily in terms of the acceptance of risk.[700] Contemporary academic wealth research has also come to the conclusion that the chances of achieving great wealth increase with risk propensity. At the same time, these researchers have not confirmed an inverse, u-shaped correlation between risk and success.[701] This relates to the second theory proposed by researchers.

- **Hypothesis No. 2: Moderate risk propensity or a non-linear correlation between risk propensity and success.** This theory claims that successful entrepreneurs are characterized by a moderate propensity for risk-taking. Too little risk is not enough of a challenge for them, but they also avoid excessive risk. The assumption is that there is a non-linear correlation between risk propensity and success. Up to a certain point, risk propensity correlates positively with success, but beyond that point, a higher appetite for risk has negative effects.

- **Hypothesis No. 3: Subjective risk perception.** A further approach addresses the subjective perception of risk. This assumes that entrepreneurs do not view their own actions as risky, even if others would perceive them as such. Hisrich, Langan-Fox, and Grant point to studies demonstrating that entrepreneurs are not distinguished from non-entrepreneurs by their elevated risk propensity – rather the difference is found far more in their subjective perceptions of risk. This would mean that entrepreneurs are characterized by a lower risk *perception*, which creates the illusion of a higher risk *propensity*.[702]

15.1. THE RISK SCALE

During the interviews, the interviewees were asked to place themselves on a risk scale. The scale extended from −5 ("the civil servant who only buys treasury securities") to +5 (the extremely risk oriented). The neutral value was set as 0. In providing their answers, many interviewees distinguished between their appetites for risk when they were younger and those at a more advanced age – this will be explored further in Section 15.3. In such cases, where different values were provided (e.g. "I used to be a +5, today I'm a +2"), the earlier value was taken as this applies to the phase during which most of the interviewees created their wealth.

According to hypotheses 2 and 3, a majority of the interviewees should have placed themselves in the neutral range. After all, hypothesis 2 maintains that they have a moderate propensity for risk and avoid excessive risk. And hypothesis 3 asserts that, while entrepreneurs do accept high levels of risk, they do not perceive the risks as high. In actual fact, only 3 of the 45 interviewees placed themselves in the neutral range. Five placed themselves in the negative range (−1 to −5), which means they view themselves as prudent and safety-oriented. A substantial majority, namely 35 of 45, grouped themselves in the positive range. It was surprising to find that 25 of 45 interviewees even placed themselves at the highest end of the risk scale, between +3 and +5.

This represents a significant deviation from the population at large. In response to a question posed by the AIPOR, which asked whether respondents would prefer a modest lifestyle and security, or a life filled with significant financial opportunities but at high levels of risk, 77% of Germans said that they would prefer security and only 12% said that they were willing to accept higher levels of risk in order to achieve more ambitious financial goals.[703]

RISK ORIENTATION OF THE INTERVIEWEES
- **High risk orientation (+3 to +5): 25** of 45 interviewees
- **Positive range (+1 to +5): 35** of 45 interviewees
- **Neutral range (= 0): 3** of 45 interviewees
- **Negative range (−1 to −5): 5** of 45 interviewees.

---

699   See Lackner, *Voraussetzungen und Erfolgsfaktoren*, 18 et seq.

700   Ibid., 21.

701   Böwing-Schmalenbrock, *Wege zum Reichtum*, 229.

702   Hisrich, Langan-Fox, and Grant, "Entrepreneurship Research and Practice," 583.

703   Institut für Demoskopie Allensbach, AIPOR survey 11050.

While these results do not confirm hypotheses 2 and 3 above, there were some interviewees whose responses matched these hypotheses exactly. The difference between subjective risk perception and real risk propensity was made clear by a number of interviewees who explicitly stated that their self-assessments, namely as people who are far less willing to accept risk, would differ significantly from the assessments of those around them.

Contrarian investors, in particular, often perceive something as relatively safe, whereas others would describe the same thing as highly risky and, vice versa, something that others would describe as relatively safe, the contrarian investor would perceive as being loaded with risk. One interviewee described his investments as follows:

> **Interviewee 19**: Others viewed that as loaded with a huge amount of risk; they were saying, light industrial real estate in Berlin and so on, my goodness, does he have any idea what he is doing? The property tax on such huge buildings is more than the rental income. Things like that. But when I was buying real estate somewhere in Berlin for EUR 80 per square metre, based on the gross floor area, that wasn't something I viewed as in the least bit risky. Others thought it was risky, but not me..., I didn't even see a sliver of risk in what I was doing. I thought to myself, "You're the ones who are crazy. You're buying at price-to-rent ratios of 24, based on rents of EUR 180 per square metre, on Kurfürstendamm,[704] which I would never even dream of doing. I'm not drunk."

One interviewee, who operates in stocks and real estate, rated himself as "+1 to +2" while admitting that others would more likely rate him with +4. He explains this discrepancy as follows:

> **Interviewee 43**: That's a tough one. I'd probably say I am only a +1 to +2. Which might surprise you, that I don't give myself a higher score, but let me just explain: many of the risks that I take on, both in my career as well as with my investments, are very well considered risks, analysed risks, which means they are ultimately nowhere near as risky. I'm not a gambler. That's one point. And I think that the second point, and the skill of the whole business, is to accept the risks that you know you can bear and where you'll be suitably rewarded. By doing that, the actual risks become less risky. For example, if I have a really long investment horizon, then I can accept certain liquidity risks, such as with small caps on the stock market, or perhaps with bonds in distressed small- and medium-sized enterprises, or even with real estate, which you can only sell every three years anyway. When I do things like that, they might appear to be very risky, but they're not actually risky,

because I know the duration of my investment, and I know that I will be able to ride it out and that the cash flow you generate is so well risk-adjusted that it is not actually very risky. [...]

Interviewer: And others, how would they assess you?

Interviewee 43: They only ever see the results; they would likely rate me at +4. [...] As far as I see it, the classic entrepreneur accepts three risks. Firstly, his investments are concentrated in one thing, mostly 100% concentrated, not at all diversified. Secondly, his sole asset is totally illiquid, and his fortune is tied to that one asset. And thirdly, he is extremely highly leveraged. So, when I consider these three things for myself, yes, my investments are in a way very concentrated. On the one hand, almost my entire fortune, directly or indirectly, is invested in German real estate. On the other hand, my investments are widely diversified across a lot of different properties. And I would never have made many of these investments as stand-alone investments, only as part of a diversified portfolio. So I'd say, 50/50 between concentration and diversification. Secondly, of course my portfolio is illiquid, but nowhere near as illiquid as it might be for many other entrepreneurs. If I wanted to, I'm sure I could liquidate half of my portfolio within a year. Which is something. Of course, it's not very liquid, but still. And in terms of leverage, I'm only moderately leveraged.

Another interviewee explained that he views himself as moderately risk averse. On the risk scale, he rated himself with a -1. However, he also admitted that others view him as being extremely willing to accept risk and would rate him at $+3$:

Interviewer: Risk. Let's take a scale with -5 as the total safety fanatic, you know? And $+5$ is someone with a great appetite for risk. And if you had to place yourself on that scale, between -5 and $+5$?

Interviewee 27: So $+5$ is the risk junkie? I would personally place myself at -1. But you also have to think about the question, where would others place you? Then I would say $+3$.

Interviewer: And where does that discrepancy come from? [...]

Interviewee 27: Well probably... I'm not really sure. First of all, anyone who is an eventing rider, others will always say, "He's brave, not afraid, takes on lots of risk." To counter that, I always have the example of my really crazy brother. He's a total risk junkie. Whereas me, I have only ever done things when I've been confident that I have the abilities to do them successfully.

---

704   Kurfürstendamm is Berlin's most prestigious downtown shopping street, lined with prime retail and office space, the German equivalent of New York City's Fifth Avenue.

There's a massive difference between standing on top of a high mountain and believing that you'll get back down somehow, on the one hand. Or, on the other hand, practising three times in less mountainous areas and then saying, "Okay, now it's time for the steep mountain." And in the things I do, I always feel well prepared. The same applies to professional life. [...] Okay, today we have processes and people that are able to assess it all far better. And the risks, I can anticipate those after almost 2,000 completed projects, and they're not as great as you might imagine. Which means that I assess the risks differently to someone standing on the outside.

These last three interviewees could be presented as case studies by the advocates of hypothesis 3, so divergent are their subjective and outside risk perceptions.

A majority of the interviewees viewed the risks they accept as manageable. Very few consciously follow an 'all or nothing' strategy. In contrast to many other interviewees, the following interviewee described himself as being more safety oriented than risk oriented. He is not willing to accept risks that could knock him out completely. "I accept risks that are manageable":

Interviewee 22: You know, I try to position myself so that I'm in what I think to myself is a good position, if I can put it like that. That means that I would never put myself in a position where it's either all or nothing. Depending on how the unknown future unfolds, you know? That would be an extremely uncomfortable position for me. That's the position gamblers put themselves in. But I want to be in a position where, even with all the known unknowns, I'll still, at worst, have an okay result.
Interviewer: And now you have had a result that is much better than just an okay result, haven't you?
Interviewee 22: Sure, okay. And that can all be traced back to what I was saying about manageable risks. When I look at the alternatives, I dismiss those that look like they could lead to a total loss or total gain, because one is normally closely linked with the other. Of course, I also try to keep my options open as much as possible, and to keep the risks within manageable bounds. I'll say it once more, I do take on risk, but I prefer it to be the kind of risk that I believe I can manage.
Interviewer: You created a huge safety margin, but never had to use it in practice, which is why your results are so good. Would that be a good way to put it?
Interviewee 22: Yes, that is true to a certain extent, because the minimum that I aim for is a high probability, while at the same time ensuring that there's no upper limit to the pay-off. When everything works out well,

then you can stand back and let it work for itself, but at the same time I want to be sure that there is at least a minimum positive result that I can be relatively sure of.

In contrast to the interviewees cited above, a majority of the interviewees viewed themselves subjectively as extremely tolerant of risk. They often described this as a weakness, or spoke about phases in their lives when they had lost considerable amounts of money as a result of their elevated risk orientation. The following interviewee, who placed himself at +5 on the scale, made an extreme statement, emphasizing on numerous occasions during the interview, "I'm a gambler." "I bet on a card and fight to make sure that I win." And he continued: "My job is the game, you know? I place my bets and can never know how it will end, but I fight for it." But he would never set foot in a casino because he views his investments as his game, in particular his real estate investments:

Interviewee: There have been days when I've lost tens of millions, but I never let my emotions show. [...] I think the biggest loss I ever made was 50 million on one thing. [...] That was in real estate. But it didn't kill me. I was more bothered by the fact that I didn't win the game. [...] What people say about me is, "Bombs could be dropping everywhere, to the right and to the left, and he'd carry on as normal, he wouldn't even bat an eyelid [...] At most, he might take a handkerchief and wipe some of the dust away." [...] You fight for a year for something, or even two or three years. Of course that makes me nervous and stresses me out. But when I finally find out whether I've won or lost 50 million, it's more like when you're at school and you study really hard for something, take your exams and pass. On the day after your exams, everything is forgotten. The tension evaporates. I think I'm someone in the industry who has won and lost similarly big sums. You can only lose big money if you've previously earned big money. [...] It's just like in the Old Testament, "The Lord giveth and the Lord taketh away." You can't influence it. [...] But what I do believe is that people *think* and God *directs*. People *think* and God *laughs*. I have never previously experienced that you can accurately predict things. I have my opinions, and sometimes they are right, but I have to say that it's nothing more than speculation every time. [...] You know Dostoyevsky's *Gambler*. Sure, that's not the image I project. And I wouldn't want to tell my family this. But, ultimately, it's all a game.

The above interviewee's attitude was not typical, and most of the other interviewees would have rejected it out of hand. However, there were several who confessed to an extreme risk orientation. This tolerance of risk is often manifested in their decisions to abandon secure professional positions in favour of far riskier challenges:

> **Interviewer**: Could you tell me something about your relationship with risk? If you were asked to rate yourself on a scale from, say, –5 is the safety freak and +5 is the risk junkie, where do you see yourself?
>
> **Interviewee 7**: I'd give myself a minimum of +4.
>
> **Interviewer**: At least +4. And have you ever made a major economic decision where you would now say, sure that ended well, but the risks were actually far too great? Have you made any decisions like that?
>
> **Interviewee 7**: Sure, of course. When I quit at the xxx bank and went to xxx, that was one of those decisions. I was earning a large salary and gave up a senior management position with xxx bank, and right in the middle [of the crisis], which also hit us in 2001, we had [a company] that was in a really difficult market position.
>
> **Interviewer**: So that means, and this is always a crucial point, you were basically an employee, and what were you earning then, roughly?
>
> **Interviewee 7**: I'm not entirely sure, but it must have been around half a million.
>
> **Interviewer**: And you gave that up, your secure job.
>
> **Interviewee 7**: Yes, and my career at xxx bank...
>
> **Interviewer**: You could have made a good career for yourself there. [...]
>
> **Interviewee 7**: Yes, and all to move into an industry that I knew nothing about.
>
> **Interviewer**: Yes? But there must be a reason why you did it despite all of that?
>
> **Interviewee 7**: Sure, the challenge.

Several interviewees reported that they have a propensity for very high levels of risk in their private lives, for example pursuing extreme sports. This is the case for the next interviewee, who placed himself at +5 on the risk scale and even talked about an "addiction to high risks":

> **Interviewee**: I hate this safety-first mentality. I am convinced that we have a safety mania in Germany that is really holding us back. A totally over-the-top craving for safety.
>
> **Interviewer**: So does that mean that you don't mind, or even enjoy, a certain degree of entrepreneurial risk – naturally approaching risks consciously and in full awareness?

Interviewee: Yes. When I was younger I used to do a bit of auto racing, a bit of extreme skiing, beyond what people might normally do, you know? Let me tell you, I accepted extreme risk on a number of occasions. Unfortunately, someone even had a bad accident. Anyway, when I was younger I had a massive craving for risk, basically an addiction to high risks. And that prompted many discussions with my friends and family.

Interviewer: Was that just in terms of extreme sports? Or how did your addiction manifest itself?

Interviewee: For example, I climbed mountains in the Alps without any equipment, without any safety equipment, where you would normally need to use a rope, ice pick, and crampons. But that just drew me, almost magically. I had to climb, so I did. I got to the top. And I got back down alive too. But the groups that were on the mountain at the time, they just said, "He is totally crazy, he wants to kill himself." But it all worked out well. And when I was skiing I also came hurtling down channels. I got such a kick, doing things that I knew, if I made just one mistake, I could end up paying with my life. That awareness, it sharpens life, doesn't it? Getting closer and closer to risk. You've never concentrated on something so intensely in your life as when you take on that risk, that point that is purely in the now, on getting it right. And be a bit addicted to that, although everything you do is relative, isn't it?

Another entrepreneur also detailed his high appetite for risk in his private life. His mother even predicted that he would one day die an unnatural death. Clearly, this is not merely a personality trait that is expressed only in his business life:

Interviewee 1: I am quite tolerant of risk. Too tolerant sometimes for my friends. Even in my private life I have been known to accept relatively high levels of risk, and sometimes I've even fallen flat on my face, although, thank goodness, never too badly. But I'm definitely risk tolerant.

Interviewer: And what do you mean, in your private life?

Interviewee 1: [...] I dodged death about half a year ago, when a buffalo was trying to kill me. That's not something you need to have happen to you at my age. When I'm doing sports, or riding horses, I'm not always careful. My mother used to say that I would die an unnatural death. She's now dead, and I'm still here. I've never been regarded as particularly careful. And I'm not.

High levels of risk tolerance are associated with the self-confidence of knowing that you will be able to get back up onto your feet after a fall. One interviewee, who also described his readiness to accept high levels of risk, has frequently had to register his businesses as insolvent. Nevertheless, from the very beginning he has always had the attitude that he would be able to earn back his losses, because he knows "how to do that":

> **Interviewee 29**: That means that when you have never had the experience of being an employee you have also never known the fear of having something to lose, because you never had anything to lose to begin with. And on the other hand I have always said to myself, "Okay, if you lose everything you have, once it's gone, you can earn it back tomorrow because you know how to do that," you know?

15.2. THE ILLUSION OF CONTROL: "I'M IN THE DRIVER'S SEAT"

The interviewees were asked whether there were any discrepancies between their descriptions of their subjective risk propensity and their actual risk behaviour. One indication of this is the percentage of their own fortune that someone has tied up in their own company, and the extent to which this is perceived as risky. A number of interviewees had systematically built wealth independent of their own companies – in stocks and real estate, for example. Even if their businesses were to collapse, this would not lead to personal financial ruin. Highly safety-oriented entrepreneurs tend to distribute large sums as dividends, which they then invest in 'safe' assets, such as real estate.

This means, of course, that the growth opportunities of one's own company are more limited than in the alternative case, when an entrepreneur reinvests or retains a large proportion of their company's earnings. Several interviewees refrained from taking money out of their companies for long periods of time, reinvesting almost every cent of their profits, in order to finance expansion and growth. The result was that a large share of their wealth was tied up in their businesses.

Both of these strategies can be effective – namely, either distributing small sums as dividends or a more dividend-oriented strategy based on extracting profits in order to build wealth outside the company. In many cases, the strategy of reinvesting profits does lead to growth, but it is also linked to higher levels of risk.

One interviewee explained that he would place himself on the risk scale at 0. When asked how others might rate him, he confessed that his girlfriend would place him at +5. He confessed that his risk behaviour sometimes has the character of 'hara-kiri' or riding the razor's edge, because he has such high costs that he would not be able to fulfil his obligations if he suddenly lost a contract. He also accepted that it is a risk that 75% of his personal fortune is tied up in his business, the result of eight out of ten years in which he has "not taken a single cent out of the business" and has instead simply paid himself a fixed salary. He is currently considering selling the business because he views the 75% of his own money tied up in the company as too high a risk. In addition, he believes that the synergies he could achieve with a potential buyer would allow his business to grow at an even more accelerated pace. However, the view that it is a risk to have so much of his personal wealth based on the value of his company makes this interviewee an exception among the interviewees.

The majority of the interviewees did not share this view. They were asked whether they viewed it as a risk when large proportions of their personal wealth were tied up in their companies. After all, such behaviour is equivalent to that of an investor who places all of his money in a single stock, rather than spreading it widely in a diversified portfolio. In fact, the behaviour of such an entrepreneur is even riskier, as their wealth is relatively illiquid and non-fungible when it is tied up in an entrepreneur's own company, as opposed to a stock, which can be bought and sold at any time. The interviewees tended not to accept this warning, dismissing it by pointing to the fact that the major difference lies in the fact that they have control of their own companies – and, as one interviewee expressed it, are "sitting in the driver's seat". This is an example of what is frequently described as the phenomenon of 'over-optimism' and the failure of subjective risk perception in relation to actual risk – the research on this subject has been presented in detail in Chapters 3.2.b, along with 4.2 and 4.3.

Here follows an example from the dialogue with one of the wealthiest inter-viewees in the group, who does not recognize the fact that a large proportion of his wealth is tied up in his company as a substantial risk, because he manages the business himself. He does not acknowledge any risk, as long as you "manage the company yourself" and "don't make any mistakes". He is an extremely successful entrepreneur, one of the 1,000 richest individuals in the world. Understandably, this leads to a high degree of self-confidence. On the other hand, how realistic is it to assume that, in future, you are not – as he himself conceded – going to make any major mistakes?

> **Interviewer**: And what I asked earlier, about having practically everything tied up in the company for a very long time, being dependent on the company, did you ever perceive that as a risk and say, "That's a risk I'm willing to accept"? Or did you never view it as a risk?
> **Interviewee 26**: Never. Never as a risk.
> **Interviewer**: Can I ask why not?
> **Interviewee 26**: Well, because you manage it all yourself. [...] As long as you manage the company yourself and don't make any mistakes.
> **Interviewer**: But everyone makes mistakes, don't they?

Interviewee 26: Yes, but not major mistakes, you understand? Small mistakes, lots of little mistakes, that's okay, you know? But a really big mistake, that'll knock you down. But if you have the business in hand, that can't happen, can it?

Interviewer: I guess it all comes down to how highly leveraged you are. Were you highly leveraged?

Interviewee 26: As little as possible. Otherwise you are too dependent, aren't you?

However, this entrepreneur has sold his company and is now running his own asset management firm on the basis of a diversified portfolio of stocks.

Many of the interviewees operate in the property development sector. To fully appreciate this fact, it is necessary to recognize that, within the real estate segment, developers have the most extreme risk–reward profiles. This means that they have the opportunity to earn huge profits but that the number of firms that fold is also extremely high. One interviewee who operates in this sector, which is as rich in opportunities as it is in risk, and who has so far hardly been able to build a fortune outside his own company, reported as follows. When his asset manager says to him, "Mr xxx, you have placed everything on a single horse," he answers, "Yes, but I have everything under my own control." His counterargument: "I'm steering the boat […] If I were to invest in a real estate fund or an equity fund, I wouldn't know how well they were going to manage their fund." At the same time, he did admit that he was planning on reducing his risk exposure over the next few years – also via a process of diversification and acquiring assets outside his own company.

The following entrepreneur, who became rich in medical technologies, belongs to the group of interviewees who have seldom extracted profits from their core businesses, preferring instead to reinvest everything in further growth. He started off by saying that this does not represent a risk, as long as "I am in charge" in the company. However, he went on to concede that this was, in fact, the very reason that led him to diversify and invest in real estate, in order to build wealth independent of his core business:

Interviewer: So that means that you have never really taken big dividends out of the company?

Interviewee 23: No, very little. With one exception, not personally, but for the real estate company at the very beginning. We had to take a dividend, and that was a personal withdrawal because we needed to be able to invest the equity in the new company in order to be able to grow. You always need start-up financing, you need to have that in place at the start. But, apart from that one time, we always retained and reinvested all earnings.

Interviewer: Did you never perceive that as a risk, having so much money tied up in the company?
Interviewee 23: No, as long as I am in charge.
Interviewer: This might sound a bit provocative, but isn't that like investing everything in a single stock? No one would normally do that, would they?
Interviewee 23: That's right, but we have since diversified. I started the real estate business in [19]75. And since then I have also set up another investment company; we set that up and now invest in other companies.

Another entrepreneur, who also has a large portion of his wealth tied up in his own company, also in the field of medical technologies, rates himself with a +4 on the risk scale that extends from −5 to +5. As with many other interviewees, he said this with a special smile on his face: "Yes, I've never been afraid of risk." His fatalistic attitude was not untypical of many of the interviewees – perhaps fatalism is one approach to dealing with high levels of risk:

Interviewer: So you never really worried about it, placing all of your money into your company? What would have happened if, for whatever reason, the company had fallen off a cliff?
Interviewee 32: Then I would have been unfortunate. Unlucky. But I was never afraid. I expected success and I was always certain that, if anything happened, I could set myself up with my own law firm.

The same resigned attitude was clearly evident in the case of the following interviewee:

Interviewee 25: There's no way I'll ever slip into poverty. But I would accept it, if I had to, because of some process that I have no control over, if a world economic crisis hits and I lose everything. If that happened, then my personal real estate would also suffer. That would be a real crisis situation. One where we had no idea how things would work out in the end, how we would get through it. Then I would accept it and say, "Fine, I'll live out the rest of my life in a small house in Spain and be happy with that." I wouldn't really have a problem with that. I'm not so focused on status, which is why I wouldn't really miss any status symbols of wealth. I'd be more likely to look back and say to myself that I'd had a really good time, developed some amazing projects, and that was it. That was it.

15.3. "I CERTAINLY THINK ABOUT THINGS MORE THAN I USED TO"

In Section 3.2.b the distinction was made between the risk that someone takes when they go into business for themselves and the risk they bear when working within an existing company. It is also necessary to differentiate between the risk an entrepreneur bears, or is willing to bear, during the start-up phase of their business, and their tolerance of risk once the company is established and growing steadily. Many of the interviewees revealed that their relationship to risk had changed over the course of time. As the years have passed, they have become less tolerant of risk. This may actually be one of the secrets of their success: building up a company and a fortune takes a greater willingness to accept risks. Once this has been achieved, it is then important not to put either of these at risk with excessively adventurous behaviour. As a result, an individual's risk exposure decreases.

This type of development can be seen clearly in the example of a property developer. When they are first starting out, they often take on financial liabilities far in excess of the value of their assets. The collapse of a single project could mean complete financial ruin. As their careers progress, they steadily reduce the level of risk they are exposed to, which, in concrete terms, means:

- Rather than accepting full liability, they use non-recourse financing
- Rather than using their own equity, they use more mezzanine capital
- They build an asset base outside their own companies.

However, the subject of risk reduction is highly relevant for interviewees from other industries as well. The reasons stated for becoming less likely to take risks were varied. One interviewee, who built her fortune in the food and retail industries, said: "When I was young I frequently worked with debt capital. Looking back at it now, I was very brave. […] I was very brave and my father was often very worried." As she got older, her tolerance of risk decreased. "Yes, because you get better at assessing the risks, because you are more experienced and can see where things went wrong, or might go wrong. That's something that, when you are younger, you maybe don't really think so much about." One reason for becoming more risk averse is therefore the fact that gaining more experience enables you to recognize risks that, earlier in life, you might not have identified as risks.

An entrepreneur who became rich in the finance industry views this as a natural progression, having become more cautious with age:

Interviewer: So that means that, with time, you have become somewhat more cautious. At what age would you say that happened, when would you say you started being more cautious?
Interviewee 1: I would say I was in my mid-50s. Yes, that'd be about right.

Interviewer: Because you no longer want to take risks with what you have.
Interviewee 1: No, that's not really it, I've never really thought like that. No, it's just that you develop a different feeling towards risk. It's not that you don't want to risk what you have; I've never really thought of it in those terms.
Interviewer: Rather?
Interviewee 1: Rather, there were good reasons for sending the younger officers off to fight in wars and sending the older officers back home when they turned 50. The older you get, the more you think, and your view of risk is different to when you were younger.
[...] When I was younger, I did think that things would only ever get better and better, and I took on personal financial liabilities that I would never accept today. Everything worked out, but it could have all gone very wrong. So, in terms of talking about caution, age-related caution, I would never expose myself to such great personal liabilities today, not to the extent that I did back then.

Many of the interviewees stated that they no longer wanted to jeopardize what they had managed to create:

Interviewee 4: [I would rate myself as] +5, although I have to qualify that by saying that I have of course developed and adapted my style somewhat, constantly reminding myself, on a daily basis, "Just a minute, now. You've achieved a certain level of security here, you have a secure life, please don't take any more 100% risks."
Interviewer: That's something I have seen with my other interviewees, who have said, "As I've grown older, my appetite for risk has decreased, as it were."
Interviewee 4: Yes, yes, yes. That's something I don't do anymore. When I was younger, employees said to me, "Mr xxx, you can't do that, we can't do that. I mean, we can't pump all of the company's profits into this single advertising campaign, or risk everything on this one strategy." Of course, I always did it anyway, and not always successfully. But I always bet everything. I can't do that today. I'm responsible for a large company with 180 people.

Being aware of just how much effort it would take to rebuild everything from scratch naturally leads one to act with a greater degree of caution:

Interviewee 9: Because I say to myself, "If I fall flat on my face here I won't have the energy for the back-breaking work it would require to go back to the beginning and build it all up again." It's totally clear, I was much more open to risk when I was younger.

One entrepreneur offered the following comment on his risk profile: "I used to be at +5 and today I'm at 0." His reasoning:

> **Interviewee 21**: My desire for security has changed. Once upon a time, what I most wanted was to behave creatively. I used to think it was better to risk breaking the bow than to never take it in your hand and draw back the bowstring. Today, one of my strongest desires is for security. First and foremost I have to be sure of something. I weigh up the security and the risk. There's some risk in every project, but it has to be manageable.

Several interviewees mentioned the responsibilities they have towards their families as the reason they have become more risk averse. Commenting on his risk profile, one entrepreneur explained that, with the passage of time, he has shifted from +5 to +3. His reasoning:

> **Interviewee 42**: Yes, I definitely used to be a +5. [...] Now I honestly have to say, my daughters are 11 now. I have four children in total and the first time I held one of my daughters in my hand, that changed me. [...] That really drives home to you that you are no longer alone in the world, no longer only responsible for yourself.

A number of the entrepreneurs were worried that risky investments could potentially endanger their children's inheritances, burdening their families with excessive levels of risk:

> **Interviewee 31**: No, my appetite for risk has certainly decreased with the passage of time. Now, at the age of 75, I don't take on any more significant risks. That's because I have very capable children and a wife who is always in my thoughts, and I don't want to expose myself to any risks that might make things difficult for them as my heirs.

When considering the risk scale from −5 to +5, another entrepreneur, who works in private equity, assessed himself as having been a +4 earlier in his life, and a 0 today. Like several other interviewees, he admitted that he has become more risk averse during the course of his life. He points out that it is important to recognize the amount of risk someone has accepted in order to achieve a certain result:

Interviewee 28: Every year, Ernst & Young crowns the Entrepreneur of the Year. It's often the case that, just two years later, these Entrepreneurs of the Year have vanished into thin air. So you have to ask yourself, "Why?" In my opinion it has a lot to do with the fact that they can only generate the exorbitant profits you need to become the Entrepreneur of the Year with a completely misguided risk structure. Putting it in other words, that means that an entrepreneur walks into a casino, heads straight to the roulette table, and bets everything on the number 13. And then the entrepreneur comes home and says, "Actually, I'm a really good entrepreneur." And then xxx also says, "You're a really good entrepreneur." Such people would never say, "I've just been really lucky." No, what they say is, "I'm just a lot cleverer than everyone else." That's just how it is, and this perception leads him back to the casino the following year, where he again bets everything on a single number. This time he places everything on 4, because he knows that, according to all the criteria of calculating probabilities, and with a chance of 37 to 1, there's no way the same number should win twice. So, he places everything on 4 and, in one stroke, he's lost everything and is wiped out, because he couldn't accept that his earlier winnings were the result of luck, circumstances beyond his control. No, he is convinced that it was all due to his cleverness. [...] There are lots of young entrepreneurs who bet everything on the turn of a single card. And it might work out for one in a hundred. And that one in a hundred gets an award. But there are 99 others, who also tried but didn't make it. They are either cleverer, or not quite as smart, or dumber than the others. [...] What I'm trying to say is that I've changed. As you get older, you just don't want to have three balls in the air at the same time. If your business is juggling with three balls in the air at the same time, and each ball is in a risky position, and those risks could accumulate, everything could implode. So I throw one risky juggling ball up in the air and it's only once it's back safely in my hands, and the risk has passed, that I throw the next ball.

Finally, there is another motive that comes into play. Higher risks are usually associated with taking on higher levels of debt capital. However, as "freedom and independence" was the prime motive of most of the interviewees, this leads to conflicting goals. One entrepreneur from the food industry revealed that he has rarely used debt financing, and typically financed his company with his own money. His company is worth billions but has only EUR 50 million of debt on its balance sheet. He has competitors who took a very different approach and were able to grow at a more accelerated pace, but at the price of billions of euros of debt on their books. "And I don't have any debts." He is worried that he would sacrifice his entrepreneurial freedom if he got into debt. He mentioned that he currently has the opportunity to buy another company for EUR 2.5 billion, and he would certainly be able to secure the financing he would need. "But that would cause me so many headaches because it would mean losing my freedom."

INTERIM FINDINGS

Researchers have intensively considered the issue of the risk orientation of entrepreneurs and the wealthy. Some researchers have identified a strong positive correlation between risk propensity, entrepreneurial success, and wealth. In contrast, others have found that entrepreneurs characteristically only have a moderate appetite for risk. A third group of researchers support the hypothesis that, while entrepreneurs' actions may objectively be classified as risky, the entrepreneurs themselves do not perceive them in this way.

There is much to indicate that the conscious acceptance of risk – particularly throughout the business start-up phase – combined with the progressive reduction of these risks, is a requirement for sustainable financial success. Anyone who is not prepared to bear an elevated level of risk is unlikely to become an entrepreneur or investor. On the other hand, anyone who exposes themselves to extreme levels of risk over an extended period of time runs the risk of losing most, if not all, of the wealth they have accumulated. The later in life this happens, the lower the chances of rebuilding everything from the ground up would appear to be. Many of the interviewees reported that their appetite for risk had decreased with age. It is important to bear in mind at all times that the UHNWIs interviewed during the research for this book are those who have maintained their success to the present day. There are, of course, large numbers of entrepreneurs who have not enjoyed long-term success – possibly because they constantly exposed themselves to excessive levels of risk and didn't implement measures to reduce their risk exposure in time.

The hypothesis that entrepreneurs and wealthy individuals are characterized by a moderate risk profile was not confirmed by the interviews. It definitely does not apply to the phases in which these UHNWIs established their companies and built their fortunes. A substantial majority of the interviewees assessed themselves as having an elevated risk profile. This contrasts with the phases in which they consolidated their businesses, at which point their willingness to take on risks decreased. It is in relation to this phase of an entrepreneur's life that the hypothesis of moderate risk propensity has its justification.

The hypothesis that entrepreneurs and the rich tolerate objectively high levels of risk, but do not perceive the risks as such, was not entirely confirmed by the interviews. Most of the interviewees were fully aware of their high risk profiles. At the same time, there were a number of interviewees for whom this hypothesis is valid – they rated their own propensity for risk as moderate, while also admitting that the outside world would classify them as extremely tolerant of risk. Furthermore, the interviews confirmed that many interviewees are objectively exposed to high levels of risk, due to the concentration of their wealth in their own companies, but that they do not perceive this as risky. This is where the illusion of control comes into play, which is, in turn, the product or expression of the interviewees' over-optimism.

16 Decision-making: Gut Feeling or Analysis?

A wide range of studies cited in Section 4.1 unanimously concluded that senior executives, in particular, often rely on their gut feelings when making decisions. According to the hypothesis, this should apply to an even greater extent to entrepreneurs than it does to senior executives, as entrepreneurs do not have to justify their decisions in the same way to third parties (committees, supervisory boards, etc.), and entrepreneurs are less likely than executives to have a background in business administration. One of the research projects presented in Section 4.1, which interviewed and psychologically tested serial entrepreneurs, confirmed this finding. Serial entrepreneurs were specifically chosen because it was believed that their repeated entrepreneurial success was less likely to be the result of luck or serendipitous external factors. Respondents were subjected to a test that measured whether they tended to make their decisions based on analysis or intuition. Further studies were carried out in a variety of countries, using the same test, and confirmed the importance of gut feeling in the decision-making of top-ranking executives and entrepreneurs.[705] In fact, as has been demonstrated, gut feeling is not a mystical property. It is actually the expression of implicit knowledge, the outward representation of implicit learning.

The series of interview questions on decision-making behaviours was therefore of great importance. To what extent would the interviewees make their decisions based on gut feeling – when would they rather rely on their analytical skills and when would they trust their intuition? The interviewees were asked by what percentage gut feeling or analysis dominated their decision-making:

DOES GUT FEELING OR ANALYSIS DOMINATE?

1. G 60% gut feeling
2. G Mostly gut feeling
3. G 70% gut feeling
4. G 90% gut feeling: "I approach things absolutely intuitively"
5. G Gut feeling plays the decisive role, along with astrology
6. G 50% gut feeling: "More gut feeling than analysis"
7. U "I base a lot of decisions on gut feeling, but I'm more analytical when it comes to complex decisions"
8. A "Two thirds of my decisions were based on analysis, but that was a mistake; if I'd paid more attention to my gut, I would have been spared some losses"
9. G 90% gut feeling
10. G "I make gut decisions; I place my hand on a file and know whether or not it's a scam, or lies, or nonsense"
11. A 70–80% analytic
12. G 80% gut feeling
13. G 60% gut feeling
14. G "Gut feeling is far better than reasoning"
15. G "In the past, 70% gut feeling, 30% reason – today 30% gut feeling, 70% reason"
16. U "Everything is always first and foremost based on analysis, but then the gut decides 100%"
17. G 60% gut feeling
18. U 50% gut feeling
19. A 100% analysis, not gut feeling
20. G 70–80% gut feeling
21. U 50% gut feeling
22. A 70% analytical
23. G "In critical situations" maximum 60/40 with the gut
24. A 20% with the gut
25. G Predominantly with the gut
26. A Mostly analytically
27. A 70% analytically (for everyday decisions, gut feeling plays more of a role in major decisions)
28. G Predominantly gut feeling

---

705   Allinson, Chell, and Hayes, "Intuition and Entrepreneurial Behaviour," 41.

29. G 60% gut feeling
30. A Mainly analysis
31. A Two thirds analysis, but more time is spent getting to know the person with whom he will potentially be doing business
32. G 80% gut feeling
33. G At least 75% gut feeling
34. U 50/50
35. A 40% gut feeling, 60% analysis
36. G No longer makes any decisions against his gut instincts
37. A 70% analysis
38. A 70% analysis due to requirements imposed by banks
39. U (No assessment)
40. G 70% with the gut
41. A 75% analysis
42. G Two thirds gut feeling
43. G 80% analysis
44. G 70% gut feeling
45. A 80% analysis ('unfortunately')

G = predominantly gut feeling; A = predominantly analysis; U = 50/50 or no clear category. If an interviewee's decision-making behaviour changed over time, the earlier behaviour was used in the findings.

More than half of the interviewees (24 of 45) said that their decision-making was dominated by gut feeling. One third (15) preferred to rely predominantly on analysis. In the case of six interviewees, either they relied equally on gut feeling and analysis or it was not possible to assign their response to one of the two main categories. Only one of the interviewees declared that gut feeling has no bearing whatsoever on his decision-making behaviour. Even those interviewees who stated that their decisions are overwhelmingly dominated by analysis said that between 20% and 40% of any decision is based on gut feeling.

In comparison: surveys carried out by the AIPOR reveal that between 39% and 51% of the German population say that they "listen more to reason" and between 27% and 36% say that they "listen more to their feelings" when it comes to making decisions. The rest are undecided.[706]

16.1. "GUT FEELING MEANS THAT YOU JUST DON'T FEEL CERTAIN"

How did the interviewees – irrespective of whether they generally tend towards basing their decisions on analysis or intuition – actually describe what is commonly referred to as gut feeling? How did they perceive and define it? One interviewee, who said that two thirds of his decisions have been based on analysis, has come to regret this fact and believes that, had he listened more frequently to his gut, he would have made fewer mistakes with his investments, as "unfortunately, the gut is sometimes right". It is interesting to consider his description of the gut as a "type of computer, but one whose calculations you can't necessarily understand". In response to a question about the instances when it would have been better to listen more to his gut feeling, he replied:

> **Interviewee 8**: Sure, so when you make any investment, buy a piece of real estate or a stock, which I have done very often, then looking back, I would say that on those occasions when I had a certain uneasiness in my gut, I would have been better to step back from the investment, wouldn't I? And in all of those cases, the analysis came out clearly in favour of those investments. But maybe the analysis was never really complete, after all, no analysis can fully take into account changes in the environment, can it? Coincidence is often neglected in any analysis, you know? Because analysis can only ever express things in terms of percentages. The risk that I will be run over on my way back home from here, that's about 5%, isn't it? If it actually happens, the percentages don't really matter, do they? And that's where gut feeling can be better, because things don't always work out in terms of percentages. Your gut is less rational, it works differently, somehow. It's less rational and is like a type of computer, but one whose calculations you can't necessarily understand. [...] But it's still right a lot of the time.

Many of the interviewees emphasized that gut feeling is not innate; rather it develops as a result of accumulated experience. This correlates with the theory presented in Section 4.1, which claims that gut feeling is the product of implicit knowledge. A flash of insight will appear in a fraction of a second, triggered by the recognition of a pattern, an awareness that is, in turn, the result of many years of experience. When asked whether he tends to base his decisions on analysis or gut feeling, the following interviewee, who described himself as making decisions based on gut feeling, responded:

---

706   Institut für Demoskopie Allensbach, AIPOR surveys 7058, 10062, and 11044.

Interviewee 10: I would say that I tend to rely on my gut feeling. Although gut feeling isn't something you have developed at the age of nine months. The gut is also the sum of your past judgements, isn't it? It's like this, there are lots of people, and I count myself as one of them, and if you tell them, look, here's a whole file on this deal you're considering – now this is slightly exaggerated, but I place my hand on that dossier and know whether or not it's a scam, or lies, or nonsense. And others study the dossier endlessly and find something in it. And, in most cases, I only need ten minutes to tell them whether it's all a load of nonsense, or not.

A very successful real estate investor explained that his decisions are 70% based on analysis, while at the same time acknowledging that gut feeling plays an important role. However, he also recognized that this feeling is the product of many years of experience:

Interviewee 22: I think that gut feeling is just another word for experience and emotion and an understanding of where exactly you stand. I would go as far as to say that what we are describing here as gut feeling is something that a fresh university graduate hasn't got yet. It doesn't exist yet. So, alongside the purely computational analysis that you mentioned, gut feeling is the sum of everything else you have ever experienced.

The next interviewee also associates gut feeling with experience and "things that have happened to you during your professional life". For this reason, the proportion of the decisions that he has made on the basis of his gut feelings has increased during the course of his professional life. When asked whether his decision-making behaviour was dominated by gut feeling or analysis, he responded:

Interviewee 29: I think it's true to say that, as a result of the experience you gain over time, my gut feeling now plays a much bigger role.
Interviewer: And if you tried to put a percentage on it, what do you mean by "a much bigger role"?
Interviewee 29: 40% gut feeling. 60/40. If my gut says no, then I don't do it.
Interviewer: I see. And what do you think gut feeling actually is? Do you think you can explain it in more detail? [...]
Interviewee 29: There are a number of factors that play a role. Firstly, you've got the experience that you have mentally stored. And experience doesn't have anything to do with numbers, it's all about the experiences and things that have happened to you during your professional life.

Secondly, you've got the people who are involved. That's really important for me. If I get a funny feeling, then I'd rather turn my back on the business, because my experience has taught me that there are some things that can turn negative. So it's when I get a good vibe, you know? And if there's something negative there, then I'd rather walk away. And I've got another experience to add to my gut feeling for future reference.

Interviewer: What you've just said is interesting. That as time has passed, your reliance on gut feeling has grown.

Interviewee 29: Yes.

Interviewer: That's probably because you've gathered more experience, isn't it?

Interviewee 29: Yes.

Interviewer: So does that mean, going back to the percentages, that earlier in your life, the percentages would have been different?

Interviewee 29: Yes, for sure. I was maybe a bit more innocent then, and either did something or not. And I was lucky. But I would say that, at the very beginning, it was all about the bare figures. Back then, it was completely the other way around. I would say, 40% gut feeling and 60% [analysis], you know?

Interviewer: I recently spoke to an extremely successful investor and he said that, when you are a student, you can't have the gut feeling because you haven't had a chance to gain the necessary experience.

Interviewee 29: Absolutely, yes. Exactly.

The following interviewee also reports that the proportion of his decisions based on analysis has decreased somewhat with the passage of time – with a corresponding increase in decisions based on gut feeling. He admits that, while he still bases his decisions on 75% analysis, the figure used to be higher, at 90%. He also supports the hypothesis that gut feeling is the product of accumulated experience:

Interviewee 41: Yes, for me it's a high percentage of analysis, definitely 70 or 75% analysis. [...] And it used to be even more. When I was starting out, it was more like 90%. I'd say it was 90% analysis.

Interviewer: And why did that change?

Interviewee 41: Maybe I've become a bit more relaxed, a bit more secluded, and maybe it's also because I don't invest quite so much time in dealing with the details, so that maybe, on the basis of my experience, I believe more now that gut feeling is sufficient.

Interviewer: And maybe because gut feeling is a form of coagulated experience gathered over many years. Could that be the reason?

Interviewee 41: Yes, yes.

Interviewer: So that you can say to yourself, "I have so many years of experience, and that's all come together and that's what I call gut feeling."

Interviewee 41: I can make decisions relatively quickly nowadays. And I don't need to say, "Okay, I'll start by sitting myself down and reading and joining up all the dots," like I used to.

Interviewer: And at what point, or in what way, would you say, "That's something I'm going to decide analytically"? Or as you just said, there's a certain percentage of gut feeling, which depends on the situation, the facts on the ground.

Interviewee 41: Yes, I would say it's one of my strengths that when I am confronted by a problem, a puzzle, from the start I can quite quickly tell you where the individual pieces of the puzzle belong. Which means that I am better at dealing with problems. When you are always able to see the big picture, complete, as well as the individual pieces of the puzzle, and how they will fit together, then you can deal with things better. And that is where I would say my strength lies, why I generally believe that I am in a better position than the person I am talking or negotiating with. And that is something that has solidified more and more over the years, so that now I would say that when I negotiate with someone, whatever industry they are from, because I can see the big picture and put myself in their shoes, that gives me a certain advantage, which I will usually exploit.

Many of the interviewees ascribe a warning or cautionary function to their gut feelings, because their intuitions have saved them from a number of bad business decisions. When it comes to business and investments, several interviewees stressed that the best business is often the business you never get involved in the first place. In such situations, the warning signals sent out by the gut can play a crucial role. The following interviewee, who pursues a profession that is almost exclusively dominated by analysis, explains that in relation to his investments – which are the source of his fortune – his gut feeling pays a decisive role:

Interviewee 17: I am firmly convinced that the best business can be the business you decide not to get involved in. I have turned down lots of business opportunities in my life.

Interviewer: And did you turn these opportunities down because your gut was saying "no", or because of the results of your analysis?

Interviewee 17: Because my gut was against it. And what does gut mean, after all? Gut feeling just means that you don't feel confident. That you're not sure about something.

The following interviewee from the real estate industry, who has already been quoted above, makes his decisions on the basis of 70% analysis. He also stresses the role of gut feeling as a warning system. He uses the example of real estate investment decisions to illustrate that relying purely on an analysis of numbers can lead investors astray – and in particular those who are less experienced – because lower-quality real estate can often seem to be more profitable at first glance. In such cases, gut feeling performs a cautionary function, requiring an investor to take another, perhaps more considered, look at the numbers, which may lead to a different conclusion:

> **Interviewee 22**: Without drilling down analytically, I don't trust my gut feeling at all, but once I've really got to the bottom of things analytically, my gut feeling becomes really important [...] That is when I say, once the analysis has arrived at a positive result, that's when my gut feeling becomes really important. That's when I say, right that's exactly how I'm going to try and do it. [...] I mean, in any analysis you have to ask whether the conditions, the assumptions that you have made are realistic enough and what would happen if things turn out to be different. Even when I have a positive gut feeling about something, I still demand that things are as close to reality as they can be.
>
> **Interviewer**: [...] So even when the numbers are more or less good, you could still reach a point where you have a negative gut feeling, when your gut tells you...
>
> **Interviewee 22**: That happens quite often in the real estate business. [...] That happens time and time again with inexperienced employees in relation to lower-quality real estate, which often, at least at first glance, seem to be cheap, a bargain, you know? In such cases it's easier to make your analysis. But when you have a really expensive piece of real estate, in the premium plus sector, then it's not so easy to make the figures add up, to arrive at a positive result, because the pure analysis of the figures is more difficult. In the first case it is more about saying, okay, when something is cheap, a bargain, there's usually a reason. So, if you spot a bargain, then you have to ask yourself, "Is this really a bargain or is it not actually very expensive because the negative aspects have been given short thrift in our analysis?" Why is it as cheap as it is? Why, for example, is the vacancy rate so high? And if you say, fine, that's something I can have dealt with within the next two years, then maybe you're being a bit naive. It's potentially far more difficult than you at first think, and when you walk through the rooms and see how badly lit they are, then maybe you need to change your assumptions. That's when the analysis and your gut feeling tend to come together.

The following interviewee, who makes two thirds of his decisions based on his gut feelings, also emphasizes the warning function of gut feelings. For him, an uneasy feeling is an indication that you have not thought something through well enough. He believes that it would be a mistake to ignore these warning signals; in fact, it is extremely important to "recognize these feelings and take them seriously". Such feelings have saved him from making a number of bad decisions:

Interviewer: Can you explain in more detail what you mean by gut feeling? What happens at the moment you experience a gut feeling?

Interviewee 42: Now that's an important point. In my opinion, it is the ability to listen to the intuition that resides within everybody. You frequently get into situations where you have to make a decision, or do something, or think about how best to do something, and then when you are considering certain scenarios, you get an uneasy feeling. And you end up saying to yourself, "There's something here I haven't really considered, there's something wrong with the solution I have in mind." And then there are some people who say, "It doesn't matter, this is definitely the way, the process, that's what I'm going to do, it's the only solution." There is never only one solution. And the solution is always tailored to the individual person or those involved. There are always a number of solutions that will get you to your goal. But you have to be open to recognize these feelings and take them seriously, that is a really important point. And there are many cases where that saved me from making bad decisions.

It became clear that so many of the interviewees take the warning function of their gut feelings so seriously because ignoring them has resulted in negative experiences in the past. One interviewee, who assesses the relationship between gut feeling and analysis in his decision-making as 50/50, admitted that it is sometimes his gut feeling that prevails and sometimes his more analytical side:

Interviewee 18: No, sometimes you have to make gut decisions, don't you? I mean, analysis can only show you the best possible results in terms of the figures and all the components. But alongside that, you need to have a feeling, and that's where the gut comes in. You need a feeling for a specific market situation. You can't analyse, for example, whether a certain politician will still be in charge of something in two years' time, can you? You can't analyse that. You can only estimate something like that. Take xxx, here in Düsseldorf, that was a close call. If he'd died three months earlier, we would never have been able to realize our xxx, would we? Those are the kinds of things you can never analyse, that's when you need your gut. 50/50.

Interviewer: [...] Someone recently said to me, "I sometimes ignored my gut feeling and I regret it, with hindsight I know that I should have listened to my gut more often, when I had a bad feeling but went ahead anyway." [...]
Interviewee 18: Yes, that has happened to me too. I have a really good example for that, where I had a bad gut feeling but went ahead anyway because of a positive evaluation from my adviser. And it went wrong. Or not entirely wrong, but it wasn't a profitable property, more of a, how can I put it, more of a zero property. But there are other examples where I would say that, if I had listened to my gut, if I had gone ahead, then things would have been even better. There are enough examples for both. But I believe that, for me, first I have to be given a framework for my decision. That's the analysis. And then, it's not just me, I have to let the gut feelings of others be heard. But I then have to be able to judge, what they are feeling and how did they arrive at their gut feelings? But property development can't work without gut feelings. And in some cases, instead of 50/50, it might then be 70/30, you know? And the same applies to recruiting employees, doesn't it?

Another of the UHNWIs confessed that he had once lost EUR 6 million because he ignored what his gut was telling him. He has never made another decision his gut feeling warned him against:

Interviewee 36: I've experienced that myself. We once lost over EUR 6 million because we made a decision against our gut feeling and another time we headhunted someone from xxx bank as a managing director or authorized representative, also going against our guts, and since then I haven't made any other decisions against my gut feelings. I learned my lesson.
Interviewer: How would you describe using your gut? Is it a feeling, an experience, or what is it with the gut?
Interviewee 36: It's a feeling. I think that gut feeling and senses are much shrewder. At least that's what I've read, and I've experienced both. Your gut can appreciate far more impressions and sensations. Whether you have a good feeling about something, or a bad feeling. That's where everything comes together. It's no different to when someone walks into the room and you can say whether you have a good or bad feeling about them. Incidentally, that's something that is easier to do with men than women. With women, you sometimes get it wrong. Men make an impression the moment they walk into a room. Your chance of sizing them up correctly – whether they are okay – is at almost 80%, based on just first impressions.

The following interviewee explained that he makes 80% of his decisions with his "head" but regrets this fact. He believes that he should have made far more of his decisions on the basis of his gut. On occasion, his gut feeling registers, and he does not act against it. But he believes that he needs to learn "to ask" his gut more frequently, and to have more confidence in its signals:

> **Interviewer**: Let's move on to a different question. We are all people who make decisions based on both our guts or more analytically. So both play a role. If you had to say for yourself, what percentage of your decisions do you base on your gut, and what percentage is analytical?
> **Interviewee 45**: I rely far too much on my head, unfortunately. 80% head.
> **Interviewer**: What makes you say "unfortunately"?
> **Interviewee 45**: I think I need to let my gut make decisions far more often.
> **Interviewer**: So why don't you?
> **Interviewee 45**: That's just me, that's where my inner pessimist comes to the fore. Because I worry that I haven't considered things carefully enough.
> **Interviewer**: So you don't really trust your gut feelings.
> **Interviewee 45**: Exactly.
> **Interviewer**: You need to have it all analysed, so to say.
> **Interviewee 45**: Right. Spot on.
> **Interviewer**: Okay. And have you ever done something where your head has said, "Right, I've analysed this and this is how I'm going to proceed," but you had an odd feeling in your gut? Or would you then say, "No, when my gut tells me not to go ahead, then I won't do it"?
> **Interviewee 45**: Then I just don't do it.
> **Interviewer**: So, in that respect, your gut plays a major role.
> **Interviewee 45**: When I ask it to, yes.
> **Interviewer**: I see, so only when you ask. And if you don't ask, don't you sometimes get the feelings anyway?
> **Interviewee 45**: No.

As the review of the theories of behavioural economics in Part A of this thesis has shown, scholars who stress the importance of gut feeling in decision-making, such as Kahneman and Gigerenzer, place particular emphasis on the fact that such behaviour has the advantage of speeding up decision-making processes. This matches the views of an interviewee from the real estate industry, who was previously an independent entrepreneur and, following the sale of his company, had to start making decisions from inside the hierarchical structures of a large corporation. He frequently found himself forced to make decisions that ran counter to his gut feeling, because analysis had suggested that these were the correct decisions:

Interviewer: Every one of us has both components. But if you had to assign a percentage, to say what percentage tends to be based on your gut feeling and what percentage is based on analysis, what would you say?

Interviewee 20: 70% to 80% gut.

Interviewer: [...] And have you ever said to yourself, "When I refused to listen to my gut, I made a bad decision," or vice versa?

Interviewee 20: Then I feel uneasy. There are some things I've done, not relying entirely on my gut, where my gut would have said, "Ah." And where I ignored my gut and caved in. That has never been my element, the corporate decision-making process. I have always felt uneasy doing that. I felt quite uncomfortable while I was there. That was one of the problems while I was at xxx. I had the gut feeling that I wanted to do something, but I had to fill out hundreds of forms and had to submit all of my proposals for approval. And the deals that I wanted, they had all disappeared by the time I was authorized to go after them. The deals that involved quick gut reactions and decisions, they were really good. And the deals that involved hundreds of forms and describing things over and over again, that mostly ended in nothing.

The same was the case for the next interviewee, who said that he makes 70% of his decisions with his gut and described himself as someone who arrives at decisions quickly:

Interviewer: What does gut mean to you? Could you describe it for me in a bit more detail?

Interviewee 40: It's a feeling. That means, in business, making decisions. Of course, any decisions are based on a certain degree of analysis, but then I think you also say, we'll do it this way because I have a good gut feeling. [...] And I make decisions really quickly, you know? Shall we do it this way? Then we do it this way. And I always live according to the motto, if you say A then you have to also say B and then live with C. That's how it is, isn't it? I've made lots of decisions that turned out to be wrong, but never wasted time complaining, then I'm an optimist and life goes on and you have to live with the situation. That's basically my motto in life.

Interviewer: Have you ever been in a situation where, purely analytically, you would say we should do it this way, and even with a bad gut feeling you have gone ahead, against your gut?

Interviewee 40: I don't think so. Strictly analytically there have been decisions that I should have made, because something looked like a good investment, or someone looked like they could be a good employee, but I had a bad feeling in my gut, so I didn't go ahead.

Interviewer: So you wouldn't go ahead.
Interviewee 40: Not really, no.

16.2. "YOU CAN'T ASK AN AUDITOR TO ANALYSE SOMEONE'S CHARACTER"

When asked what types of decisions made on the basis of gut feelings played a major role for them, many interviewees mentioned decisions that were strongly based on an assessment of the character of others. An investor from the private equity sector explained why he makes 70% of his decisions with his gut:

Interviewee 44: You have to understand that an overwhelming majority of my decisions are related to people. When I'm deciding whether to invest in a company, the figures might look great, but I always ask myself, "Do I really trust them? Do I believe they can do what they say they can do?" It boils down to reading people, assessing people, but you can't measure them, weigh them, put figures on them. It's not like you can look to see if they have an official stamp of quality on them, can you? You can't ask an auditor to analyse someone's character. You can't audit character on the basis of numbers. So, behind any business decisions, any investment, it comes down to the people involved, and those are business decisions where you have to rely on your gut. I look at the numbers; if you have a totally unsuitable product or the numbers are really bad, that's a rational framework for any decision you use to make sure that things add up.
Interviewer: One could say, filtering decisions based on figures.
Interviewee 44: But after that, it comes down to your gut feeling. [...] I have had some investment opportunities, where I thought the product looked good, the market was fantastic, but where I said to myself, "I don't want to work with this person." He can't listen, he can only talk, he is not open to accepting advice from others. So I walked away.
Interviewer: And back when you were starting out, if you cast your mind back, are there any other situations, apart from in relation to people, where you would say that your gut feeling played a major role in your decision-making? Sure, evaluating people is the obvious one.
Interviewee 44: When we were expanding. Then you have the craziest statistics. I can still remember when we entered the market in [country]. [...] time again, I said, "My gut feeling is telling me [...] we'll be fine. [...] Let's get into that market." In contrast, the statistics were all stacked up against us being successful, but we were incredibly successful. That was all gut feeling.

The following interviewee also makes his money in the private equity sector, buying companies or stakes in companies. In explaining why he makes a majority of his decisions based on gut feeling, he reasoned that in his business everything ultimately comes down to people and that it is impossible to evaluate people analytically, on the basis of a checklist, so you are forced to rely on your gut feeling. When asked what percentage of his decisions are made "from the gut" or analytically, he responded:

Interviewee 28: Well, as the key factor is the people involved in the business, and what they do in the business, it is only natural that any assessment of the people is crucial, and you just can't do that analytically. So gut feeling is something you have to rely on. I'd much rather do business with great people, reliable people, clever people, even if their product is only second best, than get involved with the best product and the second-best people. [...] I try to meet two, three, four, or even five times with the people involved. That's my priority, especially when it's a people-based business, and, particularly with smaller companies, where you know that a lot depends on the individual people. [...] Unfortunately, those are not things that you use a checklist for, you know, a catalogue with 20 points, like you can when you are assessing a business plan. No, these are aspects, like you said, where you ultimately have to rely on your gut feeling, because you can't fit them into a rigid system of assessment. You have to see the big picture, by which I mean both the business plan and the people involved. And I would say that the people are actually more important than the business plan, which means that the overall decision is also a gut decision. [...] In our case, that's particularly true, because we're not involved in multi-billion takeovers in the chemical industry, where you could more or less swap people around; they're basically interchangeable. But in smaller businesses the people or the individual who is running the company are far more important than when xxx goes off and buys a huge chemical company in the US.

Another interviewee, who makes his money by financing real estate developments, emphasized just how important it is to take the time to get to know people properly. His father once told him that he had almost never made a decision to hire someone without first taking his wife (i.e. the interviewee's mother) with him to meet the potential employee, because he believed that women often have better instincts about people. When a decision needed to be made to hire a senior executive, the interviewee's parents would usually go for a meal with the candidate and his wife. He feels that nowadays many people simply do not take enough time before making decisions, which has a detrimental impact on their decision-making:

Interviewee 5: Things didn't used to move so quickly in the past; people allowed themselves much more time for things. Looking back now, I have to admit that I lost money in a company when I was at xxxx; it was a flop, even though it wasn't a new business. My then wife had always said, "I would never touch xxx." In the end, my stake was a flop, although my overall engagement with xxx was a success because I had a number of joint ventures with them and got something out of those, that was okay. But let's get back to your question about gut feeling. First of all, my gut does play a role. Secondly, I want to know what a woman's gut feeling is telling her, that's very important to me. Because I believe that women have a different sense for things than we men do. [...]

Interviewer: Can you give me an example of something you have seen in a person that others might not be able to see?

Interviewee 5: For example on the topic of "Can you trust this person or not?" That's what I'd call a soft fact, you know? And it's extremely important. And you have a gut feeling. Your gut tells you, "He might be a great person and all that, but do you really trust him? He doesn't exactly inspire my trust." That's the kind of thing I mean, you know?

This interviewee went on to describe how he judges people based on his evaluations of them in their natural environments:

Interviewee 5: I think I could write you a relatively accurate psychogram of a company and the people I am dealing with, with a very high hit rate, after I have been to see them at work in their offices. It starts with things like their reception. What their restrooms look like, how they have arranged their hand towels, what the conference room looks like. What's on the table, how it's been laid out. I've developed a sense, if there's somewhere it's not even worth me going to, I can smell from 1,000 metres away, because I know they won't be able to afford to pay me anyway. [...] Xxx needs to show me what he has, what he can do. What I'm taking about now is offices, about self-presentation, or what is the secretary like, how do they serve the coffee, how do they present themselves, are they small-minded, petty. So when you ask me about gut feeling, that's what I mean. I'm in acquisitions. In every bit of business, it comes down to whether I take a stake or not. And the most important thing at the outset is to decide what I am going to focus on, because I don't want to waste a lot of time focusing on the wrong things, the things that don't result in anything good. And vice versa. [...] It starts with how someone arranges a meeting with me. How does his secretary deal with that? There are a multitude of soft facts that allow me to very quickly develop a picture of the situation, and that has always really helped me. So, when it comes to deciding whether to take a stake in a company or not, I look to see how they put together their business plan, how they present it, how the people present themselves.

The next interviewee, who built his wealth in stocks and real estate, is among the group who describe themselves as two thirds analysts. Still, he admits that gut feeling plays an important role when it comes to judging people. He spends far more time nowadays considering his potential business or negotiation partners than he does on the actual business proposal. And this is where gut feeling applies:

Interviewee 31: No. No, I'm two thirds an analyst. And one third is gut feeling. But gut feeling definitely plays a role for me

Interviewer: In what situations does it play a role?

Interviewee 31: For example, when I look really closely at the person sitting across the table from me. There are definitely deals that looked very promising on paper but I didn't get involved because I didn't trust the person sitting opposite me.

Interviewer: And how does that manifest itself? In what way do you experience your gut feeling?

Interviewee 31: There are lots of things that come together. One is experience, then there's the way he acts, the way he answers questions. Does everything feel right, or not, or only partly? That all comes together into a single picture. Which is why, later in my business life, I said to my employees, "I spend more time deciding whether I want to go into business with someone than I do on the actual business proposal."

Interviewer: I see. Tell me more about how you determine whether you want to go into business with someone. I find that really interesting.

Interviewee 31: It's as I just described it. Let's take a standard scenario: someone owns a piece of real estate and the starting position is that he wants to sell it for the highest price possible and I want to buy it at the lowest price possible. So, you have to try to find a way to bridge this difference. That's where you start to analyse. What is the location like? What condition is the property in? What do the leases look like? What potential for rental increases do they allow for? And so on. And during that process questions will arise that you have for the owner. And if you just get wishy-washy answers, or no answers, or maybe even incorrect answers, then you naturally get the impression and say to yourself, "Watch out. You need to be a bit careful here." And it's at that point that a number of deals have fallen apart.

The specific industry in which the interviewees are active has no impact on whether they rely more on gut instinct or careful analysis. Gut feelings can dominate even in industries where one would assume that decisions would tend to be based on analysis. An entrepreneur who became rich within the IT industry explained why he makes 75% of his decisions based on his gut feelings:

> **Interviewee 33**: Yes, it's about clients, how I feel when I'm dealing with them. How I annoy them. How I get some expert to fill in some data field. That's the gut feeling component. You could say that software projects are brought to life by the users, that they accept new developments, that they feel supported. And that involves a great deal of gut feeling. Today, we have almost as many UX designers – the UX stands for user experience – as software developers. Because software has to look good today, it has to be fun. The right elements have to be in exactly the right places. And the software industry as a whole is just about as far along as the car industry was when Henry Ford made his Model T. I think that was the last car that was developed by engineers. After that, it was all about the designers. And they are now slowly moving into the software world and, of course, that creates conflicts. You've got software engineers who have been sitting there for the last 20 years and here come the young designers straight out of art school and start to tell them what to do. And the software developer turns around and says, "Hooray. I've been waiting for you all my life."

The fact that the industry is nearly irrelevant is demonstrated by the following four excerpts from interviews with investors, all of whom are involved in the real estate industry. The first explained (the only interviewee to do so) that he arrives at his decisions 100% analytically. For the second real estate investor, this is 80% the case. Both investors view this as a clear advantage as they believe that many other real estate investors make decisions based almost entirely on their gut feelings. Following the statements from these two investors, two further interviewees are quoted, who explain why they make a majority of their decisions from the gut:

> **Interviewer**: We all have two things, we have an analytical, rational side, and we have the gut, that we make decisions based on gut feeling, and both are important. What would you say for yourself, which dominates?
> **Interviewee 19**: Analytical, definitely.
> **Interviewer**: So more the analytical side?
> **Interviewee 19**: Yes. For everything I do, before I buy a piece of real estate, I have a computer program that I wrote myself. With that, I rate the property

according to a raft of criteria, in comparison with other properties that are on the market, and it would have to offer significantly better value.

Interviewer: In terms of the figures...

Interviewee 19: Yes, in terms of the figures.

Interviewer: And what happens when you have a good or a bad gut feeling about something – let's assume your analysis is in favour of a property, but in your gut you have a less certain feeling, do you ignore that feeling?

Interviewee 19: Yes.

Interviewer: Or do you never even get such a negative feeling?

Interviewee 19: No.

Interviewer: So you don't get anything like that.

Interviewee 19: No. [...] Yes, nobody would buy a property without a gut decision. But me, I have zero interest in the property as such. Before I even start to think about a property I send one of my construction guys, I know what the planning restrictions are, how many square metres, what would the construction costs have been in 1913 for this standard of building, those are the figures I can calculate with. How far away is the average rent in the leased sections of the property from the market rent in the surrounding area. And then I put all those figures down on a piece of paper and, as long as all of the figures look good, then my gut feeling says yes, 100%. But if there's something wrong with the numbers, then my gut feeling is of little to no use anyway.

The next interviewee has a very similar perspective on things. He says that his decision-making is 80% analytical and regards this as a distinct advantage over the many other investors who are governed by their gut feelings. He believes that too many people are led by emotions when it comes to making decisions on real estate, which creates distortions that he can take advantage of:

Interviewee 43: Of course, it depends. I mean, it's a question of what you are doing. The real estate business, in my opinion, is a numbers game. And the numbers never lie. And the gut feelings relate more to, what do I think of a certain location, what do I think of one of my tenant's business concepts, what do I think of my tenant as a person. That's where the gut comes into it. But I'll tell you, an 8% yield is an 8% yield, and if a building costs x, that's what it costs. And the four basic principles of arithmetic are what they are. And I think that, especially as real estate is such an emotional product for so many people, I think that creates market distortions, which is exactly why you need to take such an analytical approach. If we were talking about a B2C [business-to-consumer] internet start-up somewhere, then maybe my gut feeling would play a bigger role, but the real estate market, at least as I see it, is one where you have to take a far more analytical approach.

Interviewer: So you're saying that opportunities arise because other people sometimes make irrational decisions with their guts, which you can then benefit from with your analytical approach?

Interviewee 43: That's it, exactly.

The next interviewee is also active in the real estate market and is convinced that he has benefited greatly from the fact that he makes 90% of his decisions based on his gut feelings. In contrast to the previous interviewee, he did not offer any analytical foundation for his position, but simply stated that in his experience people who "analyse everything and subject everything to extensive critical investigation" can never achieve true success:

Interviewee 4: I approach things completely based on intuition.

Interviewer: Does that mean 90%?

Interviewee 4: 90% based on intuition.

Interviewer: I see, and what does that mean for you? Could you describe that a little for me? What do you mean?

Interviewee 4: For example, when I buy something, buy apartment buildings, then I used to go and look at them, which I don't do now. I used to go and take a look at them from the outside. I never went into them, I just looked and said, "I like the area, it feels good, I'll buy it." And when it came to hiring employees, whether I would hire them or not, I took a look at them, is there a chemistry there, do I like them. They're capable, we can do something together. It's something I've experienced myself, you know? Other people saw things in me, liked me, helped me.

Interviewer: You must have lots of positive experiences approaching things in that way, or you wouldn't have carried on with it. Bad experiences, too. Have there been times when you've felt vindicated or proved wrong with your approach?

Interviewee 4: I've overwhelmingly only had good experiences. And the people who analyse everything and subject everything to extensive critical investigation, they make things difficult for themselves and can never achieve true success. That's just my perception. My way of thinking, if I can put it like that.

It is interesting that the next interviewee – just like interviewee 43, who decides 80% analytically – was also active in stocks and real estate. In contrast to the latter, however, he concluded that in the real estate sector it is right to take more decisions based on gut feeling, while on the stock market it is not. When asked about the relationship between gut feeling and analysis, he responded:

Interviewee 12: Gut feeling: 80. Analysis: 20.

Interviewer: And can you provide me with an example? It's not easy to say exactly what gut feeling is, so maybe you could give me an example of such a decision.

Interviewee 12: Of course. In concrete terms, it has always been the same. I make real estate investments and then I maybe say to myself, analytically, that I monitor where the prices are at, how are things developing, what are the demographics doing, and so on. And my gut feeling is when I go and look at a property, drive up to it, I don't really drill down very deeply, but I say to myself, "Okay, let's do this deal."

Interviewer: Yes, there was someone else who said to me recently, someone with a few hundred million, also in the real estate business, he said, and maybe it's the same for you, he said, "There are some people who wade through all the data and figures." And he said, exaggerating a bit, "I place my hand on a dossier and know whether it's a good deal or not."

Interviewee 12: Yes, yes, that's exactly how it is with me. It's happened to me a lot, especially in bidding processes, if I think a building is good, and the bids are getting higher and higher, I don't even think about whether I make 100,000 more, or 100,000 less, I just say, "Okay, we're doing this deal. I have a good feeling about this, let's do it." It has always been based on gut feeling.

Interviewer: I guess everyone makes mistakes, so have you ever suffered a big reversal or made a big mistake, one where you would say, "Things would have been better if I hadn't trusted my gut"? Or vice versa, "It would have been better if I had paid more attention to my gut feeling"?

Interviewee 12: Let's put it this way, I haven't lost much money on real estate. In fact, I haven't actually lost any money with real estate. At most, there were some profits that I maybe didn't realize, let's say it like that. Maybe that I sold a property for too little, something like that, you know? And in many ways, that's the same as a loss, isn't it? I got things wrong with some stocks though, because I listened to my gut. For example, I bought stocks in Greek banks, and that didn't work out. But never with real estate. I think you have to make some distinctions. With real estate, you can trust your gut, because you get a feeling. But that's not a feeling you get with stocks.

16.3. THE ROLE OF ANALYSIS

Although a majority of the interviewees primarily rely on their gut feelings in their decision-making, there is a significant minority of one third who approach their decisions largely analytically. And even among the gut decision-makers, there was not a single interviewee who said they decide entirely on the basis of their gut feelings. A selection of the arguments raised by the analytical thinkers have already been outlined in the sections above. These analytical interviewees are the initial focus of the following section. In addition, it will be shown from the interviewees' own perspectives at which stage in the decision-making process analysis plays the most important role – even in cases where they ultimately make their decisions on the basis of gut feeling.

The following three interviewees each own global corporations with thousands, if not tens of thousands, of employees. It therefore comes as no surprise that the decision-making processes within their organizations are markedly different from those in the medium-sized enterprises owned by many of the other interviewees, who often employ just a few dozen or a couple of hundred employees. For such interviewees, formal decision-making processes, committees, etc. play a much more limited role than for the three owners of international corporations.

The first of these three interviewees is the owner of a very large, globally active business in the food industry. In the past, when his company was much smaller, he based a much larger proportion of his decisions on his gut feelings; today his decisions are largely based on analysis:

> **Interviewee 15**: At the beginning it was definitely based on a feeling, we'll do it this way, end of discussion, it'll work out. But today, of course, reason plays by far the greatest role, no question about it.
> **Interviewer**: Ah, so that has changed for you with the passage of time, has it?
> **Interviewee 15**: Yes. Yes, yes. Yes, of course. Now I have to think: "Is that something consumers will benefit from? Does it make sense?" and so on. Market intelligence, what's being offered, what else there is on the market, and the connections between the things you are doing, you know? For example, knowing that there are structures there that won't last in that form much longer. A really typical example was the [food product]. Structural change passed them by until well into the 1990s. There were lots of small operations, they had maybe 10 or 15 employees, making [food product]. And we looked at things and said, things can't stay like this, we could do this very differently. So when you recognize structural weaknesses, you understand? Structural weaknesses. And then you look at how you could do things better. And then you seize the initiative, and that worked out really well. It also worked out really well with [food product], but that was [competitor], that wasn't me,

you know? He bought up five operations and started doing the same as me, same volumes, just with 1,000 fewer people. One thousand fewer people.

Interviewer: And how do you do it then? Do you have employees to whom you can say, "Analyse that for me." Is that how it works?

Interviewee 15: Yes, yes, but you have to understand it for yourself. That's an incredibly important point, that you get involved and say, "I want to understand this." [...]

Interviewer: Let's just go back to the question of gut feeling and analysis. If you had to say, back when you were younger, was it 70% gut feeling and 30% reason, and is it the opposite today?

Interviewee 15: Yes, you could certainly say that.

Interviewer: And have you ever realized and said to yourself, "I listened to my gut feeling in that case and, in principle, I was wrong to do so, I would have been better thinking that over a bit more and I was too quick in making my decision"? Or vice versa?

Interviewee 15: Yes, I've sometimes let people talk me into things, or I haven't got my way. That happens from time to time.

Interviewer: And can you give me an example?

Interviewee 15: So, in [year] I made a proposal for how we could expand our capacities. That would have cost around 13 million. If we had gone ahead, we would have been able to start production a year ago. But my employees came to me and said, "Stop, that's not a good idea, what you are planning. It won't work out, it's a waste of time. We've got a different solution." So we decided to go ahead with something that has ended up costing 180 million. And whether that's going to end up being profitable, I have significant doubts. If we'd gone ahead with the other solution, we'd already have earned 50 million in profits. I'm annoyed now that I didn't push harder, didn't get my own way, you know? Or another case related to investments, whether you make certain investments or not, and there's always the details, the details. People make investment calculations and they look back into the past and assume that the future will be just like the past. They go back five years and extrapolate that five years into the future, you know? That's when I say, the last five years were great, but whether the next five will be the same, there I have real doubts. So that's reason, knowledge, understanding, knowing the market, that's a really crucial factor.

The next interviewee is another owner of a global business, where analytical decisions naturally play the far greater role, although he does draw a distinction between analysis-based strategic decisions on the one hand and decisions related to sales and marketing, where he relies on his gut to a greater extent:

Interviewee 26: I am analytical, yes. [...] Yes, but in relation to design, marketing and the like, there's a lot of gut involved. [...] The analytical part decides in which direction you should sail the ship. Yes, that's it. Sailing in the wrong direction doesn't help you at all, no matter how efficient you are. So the most important thing is that you've got the direction right. That's the analysis, isn't it? Your gut can't help you there. But everything after that, while you're on the ship, what you cook and eat, that's the sales and marketing stuff. And there's lots of gut feeling in all of that. And I see it with my employees, all you need to do is throw lots of different designs up on the wall and then I let them vote on the designs and I ask, "So, what do you think? Which is the right one?" That's when you see what kind of feeling they have. And I was lucky enough, in Heidelberg, to have someone, unfortunately he's two years older than me, but in 95% of cases we had the same opinion on things. Without even really needing to talk about things. He'd say, "This is the xxx and this is the other option, what would you take, which design?" Or, "There's this film and that film, which is better?" Agreed, just like that, you know. And other people never get it, do they?

The third interviewee, the owner of a globally active family business with a rich tradition, only relies on his gut for 20% of his decision-making. Decisions made within the family business are overwhelmingly prepared for on the basis of analysis. Gut feeling plays a role on occasion, simply because the analyses may over-emphasize the risks involved with something:

Interviewee 24: Within the business, the proportion of gut feeling involved is not so great, especially when I consider the amount of preparation and analysis. I think the proportion of [unintelligible] was far greater. So, in terms of gut feeling, at most 20%. [...]
Interviewer: And do you have the feeling that your approach has proved to be the right one? You wouldn't say that it might have been better to rely more on gut feeling, or even less so, when you look back?
Interviewee 24: No, I wouldn't say so. I'm more of an analyst. As far as that takes you. And then I take a leap and don't get paralyzed by fear and say, "No, that's it, no more." Of course, any analysis really emphasizes the risks, depending on the mentality of the people who have produced it for you. Naturally, you need to take that into account and you have to be able to read things correctly, understand every nuance. But even with the overall responsibility that I have, I'm strongly in favour of taking a very precise and detailed look at things, but then you really do it, bravely and with all of your strength, not half-heartedly.

The next interviewee is the owner of a medium-sized enterprise with several hundred employees. He says that he makes 70% of his decisions based on analysis. He nevertheless adds that he tends to rely more on gut feeling when it comes to major decisions, such as whether to sell his company or not. When asked what percentage of his decisions are made on the basis of analysis and intuition respectively, he answered:

Interviewee 27: 70% analysis.
Interviewer: 70% analysis. And in what decisions does gut feeling play a role? Which 30% is that?
Interviewee 27: Well, there are a huge number of decisions that you just can't arrive at from analysis alone. There are some things I can discuss a hundred times, but in the end it all comes down to a gut feeling.
Interviewer: Can you give me an example, from your business life?
Interviewee 27: When we were discussing selling the business over the last few years. That's a really good example. We hired coaches to help us answer exactly that kind of question. And I would have really liked it if someone had been able to say to me, "With your risk–reward profile, your type, how you are personally, you should sell." Or the opposite, "It's completely clear, keep hold of the company." But you'll never get those kind of answers. Not even to the extent of 51 to 49 for or against. We were always stuck rigidly at 50/50. So when it came to the crunch, I had to be led by my gut feeling.
Interviewer: So, if I've understood you correctly, it's the gut feeling that you're unavoidably left with. If it were possible, you'd prefer to do things 100% based on analysis.
Interviewee 27: Yes, and it depends on how important the decision is. There are some business decisions where I know I don't need 100 different analyses. There are still a number of decisions where I can say, "Come on, let's just do this." After all, if I analysed everything, based every decision on analysis, we wouldn't make any progress. If I had to take just those two dimensions and say how much gut feeling is involved, then I think that in the truly relevant decisions the gut plays more of a role than it does when it comes to basic, unimportant decisions, even though those decisions can also have a bearing on business processes.

The following property developer states that he bases 70% of his decision-making on analysis. He explains that this is largely the result of requirements made by banks. As real estate projects always require some form of outside financing, it is important for investors to anticipate how the project will be evaluated according to the analytical schemata of the bank before they greenlight funding for a project. They will not even consider a project that fails at this stage. This is why such a high proportion of his decisions are founded on analysis:

Interviewee 38: Of course, my approach has changed over the years. I used to make a lot more of my decisions based on gut feeling. I can't do that anymore; nowadays you have to analyse everything and provide every conceivable expert opinion or report in order to secure bank financing.

Interviewer: These expert opinions, you need them for the banks, I understand that, but couldn't your original decision be a gut decision?

Interviewee 38: That will always be a gut decision. You always need a gut decision, but any decision has to be so well prepared today. I can't just say, I know I'll buy this piece of land, irrespective of the planning permits, for example. Which I might have done in the past. Take xxx, for example, he bought up pretty much everything, every forest, every meadow. He knew that at some point he would get the planning permits he needed. We can't do that nowadays. You wouldn't get the financing you need for something like that today. You could do it with your own money, but nobody does that now.

Interviewer: But, ignoring the way you have to present things to secure the financing you need for one moment, and focusing on the decision itself, what would you say, what percentage is based on your gut feeling and what percentage is analytical?

Interviewee 38: Nowadays I would definitely say that 70% is analytical, based on all of the calculations. You need business plans, even though they never tell the full story. We all know that. Nobody has ever stuck to a business plan from beginning to end, but if you don't have a business plan, you can't do anything today. You have to manage the expectations. And then, it all depends on the market. If property prices fall and rents fall, then you make a loss, and you can't know that in advance, that's just speculation.

The following interviewee also operates in the real estate industry. He believes that it is a mistake to rely primarily on gut feeling when making decisions. In any decision, he stresses that there are always three aspects to consider: "the mathematics, the concept and the people". He adds that, in many cases, he has neither had a good feeling nor a bad feeling about something; rather he has had no feeling whatsoever. In such cases he continues to monitor the situation, and waits before he takes any action:

Interviewee 21: We have many aspects to consider. First of all, I have the mathematics. Secondly, the concept. And thirdly the people I am involved with. All of that amounts to about half of it. Then I have a feeling and I project into the future with this development and say to myself, "It'll work." That gives me a good feeling and it does work. But I'd estimate that represents about 50%.

Interviewer: Have you ever realized that you have listened to your gut feeling or your intuition and something has gone wrong as a result?

Interviewee 21: That's something I have often observed. That I had no feeling about something whatsoever. I didn't have a bad feeling. But I didn't have a good one either. I couldn't move forwards like that. So I said, "Don't do it. Stand still. Wait. See how things develop." I monitored the situation. And in some cases I waited for two years, five years, ten years, until I saw a chance to make it work. Time is definitely a factor. I mean it used to be a factor because of the interest rates. We don't really have interest rates anymore, but time is still a factor for me. When you are [around 70 years of age], time becomes a factor if you're being totally honest. Because you say to yourself that you don't want to create problems, you want to go out into the world with a focus on finding solutions.

Many of the interviewees emphasized that their decision-making is based on a distinct series of processes. The first stage involves analysing the figures. If at this stage a project is identified as not being worth further consideration, because the figures just do not add up, it is dismissed. But after this stage, it is the gut that decides:

Interviewee 16: In mathematics there's something quite interesting, there's the necessary condition and the sufficient condition, you know? And analysis is always a necessary condition. If the numbers don't add up, and the analysis doesn't arrive at positive results, then I never even get into a situation where I want to make a decision. But after that, the decision is 100% gut feeling. I would say that my decisions always follow a process. First, do the figures make sense? If the numbers don't add up then I don't think about it any further. So firstly, do the figures make sense? If they do, the next question is, "What does my gut say?" And my gut always has the final say.

INTERIM FINDINGS

The interviews confirmed the hypothesis derived from entrepreneurship research and behavioural economics, namely that entrepreneurs and investors primarily make their decisions on the basis of gut feeling. Of 45 interviewees, 24 stated that gut decisions dominate, 15 said that analysis takes the fore, and six said that they gave the two equal weighting, or it was unclear from their statements which dominated. In other words, one third said that analysis played the primary role, whereas more than half stated that gut feeling was the major factor in their decisions. However, only a single interviewee said that gut feeling has no influence whatsoever on his decisions. Even those interviewees who asserted that analysis clearly dominates rely on their gut feelings for between 20% and 40% of their decisions. In comparison, in surveys of the general population, the proportion who said that they tend to make their decisions based on reason outweighed the proportion who said that they tend to make decisions based on their feelings.

Who are the people who primarily base their decisions on analysis? One interviewee is the owner of a research company, which makes his answer somewhat unsurprising. Three were or are owners of international corporations, in which it is natural that well-prepared analysis and committee decisions play a more significant role than would be the case in owner-managed enterprises. Several of the interviewees who explained that they are predominantly analytical are not actually entrepreneurs; they are senior executives or people who used to work for large corporations. One interviewee said that 70% of his decisions are based on analysis, but admitted that this related to everyday decisions, whereas in relation to major, key decisions (such as whether to sell his company or not), his gut feelings play a far larger role. A real estate investor explained that analysis takes precedence due to the stipulations of banks' financing eligibility criteria. In such cases, external constraints – the dependency on bank financing – leads to the dominance of the analytical. Two interviewees who firmly declared that they arrive at their decisions primarily on the basis of analysis said they regretted this fact and wished that they had listened more to their gut feelings.

However, many of the interviewees stressed that gut feeling is not something innate; rather it is the sum of an individual's experience. This corresponds to the theory that gut feeling is the product of implicit learning: flashes of insight will appear in a fraction of a second, triggered by the recognition of a pattern, an awareness that is, in turn, the result of experience gathered over many years. Accordingly, a number of interviewees also explained that the proportion of their decisions based on gut feeling increased during the course of their lives.

Many of the interviewees ascribed a warning function to their gut feelings, and credited these alarm signals as having prevented them from making a number of poor business decisions. They regarded an "uneasiness in the gut" as an indication that they should proceed with an elevated degree of caution and should, at the very least, reassess their decision one more time. Some of the interviewees described making decisions against their gut feelings, decisions that they went on to regret because they led to mistakes being made. The conclusion they drew from such experiences was to never again make a decision counter to their gut feelings.

The industry in which the interviewees are involved had no bearing on whether they rely more on gut feeling or analysis when making their decisions. This was clearly illustrated by the example of four real estate investors: the first went as far as asserting that he (alone among the interviewees) makes all of his decisions 100% based on analysis. For another real estate investor, this applied to 80% of his decisions. These two investors even saw themselves as holding an advantage over their competitors precisely because so many real estate investors rely primarily on their gut feeling. In contrast, other interviewees from the same industry said that they make 80% to 90% of their decisions on the basis of gut feeling, and that, in their experience, people who rely too heavily on analysis are less successful.

Almost all interviewees agreed that decisions involving the assessment of people can only be made on the basis of gut feeling. One investor from the private equity sector said: "It boils down to reading people, assessing people, but you can't measure them, weigh them, put figures on them. It's not like you can look to see if they have an official stamp of quality on them, can you? You can't ask an auditor to analyse someone's character."

Many of the interviewees stressed the fact that their decision-making follows a set series of processes. This begins with a careful analysis of the figures. If a project is identified as not being worth further consideration, because the figures just do not add up, it is immediately dismissed. If the figures line up in favour of the project, gut feeling dictates the remainder of the decision-making process.

As demonstrated in Part A, gut feelings are a manifestation of implicit knowledge, which is, in turn, the product of implicit learning. It is therefore unsurprising that, as shown in Section 9.4, academic qualifications do not play the decisive role in the creation of wealth. The interviewees acquired the implicit knowledge that would later manifest itself as gut feeling in informal rather than formal learning situations, namely – as shown in Chapters 9.5 and 9.6 – through competitive sports, for example, or early entrepreneurial activity while they were at school or university. Thus, a variety of different elements from the analysis in Part A dovetail with the interviews analysed in Part B.

The Big Five:
Conscientiousness, Extroversion, Openness to Experience, Agreeableness and Neuroticism

17

According to the Big Five model presented in Chapter 6, the extent to which Neuroticism, Extroversion, Openness to Experience, Agreeableness, and Conscientiousness dominate their personality is the prime differentiator between individuals.

This model has been applied to entrepreneurs and the rich in both the entrepreneurial and the academic wealth research. As this study focuses exclusively on ultra-high-net-worth entrepreneurs and investors, the expectation was that the findings of the entrepreneurial and academic wealth researchers, which state that these two groups are characterized by particularly high levels of conscientiousness, in combination with openness to experience and extroversion, and low levels of neuroticism and agreeableness, would be confirmed.

The questionnaire used for this book was modelled on the Big Five model developed by McCrae and Costa. It is made up of 50 questions with five possible answers ranging from 'strongly agree' to 'strongly disagree'.[707] The questionnaire, which is reproduced as an appendix to this book, was filled out by all of the interviewees, apart from one, and the answers of one of the interviewees were not included in the final evaluation. This meant that 43 completed questionnaires were evaluated. The author is not aware of any other study in which a similar number of UHNWIs have completed such an extensive personality test.[708]

In analysing the questionnaires, scores between 0 and 40 points were awarded for each personality trait for each of ten questions. A score of 0 was used to indicate that there was an extremely low level of a specific trait, whereas 40 indicates an extremely high level of this trait. Scores above 25 points indicate that a specific trait is exhibited to a very strong degree, while fewer than 20 points indicates a weak trait.

- **Neuroticism** is a weak trait among the interviewees. All of the interviewees scored in the category from 0–19 points, and 36 of the 43 scored as low as 0–9 points.
- **Conscientiousness** is the dominant personality trait: 39 of 43 interviewees had between 25 and 40 points, which indicates a very high level for this characteristic.

- **Extroversion** is also very common among the interviewees: 29 of 43 interviewees are exceptionally extroverted.
- **Openness to Experience** is very common and is characteristic of 28 of the 43 interviewees.
- **Agreeableness** is less pronounced than Conscientiousness, Extroversion, and Openness to Experience, but is nevertheless still more pronounced than Neuroticism. The results of the personality test indicate that this trait is strong among 21 of the 43 interviewees, and only present at very low levels for nine of the interviewees.

These findings correspond to a large extent with previous research carried out by entrepreneurial and academic wealth researchers. The only exception is agreeableness, which proved more dominant or widespread than might have been expected on the basis of previous research. The findings of previous studies of UHNWIs were confirmed, in that conscientiousness was the most dominant personality characteristic and neuroticism the weakest.

As agreeableness proved to be the only trait for which the results of this test were at variance with the findings of prior research, additional questions were posed during the interviews in order to explore this trait further. This revealed that the test questions did not sufficiently distinguish between agreeable and conflict-oriented individuals within this test group. This will be addressed in greater detail in the next chapter.

The following lists questions from among the catalogue of 50 questions which most frequently received consistently similar answers from the interviewees. For each of the 50 test questions, respondents were asked to choose between five possible answers (A, B, C, D, E), with A representing strong disagreement and E representing strong agreement with the respective statement. The following questions most frequently received consistently similar answers from the interviewees.

NEUROTICISM

"I often think I am inferior to other people." (Question 1)
None of the interviewees agreed with this statement. In fact, 36 of 43 strongly disagreed with this statement and four disagreed. Only three neither agreed nor disagreed. This was to be expected. During the interviews, all interviewees exhibited extraordinary

---

707   Hesse and Schrader, *Persönlichkeitstest*, 88 et seq.

708   Unfortunately, it was not possible to compare the results here with results from other groups who have completed the same questionnaire. The publisher that holds the copyright to the questionnaire was kind enough to grant the right to reproduce the questionnaire here, but, despite repeated attempts, it was not possible to contact the authors of the questionnaire directly.

self-confidence and were themselves convinced of their exceptional skills. They viewed their professional and financial success as proof of this.

"I am not easily discouraged if things do not go so well." (Question 21)
Of the 43 respondents, 32 agreed very strongly with this statement, while ten indicated that they somewhat agreed. Only one interviewee was undecided. This finding will be addressed in more detail in Chapter 20, which focuses on the way in which the UHNWIs react to crises and setbacks. A high tolerance to frustration is one of the most characteristic personality traits of this group.

"There are days when I feel totally worthless." (Question 6)
None of the respondents agreed with this statement. In fact, 35 of the 43 very strongly disagreed and six strongly disagreed. Only two were undecided.

"I often feel depressed or abandoned." (Question 16)
Only four of the group often felt depressed or abandoned; three provided undecided responses and 33 of the 43 strongly disagreed, while three disagreed.

EXTROVERSION
"I am more of a pessimist." (Question 32)
Answers to this question were more consistent than for any other question. Of the 43 respondents, 38 strongly disagreed with the statement. A further three partially rejected the statement. Only two registered partial agreement, viewing themselves as tending towards pessimism. This personality trait has already been explored in detail in Chapter 14, where it was shown that optimism is among the interviewees' most dominant traits. It was demonstrated that the definition of optimism used by the interviewees describes the same attitudes that psychologists define as self-efficacy.

"I would describe myself as someone who prefers to go my own way." (Question 22)
Of the 43 interviewees, 30 registered very strong agreement with this statement and 11 partially agreed. Only two provided an undecided answer. This dimension is described in detail in Chapter 19. The test result confirms the findings of Schumpeter and others, who primarily characterize entrepreneurs as being prepared to swim against the current and make their decisions irrespective of majority opinion.

OPENESS TO EXPERIENCE

"I like to play out unusual ideas or new theories in my head." (Question 28)
Of the 43 interviewees, 28 expressed very strong agreement with this statement and a further 11 agreed partially. Only three provided undecided responses and one disagreed.

"I believe that you should constantly broaden your knowledge." (Question 33)
Of the 43 interviewees, 36 very strongly agreed with this statement and five partially agreed. Only two respondents provided undecided answers.

AGREEABLENESS

"I try to treat other people impartially and with friendliness." (Question 29)
Among all of the statements related to the dimension of agreeableness, this was the only one that more than half of the interviewees agreed with. Very strong agreement was registered by 26 of the 43, and a further 14 expressed partial agreement. Two were undecided and one signalled partial disagreement. The formulation of the statement itself is relatively weak ("I try to") and is composed of two very different elements (impartially and friendliness). It is therefore possible that, while an interviewee might treat other people impartially, they may do so without being especially friendly. In response to the other questions on agreeableness, the interviewees' answers varied strongly and no clear pattern emerged. In the next chapter, it will be demonstrated that the questions in this test related to agreeableness did not differentiate sufficiently between agreeable individuals and those with more conflict-oriented personalities.

CONCIENTIOUSNESS

"I work steadily and conscientiously in order to achieve my goals." (Question 15)
29 respondents very strongly agreed with this statement and nine registered their strong agreement. Only four were undecided and one disagreed. This characteristic was covered extensively in Chapter 11, which shows that a consistent goal orientation plays a very important role for many of the interviewees.

"I always keep my promises." (Question 35)
Of the respondents, 31 registered very strong agreement and 11 agreed strongly. Only one was undecided. Many of the interviewees said that they believed that a high degree of reliability was a crucial contributor to their professional and financial success. Thanks to a high level of reliability, they have gained the trust of business partners and, in particular, financiers.

"I often waste a lot of time before I start a task." (Question 50)
This statement was very strongly rejected by 27 of the interviewees, while a further eight partially disagreed. Three were undecided and five partially agreed.

INTERIM FINDINGS

The findings of the entrepreneurial and academic wealth research presented in Part A were largely confirmed by the interviewees' answers to the 50 questions of the Big Five test.

Among the interviewees, conscientiousness was found to be the dominant personality trait. As shown in Chapter 6, the Big Five theory's definition of conscientiousness includes dimensions such as devotion, precision, and thoroughness, along with diligence, discipline, ambition, and stamina. This was a very strong trait for 39 of the 43 respondents, who scored between 25 and 40 points for this trait. In the answers they provided to these questions, a high degree of determination and reliability were particularly evident.

Extroversion was widespread among the interviewees, but less so than conscientiousness. Of the interviewees, 29 of the 43 are exceptionally extroverted. They describe themselves as very optimistic people who prefer to forge their own paths.

Openness to experience was also very strong among the interviewees, as 28 of the 43 were very open to new experiences. The interviewees strongly agreed with the statement that they like to mentally experiment with unusual ideas.

Neuroticism is a weak characteristic among the interviewees. All of the interviewees were in the category 0 to 19 points, with 36 of the 43 even scoring as low as 0 to 9 points. This confirms the UHNWIs' exceptionally high levels of mental stability. Statements such as "I often think I am inferior to other people" were unanimously rejected by the interviewees. Strong assent, however, was given to the statement "I am not easily discouraged if things do not go so well".

According to the test results, the personality trait agreeableness was somewhat weaker than conscientiousness, extroversion, and openness to experience. However, agreeableness was still more pronounced than neuroticism. Agreeableness was a very strong trait for 21 of the 43 interviewees, while it was a weak trait for just nine respondents. According to the findings of previous entrepreneurship research, this trait should have been expected to be even weaker. This discrepancy is addressed in more detail in the next chapter.

Antagonism and Agreeableness | 18

Entrepreneurship research supports the hypothesis that the wealthy and entrepreneurs are less agreeable. Numerous studies show that agreeableness is negatively correlated with entrepreneurial success. In the early 1980s, David McCelland developed the hypothesis that 'affiliation', a component of agreeableness, could limit career development in management positions, as a manager with this trait would find it more difficult to make decisions that could potentially lead to conflict. Hao Zhao and Scott E. Seibert demonstrated that this is true for entrepreneurs to an even greater extent.[709]

Analysis of the biographies of billionaires such as Steve Jobs, Bill Gates, Rupert Murdoch, Ted Turner, and George Soros demonstrates that they were all highly antagonistic and intolerant.[710] Even as adolescents, they exhibited rebellious qualities and came into massive conflict with the people in their immediate environment, in particular with those in positions of authority.

In the course of the interviews, the interviewees were therefore asked whether they would generally characterize themselves as more harmony-oriented or more conflict-oriented. Agreeableness was also one of the five personality traits measured by the Big Five test.

18.1. NECESSARY CORRECTIONS TO THE BIG FIVE TEST

The results of the test indicated that agreeableness was a strong characteristic for 20 of 42 interviewees (minimum scores of 25 out of 40 possible points) and a weak characteristic for nine (0 to 19 points). Thirteen of the interviewees scored in the medium range with between 20 and 24 points. According to the test's findings, agreeableness was certainly less pronounced among

---

709   Zhao and Seibert, "The Big Five," 264.
710   See also Zitelmann, *Dare to be Different*, Chapter 6.

these wealthy individuals than the other personality traits (with the exception of neuroticism, which was even weaker). Nevertheless, a more detailed review of the test's results seemed required.

It is not possible to accurately assess the interviewees' levels of agreeableness or antagonism based solely on the test results. Rather, the findings here need to be combined with an analysis of the actual interviews, in which a willingness to engage in conflict is discussed at length. As the results of the test tended to contradict the findings of the previous research in the field, it was particularly important not to rely exclusively on the test questions, especially as there were doubts as to whether affirmative answers to some of the questions should really be accepted as a reliable indication of the agreeableness in the field of business (see below for more detail). Based on the test results alone, the interviewees were divided into four groups:

- A = low degree of agreeableness (0 to 19)
- B = average degree of agreeableness (20 to 24)
- C = high degree of agreeableness (24 to 34)
- D = very high degree of agreeableness (35 to 40).

A comparison of the test results with the evaluation of the interviews revealed that 13 of the interviewees who scored highly for agreeableness on the Big Five test actually described themselves as conflict-oriented individuals. According to the content of their interviews, seven of the individuals who were placed in groups C and D (high degrees of agreeableness) based on their test scores should clearly be classified as conflict-oriented. In terms of the statements made during their interviews, a further six of the interviewees assigned to group B (average degree of agreeableness) must also be reassigned to the conflict-oriented group. The following excerpts are taken from the interview transcripts of those interviewees with high or average test scores for agreeableness, but who clearly describe themselves as more conflict-oriented:

Interviewer: If people who know you well were asked to describe you, what would they say? That you tend to be a harmony-seeker or rather...?
Interviewee 1: No, I'm not a harmony-seeker.
Interviewer: So you don't shy away from conflict?
Interviewee 1: I stand my ground, that's right.

Interviewer: If you had to assess yourself on another scale, this time –5 is an absolute harmony-seeker and +5 is a very conflict-oriented individual, what would you say...
Interviewee 7: That depends. In business, +4 or +5.
Interviewer: So you don't shy away from conflict?

Interviewee 7: No, I don't. I get stuck into every conflict, yes. But in my private life, that's not such a strong characteristic, you know?

Interviewer: What do you mean, you get stuck into every conflict?

Interviewee 7: Well, I don't have any latent conflicts. There are conflicts that are resolved and there are conflicts that remain unresolved. I don't have any that haven't been resolved.

Interviewer: So, as an example...

Interviewee 7: Well, if I had a problem with you, I would say: "Dr Zitelmann, I have a problem with you. Last week, when we went out to dinner, there was this and that, and I didn't like that at all!" And we would discuss it and put it behind us, you know? So I don't have any simmering conflicts. Which is why I get stuck into discussions, confrontations, conflicts – to solve them, you know? I don't leave things unresolved.

Interviewer: Would others describe you more as a harmony-seeker or as someone who stands their ground?

Interviewee 11: As belligerent, combative, more of a conflict-oriented person.

Interviewer: So, people who know you well, would they describe you more as a harmony-seeker, or as someone who stands their ground?

Interviewee 26: I don't shy away from conflicts.

Interviewer: So, more belligerent.

Interviewee 26: Yes, certainly. You can't be successful without conflicts. People who are desperate for harmony will never make it to the top. [...] The route to the top is strewn with conflicts. It's all conflict.

Interviewer: If other people who know you well were to describe you, are they more likely to say that you always seek to maintain harmony, or that you are a more combative person who looks to get stuck into conflicts?

Interviewee 34: More likely the second one.

Interviewer: The second one. And how does this manifest itself? In your business or with your employees, or how?

Interviewee 34: It was evident from very early on. I'm not someone who goes chasing after conflicts, but I have a very clear idea of what is right and what is wrong, and I'm perfectly willing to articulate what I think. And that sometimes means that you bump heads with other people, doesn't it? There are some people who prefer to hold their tongues, so that they don't rub others up the wrong way. But when I feel strongly about something, when I am convinced that it is right to say something, then I prefer to get it said and harmony has to take the back seat.

Interviewee 43: On a purely business level, I don't shy away from any conflicts. On the contrary, in business I do not shy away from going in unorthodox directions, attracting criticism, having to defend myself for things that I think are right. I have no problems at all with any of that.

These and similar statements prove that a number of the interviewees who recorded average or high scores for agreeableness in the Big Five test tend, at least in business, to be far more conflict-oriented. The test found that agreeableness was a strong characteristic for 21 of the 43 interviewees (who scored at least 25 of a maximum 40 points) and a weak characteristic for nine (0 to 19 points). There were 13 interviewees in the medium range, scoring between 20 and 24 points. Taking the nine interviewees who, according to the test, were less agreeable, together with the 13 interviewees who were categorized as moderately or highly agreeable according to the test (but described themselves as more conflict-oriented in their interviews), then the group of more conflict-oriented individuals expands from 9 to 22. The group of interviewees classified as highly agreeable (C and D) thereby shrinks from 21 to 14. The corrected results are as follows:

- Low degree of agreeableness, conflict-oriented: 22 of 43
- Average agreeableness: 7 of 43
- High degree of agreeableness: 14 of 43.

The corrected results show that the number of conflict-oriented interviewees is significantly larger than the group of agreeable interviewees. In this corrected form, the results correspond far more closely with the findings of the previous research, which have shown that entrepreneurs and the wealthy are not especially agreeable. But what was it that led to such stark discrepancies between the test results and the interview findings on this point? Closer analysis reveals that the questions designed to measure agreeableness in the Big Five test are not necessarily fit for the purpose of assessing conflict orientation in a business context. The following ten statements are used in the Big Five test to measure agreeableness:

- "I prioritize respect and sensitivity in my actions towards others."
- "My co-workers and my family view me as an argumentative person" (reversed).
- "I am usually unyielding and uncompromising in my decisions and opinions" (reversed).
- "I think it is okay to tell somebody that you do not like them" (reversed).
- "I would never call myself a sceptic or a cynic."
- "I try to treat other people impartially and with friendliness."
- "Many people think that I am cold or arrogant" (reversed).

- "In order to achieve a specific goal, I can sometimes be extremely ruthless" (reversed).
- "Some people would describe me as egotistical and arrogant" (reversed).
- "I am someone who prefers cooperation to competition."

It is understandable why these questions do not adequately differentiate between conflict-oriented and more harmony-oriented persons in the field of business. Individuals who are typically 'uncompromising' in business will rarely be successful, since negotiations often involve making compromises. Thus entrepreneurs could not be expected to describe themselves as uncompromising. 'Argumentative' is a term with an extremely negative connotation – the term 'stand your ground' would probably have elicited different responses. And somebody might well state that they treat others impartially but are still very willing to stand their ground. Moreover, competition is one of the central pillars of economic life, and it is clear that not everything can be based on 'cooperation' – so entrepreneurs could not be expected to agree with this statement.

Nevertheless, and despite the clear inability of the test questions to accurately differentiate between conflict-oriented and harmony-oriented individuals, the UHNWIs exhibited lower levels of agreeableness (even *without* the correction described above) than any of the other personality traits, with the single exception of neuroticism.

18.2. THE AGREEABLE INTERVIEWEES

Despite the prevalence of more conflict-oriented personalities, it would be inappropriate to characterize the group as being defined by high levels of intolerance and antagonism. It is very clear not only that several of the UHNWIs consider themselves to be extremely agreeable but also that their test results in the Big Five indicate that this is indeed the case. The highest score for agreeableness was registered by an interviewee who described herself as "terribly harmonious". Yet this interviewee, who is now in her 70s, admitted that she had been tougher and more willing to stand her ground when she was younger. This corresponds with the findings of personality research that indicate that agreeableness increases with age:[711]

Interviewee 14: I am terribly harmonious, but in my dealings with the outside world I tend to be more stubborn. It's not easy, because I much

---

711   McCrae and Costa, *Personality in Adulthood*, 62.

prefer harmony, but on the other hand, at some point in business you need to be strong-willed. How shall I put it? You need to be able to say "no".

Interviewer: Could you expand on that a little, what you just said about saying "no"? Maybe with an example.

Interviewee 14: Certainly. For example, when it comes to staffing decisions, there are occasions when you simply have to say: "No, that is definitely not good for the company." When you have someone in charge in a branch, and the figures are always bad, you have to be able to say, "Right then, now I have to take action and make a change."

Interviewer: So that means that although, as you said, you valued your employees and had a good relationship with them, that was never really your objective. I am actually a little sceptical when people say that you have to be popular with your employees. Or don't you think that the one thing sometimes excludes the other, because you do have to be tough sometimes?

Interviewee 14: All in all, I would say that I am popular, but that might have something to do with my age. When I was younger I was probably...

Interviewer: Were you tougher?

Interviewee 14: Tougher. Yes, I was tougher.

Interviewer: Were you? And maybe also more confrontational?

Interviewee 14: Yes, yes, of course I was. Very much so.

Interviewer: [...] And did you ever get angry, when things were particularly difficult, and really lose your temper?

Interviewee 14: No, I never did that. I never get loud. But I can be resolute and say: "That is unacceptable." And then you either have to go your separate ways or make a decision that the other party might not like. It's the same in negotiations. I was always described by other people as a bit of a toughie.

Another interviewee, who tends towards agreeableness according to the test results, also reported that it took him a number of years to "get it out of his system", and has since become more agreeable.

Interviewee 6: So, you know me as a totally peaceful person. But in our federation, for example, I am seen as the troublemaker, the bolshy one, the difficult one, the rude one, the argumentative one, the one who is always a bit stressful to deal with. And it's only really in the last five years that I've shed all of that. I think that everyone used to view me as very confrontational.

Interviewer: Oh, I see. And what changed you, how did that come about?

Interviewee 6: Because I got it out of my system. I put all of that butting heads with other people and having to get my own way behind me and realized that it was better to avoid discussing controversial politics with my family over coffee and cake, that kind of thing.

[...]

Interviewer: So, one could say that you changed to some extent?

Interviewee 6: Quite a lot; I've taken a big step back from being someone who used to pretty much go around looking for arguments.

The next interviewee was classified as highly agreeable and conflict-averse by both the Big Five test and the statements he made during his interview. However, his self-description stood in very striking contrast to his accounts of his school days, where he explained that he was always in trouble and was expelled from five schools, which does not exactly tally with the image of a highly agreeable person.

Interviewer: Would other people tend to describe you as a harmony-seeker, or would they say you tend to be more confrontational?

Interviewee 40: It's all about harmony for me. As far as arguments are concerned, I was always the cheerful, carefree one. That's just how it was.

Interviewer: But that doesn't really match up with what you told me about your schooldays.

Interviewee 40: No, I'm a bit of a rascal, you know? That's simply how I am. It's not something I can easily explain. My teachers had to do what teachers have to do, but they liked me as a person. They said: "Come on, you're such a great kid, why do you do things like that?" And, because I was so pig-headed, I said, "But, that's what I do." So that's probably the best way to describe me. I think that I have a really big circle of friends and acquaintants, and I don't think that I have many enemies or people who hate me. I really don't think that at all. Even in the business world. And I think that, in relation to business, if you ask around, there are lots of people who will say that I stick to my guns, but that I'm a smart guy.

A number of the interviewees described themselves as agreeable (which corresponded to their test results) while at the same time admitting that the people around them would see things very differently. This is true for the following interviewee:

Interviewee 35: Well, I would say opinion is divided. Because I would tend to describe myself as more of a diplomat, as a consensus builder, but from the people around me I always hear the exact opposite. That I'm permanently oriented towards competition and confrontation. And they are right, I like to discuss things and, of course, I'll fight for the best solution.

My motto is always: thesis, antithesis, synthesis. Which naturally requires that you formulate an antithesis, and that constantly rubs lots of the people in my closest circle up the wrong way and they say: "There's always battles and no harmony." So there's a real dichotomy between my own assessment and what the people around me say and think. And I sit down every evening and have to say to myself, "You know what, somehow the others are right."

In a majority of cases, the behaviour of the interviewees cannot be reduced to a common denominator. There are interviewees who describe themselves as extremely confrontational in their dealings with competitors or within their own company. In their dealings with customers, however, this is of course not the case, as, if it were, they would hardly have enjoyed the success they have. This applies, for example, to the next interviewee, who is also agreeable according to the test, but who makes the following distinction: within his own company he is considered to be very aggressive, even "the most aggressive of the partners", while he describes himself as "if anything, too harmonious" when it comes to dealing with clients:

Interviewee 17: I think the answers to that question are very different. [...] In my role as managing partner, for example, I have a duty to address painful subjects, which means I am viewed as very aggressive.
Interviewer: Yes? Okay, I understand. And what really gets your blood boiling? What makes you blow your top, go crazy?
Interviewee 17: Well, when things are just not working as they should. Or when partners are undisciplined. I'm well known for the fact that I don't shy away from anything. That's something that a lot of people just can't deal with. [...] And then you have to confront things head on, because there's no other way. I'm sure that I'm regarded as the most aggressive of the partners. But when it comes to personal contact with [clients] and friends, I actually tend to be too harmonious.

The following interviewee, who is very agreeable according to the test and describes himself as a profound seeker of harmony, recognizes this as a flaw in himself:

Interviewee 18: Well, I know myself that I'm a harmony-seeker and not so confrontational. But I'm not entirely sure what others would say about me.
Interviewer: Fine. So, you say that you have had many serious arguments or confrontations, for example with employees?
Interviewee 18: No.

Interviewer: Never got angry.

Interviewee 18: That was one of my mistakes, that I didn't confront my employees often enough. I was too generous to my employees. I needed harmony. Harmony was more important than conflicts.

Another interviewee, who has been highly successful as a stock and real estate investor and scored highly for agreeableness in the Big Five test, describes himself as being a person who tends to seek harmony. He justifies this by explaining that "arguing doesn't get you anywhere" because it achieves nothing. Instead, one should seek to create 'win–win' situations, which he believes he can better achieve through a strategy of consensus rather than conflict:

Interviewee 31: No, more of a harmony-seeker, although harmony itself was never that important to me, it's always been far more about creating a consensus between divergent interests and parties. Throughout my career, I have always been described as someone who follows a strategy based on hugs rather than arguments. But that was always more directed at building consensus. I very quickly became convinced that arguing doesn't solve anything. First, it's stressful and second, it doesn't bring you any closer to your goal. You have to try to understand your opposite number's situation and make something constructive out of it. To create a win–win situation.

18.3. THE CONFLICT-ORIENTED INTERVIEWEES

There are, however, several interviewees who describe themselves as extremely confrontational and whose test results also indicate that they are not particularly agreeable individuals. This interviewee from the real estate industry registered low levels of agreeableness in the test and views himself as more of a conflict-oriented person. He regards conflict as an essential "filtering" mechanism, which he uses to keep people who may represent a danger to him or his business at arm's length. He believes it is often necessary to resolve conflicts early on in order to then enjoy a conflict-free relationship. When asked how others perceive him, he responded:

Interviewee 16: They would describe me as someone who stands my ground. [...] Anyone who knows me well would say, "Tough skin, soft on the inside." I use conflicts as a filtering mechanism, so that I can go on to live in harmony with the people I'm close to. So, arguments are almost a filtering process that allow you to keep away from people who might represent a threat. [...] In that regard, I'm a sportsman. The sporting spirit is also combative. I don't argue for the sake of arguing, but it makes sense to get it over and done with, to know how things stand, so that you can then have a conflict-free time.

The next interviewee, who comes from the IT industry, describes himself as conflict-oriented, which matches the low rating for agreeableness he received from his test result. He reported that counselling has helped him control his anger issues. When asked to describe himself, he said:

> **Interviewee 33**: Confrontational. [...] I enjoy debating. I also enjoy hearing different opinions. That's how I like things. If we sat down with each other three times and agreed on everything, that would be boring. But if we can discuss different opinions on politics, on anything, then, for me, we've had a rich and enjoyable conversation. I tend to get bored if I sit down and talk with people who think the same as me on all of the questions of life.
> **Interviewer**: That's one side of it. Let's come to the other side, which is that lots of entrepreneurs really lose their tempers and blow up. [...]
> **Interviewee 33**: Yes, I used to lose my temper quite often. But I managed to get myself under control. It's very rare that I lose my temper nowadays.
> **Interviewer**: I find that really interesting. How did you manage to gain control over your temper?
> **Interviewee 33**: Well, essentially, of course, via counselling, by asking myself, why do I do that? It's often the result of a feeling of helplessness, of uncertainty. So, once you understand the "why" of it, you don't need it anymore. [...] And that's something you're more likely to achieve from counselling or the like.

The highly conflict-oriented interviewees did not limit their confrontational behaviour only to their business lives. According to the results of the Big Five test, the following interviewee scored poorly for agreeableness, which matches up with his own description of himself. He simply loves "the rough and tumble" and will argue with anyone. He views it as a kind of sport and associates it with assertiveness and getting his way – "it doesn't matter [...] if I'm doing business or riding my bike." He clashes with everyone who "unwittingly crosses" him:

> **Interviewer**: If other people were to describe you, would they say you are someone who always looks to keep the peace, or someone who stands their ground?
> **Interviewee 37**: Someone who stands their ground. [...] I just love it, the rough and tumble. I love it. I'll argue with anyone, in a positive way.

I have to admit, I view it as a bit of a game. I want to assert myself, you know? And it doesn't matter whether it's a difference of opinions, or if I'm doing business or riding my bike.

Interviewer: So, who do you argue most often with?

Interviewee 37: Well, with anyone who unwittingly crosses me.

Interviewer: I meant more in business.

Interviewee 37: In business? Well I'm not in sales anymore. That means it's my suppliers, then the people who work for me, my management team. Then my competitors. I take a very close look at them. I'm aiming for world domination, you know? I can't afford to take any prisoners. [...] I'm a real fighter. No doubt about it.

The next interviewee, whose test result indicates average levels of agreeableness, believes that he has become calmer over the years, but described his own highly aggressive behaviour. He answered in the negative when asked whether he sometimes "explodes" and described himself as "quite calm now", before going on to describe how he recently threatened a party guest: "I'll hit you so hard in the mouth that your teeth will fly out." This is what he means when he talks about sorting things out "calmly":

Interviewee: I'm really calm nowadays. I can give you an example. My name won't appear here, will it? I hosted a party and there was lots going on. And there was one guest, who hadn't behaved himself well. And he hadn't even been invited, someone else had brought him along to the party. And, at some point, one of the other guests let me know that this guy had done something. So I went over to him and said, "Who are you?" And he answered, "That's none of your business!" I said, "Of course it's my business, this is my party." So then I said, "Look here..." And he said, let's say, "My name's Frank." So I said, "Look here, Frank. You have two options." I smiled at him. "We smile at each other, I smile, you smile. Then you get your things together, it was a great party, you had some nice food, something to drink, and now you're going home after a nice evening." "And what's the second option?" Which is when I told him, "The second option is that you decide not to leave, and I'll give you 30 seconds to make your decision, but then I'll punch you so hard in the face that your teeth will fly out." "Then I'd better leave." To which I replied, "Good decision." [...] And that's that. And I never raised my voice to him, you know. When I was younger...

Interviewer: Were things different when you were younger?

Interviewee: Yes. I used to be much more impulsive. Today I approach things calmly, but I still assert myself, you know?

INTERIM FINDINGS

The hypothesis proposed in entrepreneurial and academic wealth research, namely that entrepreneurs and the wealthy are less agreeable, was only partially confirmed. According to the Big Five test, agreeableness was a less pronounced personality trait than conscientiousness, openness to experience, and extroversion. Nevertheless, the test results showed agreeableness was a trait of a majority of the interviewees. There were, however, well-founded doubts as to whether the test questions adequately differentiated between those who tend to be more conflict-oriented and those who are more harmony-oriented in the field of business.

The test results were therefore compared with the analysis of the interviews. During the interviews, the interviewees were asked whether they would tend to characterize themselves as harmony-seekers or conflict-oriented. Taking the interviewees who were classed as conflict-oriented by the test, together with those who described themselves as conflict-oriented in their interviews, despite having scored more highly for agreeableness in the test, leads to the following: of the 43 UHNWIs who took the test, more than half (22) received a low agreeableness rating and can be classified as tendentially conflict-oriented, seven registered average levels of agreeableness, and 14 exhibited high levels of agreeableness. The corrected results show that conflict-oriented individuals outnumbered agreeable individuals by a significant margin. The findings thus correspond more closely with the existing research findings, which have shown that wealthy individuals and entrepreneurs are not very agreeable.

The interview questions also showed that a few of the interviewees who described themselves as very harmony-oriented (matching the results of their Big Five tests) used to be far more conflict-oriented. This corresponds to research results that find that agreeableness increases with age. Other interviewees exhibited striking discrepancies between their own self-perceptions and the ways in which they are viewed by others. The interviewees reported that they perceive themselves as harmony-oriented, but are viewed as more conflict-oriented by the people around them. In addition to this, many of the interviewees painted a more differentiated picture – in relation to their customers, for example, they are very focused on harmony, while they may be perceived as highly aggressive within their own companies.

The highly conflict-oriented interviewees described behaviours that suggested that their aggressive tendencies are not only confined to their working environments but also exhibited in other areas of their lives, where they hardly ever make efforts to avoid a confrontation. For many of the interviewees, this readiness to meet conflicts head on corresponds with the fact that, with their investments and business decisions, they often position themselves in opposition to majority opinion and swim against prevailing currents – which is the subject of the next chapter.

Nonconformism: "Swimming Against the Stream" 19

In his analysis of the lives and success strategies of 14 billionaires, Martin S. Fridson came to the conclusion that those who always comply with conventions and the societal code of conduct, or who are unable to deal with massive criticism and hostility, are unlikely to achieve great wealth. Fridson uses a host of examples to demonstrate that billionaires such as Bill Gates, John D. Rockefeller, Carl Icahn, and others were frequently the target of intense hostility, which, however, did not deter or intimidate them. "Imperviousness to such criticism has been a key to Icahn's success. Although by some accounts he wants to be well-liked, making pals is hardly the central focus of his business activity. 'If you want a friend on Wall Street,' he advises, 'get a dog.'"[712]

According to Fridson, self-made billionaires have always forged their own paths. Anyone who orients themselves according to majority opinion does not have much chance of becoming wealthy. "Doing the same thing in the same way as everyone else is decidedly not the way to overcome the leveling effects of competition," writes Fridson.[713] In Fridson's view, people who always obey society's unwritten rules and codes of conduct therefore rarely achieve substantial fortunes.[714]

The entrepreneurial type described by Schumpeter, as detailed in Section 3.1, swims "against the stream".[715] "The fact that something has not yet been done is irrelevant to him as a counterargument. He does not feel the inhibitions which otherwise constrain the behaviour of economic agents."[716] Schumpeter's entrepreneur "is quite indifferent ... to what his peers and superiors would have to say about his business."[717]

---

712 Fridson, *How to Be a Billionaire*, 12.
713 Ibid., 216.
714 Ibid., 11.
715 Schumpeter, *Theorie*, 121.
716 Ibid., 132.
717 Ibid., 163–164.

More recent entrepreneurship research also emphasizes the importance of nonconformism, even if the term itself is not used. George G. Brenkert showed that academic scholars have frequently characterized entrepreneurs as "rule breakers".[718]

One of the hypotheses developed in Part A is that a specific form of nonconformism is a typical trait of UHNWIs. This was based on the assumption that it is difficult to become rich by operating in the same way as all other competitors and making the same investments as the majority of other investors. The entrepreneurs and investors were therefore asked for examples of instances where they had deliberately set themselves in opposition to the opinions that prevailed within their social peer group.

More than half of the interviewees emphasized that their habit of swimming against the prevailing current had been a key contributing factor for their success. Only four explicitly refuted this. And few of the 50 questions in the Big Five personality test were met with as unanimous a response as the statement "I would describe myself as someone who prefers to forge my own path": 30 of the 43 interviewees agreed strongly, while 11 expressed partial agreement and only two were undecided. Not a single interviewee disagreed.

It should, however, be noted that most of the pronounced contrarians were investors, often from the real estate sector. Therefore, the findings cannot necessarily be generalized. In addition, two different types emerged from the interviews.

Type A quite obviously enjoys swimming against the prevailing current and standing in opposition to the majority opinion as a matter of principle. Type B, on the other hand, is indifferent to majority opinion and is prepared to frequently swim against the current, without elevating this attitude to the level of a principle, or gains no specific pleasure from taking such a contrarian position.

19.1. "I HAVE MADE IT MY ABSOLUTE MISSION TO THINK DIFFERENTLY FROM EVERYONE ELSE"

For the first type, swimming against the current and disagreeing with majority opinion is almost a knee-jerk reaction. This attitude is evident in the obvious enjoyment the following interviewee takes in the role of outsider or misfit:

> **Interviewee 4**: I have always seen myself as someone who experiences things differently, sees and thinks differently, even if I haven't always broadcast the fact.
> **Interviewer**: And can you give me an example of what you mean?
> **Interviewee 4**: I can. It started when I went to the Chamber of Commerce here and told them that I wanted to get involved in real estate. That was in the 1980s and they said, "For God's sake, Mr xxx, you've missed the boat.

I would strongly advise you against getting involved in real estate. Real estate is dead. It's over." And that's what made me realize that I really had to do it. And it's always been like that when anyone tells me not to do something, or that I can't do it. What did people in the industry say to me? "Mr xxx, trying to sell apartments is the stupidest idea, you'll never make any money that way." Yes? And for many years I didn't earn much money from them, but I stuck at it, didn't I? And I did it even more when I saw that it was difficult, that's what appealed to me, isn't it?

Interviewer: I have what might be a very personal question in relation to this outsider role. As far as I know, you are gay.

Interviewee 4: Yes.

Interviewer: And as a gay man, you must have been used to being in the role of an outsider from very early on.

Interviewee 4: Yes.

Interviewer: Do you see a connection there? Could you say, "I was already used to not conforming to the norm, not being like all the others, so that made it easier to do the same in business."

Interviewee 4: Yes, that's true. It reinforces that, you know? It reinforces what you learn, to avoid following certain tendencies, schools of thought, patterns of behaviour. I eat completely differently to everyone else. I sleep differently. I think differently. I have made it my absolute mission to think differently from everyone else, you know? I listen to music differently; when I'm at a concert, I criticize internally – lovingly, because I don't want to be aggressive – but I criticize the conductor from the second he picks up his baton. [...] And it's something I enjoy. I have learned to adopt that as my role, as a provocation. Even within the industry, you know? And there are lots of people out there who like me for exactly that reason, because I think differently from the majority.

For such people, there is nothing negative or indecent in being a misfit or outsider. On the contrary, they appropriate this label proudly and perceive it as something to boast about. One of the wealthiest interview partners confesses:

Interviewee 21: I have always been an outsider. I always did things that no one else would do. The others, they said, "The economy will pick up." And I said, "It's heading downwards, in two years it will start to go down.

---

718   Brenkert, "Innovation," 4.

So, what can I do today to make sure that I'm well positioned when the economy starts to decline?"

Interviewer: And did it give you a certain inner joy when you said, "Everyone else says to go left, so I'm taking a turn to the right"? Would you agree?

Interviewee 21: That was my way.

In reality, type A – in contrast to type B – does not operate completely independently of majority opinion. Rather than being indifferent to it, it is almost a knee-jerk reaction to maintain a contrarian position because one of the contrarian's key doctrines is that the "herd" often gets things wrong. The "herd" does not just refer to a majority of the population; it also frequently refers to a majority of market players in a particular industry:

Interviewee 16: Let me put it this way, as an automatic reaction I always go in the opposite direction. Because my lifetime's experience tells me that it tends to be a mistake to follow the herd.

Interviewer: And how much of your success would you say is due to swimming against the current?

Interviewee 16: 90%. [...] Swimming against the current means keeping a cool head, not allowing yourself to be caught up in prevailing opinions, to think independently and to try, in principle, to influence your own fate, doesn't it? And lining up with the masses, being pulled along with them, you're basically handing control of your fate to the masses.

Many interviewees report the pleasure they gain from going against majority opinion. While many people feel uncomfortable when they are outsiders or standing in opposition to a majority, for these individuals this is precisely the source of their greatest pleasure. One interviewee, who reports how he has placed himself in opposition to majority opinion both in his professional decisions and in his investments, admitted:

Interviewee 6: I got an almost perverse delight out of it, because after all it was part of my contrarian nature, because I was never interested in consensus. On the contrary, you could say that I was deliberately looking for the opposite.

Another interviewee talked about how much he enjoys looking for the "fly in the ointment" when everyone else thinks something is right:

Interviewer: Some people are successful because they have the courage to stand up to prevailing opinions and do things differently from everyone else.
Interviewee 11: I have absolutely no problem doing that.
Interviewer: You don't? There are people who say they get a kick out of doing just that, that it's something they enjoy in a certain way. So, how would you see yourself in that regard, let's call it 'swimming against the current', a degree of nonconformism?
Interviewee 11: I really, truly enjoy it.
Interviewer: You enjoy it, even when you express opinions that dissent from the majority?
Interviewee 11: Yes.
Interviewer: Everyone says one thing, and you say the opposite.
Interviewee 11: Yes, when everyone believes that something is right, I expend all my energy trying to find the fly in the ointment.

This attitude was not confined to the interviewees' investments. They also quite proudly reported relevant examples of minor and major successes from their everyday lives:

Interviewee 12: Off the top of my head, I can think of one example. I always try to go my own way, or at least to question everything. I have had lots of experiences like the one I'm about to tell you about. I went to Bali ten years ago. I landed and there were massive queues, 100 people in every line – 100 people here, 100 people there. And there was one desk where nobody was waiting. So, I just went over and said, "Hello there, would you be so kind as to let me through?" The man at the desk said, "Certainly, no problem." And everyone else saw this and came running over after me. Things like that happen to me all the time. If I'm somewhere where I have to stand in line, if I want a new iPhone for example, I always try to find an unconventional way around the problem to get what I want. The same with real estate, if I want to buy a property, or anything else.
Interviewer: And can you give me an example of an investment where everyone else was doing things one way and you did things differently?
Interviewee 12: I was definitely the first, or at least one of the first, to invest aggressively in B and C locations in [719][city]. [...]
Interviewer: And how did you react when other people said, "Hang on, that's stupid, why are you even doing that?" Did that spur you on?

---

719   The interviewee is referring to secondary, less expensive real estate locations.

Interviewee 12: Yes, that spurred me on. But it didn't really give me any extra pleasure, because I totally believed in myself and my strategy. I said to myself, "It's actually great that everyone else thinks that what you are doing is crap, because it means the property prices will stay low."
Interviewer: And you were never nervous or uneasy when you did things differently?
Interviewee 12: The opposite. Exactly the opposite.

Another interviewee, who has enjoyed great success in the field of medical technology, reported that he feels uneasy when everyone else agrees with him. In fact, for nonconformists, it is indeed unsettling when they see that their actions or beliefs are in alignment with the majority. The following interviewee even believes that this attitude is a general precondition for entrepreneurial success:

Interviewee 32: I've never followed the herd anywhere. I often wonder why people just plod along doing the same old things without ever questioning why or asking themselves what they could do better or differently. [...] But once I've identified what I believe is the right way, then I think of the wonderful quote, I think it's from Oscar Wilde: "Whenever people agree with me I always feel I must be wrong." Do you see what I mean? So, when I have identified what I believe is the right way, I can also see the reasons why others might think it's the wrong one, you understand? It's mostly not a question of rational arguments, but there can be other reasons. I have absolutely no problem with that. [...] As an entrepreneur, you'll never be successful if you swim with the current. No. Then you'll be following someone who changes tack, and you won't even realize until you catch up with him again. But if you set the course for yourself, then you will be successful. And that can mean swimming against the current to some extent.

Another entrepreneur, who built his fortune in the IT technology industry, reported that he was often ridiculed by others, which triggered a reaction in him: "Now more than ever!"

Interviewee 33: Yes, people were always laughing at us.
Interviewer: Why?
Interviewee 33: Because they said that nobody needed what we were doing. They said it was totally useless. [...]
Interviewer: And how did you react? Some people take an extra motivation from having others laugh at them. Others might react by becoming insecure.

How did you deal with it, psychologically? Or are you someone who says, "Now more than ever"?

Interviewee 33: Yes, I tend to be one of those who says, "Now more than ever." Although I also think that believing in something involves a degree of doubt. Every now and then, you have to have your doubts, and not everything always worked out.

19.2. "THE PICKINGS ARE SLIM IN THE MAINSTREAM"

In clear contrast to type A described above, who opposes majority opinion as a matter of principle and gains great satisfaction from doing so, type B claims to act completely independently of what the majority thinks. Majority opinion is simply irrelevant to type B individuals – they do not necessarily follow it, but neither do they necessarily oppose it. One of the most successful investors in the group of interviewees said that his frequent opposition to majority opinion had played a very important role in his success. When asked whether he views himself as a nonconformist who happily swims against the current, he resolutely replied:

Interviewee 22: No, no. It's not as if I think to myself, do I deliberately want to play the contrarian here? Rather, I try to form my opinion based on the factors that are important to me. And then I look around and work out whether that chimes with the masses or not. But I never approach anything saying, "Let's see, how would it be if I take a contrarian position, what would that involve and would it be promising?" That would be one approach. But that's not my approach. I approach things from the opposite direction and say, "This is what I think is right in this specific situation." And then I look to see if that is with the masses or against them. [...]

Interviewer: Still, there is probably a certain degree of satisfaction in seeing that everyone else goes in one direction and you head the opposite way, and you are the one who is successful. Or does that not really matter to you?

Interviewee 22: If I'm being totally honest here, at that point in time you have already taken the decision to do things in a certain way. But of course you also have doubts, because everyone else is doing things differently.

Interviewer: You sometimes think to yourself, "Am I the person driving on the wrong side of the freeway and wondering why everyone else is headed in the other direction?"

Interviewee 22: Yes, exactly. Exactly right.

Interviewer: And is that how it is for you?

Interviewee 22: No, no, nothing so intense. I've always kept my cool, but still. You could say that there was a similar situation just after German reunification.

Everyone made a dash for eastern Germany and started snapping up real estate. [...] After driving around for a day or two I just said, "We're going to keep on doing what we've been doing." And that was despite the fact that no one wanted to at the time.

Interviewer: I see. You're not like some of the other people I have spoken to who get a real kick out of it. They say, "Everyone else is heading to the left, so that really makes me want to go over to the right."

Interviewee 22: No. No, not at all. [...] In certain situations, I have gone with the herd, and, for example, I'm doing it right now in the sense that I wouldn't want to place a bet on the next interest rate rise. I believe that the majority fully expects interest rates to stay low for the foreseeable future, and I wouldn't bet against that trend because I can see a lot that speaks in favour of it at the moment. Whether the reasons are rational or not remains to be seen. But there are lots of reasons for the status quo to be maintained. [...] And that's just one example of going with the herd.

Some of the interviewees interpret successfully standing up to peer pressure as a sign of a strong character. This is clearly evident from the following interviewee, who described a situation from his youth that involved him resisting pressure from his peers. However, he also expressed opinions typical of type B, who does not instinctively oppose majority thinking as a matter of principle, but claims to arrive at decisions completely independently of what the majority believes:

Interviewee 41: I have always swum against the current and have never had a problem doing so. That was true early on, even as a student. I can give you an example. Everyone was sitting around the table and had taken a decision and I said, "No, I'm not doing that, it's complete and utter nonsense and I am not doing it." And then they all tried to pressure me into agreeing. I was the only one who didn't get involved, everyone else paid the price. I was the only one who came out of it with my nose clean. I have never had a problem with that. I trust my intellect and listen to all of the arguments, but I make my decision based on what I think, not what anyone else thinks. At the end of the day, it doesn't matter what anyone else says. I'll take it on board and consider what other people say, but my decisions are based on what I think is correct, not what other people think is correct. And I don't care if 99% of other people are against it.

Interviewer: And this ability to swim against the current, how much of your success would you say you owe to it, if you can put it so simply?

Interviewee 41: Yes, I believe that I owe a significant portion of my success to the belief that I can rely on myself more than anyone else. I'd say it's a huge part of my success – 90%, 80% at least.

For some, nonconformism may be an affectation, or even a quirk, but in many cases, it is based on serious considerations of why financial success is much more likely when you swim against the current. One interviewee, who has been successful in both investment banking and the real estate sector, credits "almost 100%" of his success as an investor to his ability to swim against the prevailing current. He also reported the "joy" he gets when everyone else is taking a left turn and he heads to the right. When asked whether this didn't sometimes make him feel uneasy, he admitted that he was by no means always free from doubt:

> **Interviewee 43**: Of course, constantly. To the outside world I might look like an aggressive risk-happy person, but I don't do that just to swim against the current. No, every one of my decisions is based on a great deal of work, analysis, thoughts, and calculations. And, of course, I am constantly asking myself whether I am doing the right thing when I'm swimming against the current. After all, the current never stops shifting and it might take a couple of years before you can say with certainty that a certain approach was the correct one. And there are always doubts, sometimes more so, sometimes less so. But there have been things that I have done, things that were regarded as controversial by others in the industry, where I had no doubts whatsoever and still don't. And there are other things that you constantly question and reconsider, you know? But it would be pretty bad if that wasn't the case. That would make you totally autistic. I may be a little autistic, but I'm not totally autistic.

His contrarian strategy is based on the fundamental premise that the intrinsic value of something will ultimately align with its market price. Contrarian investors are driven by the conviction that temporary market fluctuations, which are partly triggered or exacerbated by the effects of mass psychology, offer the opportunity to buy goods under their true, intrinsic value:

> **Interviewer**: Yes, at some point the others do have to recognize the true value of something. And even when you say that the others are stupid, you have to anticipate their stupidity when you are making your decisions. Have you ever thought about that?
>
> **Interviewee 43**: Yes, that's right. I have developed a fundamental trust in the market, probably owing to my time on the capital market in the English-speaking world. I am convinced that, in the long term, the market price of any investment will always end up at the right level. Capital always follows the best ideas, maybe not in the medium term, but certainly in the long term. Capital finds the best returns, and for the best ideas – only in the long term – capital is always available. It's just a question of time.

There are stock market investors who work according to a strategy. Some investors need a "value-add" approach, others need a catalyst. They're not wrong, thinking the way they do, but I believe that value can actually be the catalyst in the medium or long term, because at some point it becomes obvious. **Interviewer**: So you believe that it will ultimately prevail, almost like a law of nature, like gravity.

Interviewee 43: Exactly, exactly. [...] That is exactly what I believe. It might take a year, but the fundamentals can't be ignored forever. Of that, I am totally convinced. And even in completely irrational markets with completely irrational players, economic history has shown us that the market finds the right level in the long term. It's just that it can sometimes take a very long time to do so.

The entrepreneur from the food industry quoted below is one of the wealthiest interviewees. He does not belong to the group who swim against the prevailing current or stand in opposition to majority thinking for pleasure – in fact, he argued that this would be "obstructive". But he did report that he has regularly developed new products in the face of scepticism from other market players and experts. He used the following example to illustrate the systematic considerations behind his approach:

Interviewer: It is sometimes true that you can only be successful when you have the courage to do things differently from everyone else, when you take a bit of a contrarian position.

Interviewee 15: Yes, yes, of course. That's only logical.

Interviewer: Can you think of an example, one from your business? [...] A situation where everyone else just shook their heads at first and said, "What kind of a crazy idea is that?", and you responded by saying, "I don't care, we're doing it anyway"?

Interviewee 15: Sure, that applies to almost all of the products we developed. Others were always saying, "What's this then? You can't do that. Mr. xxx can't do something like that."

Interviewer: What kinds of people said that? People from within the industry?

Interviewee 15: Yes, mostly competitors, but also some of the people who worked for me, you know? And those so-called know-it-alls, they said, "Mr xxx makes things for other brands and now he wants to make his own brand products, how does he think that is supposed to work?"

Interviewer: And you did it anyway. From what I know of you, I'd say that you are probably someone who enjoys it when everyone else says to go one way and you go the opposite way. Would that be right?

Interviewee 15: A little bit. There's a great example from farming, when a herd of cows comes to a fork in the road. There's a beautiful green pasture on the left, which 100 cows head towards, and there's one cow that goes to the pasture on the right, where the grass is nowhere near as lush. And in no time at all, the 100 cows have grazed and their grass is gone. The lone cow might not have had the lushest grass, but she could take her time and eat her fill.
Interviewer: And end up having more to eat.
Interviewee 15: Yes, that's precisely what it's all about.
Interviewer: So, does that mean that when you express an opinion that diverges from the masses, that you ever feel a bit uneasy, or is that something you enjoy, swimming against the current? Just in terms of how it makes you feel.
Interviewee 15: Well, feeling on its own is not enough, it has to be based on sound foundations, doesn't it? Simply going ahead and doing something that everyone else says is not going to work, that's no way to approach anything. That would just be kind of obstructive.

Another interviewee's fortune stems exclusively from his investments, which – independent of his actual profession – he has made in real estate. In the immediate wake of the 2008 financial crisis, when the prices of real estate had fallen, he bought on a grand scale, and then sold at a huge profit seven years later once the market had become euphoric once again. He followed the doctrine for which the investor Warren Buffett is also well known – buy on panic and sell on euphoria:

Interviewee 17: I think that swimming against the current is the only way to generate really high returns.
Interviewer: I see. Are you talking primarily about the investments?
Interviewee 17: I wouldn't buy any residential real estate in the current market ... I believe that a basic prerequisite for a good investment is the acquisition price.
Interviewer: And can you give me an example of a situation where you did something and others took a different view?
Interviewee 17: I bought a lot of real estate immediately after the financial crisis.
Interviewer: Yes, there was a short gap back then, when real estate was cheaper.
Interviewee 17: Exactly.
Interviewer: So, in 2008, 2009.
Interviewee 17: I bought a lot then.
Interviewer: Yes, yes. And where, in which locations or districts?
Interviewee 17: Downmarket locations. ...
[...]

> **Interviewer**: I guess you were buying at rent-to-price multipliers of around ten back then?
> **Interviewee 17**: Cheaper.
> **Interviewer**: Even cheaper?
> **Interviewee 17**: The multiplier was six.

In the real estate segment, in particular, it is often possible to generate large profits with a contrarian strategy, as was the case for the following investor, who invests in commercial real estate. His success was due to the fact that he bought distressed property from banks, which he then upgraded and revitalized, before selling the properties at a considerable profit:

> **Interviewee 29**: I would say that swimming against the current has played an important role for me. [...] Yes, I've constantly done that, particularly as I had my greatest successes with distressed property that no one else really wanted to touch. People actually said: "He's mad." For me, the most striking example was xxx, the two high-rises in [major city]. They were on the market, everyone had the chance to buy them. But at that time, everybody was saying that the market had collapsed, and look at these two old blocks, and so on. And I said, "I'm doing it." And that is a typical example of swimming against the current, isn't it?
> **Interviewer**: Yes, sure. And did it rattle you, what everyone else was saying?
> **Interviewee 29**: No.

Not all of the interviewees are completely free of doubt. Several reported that they sometimes felt like drivers travelling the wrong way down the freeway, wondering why the other cars are all headed in the other direction. This group includes the following entrepreneur from the finance industry:

> **Interviewee 44**: I do swim against the current in the sense that I'm a contrarian investor. In mid-2005, when the gold price was so low, I bought a lot of gold. [...] In 2008, I bought lots of Swiss Francs. [...]
> **Interviewer**: And how is it in your professional life? Do you also swim against the current and do things differently from everyone else?
> **Interviewee 44**: Yes, yes. [...] Of course. When I came up with the [idea for the company], everyone said it wasn't possible. So I asked them "Why not?" And they all said, "If it was such a great idea, somebody would already have thought of it." So I said: "Well now I'm really going to do it." Everyone said it wouldn't work.

Interviewer: And did that bother you at all? I mean, sometimes you then think to yourself, "Maybe I'm the person going the wrong way after all."
Interviewee 44: Exactly, that's right. And then all of these companies [in his industry] were being sold off and I always said that I would stay independent. At some point you ask yourself, "Are they all idiots, or am I the idiot here?" But that never bothered me. It never bothered me to be different.

Another investor, who has enjoyed massive success in the hotel industry, entertained doubts about his investment, even though he was totally convinced of its profitability in principle:

Interviewee 30: Basically, I was totally convinced: I believed in it completely from day one. There's a story I tell often, I might even have mentioned it to you in the past. [...] One evening, at about ten o'clock, I drove out to the construction site and there were 14 huge cranes standing there, surrounding the building structure. And, just that once, I thought to myself, "Are you crazy? Look at what you're doing here." But that was just the once, and it only lasted about ten minutes. After that, I drove back home. And then I never thought about it again. That was the moment when I said to myself that it couldn't go wrong. I had a chance and I had worked it all out, and I was going to make money.

Banks are generally pro-cyclical in terms of their financing behaviour, so they represent exactly the opposite approach. This sometimes makes it difficult for investors because they are obviously dependent on bank financing. One interviewee reported that he even treats a bank's opinion as a contra-indicator. When asked whether 'swimming against the current' had played a role for him, he responded:

Interviewee 19: Always. All the way through. I always speak to bankers, listen to what they have to say and I know that if I do the opposite of what they tell me, I'll be pretty much right, whereas they are always totally wrong. [...] Yes. I could give you roughly 50 examples for that.
Interviewer: Could you give me the most striking one, where you did totally the opposite of what they were saying?
Interviewee 19: Yes I can. It relates to the bankruptcy of xxx in 2003. There was a huge insolvency in [city], where xxx had bought hotels and there were still 52 old buildings. [...] The bank I was doing business with was xxx and they were caught up in it, having a bit of a difficult time and they asked if I might fancy taking one of the problems off their hands. [...]

> At a dinner we were having, they were really jolly and said, "So, Mr xxx, what are you planning on doing?" So I responded, "You know, it's interesting, but with these developments, I'm just not sure if this is the right opportunity for me. I've just bought 52 apartment buildings in [city]. Just picture it. Average rent of EUR 3.90, at a multiplier of 6.3." And then they said, "Mr xxx, we've supported you here, and with xxx, and with xxx, we've stood by your side in so many deals, and now you've started buying apartments in [city]? With all due respect, we can't understand that at all and that is not the bank's policy. We can only advise you to withdraw from the contracts if you can but there's no way we can support you in this." And that's when I knew that I'd made a good deal.

There were a few exceptions who said they did not place much stock in swimming against the current. One was very successful in his field, having copied the business model of the market leader – for whom he actually worked before he became self-employed and set up his own company. When asked whether he had frequently swum against the current, he responded firmly:

> **Interviewee 18**: No, just the opposite. I have always been very careful to watch other people very closely. And to do what I thought was the right thing to do. I never wanted to reinvent the world, or reinvent the wheel. [...] That was clear to me the whole time when we were setting up xxx, our biggest competitor was extremely successful. Yes, so I said that there was no reason for us to try and reinvent the wheel, was there? We only needed to do one or two things differently. [...] So, I think we've been successful because we successfully copied a good concept.

INTERIM FINDINGS

Few of the 50 questions of the Big Five personality test elicited as unanimous a response from the interviewees as the statement "I would describe myself as someone who prefers to forge my own path". Of the interviewees, 41 of 43 expressed agreement and only two were undecided. None disagreed with the statement.

Schumpeter's definition of the entrepreneurial type as one who opposes majority opinion, or at least acts independently of what the majority thinks, emerged clearly from the interviews. A majority of the interviewees can be categorized in these terms – especially the investors. Many attributed their financial success largely to their ability to swim against the prevailing current.

Having the courage to stand against majority opinion is probably a prerequisite for making successful investments, as this is what makes it possible to buy cheap and sell high. Of course, this is no definite guarantee of success, as there is always a danger that an investor will get their 'timing' wrong – especially when such investments are highly leveraged. The contrarian investor is also dependent on other market players, at some point, following the investor's judgement. After all, it is only once this happens that prices will rise and the investor can realize their profits. But they do not have any problem with selling when the markets are euphoric, because they tend to feel uneasy when their opinion is shared by the majority. They regard majority opinion as a contra-indicator – a view they maintain both through phases of widespread market panic and through euphoric upswings.

During the interviews, two distinct types of entrepreneur and investor emerged. The first group were delighted to stand in opposition to majority opinion and to swim against the current. They were actually uncomfortable when they had the impression that their view of a situation was aligned with the 'mainstream', as they disparagingly termed it. The other group acted more independently of the majority, which was actually irrelevant to them. This means that they formed their own opinions independent of the majority view. They were neither bothered nor stimulated by disagreeing with the majority. Conversely, there were times when their actions closely resembled those of the majority. Thus, they did not view contrarianism and 'swimming against the current' as fundamental attitudes.

20 Dealing with Crises and Setbacks

Anyone who has been active as an entrepreneur and investor for many decades will usually have had to face major crises and setbacks. These can sometimes even be so great as to be existential. In entrepreneurship research, 'action orientation' has been identified as a personality trait of entrepreneurs, which is measured in terms of action orientation after failure. "Action orientation after failure means that an individual remains able to act immediately after an error or failure and does not hesitate to continue with their work."[720] A study published by Sigrun Göbel and Michael Frese found that only 3 of 29 personality traits examined correlate more strongly with entrepreneurial success than "action orientation after failure".[721] "An entrepreneur with a high score in this scale remains effective even after a failure."[722] Another study identified action orientation after failure as a key personality trait of successful people in general.[723]

An analysis of the biographies of wealthy people shows that a large number of UHNWIs, such as John D. Rockefeller, Ingvar Kamprad, Michael Bloomberg, Warren Buffett, Walt Disney, and others, grew particularly as a result of problems and crises.[724] The conviction that any defeat could be turned into an even greater success and any disadvantage could be transformed into an at least equal benefit dates back as far as Napoleon Hill's self-help classic *Think and Grow Rich*. "Put your dreams across, and never mind what 'they' say if you meet with temporary defeat, for 'they,' perhaps do not know that every failure brings with it the seed of an equivalent success."[725] According to Hill, 500 of the most successful men in America told him that most of their greatest successes were achieved immediately after they had suffered a setback.[726]

The results of the Big Five test also clearly showed that action orientation after failure was an important characteristic shared by this group of wealthy individuals. The interviewees were asked to respond to the following statement: "I am not easily discouraged if things do not go well." Of the interviewees, 32 of 43 agreed strongly and 10 agreed. Only one respondent was undecided.

In the interviews, the UHNWIs were asked to discuss in detail the setbacks they had had to cope with. They were explicitly asked whether opportunities and progress had arisen from setbacks and crises. The following interview extracts demonstrate patterns of behaviour for dealing with setbacks and crises that emerged during the interviews.

20.1. "I AM HECTIC ON THE OUTSIDE, BUT TOTALLY RELAXED ON THE INSIDE"

When asked how they have psychologically coped with difficult situations, many interviewees reported that, even in the midst of extremely serious crises, they remained calm and were able to sleep soundly. Some referred to their religious beliefs and the fact that their faith helped them. An example is the investor who said that, on some days, he had lost tens of millions, but still "never let [his] emotions show":

> **Interviewee:** There have been days when I've lost tens of millions, but I never let my emotions show. [...] But it didn't kill me. I was more bothered by the fact that I hadn't won the game. [...] I believe in something and I go all out for it. And the cards can land where they may. What people say about me is, "Bombs could be dropping everywhere, to the right and to the left, and he'd carry on as normal, he wouldn't even bat an eyelid. [...] At most, he might take a handkerchief and wipe some of the dust away." It's to do with those basic Christian values. Christians talk about the conscience – I'm not sure how it is for Protestants, but for Catholics, you have to have a clear conscience and then everything's okay, you know?

The next interviewee reported that he believes that "a universal force", the power of positive thinking, and "maybe also a belief in God" have all helped him to remain completely calm and composed, even in the midst of the most difficult situations he has faced, including insolvency. His inner peace is founded on his belief in his own ability to follow a EUR 10 million loss by earning EUR 20 million. Similar sentiments were expressed by a number of interviewees. This clearly corresponds to the observations made about optimism and self-efficacy in Chapter 14:

---

720   Utsch, "Psychologische Einflussgrößen," 102.
721   Göbel and Frese, "Persönlichkeit, Strategien," 101.
722   Ibid., 96.
723   Göbel, "Persönlichkeit, Handlungsstrategien und Erfolg," 119.
724   Zitelmann, *Dare to Be Different and Grow Rich*, 32–56.
725   Hill, *Think and Grow Rich*, 39.
726   Ibid., 21.

keeping a cool head during a crisis is a product of the pronounced optimism and high levels of self-efficacy of these wealthy individuals. When asked how he had psychologically coped with difficult situations – such as insolvency – the following entrepreneur explained:

> **Interviewee 16**: In myself, I'm not under any pressure.
> **Interviewer**: But how do you manage that?
> **Interviewee 16**: I think that I am hectic on the outside, but totally relaxed on the inside. Because I have confidence.
> **Interviewer**: And where does your calmness come from?
> **Interviewee 16**: From my belief. The belief in a universal force, maybe also a belief in God. From faith, from positive thinking. I have experienced too much, and seen too many beautiful things, and been through so many bad things, but above all beautiful things, to believe that it would go wrong. As far as the future is concerned, I am an incurable optimist. [...] That's my way, and it's why I am totally calm, even in business. Even if I lost 10 million today, I would still be totally calm, because I know I can earn another 20 million. You could break down in despair over the 10 million, or you could say, "How do I earn 20 million, so that I have the 10 million again plus an extra 10 million for the future?" It's clearly a question of always viewing things completely pragmatically, with an almost objective eye. At the moment you are analysing a situation, you need to dispel your emotions before you make your decision. And that's my fundamental approach; I am not in the slightest bit hectic. I have positive stress. I am never scared, although I am sometimes anxious. My life is not determined by these things, and if tomorrow were to be my last day on earth, I would be able to say that I have experienced everything. The only regret I would have is missing my daughters' weddings. If tomorrow is my last day, I have had the best and largest of lives a person could ever have. I have experienced everything, I've experienced love, I've experienced having children, I've experienced affection, I've experienced defeats, I've experienced success, all of the most amazing things a man could possibly experience. I've experienced everything. What would I have to complain about?

Many of the interviewees were visibly proud of the fact that they retain a cool head and calm demeanour in the midst of even the most serious situation. An entrepreneur from the food industry believes that it is crises that show "if you are made of the right stuff". He remains perfectly calm in such circumstances:

> **Interviewee 37**: I am a very calm person. I don't lose my temper. I keep my cool. Last year, for example, we were hit with a temporary injunction from a

competitor who is 20 to 30 times bigger than we are. In relation to [product]. We had to recall our product from 1,600 [vendors]. And you don't achieve anything by hurling accusations at the people who are responsible, do you? The sky's already fallen on their heads. So I stay cool. I think that it is only in a crisis that you find out what you are made of and if you have the right stuff. When things are coming up trumps, everyone can be as happy as Larry, but when things are going badly, when the roof caves in, that's when it comes down to whether people think you are good or not, and decide whether they are with you or against you. Anybody can throw a party when the company's making big money – but standing firm when things aren't working out and saying, "Come on people, that was crap, but let's go out for a meal and talk it through," that's far cooler in my opinion. And sometimes being able to do that doesn't come easy, you have to force yourself to do it. You have to apply reason and knowledge, even if it goes against your natural inclination. Of course, there are situations where you might be tempted to explode, but that doesn't achieve anything. It doesn't achieve anything. And, naturally, that's a learning curve that I'm talking about here.

Like many other interviewees, the real estate developer quoted below stated that he remains astonishingly calm in crisis situations. He observed that, especially when it comes to negotiations with banks, it is important to stay calm. His pride was obvious when he added, "You can't afford to be scared. Not everyone has strong nerves":

Interviewee 38: No, the most important thing is to go through with it. You have to go to your creditors and say, "Right, we have a problem here that we need to solve." [...] Yes, and then you need to solve it. And if they were thinking of driving me into bankruptcy, I told them that they wouldn't get a penny. They'd get nothing from me and it wouldn't hurt me one iota. I said, "We'll find something else." You have to take a risk. You can't afford to be scared. Not everyone has strong nerves.

Real estate developers are involved in a high-stakes business. The next interviewee confessed that his company would "go under" if just a single project went "belly up". But the possibility of losing everything does not burden him – he still sleeps soundly:

Interviewee 25: Yes, I sleep soundly. So no, it really doesn't stress me out. Because I think that I can manage to make things work. And we really are in the position that if one of our big projects goes belly up, we would go under.

Which means that the pressure is always there, every project that we buy has to work out. It has to.

The next interviewee is also a real estate developer. His company had to survive three extremely difficult years. In contrast to some of the other interviewees, he did suffer sleepless nights before he eventually found a way to psychologically cope with the situation by getting out of bed if he woke up in the middle of the night and composing to-do lists on a piece of paper at his bedside. Once he had done this, he was able to sleep well again:

Interviewer: And how did you cope with the situation psychologically at the time?

Interviewee 36: I can tell you exactly. I learned how to cope with huge problems psychologically.

Interviewer: That's something you have to live with for three years then, is it?

Interviewee 36: Yes, a problem, individual problem-solving mechanisms. How to stay creative, on the one hand. And on the other hand that you don't collapse or become depressed. So, just the one thing: I carried on living as I had, going out in the evenings, meeting girls, and so on. But I was frequently relieved when people wanted to draw the evening to a close at eight o'clock. And I woke up every night at around four in the morning. And I learned not to lie there in bed, thinking. Because that releases a hormone and your problem seems doubled or tripled. You see the problem, and you see it from three sides and you end up thinking that you have three problems. I'd turn the light on. I have pieces of paper all over the place, mainly in my bedroom and by the side of my bed, and I'd write it all down. Write down the first thing I was going to do, the worst-case scenario, and then a to-do list, and then I'd be calm and could go back to sleep.

Interviewer: Because it is out of your mind, because you've written it down.

Interviewee 36: Yes, because then you can see a way out. You can see the solution. A course of action. You work on the problem. And that's how I did it, but it takes a long time. It must have taken me three months at first, until I was calmer. But now I have that calm. At the end of the day, I benefited hugely, because it means you can deal with immense topics, including huge problems, without ever thinking of jumping off your balcony or anything like that. And some people get overwhelmed by it and stop doing anything at all, but you need a balance. So you have to go skiing, or do something nice one evening, something really special. You need to recharge your batteries. And if you approach things as if nothing matters, that doesn't work either. You can't be creative then, can't come up with a solution.

At the nascent stages of their companies' existences in particular, investors' potential liabilities often far exceed the value of their assets. If their companies became insolvent, they would be personally extremely highly indebted. This applied to the following interviewee, whose previous liabilities amounted to between EUR 50 and 100 million – far more than the value of the assets he owned at the time. But he told himself that if he lost the money, he would still be able to earn it again. He firmly believed that, having earned it once, he knew how to earn it again. This is where his strong optimism and self-efficacy come to bear:

Interviewee 29: I have always slept well. But that's because, when I was young, my grandfather introduced me to Buddhism. It also has a lot to do with the sports I used to do. We did sport yoga together. You learn certain breathing techniques, that kind of thing. They let you calm yourself down, or enable you to switch off and relax. On the other hand, as I've already mentioned, I was never an employee, I never had that security. I always had to make sure that there was a bit of money left in my account at the end of the month. That means that when you have never had the experience of being an employee, you have also never known the fear of having something to lose, because you never had anything to lose to begin with. And on the other hand, I have always said to myself, "Okay, if you lose everything you have, once it's gone, you can earn it back tomorrow because you know how to do that," you know?

Early on, the company of the following interviewee experienced a situation that threatened its very existence. He explained how he coped with this situation psychologically:

Interviewee 27: That really was a question of life and death for the business.
Interviewer: Yes, and how did you cope with the situation psychologically?
Interviewee 27: Psychologically it wasn't so much of a problem, I could still sleep, that kind of thing, you know? If that's what you're talking about. But of course, with a project like that, where things are spiralling downwards, at some point you realize that you can't influence things anymore. When it comes down to it, you can't influence whether it is going to hit you badly or not. Whether you see it as exciting or just bad. There are certain things that you can always have a direct influence on. When you can say to yourself, fine, I need to work harder in this, then I'll work three nights in a row. Or I'll negotiate. Or I'll get involved myself. I can develop strategies. In this case, everything happened at once, because the whole management team at our client changed in one go, because partners jumped ship and the team didn't work anymore. It all added up to a situation that we could no longer

elegantly solve and we knew that it was going to be expensive to get out of. Putting it mildly, it was a somewhat frustrating moment. But we never reacted by burying our heads in the sand. Somehow, we fought our way through, but mainly we focused on the things we could do to make money again, where we could drive the business forwards. We always focused on the future. Still, we burned EUR 3 million back then. For a fledgling business, that was definitely at the limits of what we could bear.

Another entrepreneur said that serious illness taught him humility, which enabled him to remain calm and composed through two financially very difficult business years when he parted ways with his business partner. When confronted with the statements made by another interviewee, who is quoted above, he responded:

Interviewer: One of my interviewees said to me, and I thought it was a really great image, he said, "Bombs could be dropping everywhere, to the right and to the left, and I'd carry on as normal; at most, I might take a handkerchief and wipe some of the dust away."
Interviewee 45: That's how I am, too. You have to experience a few setbacks in life and then it's much easier to deal with such situations.
Interviewer: You once told me that you had some serious health problems, if I remember correctly.
Interviewee 45: Yes. Yes, I did.
Interviewer: And did that experience help you in any way, that you would say that your health problems made you more relaxed when it came to other situations, so that you would say, "Well, the main thing is that I have my health"?
Interviewee 45: You could also call that humility, couldn't you? Knowing that everything could be over very quickly, from one day to the next.

Many of the interviewees spoke about their ability to switch off and direct their focus, even in the event of major problems. The interviewees consistently referred to their ability to focus on solutions, rather than torturing themselves with problems:

Interviewee 34: No, those things don't make me nervous. Of course, I take them on board and deal with them too. But it's not as if I can't sleep at night or experience restlessness or anxiety. At the weekend, or when I'm on holiday, it's all gone.
Interviewer: And I guess it's definitely gone once you've emerged from the situation, after all, you're not the kind of person who would dwell on things. You deal with them quickly and move on.

Interviewee 34: You're absolutely right. I recognize problems. But I'm not someone who spends a lot of time dwelling on them, I switch on quickly and ask myself how to solve the problem and then focus on solving it. I don't waste time fretting about how I got into the situation in the first place, you know? [...] That's what lots of people do, they focus too much on the problem. Sure, you have to acknowledge the problem. You have to get organized, no question. But then you have to banish the problem from your mind and programme all of your thoughts on the solution. [...] Danger recognized, danger averted. If you don't recognize it, you leave yourself open. Certainly one point, and it's one we spoke about earlier, but it's connected with another problem, which is analysing the situation thoroughly and then developing solutions, and focusing on the solution, rather than dwelling on the problem. In my opinion, that's a very key characteristic of successful entrepreneurs, just from looking at the world around me, you know?

20.2. "DON'T PASS THE BUCK"

One of the key characteristics of many interviewees in dealing with crises and setbacks is that they take personal responsibility for the situations in which they find themselves. They consider it essential not to offload responsibility onto external circumstances or other people, but to accept responsibility for themselves. This appears to give them a feeling of power and self-efficacy. The following interviewee talked about his insolvency. Here, too, it was crucial for him to assume personal responsibility. He distinguished between two types of people – those who look for the causes of their setbacks in other people, and those who seek the roots of any problems in themselves:

Interviewee 16: I became insolvent in 19xx. And do you know what? The worst thing was that I knew it was coming. [...] When you look back on it and analyse yourself and have the strength to say, "What did you do wrong? How did it happen?" And that, I think, is where there are two types of people. The first group says, "I didn't get enough money there and he didn't pay on time and the like," and the others say, "What mistake did I make? What did I do wrong?" And the ones who say, "What was my mistake and what chance do I have?", they stand a good chance of getting things right and doing better in the future.
Interviewer: [...] You take responsibility yourself and can change things yourself.
Interviewee 16: Exactly. We are the mistake. Everything that happens, apart from serious illnesses and things like that, and even on that score you can debate whether we are to blame, you make your own bed and you have to

lie in it, don't you? I had big problems when I was bringing up my son and then I asked myself, "What have I done wrong?" Not, "What has my son done wrong?" And on the very day that I stopped making the mistake I had been making, my son turned out fine.

The following interviewee has already had to face and overcome substantial difficulties despite his young age. For him, too, it is important not to look for faults in others, but within oneself. He considers this attitude crucial to experiencing personal growth as a result of problems. He reported how, early in his entrepreneurial career, he was confronted by a million-euro lawsuit. He had a large amount of money tied up in various investments, but did not have much money in his bank account. He is convinced that it was crucial not to say, "They're such greedy swine, it's all their fault." Instead he said to himself, "There's a specific reason you are in this situation; accept the situation, solve the situation, grow from it, become better at what you're doing as a result":

Interviewee 12: Whenever I'm in that situation, I start off by getting worked up. For example, one time I was sued for EUR 1 million. And that was at a time when I had a large amount of money tied up in investments, but didn't have much money in my bank account. It would have wiped me out. At first I was shocked, but then, as I always do when I suffer a setback, I analysed the situation, recognized it for what it was, and took responsibility. I went to my people and said, "Right, we can stand here and say, 'They're such greedy swine,' but we're not going to do that. We're going to be grateful for this situation, because it is going to make us stronger; they're going to turn us into something even better." [...] And that's exactly what happened; I can't change the situation, I can only accept it and, as hard as it may sound, I can only see the positive in something extremely negative and say, "Okay, I'm going to be better as a result of this." And so I always saw the negative, the bad things, because I always said, "Don't pass the buck, don't say, 'They're such greedy swine, it's all their fault,' rather there's a specific reason you are in this situation; accept the situation, solve the situation, grow from it, become better at what you're doing as a result. The situation will come again, in another environment and in other areas.

Entrepreneurs take credit for their successes, which means they do not ascribe them to fortunate coincidences or external circumstances. From their point of view, the corollary is to take responsibility for their defeats and setbacks as well. The next interviewee also looks within himself for the causes of the setbacks he has experienced:

Interviewee 37: You know what, it's really simple. There's no division of responsibility. Everything that works out fantastically, that's down to me. But I have to accept that the same is also true when things don't work out. I can't take the credit for everything that works well and then blame my wife for the things that don't work out, can I?

The resoluteness of this inner attitude of assuming personal responsibility in every situation is demonstrated by the following real estate investor. He even feels responsible for setbacks triggered by market changes, in the same way as he would if he himself were actually guilty of making errors of judgement. Many would claim that it was nothing to do with them, that it was the market, "but at the same time I also have to acknowledge that it was me who misjudged the market". He does not accept it as an excuse that everyone else had misjudged the market:

Interviewee 41: The setback itself is a result of the market. [...] Of course, you can say that it is nothing to do with you, it was the market, but at the same time, I also have to acknowledge that it was me who misjudged the market. It could well be that everyone else had misjudged the market, but that doesn't help me in the slightest. It's another example of what you asked at the beginning, that I ultimately have to be able to rely on myself. And it doesn't help me when others arrive at their assessments of the market and I am as wrong as they are. I have to be able to stand for my decision, to be able to live with my decision. That's another reason not to simply trust the masses, but to make your own decisions, based on your own convictions.

The financial crisis of 2008–2009 was a topic that was raised in several interviews. The next interviewee, who became rich from investments in stocks and real estate, believes it is a mistake to apportion the blame to external circumstances and absolve oneself of any guilt. "At the end of the day, I have to be able to identify the risks that are emerging, and to anticipate them":

Interviewee 42: Well, okay, none of us could do anything about the financial crisis, could we? But, of course, I have to be clear and say that in [date], before the capital market shut downs, we were one of the very few real estate companies that managed to secure a cash capital increase of [a few hundred] million euros. That meant we had basically managed to create a nice safety buffer for ourselves. But I still believe, with hindsight, that we should have seen the signs and maybe refinanced a few things earlier on, because we were already dancing on the deck of the *Titanic* as the ship was going down. That means, I'm not someone who blames everything on external circumstances and absolves himself of any blame. At the end of the day, I have to be able to identify the risks that are emerging, and to anticipate them. That's something I'm certainly extremely self-critical about.

One of the interviewees got into severe financial difficulties in the late 1990s as a result of his inexperience and the high levels of risk he had taken on. He had also spent far too much money in his private life. At the time, his company had two business divisions: residential real estate development and providing distressed real estate advisory services to banks. All of a sudden, neither division was making any profits. He again adopted the attitude that he needed to take personal responsibility for the negative situation:

> **Interviewee 40**: Yes, and it was my fault. There are situations where things just happen. I mean, where someone else is to blame, I'm also ultimately to blame because I have accepted the risk when I play with fire, and I have to expect that at some point I might get burned. Yes, that's just how it is. If one of my investments were to fall apart today, it's my fault because I bought it, isn't it? And that can happen from time to time. That's something you just have to live with.

Another interviewee from the finance sector goes as far as accepting personal responsibility when others perpetrated fraud against him.

> **Interviewee 9**: I have never taken legal action against anyone. [...] And we have had people who have really defrauded us, but I said, well you share the blame, you should have thought it through more carefully beforehand...

20.3. "YOU'LL SEE THIS THROUGH, WITH YOUR INTEGRITY INTACT"

In severe crises, many people tend to want to put a positive spin on things, especially in the disclosures they make to banks or other creditors and investors. The interviewees reported that it is not just a question of taking decisive action to solve major crises but that it is crucial to show the utmost degree of transparency. According to the following entrepreneur, open, timely, and honest communication with creditors is the most important factor in dealing with any crisis:

Interviewee 38: No, because the most important thing in this life is to always be honest and open with your creditors. Whereas our "friends", I won't name any names here, but you know it too, they tried to cover up their problems by doctoring their figures. And when that comes out, they are as good as dead. So it's always better to approach your creditors and say, "Look, I have a problem here, we need to solve this together."

Psychologically this is not easy. Many interviewees reported that in the midst of a crisis a bank's attitude can change dramatically from one day to the next. One entrepreneur got into a difficult situation and was shocked by the sudden shift in the way his key account manager at the bank suddenly treated him:

Interviewee 3: And Mr. xxx, he was the one who always made a big show of seeing me down to my car on Promenadeplatz in Munich, bowing and swinging the door open for me, using my academic title to address me. And it was him of all people who suddenly pushed a button to summon his secretary when I was in his office and told her that I was ready to leave. So I said, "What do you mean, we were just getting started." And he replied, "No, we were not just getting started. If you think you are going to get a single cent of equity back, no way. Full stop. End of story. Goodbye." And that was the same guy who, just three weeks earlier, had...

Throughout the company's crisis, it was crucial to deal with problems openly and transparently, and to present the reality of the situation to creditors – between 70 and 80 companies – without delay and without embellishments. He is convinced that he only managed to keep his creditors onside because he contacted them immediately and communicated openly with them, unlike many others who find themselves in similar situations and try to "dodge their problems" and talk their way out of a difficult situation:

Interviewee 3: That was a really tight spot, at the end of 1992. And it taught me a valuable lesson. I called all of the companies we were in business with and told them to listen to me. I told them that I had a problem and needed to meet with them. I told them money was coming in, but it was nowhere near enough to pay everyone. I put a plan together and proposed paying what we could immediately. I said, "The small tradesmen, we'll pay them more, and you xxx, you'll get less, but that's just how it will have to be, and I hope that I can sell the product quickly, but for the next few months, we have a liquidity problem. That's all the cash that is coming in. I know that if I pay everyone according to the terms of their contracts, if I have to fulfil all of my obligations, then I'm going bust. There's nothing I can do about it." So I made my proposal and what I thought was really great at the time was that everyone went along with it. [...] I contacted them all immediately. As soon as I got out of the bank, I sat down with our finance guys. "Okay, this is the situation, what do we do now?" I told them how much money was coming in and all of the bills, and the massive gap between the two, and then I said, "Fine, I've got to talk to everyone, tell them that we can't pay right now, that we can only pay some of what we owe."

Interviewer: But surely not everyone who saw the figures would have agreed to go along with your plan.

Interviewee 3: No, of course, there were a few who complained, but everyone, without exception, said, "Okay. We're in this with you."

Interviewer: And how did you overcome the objections of those who initially made trouble?

Interviewee 3: There really weren't any. It totally surprised me, but everyone, from small businesses to huge corporations, we informed everyone. It could have been because they said they had never had anyone contact them immediately in that kind of situation. Most people start by trying to dodge their problems, they say things like, "I've already paid" or "The check is in the post," which I never understand, but that's what they do. And I said, no, this is the situation. Why should I beat around the bush? In four weeks it will all be over anyway. Get it over and done with. And that led to us agreeing, okay, this is how we're going to pay...

At the start of his professional career, the following interviewee made the mistake of distributing funds that subsequently collapsed owing a total sum of DM 100 million. In the midst of this situation, the other distribution partners "disappeared". In contrast, this interviewee actively contacted every single investor:

Interviewee 4: Yes, it was a fund. And that was really tough for me. I even said to myself: "You'll see this through, with your integrity intact." I was there for every single customer... All of my colleagues, the company, they disappeared, didn't they? Simply disappeared. And I sat down and phoned every single customer to tell them what had happened. I was ready to talk it through with each of them. Completely open. I called them and said, "The money is gone. You can hit me if you want, I accept that I am partly to blame. I should have seen it coming, I should have approached things more critically, but this is where we are now." It was important to me, the way I dealt with the situation, and of course, what does it mean for me, what can I learn from it, how do I draw new energy from it?

The owner of a major food company reported that only the complete disclosure of all figures to the works' council had helped to establish credibility and solve the crisis his company found itself in:

> **Interviewee 26**: There was one time when we made a loss in Germany, a big loss. It was with the xxx. And naturally, because it was such a great product and the company looked like it was in a great position, nobody could believe it. And then I got the figures, called the works' council in, and said, "Look here, these are our figures." Their jaws dropped to the floor. Then, together with the works' council and the employees, and with the same management team that had got the business into such a difficult position, we got the business back on the right track. That created a completely different atmosphere, you know? And we haven't made another loss since.
> **Interviewer**: And what was the key factor in solving the problem? [...]
> **Interviewee 26**: That everyone pulled together. That we had credibility. Otherwise, if they had stood there and said, right, now we need to cut costs, people would have said, "Right, now the bigwigs want to cut costs because they dont't want to earn less." But when you say, "Look here, I'm losing 10% of sales revenues, that's the extent of the losses," then they believe you. I made it clear to them that their jobs were on the line.

20.4. "LOOKING BACK ON IT, WHAT HAPPENED WAS ALWAYS FOR THE BEST"

In crises, however, it is not just a matter of eliminating problems and re-establishing the status quo, but ideally turning bad into good and emerging from the situation with newfound strength. One interviewee summed it up as follows: "Looking back on it, what happened was always for the best." Many of the interviewees expressed similar sentiments.

This interviewee's business originally comprised only a small number of stores; today there are hundreds. It was disagreements with a wholesaler that provided the trigger for the expansion of the business:

> **Interviewer**: And what made you decide to expand on such a scale, with all of these stores?
> **Interviewee 14**: Yes, well I once had a problem with a buyer in the wholesale sector. He was always telling me that he wanted our quality, but in reality he put so much pressure on us, to lower our prices that I said, "No, no, we won't supply to you any more." But I wanted to expand, so I said to myself, "The customer, the individual customer, the end customer, they'll either come

or they won't, and then you'll know. Now is your chance." So I went and discussed it with my father, told him that I wanted to expand our network of stores. My father's first reaction was to throw his hands up in despair. [...] But he left me to get on with it and I opened between 10 and 15 stores per year and that was a complete success.

For the IT entrepreneur quoted below, a major database problem affecting roughly 1,000 customers led to an innovation that made his product suitable for major business clients:

Interviewee 33: We had a database system and the software we used wasn't really stable for our large business clients, so we had to make a major intervention in the product, so to speak, and then install a completely new database kernel. Yes, it's only after that that the product was really suitable for major businesses and could integrate with SAP and so on. None of that would have been possible with the old technology. [...]
Interviewer: Could you give me a few more details?
Interviewee 33: Well, alongside the software's core code, software is based on a database, which is where all of the data is stored. And there are relational and non-relational databases. The databases that we all know come from Oracle or DB2, from SAP or Microsoft SQL Server. Those are the best-known database manufacturers nowadays, but there are others, and they can also be good and certainly have their advantages and many are actually cheaper for customers. Well, we had a database that kept on causing crashes and system freezes for customers with more than 40 workstations. It was relatively unsystematic. We weren't 100% sure if it was because of the database, or if it was something else that was causing the problem. But the suspicion was already there, because our smaller customers weren't having the same problem, and we didn't have that many large customers. Our business tended to involve lots of small customers. And at some point, because of the problems, we decided to make a big investment, two years of development capacity I think it was, to replace the database. It's not like a car, engine out, new engine in and everything works smoothly again. The migration to a new database technology was a big challenge. We're talking about more than a thousand customers. You can't just switch them all over in one go. But we managed it. We suffered for a while, until the process was complete, but once it was finished, we were suddenly a completely different proposition and became an important potential supplier to a whole new category of customers.
Interviewer: For larger customers?

Interviewee 33: Yes, for larger companies. For companies that have a more professional IT infrastructure.

The next interviewee reports how his company's most important financing partner tore up a contract in the middle of the financial crisis, creating an existential threat to his company. Without this breach of contract, however, he would not have been able to sell his company for such a high price – for an amount that far exceeded his expectations:

Interviewee 18: It was during the big credit crunch, when [the financing partner] jumped ship. It took us two years to get things back under control; it was a really tough time. Everything I had was on the line. Everything. But I was totally sure that I would win out in the end, because I was convinced that I could get the company back on the right track. [...] Before all of this, I would never have believed that such a reputable partner would just tear up contracts like that. And these contracts were worth a few hundred million. [...]
Interviewer: Some of the people I have spoken with have told me that ultimately a problem or setback led to something great. Was it the same for you?
Interviewee 18: Yes, of course. When you compare the valuation xxx bank made of my company and the price I sold it for, that's a ratio of one to three, I would say. I always knew that it was worth more, you know? But xxx bank, they naturally saw things from a different perspective, didn't they? But I knew that the true value of the company was more than just the sum of its assets and property developments, but also our unique position in Germany. [...].
Interviewer: So, with hindsight you could say that, as bad as things got, it was actually a good thing, because otherwise you never would have been able to achieve what you did?
Interviewee 18: Yes, you could definitely say that.
Interviewer: Otherwise, you might not have made your exit, and who knows how difficult things would have been.
Interviewee 18: No, I probably wouldn't have done any of it without the credit crunch and xxx's breach of our agreement; I would have just carried on happily as before, wouldn't I? But whether I would have ended up with such a strong and attractive company, one that commanded such a premium from a buyer who was desperate to enter the German market, that probably wouldn't have happened.

The following entrepreneur's investments have had to survive three major crises over the past few decades. In one case, a multi-billion-euro investment got into serious financial difficulties. But the company "emerged stronger" out of each of these crises. New strategies were implemented to deal with the crises, and the company was left with little choice but to evolve:

> **Interviewee 22**: And that we had to develop completely new strategies and come up with completely new ideas. That's basically what led to us developing from a pure asset manager into a vertically integrated real estate company.
> **Interviewer**: And that's the basis of everything that you do now.
> **Interviewee 22**: That's right. In that respect, we embraced the crisis and said, we'll have to finish the residential development at xxx ourselves, because the developer had committed suicide and the buildings were all standing there half finished. So, to do that we needed to bring in people to handle the construction management. We had to start by hiring them. And so it went on. And then we had to hire a lettings team. And that's how we developed from an asset manager that was only ever involved with real estate at the management level, into a company that also got dirt on its hands, that was on-site, wading through the mud, managing buildings and construction, organizing the building sites and the like.
> **Interviewer**: So that means that out of each of these three crises the end result was something positive.
> **Interviewee 22**: Definitely. Yes, yes, definitely. We emerged stronger out of every crisis, not always financially stronger, but better organized, or stronger in other ways, stronger than when we entered the crises.

The following interviewee was forced into a product recall when a competitor secured a temporary injunction against his company. This was a major problem, but it led to growth because it opened up the Chinese market for his products:

> **Interviewee 37**: So there you are, surrounded by these five thousand boxes of your product. Already opened, already with price labels on. The goods were worth probably EUR 200,000, plus the costs of the recall, plus the expense of resupplying new product. All in all it must have cost between EUR 300,000 and 500,000, even more if you include the court costs and lawyers' fees. They've got you nailed to the wall, and all because you weren't quite careful enough. And then you sit there and think to yourself, "So, what can we do with all this stuff?" We weren't allowed to bring it back into circulation, were we? And then this Chinese guy came waltzing round the corner and said, "I like what you've got there. I'll buy it

all off you and I'll establish a brand for you in China." So we suddenly had a brand in China. One of the fastest growing brands in that product category in China, if not the fastest, you know? So, if none of that had happened, who would have ever had the idea to sell [product category] in China, and in such small pack sizes?

"Setbacks and catharsis have given me greater happiness," said the following interviewee. These challenges primarily brought about a personal change, because he learned humility through such situations:

Interviewer: You've already said what was important to you [the interviewee had written this down prior to the interview]: "We need success, but we also need setbacks and to fail; setbacks and catharsis have given me greater happiness." [...] Can you give me an example to illustrate what you mean? A situation where you would say, "That setback was important for me."

Interviewee 21: I have had smaller and greater catharses and setbacks. If we were to talk about the greatest, then that would be xxx. I bought the company and believed I was doing well. And the banks came in and refused to approve any more lending. In such a capital-intensive business, you need bank loans. And then the planning authorities left me a bit in the lurch, and the press got involved and wrote: "He's doing something here that isn't right. He's making money off the backs of his tenants." That made me reflect on what I was doing, because I thought they were wrong. But if I take things one step further, then I can only say that if I hadn't bought [company] [...], then I would have invested three times as much in eastern Germany, and that wouldn't have been good. So, a setback can lead to an economic solution, or it can provide the stimulus for a personal change, create humility. And so I say, courage and humility, like a mountaineer, that's what life is about. I need courage to approach tasks without fear, but then I need the right amount of humility because I know that when I'm doing something, there are lots of factors I need to consider that can't be defeated with courage, but only with humility and modesty.

Interviewer: And what does that mean, defeated with humility and modesty? That's certainly an interesting formulation. Could you explain a bit more what you mean?

Interviewee 21: Aggression grows with too much courage, with too much self-confidence. Modesty means I see people as they are, and that I don't overestimate myself, that I recognize myself as a regular human being. Those are the foundations, I believe, of a certain modesty. That means recognizing that we won't be successful unless fate smiles on us, and realizing that we shouldn't just enjoy life and all of the beautiful things it gives us, but that we should also know where they come from.

The following interviewee, who enjoyed considerable success as a competitive athlete before embarking on his entrepreneurial career, compared business defeats with sporting defeats – "I find it incredibly boring, just winning all the time":

Interviewee 27: First, crises are part and parcel of life, even in sports. I find it incredibly boring, just winning all the time. I know people who won all the time, and then, after a single poor performance, they were gone, you never saw them again. So, I find that the challenging times are actually those where you have stress and a crisis. It doesn't necessarily have to cost as much money as my crisis cost me. That really was a question of life and death for the business.

Looking back on his life, another interviewee said that the defeats and existential crises of his company had been necessary for his own development process. These setbacks only matured him – "I needed to get punched in the face for three years or I would never have grown up":

Interviewee 40: And that's why I say it was the most important thing that ever happened to me. That immature and stubborn youth somehow transformed into someone who thinks analytically, who reduced their level of risk exposure a bit and also became more mature. It's the result of lots of experience, so to speak. [...] I needed to get punched in the face for three years or I would never have grown up. Otherwise, I just wouldn't have learned. It was exactly that, you know?
Interviewer: So you would say that it was a good thing.
Interviewee 40: It was perfect. I mean, look at where we're sitting today, right?
[...]
Interviewer: And what was the main thing, the biggest leap in your learning? You said that you matured, but if you can help me to understand it better, what was the most positive lesson you learned from this whole crisis situation?
Interviewee 40: Well, first of all, what you are naturally capable of. The strengths that you possess, the finesse. What I mean by that is the ability to win people over, to assess situations correctly. You asked me earlier on, "What is it that makes you special," and that is it. Yes, that's what

I realized. I truly realized what it is that I am best at, and I went on to use that realization.

Interviewer: So it gave you confidence.

Interviewee 40: Yes, absolutely. I very clearly said to myself, this is what I can do best. I know today that I don't need to be a perfectionist when it comes to using Excel, I don't need to be a perfectionist when it comes to lots of other things. Other people can do that, can't they?

Setbacks and crises are important, said the entrepreneur quoted below, because "when people are under pressure and cornered, they are capable of far greater achievements than if they only ever walk in the sunlight". In the early 1990s, he experienced severe financial difficulties when his bank refused to honour a loan approval and he did not have access to sufficient equity capital to make up the difference. In the end, he found a creative solution, "born out of necessity, because we couldn't manage it any other way". This solution later became an important foundation and unique selling point of his company's business model:

Interviewee 41: Yes, I do believe that when people are under pressure and cornered, they are capable of far greater achievements than if they only ever walk in the sunlight. And for me, I was also shaped by my parents. I respect my mother like no other person in the world, so I really had to help her [because of the problems, caused by his father]. That was a disaster for me, while I was studying and I spent a huge amount of money, including the money I had to earn. That made a lasting impression on me. That's the one side of it. You fight harder than if you've only ever had the sun shining down on you. And the second thing was that, having seen my father's attitude to money, I practically said to myself that I would do anything in life, but never that. That was basically my safety concept.

20.5. "ON THE DAY AFTER YOUR EXAMS, EVERYTHING IS FORGOTTEN"

As shown in Section 3.2.d, action orientation after failure is an important trait of successful entrepreneurs. None of the interviewees ever spent long dwelling on crises or heavy setbacks, nor did they waste time crying over spilt milk. One interviewee, who has survived several major crises and temporarily lost a large portion of his assets, used the following anecdote to explain this attitude:

Interviewee 3: No. I basically think that the lesson is to always believe in yourself, to see the positives and to just try to deal with things and to look to the future and never look back. There's a story about an American professor who was giving his first lecture to a group of students. He just sat there, not saying a word, and poured a litre of milk down the drain while all these students looked on. Then he poured another litre of milk down the drain. That's when the first students started grumbling. Then he poured another litre of milk down the drain. The grumbling got louder. What was this nonsense? And then another litre of milk, which was met by clear protest. Unbelievable, the waste and so on, and then the professor turned to the students and said, "So, we've just learned our first valuable lesson. No matter how annoyed you get, the milk is never coming back out of the drain."

The career of the following interviewee, who has built a large fortune in the finance industry, began when his prior employer terminated his employment contract. He decided to start his own business on the way back from the same appointment in which he was informed of his dismissal. His motto is, "If you're 2:0 down, you need to score three goals. You can't just stand around and count the blades of grass on the field and tell yourself, 'Boy today has been a really bad day.'" He has always been able to "get over" negative things quickly:

Interviewee 44: It was the same way in which I dealt with difficult situations when I was kid; I knew that if I had been given a job to do as a punishment, or had been banned from watching TV for a week, I just said, "Fine" knowing that the week would soon be over. [...]
Interviewer: But at that time, in that situation, immediate action is required.
Interviewee 44: I had to take massive professional countermeasures. While controlling my emotions a bit, yes.
Interviewer: Sure. And how long it did it take you, between the time when you left the company and setting up your own business? How much of a gap was there, how quickly did you make your decision?
Interviewee 44: It was on the way back from the meeting.
Interviewer: Was it something you had already been considering?
Interviewee 44: Yes, it was something I had often thought about, what if I were the boss, if I could do things differently. So I just said, "Fine, let's do it."
Interviewer: But the idea of having your own business wasn't something you had really considered?
Interviewee 44: No, no. [...] There were certain things that I had always missed, certain things that I thought were wrong. And now I was going to set up my own business and I was determined not to make those mistakes.

Interviewer: That means that, practically at that very moment, as you were thinking those thoughts, you were once again charged with positive energy.
Interviewee 44: Yes, yes. [...] I was suffering emotionally, but as far as my drive and energy was concerned, it's like in football, going on the offensive. It wasn't about scoring a goal at any cost, of course I was suffering on the inside, but straight away I said, "So how do I get the ball in the back of the net?" [...] Yes. So, if you're 2:0 down, you need to score three goals. You can't just stand around and count the blades of grass on the field and tell yourself, "Boy, today has been a really bad day."

The next interviewee is one of the most financially successful in his industry. For him, it was very important to learn that he could forgive himself for mistakes, because "I realized that 50% of our total energy is consumed by not forgiving ourselves". He even employed a personal trainer to help to learn "the art of forgiveness":

Interviewee 21: I realized that, in 199x, I needed all of the strength a person can possibly possess. And I realized that 50% of our total energy is consumed by not forgiving ourselves. I made a mistake and it's blocking me. Now I have to reflect on the mistake and then forgive myself emotionally and in conversation with myself. I need to fully dispel it. So, if I hadn't done that, between 199x and 199x, I know it would have destroyed me, both in business and personally. That was my secret, realizing that people expend 50% of their energy, and sometimes far more, in that way, by not being able to forgive themselves or others. So, in 199x, I took on a coach, a coach who only coached me in one thing. Every week, to spend roughly three hours a night forgiving others and forgiving myself when I recognized a mistake. I definitely owe my business and my life to the ability to forgive. Definitely. [...] And here's the secret; where I draw that energy from. And this energy grows naturally as I train it, when I repeat it, when I use it. And never, "I forgive myself, I forgive them, but in the back of my mind I know I could still knock all of their teeth out." That doesn't work.
Interviewer: So, what was more difficult for you, learning to forgive yourself, or learning to forgive other people?
Interviewee 21: Forgiving myself. That's the hardest.

The following interviewee gets a kick out of taking great risks. He views investing as a game. And when he loses, he is not all that bothered:

Interviewee: You fight for a year for something, or even two or three years. Of course that makes me nervous and stresses me out. But when I finally find out whether I've won or lost 50 million, it's more like when you're at school and you study really hard for something, take your exams and pass. On the day after your exams, everything is forgotten. The tension evaporates. I think I'm someone in the industry who has won and lost similarly big sums. You can only lose big money if you've previously earned big money. [...] It's just like in the Old Testament, "The Lord giveth and the Lord taketh away." You can't influence it. [...] But what I do believe is that people *think* and God *directs*. People *think* and God *laughs*. I have never previously experienced that you can accurately predict things. I have my opinions, and sometimes they are right, but I have to say that it's nothing more than speculation every time.

Another interviewee experienced a massive setback in one of his company's most important projects when, after extensive negotiations, his business partner decided to pull out at the last minute. He said that the employee who had been handling the project was, understandably, "totally devastated" and "suffered a massive blow", while he himself is able to quickly "draw a line and move on" after such setbacks:

Interviewer: How do you cope with those kinds of situations psychologically? Nobody would simply say, "Fine, it doesn't matter," or, "Come on, it'll all be back to normal in a minute." It can have an impact, just knowing that it could happen to you. Do you have a specific way of dealing with things? Can you put things behind you more quickly than other people?
Interviewee 25: Yes, and my employee, the one who had been handling things, he was totally devastated. It hit him so hard. He felt betrayed, which I can fully understand. On the other hand, it annoyed me too, of course. [...]
Interviewer: Of course, it's only human to be disappointed and frustrated, to have the wind knocked out of your sails, but I was more interested in how long those feelings last. Or how quickly can you put them behind you and get over them, psychologically and emotionally?
Interviewee 25: Yes, I can put things behind me very quickly.
Interviewer: And would you say that's an important quality you need to have in the industry?
Interviewee 25: Yes, you need a certain frustration threshold. And I have that, guaranteed. I've experienced too many mishaps not to. And I know that they were sometimes the best things that happened to me. There have been lots of acquisitions that I missed out on at the last minute, but I've come across them later on and could only say, "You were lucky there."

The next interviewee has experienced crises and setbacks, but has overcome these situations by concentrating exclusively on the root of the problem. He believes that others are tempted to dissipate their energies by doing lots of insignificant things in such situations; they avoid the problem, or get bogged down, rather than focusing on it intensively:

Interviewee 20: Yes, just this one thing. There is nothing else on my desk. Nothing else... just this. My entire desk is empty. I just have this one topic to deal with on my desk. And I don't do anything else [...] It's the others who repress things. [...] I can tell you this, I've even developed my own A4 document, and that has A, B, and C on it, you know? What I realized is that people, when they are under pressure, they may be working more, but they're trying to work on ten tasks. In the evening, they can say, "I got a lot done today." But the true art of it is that when I'm under real pressure, I keep my cool. Why? Well, all of a sudden, I no longer have to deal with A, B, and C. I cross B and C out and only have A left. [...] That's something you have to define for yourself, because when you have pressure or real problems and you go to your people and ask them, "What have you been doing all day?" [...] This is what I learned: when you go to your management team and ask them to make a list of all the things they have been doing, you can basically cross out three quarters of the tasks on their lists and say, "That's not important for us right now." And you write two or three points on the list, far fewer than the ones you already crossed off the list, and they should just concentrate on those. And they look up and say, "What?" But those are the most important tasks for the company [...] Let me tell you, if the business is not doing so well, there are some people who come and say, "I'll get a new cellphone because I've already had mine for two years." And I say, "Will we generate more revenues if you get a new phone?" If they say yes, then they get one. But if they say no, then they have to keep the old one. [...] Everything else has a lower priority. That relates to costs, that relates to recruitment. But experience has shown me that to develop the right attitude, the entrepreneurial attitude, which I believe is the key, what they really need, that's where they need help and support. It's what I learned for myself, and it's something they become aware of for themselves, writing it down. Write down what you do all day. And when you as the boss see what someone is doing, how much time they are wasting, that they spend all day working on the homepage and crap like that, then cross it all off the list. A few quick strokes of the pen and all that is left are the two or three crucial points.

INTERIM FINDINGS

According to the findings of entrepreneurship research, action orientation after failure is a key personality trait of entrepreneurs. From the interviews, it became clear that the specific way in which UHNWIs react to setbacks and crises is an important factor in their success and a characteristic they share.

First, it is worth noting that many interviewees reported that they remain extremely calm and composed during serious crises. Some of them did report having had sleepless nights, but most stressed that they were able to sleep well and switch off, even in the most severe crises. With some pride, they declared that it takes a severe crisis to find out whether you possess strong nerves and appreciate just how strong a character you have. The great strength of their optimism and their strong belief in their own self-efficacy (see Chapter 14) also appears to have helped these UHNWIs.

What is also striking is the fundamental attitude that the blame for setbacks and crises is not to be sought in external circumstances or in other people, but in themselves. The UHNWIs interviewed for this book do not regard themselves as the victims of circumstance or of their competitors' machinations, but assume personal responsibility. They also do not use negative market changes as an excuse. They accept that they are, after all, the ones who misjudged the market.

An utterly transparent approach to problems is crucial in any crisis. The only chance of overcoming a crisis is to inform all affected stakeholders – primarily creditors, banks, and investors – about the situation, at an early stage and without embellishment.

However, dealing with a crisis is not just about solving the root problem and re-establishing the status quo. Rather, the interviewees try to turn a bad situation into a good one. They repeatedly reported how their success is a result of crises and severe setbacks. The entrepreneurs explained that the expansion of their company, the conquest of new markets, and key improvements in their company's strategy or products were achieved in response to severe setbacks and crises. Their personalities, too, were tempered and strengthened by these crises. This is plausible because, as long as things are going well, people do not question their existing strategies and procedures, while a crisis forces them to do so.

The interviewees share an ability to get over negative experiences very quickly. To put it simply, they do not struggle with things they cannot change anyway, but focus exclusively on practical solutions to any crisis. Forgiving themselves for their own mistakes is as important to them as taking personal responsibility for setbacks.

Conclusion 21

21.1. SUMMARY

Unlike poverty research, academic wealth research is still in its infancy. Initially, it only focused on individuals with high earnings, before broadening its scope to include the wealthy. But UHNWIs with net assets worth tens and hundreds of millions have not yet been systematically investigated. This is the first study to undertake such an investigation. Existing elite research has not focused on this group either. Insofar as academic research has dealt with the economic elite, the selection criteria were largely based on the size of companies. As a result, most of the previous research focused on the members of the executive boards of large corporations and major banks – employed executives, in other words. Entrepreneurs, however, have been almost entirely ignored by the existing elite research – despite the fact that even owners of small or medium-sized companies often own more wealth than employed executives in large, global corporations.

In Germany there were 16,495 income millionaires in 2012.[727] The few hundred executive board members of large corporations who are in the public eye and have been the subject of research into the economic elite represent only a small minority of these high-income earners.[728] Conversely, very few of the interviewees who appear in this book are high-ranking board members of large corporations. Most of the interviewees are entrepreneurs and investors. In most cases, their companies only have a few dozen or a hundred employees, and only a few are among the major corporations whose top executives were the subject of previous studies into the economic elite.

This study proposes a division of the concept of the 'economic elite' into two subcategories and focuses exclusively on the second group. Previous elite research

---

727 Statista, "Anzahl der Einkommensteuerpflichtigen."

728 The Potsdam Elite study examined 539 executive and supervisory board members of major companies: Wilhelm Bürklin and Hilke Rebenstorf, *Eliten in Deutschland: Rekrutierung und Integration* (Wiesbaden: Springer Fachmedien, 1997), 44. Hartmann investigated 177 individuals who, during the course of their professional careers, had occupied leading executive positions in major companies: Hartmann, *Der Mythos*, 81.

has dealt very intensively with the first group, namely top executives of large corporations, who, owing to their positions and the size of their companies, are likely to be able to influence political decisions at the national level. The second subcategory, which is the subject of this book and has so far hardly been investigated, is the wealth elite, consisting mainly of entrepreneurs and investors. It is this latter group upon which wealth research focuses.

This group is undoubtedly an elite according to a standard definition of the term, as its members have passed through a distinct selection process, emerging as superior in certain features to the other members of a social system. Whether someone advances into this elite is not decided – as is the case for the executive boards of large corporations – by committees (i.e. supervisory boards), but solely on the basis of the market success of the entrepreneurs and investors themselves.

Systematic questions were developed for the interviews with the UHNWIs. The findings of the Wealth in Germany project show that – apart from inheritances – entrepreneurship is the most likely route to wealth creation. Surprisingly, however, academic wealth research has so far paid scant attention to the findings of the far more extensive entrepreneurship research. For the questions addressed in this book, applying the findings of entrepreneurship research to wealth research was therefore an important step.

A further result of academic wealth research has been the recognition that personality traits play a decisive role in wealth creation. The questions in this book therefore also take into account the broad spectrum of American research on the personality traits of entrepreneurs. In addition to these findings of entrepreneurship research, the questions asked in the interviews also draw on other research disciplines, in particular questions raised by behavioural economics and learning theories. In the interviews, the focus was on the following topics:

- Specific characteristics of the interviewees' youths (school, university, and informal learning through sports and early entrepreneurial activities)
- Motivations for self-employment
- The role of goal-setting
- The importance of sales skills for financial success
- The role of optimism and self-efficacy
- Risk orientation
- The relationship between analytical and intuitive ('gut') decisions
- The Big Five personality traits: Neuroticism, Extroversion, Openness to Experience, Conscientiousness, and Agreeableness
- The willingness to engage in confrontation
- Nonconformism and the willingness to "swim against the current"
- Dealing with crises and setbacks.

A number of these topics, including risk orientation, the role of optimism, and the relationship between decisions based on gut feeling versus those based on analysis, have been well researched. In contrast, there has been little scholarly research on the other topics, such as the importance of sales skills for the financial success of UHNWIs, or the significance of nonconformism.

The evaluation of the interviews confirmed previous findings of academic wealth and entrepreneurship research, but also showed that some findings need to be reviewed or revised. It also became clear that research on the 'economic elite' has so far focused one-sidedly on employed executives within large corporations, which has resulted in findings that are not applicable to this investigation of the wealth elite.

Most of the interviewees come from families that belong to the economic middle class. It is striking, however, that the parents of 60% of the interviewees were self-employed – a rate that is ten times higher than that for the German population as a whole. Their parents were often entrepreneurs, small business owners, or farmers – most of them not rich, but, more significantly, not working as employees. As a result, it was something of a foregone conclusion for these interviewees when they were children and young people that they would later go into business for themselves. The remaining two fifths of the parents were employees or civil servants, but only two were blue-collar workers. The importance of role models outside the parental home should not be underestimated. The rich parents of friends, wealthy relatives, classmates at boarding school, and affluent neighbours impressed a number of these future UHNWIs with their lifestyles.

The social recruitment of the wealth elite is different from that of the 'economic elite' that has been the subject of previous research. While the parents of senior executives in large corporations, as shown by Hartmann et al., mainly come from the grand bourgeoisie, and habitus plays an important role in their careers, the selection processes to join the wealth elite are quite different. Neither does school or university education play a key role.

Admittedly, most of the interviewees did benefit from a good school and university education. But this does not set them apart from many of their contemporaries. And their formal academic achievements were largely mediocre. One important finding of the biographical interview questions was that there is no correlation between performance at school or university and the degree of wealth these individuals went on to achieve. Those who performed best at school or university did not typically later rise to the absolute peak of wealth. A third of those who went on to become wealthy had not studied, and one in seven had not even graduated secondary school.

The extracurricular activities these individuals engaged in were far more important. Almost all of the interviewees were involved in competitive sports from a young age, or they earned money in an atypical, entrepreneurial way. There were only 6 of the 45 interviewees for whom neither of these applied.

More than half of the interviewees pursued competitive or amateur sports at very high levels. In this way, they learned to cope with victories and defeats, and to assert themselves against their competitors; they acquired a tolerance for frustration and developed self-confidence in their own abilities. Most of the interviewees were not team athletes, but 'lone fighters'. They were, for example, athletes, skiers, equestrians, swimmers, tennis players, or judoka. They achieved remarkable results, winning at district and state level, or competed in national or international championships. But at some point, they realized that they lacked the genetic predispositions to reach the highest level of their sports.

The approaches these future UHNWIs took to earning money while they were at school and university are also striking. Typical jobs for schoolchildren and students, the kind that involve working for an hourly wage, were the exception. The range of ideas and resourcefulness these interviewees demonstrated as young people reveal their tremendous creativity. They sold everything from cosmetics to private winter gardens, from second-choice wheel rims to car washes, from used cars and motorbikes to insurance products and closed-end funds, from animals they raised themselves to jewellery, from DIY radios to second-hand car radios. These were undoubtedly formative experiences for the young people who would later become entrepreneurs. They learned to organize, sell, and think entrepreneurially. They learned, often unconsciously, to acquire the implicit knowledge that is so important for successful entrepreneurs and investors. And their early entrepreneurial experiences were the best preparation for their later self-employment.

The hypothesis that entrepreneurs are 'misfits' who were difficult and rebellious as employees and therefore could not have climbed the career ladder in an existing company was confirmed by numerous interviewees. They see themselves as difficult people who are too unconventional to subordinate themselves to existing structures or to other people. This nonconformism was often already evident during their school days. Many interviewees reported that they had experienced massive confrontations with figures of authority, in particular with their teachers.

These nonconformists would certainly often have had a tough time climbing to the top in existing companies. One commented that "you would have had to give [him] pills" to make him function as an employee. He considered himself far too rebellious and too much of a know-it-all. Alongside this group there were other interviewees for whom this was not the case. They had previously worked in large companies where they had made careers for themselves. But things did not move quickly enough for them in such environments, or they thought the earning potential was too low. One noted succinctly that, in view of his very high financial demands, it would not have been "financially viable" for him to continue working as a bank employee. Another said it would simply have taken too long to climb the career ladder in a large corporation. Although he had been very strongly supported and rapidly promoted, the route to CEO was a long one and he did not want "to wait in line for ten years".

A third group never even faced the decision between self-employment or employment. It was always clear to them that they would only ever go into business for themselves. One interviewee, who had not spent a single day as an employee in his entire life, earned a few hundred thousand Deutschmarks per year from sales while he was still at university. Like several others, he stated that he had never even considered the idea of working as an employee. This is also true for those interviewees who joined their parents' family businesses, which many of them considered a foregone conclusion from a very young age, so that no other option ever presented itself.

An important question addressed by this book was whether the interviewees had built their fortunes as the result of a deliberate and purposeful striving towards wealth as a specific goal (as is claimed, for example, in the popular wealth-creation literature in the tradition of Napoleon Hill) or simply as a by-product of their entrepreneurial activity. Specifying their goals in writing had been very important for many of the interviewees. A number of the interviewees had followed the guidance of popular wealth-creation literature to the letter. They set themselves precise financial goals and deadlines for achieving them. A surprising number of the interviewees reported a detailed planning process undertaken at least once a year. Many interviewees emphasized that this goal-setting needed to be done in writing, since only written and quantifiable goals are ultimately verifiable. Some of the interviewees extensively document their goals. Many reported visualization techniques and other rituals that they are convinced help them to achieve their goals. Many of the interviewees do not limit their goal-setting to financial targets, but also adopt the same approach towards other areas of their lives.

The observation that it is helpful to set ambitious and specifically formulated goals is consistent with the goal-setting theory discussed in Section 3.2.e – a psychological theory that has demonstrated in numerous studies that challenging and specifically formulated goals lead to better results than easily achievable goals, and that people who set specific goals are more successful than those who set themselves either no goals or only vaguely formulated ones.

Nevertheless, not all of the interviewees used such goal-setting techniques. Some explained that, although they defined revenue targets for their companies, they did not set personal financial goals. Other interviewees expressed general scepticism as to whether planning life targets was possible and useful at all. Thus, the hypothesis of the popular wealth-creation literature – that wealth will *only* be attained by those who set and visualize specific, quantifiable financial goals – cannot be substantiated. While this *can* be a path to wealth, it is by no means the only one. On the other hand, it would be a mistake to assume that the interviewees' career paths were largely unintended and the result of chance occurrences.

As explained in detail in Section 5.2 and Section 7.4 on methodology, attempts at self-explanation that downplay the role of purposeful planning and over-emphasize the role of happenstance can also be interpreted in socio-psychological terms as the result of unconscious envy-defence strategies or as an expression of the interviewee's desire to provide what will be viewed as socially desirable responses.

To better understand their motivations, the interviewees were asked what they associated with the concept of money. The interviewees associate money with a wide range of different advantages. The variety of their answers reveals the range of their motivations. Thus, the motivation of being able to afford the finer things (such as expensive cars, houses, or vacations) played a very important role for 13 interviewees, whereas ten stated that this was not at all important to them. This motive was neither particularly important nor completely unimportant for the remaining interviewees.

While about half of the interviewees stated that security was of particular importance to them, there were also nine who said this was not at all a motivation for them. There was only one motivation upon which almost all interviewees agreed: they associate wealth with freedom and independence. Almost all of the interviewees were united in their agreement on the importance of financial independence. No other motivation was so frequently rated so highly. On a scale of 0 to 10, only five interviewees did not rate this motivation in the highest range of between 7 and 10. In fact, 23 interviewees even decided to award this motivation the highest possible score, a 10. The second-placed motivation was the opportunity to use the money for new things, to invest.

So, from the interviewees' own perspectives, what skills and qualities were decisive in the far-above-average financial success and great wealth they have achieved? The importance of sales skills, which Werner Sombart defined with his concept of the 'trader' and which he described as one of the most important entrepreneurial abilities, has been considerably underestimated as a success factor by both recent entrepreneurship research and recent wealth research. And yet, there is almost no other point upon which the interviewees – across all industries they are involved in – are as unanimous as the fact that sales skills have contributed significantly to their financial success. Two thirds of the interviewees stated that the ability to sell successfully had a decisive impact on their success. More than one in three credited 70% to 100% of their success to their sales skills. And this is despite the fact that many of these outstanding salespeople would not be recognized as such at first glance – which is most likely one of the keys to their sales success.

For them, sales is not just the process of marketing products or services. They define sales in far broader terms. They view sales as the process of convincing other people: the government official to issue a permit, the outstanding job applicant to join their company, their employees to buy into a vision, a banker to approve a loan. "Everything is sales," as one of the interviewees put it. The interviewees did not view the "No" that they are often met with at the start of a sales process as something negative. Many report that their greatest pleasure is turning this "No" into a "Yes."

Many interviewees emphasize that, above all, a high degree of empathy is required to achieve such a turnaround. The ability to 'read' people and intuitively grasp their fears, blockades and objections, and then dispel them, is of crucial importance. Many of the interviewees describe themselves as very empathetic and capable psychologists.

Alongside empathy, professional expertise also plays an important role, but only in combination with excellent didactic skills. The interviewees describe "being able to explain things clearly" as a crucial prerequisite for success in sales. Likewise, the importance of networking is frequently highlighted. Interviewees report how, with great diligence, persistence and determination, they established the networks which then became the basis for their financial success.

The interviewees did not learn these sales skills at school or university. In addition to any innate sales talents, it was their early entrepreneurial experiences, as described in Section 9.6, that proved decisive. This shows that informal learning processes, by which implicit learning leads to implicit knowledge, were more important for the interviewees' later success than their formal education at school and university.

In addition to this knowledge, the interviewees' success was founded on a number of fundamental attitudes and dispositions. One of these was a pronounced optimism. Both entrepreneurship research and behavioural economics have devoted a great deal of attention to the topic of "optimism and over-optimism". The hypothesis that entrepreneurs are extremely optimistic is clearly confirmed by these ultra-high-net-worth entrepreneurs and investors. There was stronger agreement among the interviewees on the perception of themselves as very optimistic than on any other personality trait.

On a scale from −5 (extreme pessimist) to +5 (extreme optimist), 37 of 40 interviewees ranked themselves in the positive range, namely as optimists. Of these, 35 went as far as to place themselves in the highest optimistic range of +3 to +5. A high degree of optimism was also apparent in the results of the Big Five personality test. None of the other 50 questions was answered with the same degree of consistency as the one about optimism and pessimism. The statement "I am actually more of a pessimist" was very strongly rejected by 38 of the 43 interviewees.

In the interviews it became clear that what the interviewees meant by optimism is synonymous with what psychologists have termed self-efficacy. In their own words, the interviewees defined optimism as the conviction that "as a result of your own abilities, or the network you have built, or your intellect, you are always able to identify solutions and to overcome anything". For them, optimism is "self-confidence in one's own actions", as well as in one's own "organizational capabilities" and problem-solving competence. This confirms the findings of entrepreneurship and wealth research that high self-efficacy is an essential personality trait of entrepreneurs and the rich.

Only a minority of the interviewees have reflected on the problematic aspects of over-optimism. These interviewees recognized that the dangers of an overly optimistic attitude could lead to the acceptance of excessive risk. In this context, several of the interviewees pointed out that they had adopted corrective decision-making mechanisms, such as working with a partner whose fundamental attitude was less optimistic.

There is a close correlation between optimism and risk orientation. Extensive research has been carried out into the risk orientation of entrepreneurs and the rich. Some researchers have come to the conclusion that a high level of risk propensity is positively correlated with successful entrepreneurship and wealth, others have concluded that a moderate risk profile is characteristic of entrepreneurs, while others have argued that, although entrepreneurs' actions are objectively risky, they do not subjectively perceive them to be risky.

There is much evidence that both the conscious acceptance of high levels of risk, particularly in a business's start-up phase, and the subsequent reduction of these risks are key to lasting financial success. Only very few people who are not willing to bear increased risks become entrepreneurs or investors. On the other hand, those who expose themselves to constant high levels of risk stand a high likelihood of losing most or all of their assets. And the later in life this happens, the less likely it is that they will be able to rebuild their fortunes from scratch. Many interviewees reported that their risk-taking had decreased significantly as they got older.

The hypothesis that many entrepreneurs and the wealthy have only a moderate risk profile was not confirmed by the interviews. At least in the initial phases of wealth creation, most of the interviewees rated their own risk profiles as very high. This changes during the stabilization phase, when risk profiles decrease. In this phase, the hypothesis of moderate risk does apply.

The hypothesis that entrepreneurs and the wealthy take on objectively higher levels of risk, but do not subjectively perceive these risks to be so great, cannot be fully upheld in the context of the interviews. Most interviewees were well aware of their very high risk profiles. On the other hand, there were interviewees for whom this hypothesis is valid – they assessed their own risk propensity as moderate, but acknowledged that the people around them considered them to be significant risk-takers. In addition, it was shown that many interviewees did not recognize risks that could objectively be described as high, such as the low level of diversification and high concentration of their assets in their own companies. This is where the illusion of control, which is in turn the result or expression of over-optimism, plays a role.

The hypothesis derived from entrepreneurship research and behavioural economics that entrepreneurs and investors predominantly base their decisions on gut feeling was confirmed. Of the 45 interviewees, 24 stated that gut decisions dominated,

15 said that analysis dominated, and six either said gut feeling and analysis each contributed 50/50, or they could not be clearly assigned to one category or the other. Even those who primarily relied on analytical decisions explained that they trusted their gut for 20% to 40% of their decisions. In comparison, surveys of the German population as a whole reveal that the proportion of those who say they tend to base their decisions on reason is greater than the proportion who say they tend to make decisions based on feelings.

Many of the interviewees stress the fact that gut feeling is not innate; rather it develops as the sum of life experiences. This corresponds to the theory presented in Section 4.1, which describes gut feeling as the product of implicit learning. Flashes of insight will appear in a fraction of a second, triggered by the recognition of a pattern, an awareness that is, in turn, the result of many years of collected experiences. However, according to the interviewees, this is only possible on the basis of many years of experience, which is why some reported that the proportion of gut decisions they have made has increased over the course of their lives.

Many of the interviewees ascribed a warning function to their gut feelings, and credited these alarm signals for having prevented them from making a number of poor business decisions. Some of the interviewees reported making decisions against their gut feelings that subsequently proved to be mistakes. The conclusion they drew from such experiences was to never again make a decision against their intuition. At the same time, the industry in which the interviewees are involved had no bearing on whether they rely more on gut feeling or analysis when making their decisions. This was clearly illustrated by the example of four real estate investors. The first went as far as to assert that he (exclusively among the interviewees) makes all of his decisions 100% analytically. For the second real estate investor, this applied to 80% of his decisions. These two investors even saw themselves as having an advantage over their competitors, because they believe that so many real estate investors rely primarily on gut feeling. In contrast, industry colleagues said that they make 80% to 90% of their decisions on the basis of gut feeling, and that, in their experience, people who rely too heavily on analysis are less successful.

The interviewees were almost unanimous in believing that decisions involving the assessment of people can only be made on the basis of gut feeling. One investor from the private equity sector expressed it thus: "It boils down to reading people, assessing people, but you can't measure them, weigh them, put figures on them. It's not like you can look to see if they have an official stamp of quality on them, can you? You can't ask an auditor to analyse someone's character."

As demonstrated in Part A, gut feelings are a manifestation of implicit knowledge, which is, in turn, the product of implicit learning. It is therefore unsurprising that, as shown in Section 9.4, academic qualifications do not play the decisive role in wealth creation. The interviewees did not primarily acquire the implicit knowledge that would later manifest itself as gut feeling from their formal learning, but in informal learning situations, such as competitive sports or early entrepreneurial activity while they were at school or university.

The findings of entrepreneurship and wealth research presented in Part A of this book were largely confirmed by the interviewees' answers to the 50 questions of the Big Five personality test. Conscientiousness was the interviewees' most dominant personality trait. It is important to remember that the Big Five theory's definition of conscientiousness does not just include qualities such as duty, precision, and thoroughness, but also emphasizes diligence, discipline, ambition, and stamina. Conscientiousness is therefore a very strong trait. Of the respondents, 39 of 43 scored between 25 and 40 points for this trait. In the answers they provided to these questions, a high degree of determination and reliability were particularly evident.

Extroversion was also widespread among the interviewees, although slightly less so than conscientiousness. Of the interviewees, 29 of 43 proved to be distinctly extroverted, describing themselves as very optimistic people who prefer to forge their own paths. Openness to Experience was also widespread, with 28 of the 43 interviewees very open to new experiences. The interviewees strongly agreed with the statement that they like to conduct thought experiments with unusual ideas.

The interviewees scored very low or low for neuroticism. All of the interviewees were in the category 0 to 19 points, with 36 of the 43 even scoring as low as 0 to 9 points. This confirms the interviewees' exceptionally high levels of mental stability. Statements such as "I often think that I am inferior to other people" were roundly rejected by the interviewees. Strong assent, however, was given to the statement "I am not easily discouraged when things are not running entirely smoothly."

The thesis proposed by entrepreneurship and wealth research, namely that entrepreneurs and the wealthy are less agreeable, was only partially confirmed. According to the Big Five test, Agreeableness was a less pronounced trait than Conscientiousness, Openness to Experience, and Extroversion. Nevertheless, a majority of the interviewees tended towards agreeableness. There were, however, reasons to doubt whether the test questions adequately differentiated between those who tend to be more conflict-oriented and those who are more harmony-oriented in the field of business. The test results were therefore compared with the analysis of the interviews. During the interviews, the interviewees were asked whether they would tend to characterize themselves as harmony-oriented or conflict-oriented. Taking the interviewees classed as conflict-oriented by the test together with those who – despite having scored more highly for agreeableness in the test – described themselves as conflict-oriented in their interviews, the following findings emerge: of the 43 UHNWIs who took the test, more than half (22) received a low agreeableness rating and can be classified as tendentially conflict-oriented, seven registered average levels of agreeableness, and 14 exhibited high levels of agreeableness. The corrected results show that there were significantly more conflict-oriented individuals than agreeable individuals. This corresponds more closely with the existing research findings, which have shown that UHNWIs and entrepreneurs are not particularly agreeable.

The supplementary interview questions also revealed that some of the interviewees who described themselves as very harmony-oriented (matching the results of their Big Five tests) used to be far more conflict-oriented earlier in their lives. This corresponds with research findings that agreeableness becomes a stronger trait with age. For other interviewees, there were striking discrepancies between their self-perceptions and the ways in which they are viewed by others. These interviewees reported that they perceive themselves as harmony-oriented but are viewed as more conflict-oriented by the people around them. In addition to this, many of the interviewees paint a more differentiated picture – in relation to their clients and customers, for example, they are very keen on maintaining harmonious relationships, but at the same time, within their own companies, they can also be regarded as highly aggressive.

The highly conflict-oriented interviewees described behaviours that suggest that their aggressive tendencies are not only confined to their working environments but also exhibited in other areas of their lives, where they make very little effort to avoid conflict. For many of the interviewees, this readiness to meet conflicts head on corresponds with the fact that, in their investments and business decisions, they often position themselves in opposition to majority opinions and swim against prevailing currents.

Few of the Big Five personality test's 50 questions elicited as positive a response from the interviewees as the statement "I would describe myself as someone who prefers to forge my own path." Of the interviewees, 41 of 43 expressed agreement. Not a single interviewee disagreed with the statement; the remaining two interviewees were undecided. Many interviewees – especially the investors – attributed their financial success to a large extent to their ability to swim against the current. They confirmed Schumpeter's diagnosis that successful entrepreneurs oppose majority opinion, or at least act independently of what the majority thinks.

This pattern of behaviour is probably what helps them to buy low and sell high. Of course, this is no definite guarantee of success, as with highly leveraged investments in particular, there is always a danger that an investor will get their timing wrong. The contrarian investor is also dependent on other market players at some point following the investor's lead. After all, it is only once this happens that prices will rise and they can take their profits. But they do not have a problem with selling when the markets are euphoric, because they tend to feel uneasy when their opinion is shared by the majority. They regard majority opinion as a contra-indicator – a view they maintain both through phases of widespread market panic and through euphoric upswings.

During the interviews, two distinct types of entrepreneur and investor emerged. The first group were delighted to stand in opposition to majority opinion and to swim against the current as a matter of principle. They were actually uncomfortable when they had the impression that their view of a situation was aligned with the 'mainstream', as they disparagingly termed it. The other group acted more independently of the majority, which was essentially irrelevant to them. This means that they formed their own opinions independent of the majority view. Disagreeing with majority opinion neither bothered nor stimulated them. Conversely, there were times when their actions were closer to those of the majority. Thus, this subgroup did not view contrarianism and 'swimming against the current' as fundamental stances.

According to the findings of entrepreneurship research, action orientation after failure is a key personality characteristic of entrepreneurs. From the interviews, it became clear that the specific way in which UHNWIs react to setbacks and crises is an important factor in their success and a unifying characteristic.

Firstly, it is worth noting that many interviewees reported that they remain extremely calm and composed during serious crises. Some of them did report having had sleepless nights, but most of the interviewees emphasized that they were able to sleep well and switch off, even in the midst of the most severe crises. It was not without a certain pride that they declared that it was only in a serious crisis that you learn whether you have strong nerves and come to appreciate just how strong a character you have. Obviously, these wealthy interviewees were helped by the great strength of their optimism and their strong conviction in their own self-efficacy.

What is also striking is the fundamental attitude that leads the interviewees not to seek the blame for setbacks and crises in external circumstances or in other people, but in themselves. The interviewees do not regard themselves as the victims of circumstance or of their competitors' machinations, but assume responsibility for their own failures. Nor do they use negative market changes as an excuse, but instead accept that they are to blame for misjudging the market.

They strongly believe that an utterly transparent approach to problems is crucial in any crisis. Accordingly, the only chance of overcoming a crisis is to inform any and all affected business partners – primarily creditors, banks, and investors – about the situation, at an early stage and without embellishment. However, dealing with a crisis is not just about solving the root problem and re-establishing the status quo. Rather, the interviewees try to turn setbacks into opportunities. They repeatedly reported how their crises and setbacks only served to make them even more successful. The entrepreneurs explained that the expansion of their companies, the conquest of new markets, and decisive improvements in their company's strategy or products were achieved in response to severe setbacks and crises. Their personalities, too, were tempered and strengthened by these crises.

The interviewees are united in their ability to 'get over' negative experiences very quickly. Rather than struggling with things they cannot change, they focus exclusively on practical solutions to any crisis. To forgive themselves for mistakes is as important to them as taking personal responsibility for setbacks.

This book has demonstrated that it would be equally as wrong to assume that all UHNWIs share identical personality traits as it would be to assume that there are only differences and very few similarities. In addition to the differences, there were numerous repeating patterns in the interviewees' biographies, personalities, and behaviours. And there is a correlation between the various behavioural patterns demonstrated here: people with a higher risk propensity are more likely to swim against the current and break the rules. After all, more optimistic individuals with a high degree of self-efficacy are also more willing to take risks because they are convinced that their efforts will be rewarded with success. And individuals who trust their gut feelings are more likely to question and break established conventions than individuals who rely exclusively on their analytical skills.

This book has integrated the findings of entrepreneurship research, behavioural economics, and wealth research. The concept of the wealth elite was developed and it has been shown that this elite is different from the 'economic elite' that has so far been the subject of academic research into elites. For the classic economic elite, Hartmann and others showed the importance of habitus. Evidence suggests that for the wealth elite the role of habitus is less important, as is that of education. For, while it is committees (supervisory boards) who ultimately decide whether someone is admitted to the ranks of the traditional economic elite or not, membership of the wealth elite is determined solely by entrepreneurial market success.

21.2. LIMITATIONS OF THE STUDY AND RECOMMENDATIONS FOR FUTURE RESEARCH

A comparison between the economic elite, which is mainly composed of the high-ranking executives of large corporations, and UHNWIs, who are mainly entrepreneurs and investors, would be a worthwhile undertaking for future research. A systematic and empirical comparison of this kind should, for example, consider social background, personality traits, educational background, and habitus.

An important finding of this work was the key importance of sales skills for the financial and professional success of the interviewees. As no investigations have so far been carried out into this topic, it should be pursued more intensively in future. Here, it would be useful to identify links to the theories of implicit learning, implicit knowledge, and the importance of intuition or gut feeling, as essential components of the successful sales process are not based on particular analytical abilities but on qualities such as empathy and sensitivity.

Wealthy individuals who owe their great fortunes primarily to inheritance were not the subject of this investigation. A comparative study of the personality traits and behavioural patterns of ultra-high-net-worth heirs with the group examined in this book would also be of great interest.

After all, this book is only a first step towards understanding the wealth elite. The real estate sector is strongly represented in the group examined here. It would be interesting to take a closer look at individuals from other sectors, such as young start-up entrepreneurs who have attained great wealth in the new technologies sector.

The findings of this book are also relevant to educational research. As shown in Section 4.5, the importance of informal learning outside educational institutions has been increasingly emphasized and researched in recent years. The analysis of the biographies of UHNWIs has shown that school and university education, as important as they are, were less important for creating wealth than informal learning experiences – for example, through early entrepreneurial activity or competitive sports. Furthermore, implicit learning has been shown to play a key role. The relevance of the implicit knowledge gained in this way was demonstrated in the great importance the entrepreneurs and investors interviewed for this book attached to making gut decisions. Thus, this work has confirmed research results, such as those from Kahneman and Gigerenzer, that have stressed the importance of gut decisions. How informal learning occurs, for example through early entrepreneurial activity, would be an interesting research topic for future interdisciplinary work within the framework of entrepreneurship, wealth, and education research, as well as business administration.

Finally, attention must be drawn to the scope of this research and its limitations, which result from the methods employed. As with many qualitative studies, this work describes the mindsets, biographies, self-image, and personalities of the interviewees. The exploration of the economic success of UHNWIs is still at an early stage. In this early research phase, it was first of all important to reconstruct the self-image of UHNWIs and to learn more about their biographies, personalities, and behavioural patterns. In this context, the study has also sought to describe possible cause-and-effect relationships and to form new hypotheses and critically assess existing ones. A causal explanation, as provided in standardized approaches in the social sciences, would have required the formation of control groups and, for example, a comparison between this group of interviewees and the "millionaire next door" or other social groups who are less financially successful. This gap in the existing research remains to be filled.

The author has repeatedly pointed out that, as is always the case with elite research, the investigation included only those who have succeeded – that is, those who are among the winners of an economic selection process. However, this presents the problem of 'undersampling of failure', which Jerker Denrell referred to in 2003. This is a problem that, for example, affects a large amount of the work dealing with successful companies or successful executives. "In addition, there is a strong tendency to focus on successful firms and individuals in books, cases, and the business press. Such sample bias implies that the examples that managers encounter and attend to undersample failure. Practicing managers observe the performances and practices of other firms, but they may not observe the practices of firms that have failed."[729]

This methodological problem is characteristic of best practice studies as well as of the bulk of the literature on management and success, and the popular wealth-creation literature. Therefore, it should again be emphasized that – contrary to what popular wealth-creation books would have their readers believe – the traits of UHNWIs described in this work are by no means a formula for success, the application of which would definitely lead to great wealth.

Denrell points to the largely underestimated methodological problem of undersampling of failure, which he demonstrates with examples that are also relevant to this work:

Very successful companies are often those that have taken very high risks. There is, however, some evidence that the companies that take on particularly high levels of risk are also the companies that fail, namely when these risks materialize. These exit the market and are therefore not usually the subject of research – and certainly not the subject of investigations into successful companies.[730] Therefore, it has been pointed out repeatedly in this book that, for example, an elevated risk propensity may be a prerequisite for extraordinary success, but, of course, there is no guarantee that an increased tolerance of risk will result in vast wealth. It is likely that a very high propensity for risk will lead to economic failure in at least as many (if not even more) cases – but existing research mainly deals with the victors. To be successful, a more moderate willingness to take on risk is probably the best prescription, and works more often than a highly elevated risk exposure. In order to be extremely successful, however, a much higher willingness to take on risk is likely to be an advantage, but this can also lead to failure (probably even more frequently). Therefore, studies on failed entrepreneurs and investors would be revealing.

Another example is the significant role that gut decisions play for many successful entrepreneurs. "If undersampling of failure implies that the potential of risky management practices will be overestimated, it follows that certain risky decision-making processes are likely to be overestimated. For example, undersampling of failure could result in potentially misleading evidence for the benefits of rapid and intuitive decision-making processes."[731] According to Denrell, rapid, intuitive decisions could lead to an advantage in market situations in which it is important to gain market share and market domination quickly. The companies that did so

---

729 Jerker Denrell, "Vicarious Learning, Undersampling of Failure, and the Myths of Management," *Organization Science* 14, no. 3 (2003), 227.

730 Ibid., 230.

731 Ibid., 238.

would have a temporal advantage and would then possibly emerge as winners. "Nevertheless, in this type of situation the top-performing companies will be those companies that, without any analysis, launched a product that happened to appeal to customers. Thus, the top performers will seem to have acted on intuition. It is possible, however, that the worst-performing companies will also be companies that acted without analysis, and happened to launch a product that did not appeal to customers."[732]

The same is true of many of the traits mentioned in management literature and how-to guides to success as a prerequisite for above-average success, such as single-minded focus and strong perseverance in difficult situations. This is certainly true, as this study has confirmed. However, as Denrell points out, "Thus, if we only observe successful entrepreneurs, it is likely that we overestimate the benefits of a persistent and single-minded focus. The individuals who persistently and single-mindedly focused on a scenario that never materialized will be forgotten or will be classified as cranks rather than visionaries."[733]

But even Jerker Denrell and Chengwei Liu, who emphasize that extraordinary success does not necessarily have to be an indicator of extraordinary abilities,[734] concede that this is especially the case when chance plays a major role. In contrast, in competitive situations where luck and random events are of little importance – the authors suggest a marathon as an example – performance is an indicator of special abilities. "In such settings, performance is a good indicator of skill and … extreme performance may be especially informative."[735]

There is much evidence that the behavioural patterns and personality traits described in this book are prerequisites for becoming extremely rich. However, they are not a guarantee, because the same behavioural patterns and personality traits (i.e., very high optimism, high risk tolerance, gut decisions) could also lead to failure. It is therefore no coincidence that, for example, many interviewees stated that their propensity for risk had decreased significantly during the course of their lives. Their high propensity for risk in the initial entrepreneurial phase was a precondition for their financial success. The fact that they were more cautious later on was the necessary prerequisite for not jeopardizing this success. Individuals who did not reduce their propensity for risk over their lifetime may well have experienced financial ruin – and would therefore not have been interviewed for this book.

This is only the beginning of scholarly research into UHNWIs. The findings presented in this book are intended to pave the way for further scholarly efforts to approach a group who remain unfamiliar to many.

732   Ibid., 238.

733   Ibid., 236.

734   See Jerker Denrell and Chengwei Liu, "Top Performers Are Not the Most Impressive when Extreme Performance Indicates Unreliability," *Proceedings of the National Academy of Sciences* 109, no. 24 (2012).

735   Ibid., unnumbered.

Appendix

GUIDED QUESTIONS FOR THE 45 INTERVIEWS

TOPIC AREA 1: BIOGRAPHY, YOUTH – TIME AT SCHOOL AND UNIVERSITY

First of all, I would like to start by asking you some questions about your youth, especially about your time at school and university.

1. What was your father's job?
2. Many children and young people already have career aspirations or dreams. If you can remember, what did you want to be when you grew up?
3. Some individuals who have gone on to be successful are reported to have had conflicts with their fathers or parents when they were young. But there are many other cases where familial relationships were harmonious. How was your relationship with your parents during your youth?
4. During your time in school: How was your overall performance in school and what were your grades in your final exams?
5. During your time in school: Did you have conflicts at school or with teachers, beyond what is usual for many schoolchildren? Or were things predominantly harmonious?
6. Have you intensively pursued a particular sport? If so, did you participate in championships and with what results?
7. Did you earn money in some way during your school time? How?
8. What did you do after you left school? (For example, university studies.)
9. Did you graduate from university?
10. Were you among the best at university, or more of an average student?
11. Did you make money while you were at university – how?

TOPIC AREA 2: PROFESSIONAL AND FINANCIAL ADVANCEMENT
(If interviewee started their career as an employee.)
1. As an employee, did you get on well with your former bosses or were things more difficult?
2. Did you climb the career ladder quickly as an employee? Could you have imagined continuing to pursue a career in the company where you were working, or even getting to the top?
3. Why did you decide to become self-employed?

TOPIC AREA 3: FINANCIAL GOALS, MONEY
1. Some financially successful people report that they set themselves a financial goal early on – for example, "By 30 I will have my first million." But there are also people who became financially successful later in life and who did not set this as their goal. Can you remember how it was for you?
2. What were the key factors in building your current wealth? What would you say?
   - What percentage was inherited?
   - What percentage was from money saved during employment?
   - What percentage of the money was from dividends/entrepreneurial activity?
   - What percentage of the money was from investments (real estate, stocks, etc.)?

In case of goal-setting, supplementary questions:
1. Did you write this goal down?
2. Do you generally formulate specific goals?
3. And how often do you formulate your goals?
4. Did you somehow 'visualize' these goals, seeing them in front of you?
5. People associate money with many different things. On a scale of 0 (completely unimportant) to 10 (very important), how would you rate the following benefits of being financially independent?
   - Security, namely that "I won't have any financial problems unless I make a massive mistake"
   - Freedom and independence
   - The opportunity to use the money for new things, to invest
   - Being able to afford the finer things in life
   - Having money is personal confirmation that you got a lot of things right
   - With a large amount of money, and despite the envy the wealthy are sometimes confronted with, you receive greater recognition and have the opportunity to meet interesting people.

Open: Or are there other things that you associate with 'money' that have not been mentioned here?

TOPIC AREA 4: DEALING WITH CONFLICT, NONCONFORMISM, AGREEABILITY

1. How would people who know you well describe you?
   a. As someone who is very much in need of harmony?
   b. As someone who tends to be conflict-oriented?
2. Looking back, have other people initially responded with scepticism to any of your business decisions or investments, because you challenged prevailing opinion?
3. If you express disagreement with majority opinion, does that make you feel uncomfortable? Or have you ever taken a certain pleasure in swimming against the current?

TOPIC AREA 5: RISK BEHAVIOUR, OPTIMISM

1. Where would you place yourself on a scale from −5 (the extremely security-oriented person) to +5 (the risk junky)?
2. Would others also place you in a similar category?
3. If you look at your total net worth, roughly what percentage of it is tied to your own company?

If the percentage is very high, follow up by asking whether the interviewee perceives this as risky.

4. On the subject of optimism: If you had to place yourself on a pessimism–optimism scale (−5 = extreme pessimist and +5 = extreme optimist), where do you see yourself? And what do you personally mean by 'optimism'?
5. Follow-up question: if the interviewee assesses themselves as very optimistic: Optimism is an important characteristic for entrepreneurs and investors, but there is also the opinion that, especially in difficult situations, too much optimism can be dangerous. Have there been situations in which you would say your optimism was not necessarily a good thing?

TOPIC AREA 6: ANALYTICAL DECISIONS VERSUS GUT DECISIONS

1. Some people tend to proceed analytically, making decisions based on detailed analyses, while others are more likely to base their decisions on gut feeling. I am sure that you have experienced both. If, however, you were to weigh up what is more dominant in your decision-making process – the analytical approach or gut feeling – could you express that in percentage terms?
2. When or in what situations do you decide more analytically and when do you base your decisions more on intuition?

TOPIC AREA 7: SALES SKILLS, NETWORKS

1. Would other people call you a 'good salesperson'?
2. Follow-up question if interviewee has a lot of sales talent: To what extent has this ability contributed to your success? What would you say are the most important skills and strategies that make you a 'good salesperson'?

TOPIC AREA 8: CRISIS MANAGEMENT, DEALING WITH SETBACKS

1. Please tell me about the biggest setbacks and crises that you have experienced on your way to business/financial success.
2. It is sometimes said that crises and setbacks are the starting point for even greater success. Are there examples from your life that confirm this, or are there no such examples?

FINALLY: PERSONALITY TEST, BIG FIVE: NEO-FFI

"I have a request. There are some questions that allow you to work out your personality type. You should answer spontaneously and quickly; it takes about 15 minutes. Would you please fill out this questionnaire? If you are curious about the results, I can give you a quick summary, and then of course I would be interested in your opinion as to whether you feel the results accurately reflect your personality or not."

At the very end:
Please place yourself in one of the following wealth categories:
- EUR 10–30 million
- EUR 30–100 million
- EUR 100–300 million
- EUR 300 million–1 billion
- EUR 1–2 billion
- More than EUR 2 billion

THE NEO-FFI TEST [736]

In the following test, there are 50 statements which you should evaluate according to your agreement or rejection. These include:
A) Strongly disagree
B) Disagree
C) Neither agree nor disagree
D) Agree
E) Strongly agree.

Please decide spontaneously which value most closely expresses your opinion, and write down the respective score according to the symbols.

1. I often think I am inferior to other people.
   A) 0 B) 1 C) 2 D) 3 E) 4 -points □

2. Conversations with other people give me pleasure.
   A) 0 B) 1 C) 2 D) 3 E) 4 -points ▱

3. I like to take creative inspiration from nature or objects that I find in museums.
   A) 0 B) 1 C) 2 D) 3 E) 4 -points ○

4. I prioritize respect and sensitivity in my actions towards others.
   A) 0 B) 1 C) 2 D) 3 E) 4 -points △

5. I strive for perfection in everything I do at work.
   A) 0 B) 1 C) 2 D) 3 E) 4 -points ▭

6. There are days when I feel totally worthless.
   A) 0 B) 1 C) 2 D) 3 E) 4 -points □

7. I am definitely a cheerful person.
   A) 0 B) 1 C) 2 D) 3 E) 4 -points ▱

8. I sometimes get goose bumps when I am listening to music or reading a book.
   A) 0 B) 1 C) 2 D) 3 E) 4 -points ○

9. My co-workers and my family view me as an argumentative person.
   A) 4 B) 3 C) 2 D) 1 E) 0 -points △

10. I find it easy to meet the deadlines set for me at work.
    A) 0 B) 1 C) 2 D) 3 E) 4 -points ▭

11. I rarely feel anxiety or fear.
    A) 4 B) 3 C) 2 D) 1 E) 0 -points □

12. I like to surround myself with pleasant people.
    A) 0 B) 1 C) 2 D) 3 E) 4 -points ▱

13. When travelling, I like to try exotic dishes.
    A) 0 B) 1 C) 2 D) 3 E) 4 -points ○

14. I am usually unyielding and uncompromising in my decisions and opinions.
    A) 4 B) 3 C) 2 D) 1 E) 0 -points △

15. I work steadily and conscientiously in order to achieve my goals.
    A) 0 B) 1 C) 2 D) 3 E) 4 -points ▭

16. I very rarely feel depressed or abandoned.
    A) 4 B) 3 C) 2 D) 1 E) 0 -points □

17. My lifestyle could be described as very busy and slightly chaotic.
    A) 0 B) 1 C) 2 D) 3 E) 4 -points ▱

18. I sometimes get emotional when reading poetry.
    A) 0 B) 1 C) 2 D) 3 E) 4 -points ○

19. I think it is okay to show somebody that you do not like them.
    A) 4 B) 3 C) 2 D) 1 E) 0 -points △

20. I am always very systematic in everything I do.
    A) 0 B) 1 C) 2 D) 3 E) 4 -points ▭

21. I am not easily discouraged if things do not go so well.
    A) 4 B) 3 C) 2 D) 1 E) 0 -points □

22. I would describe myself as someone who prefers to go my own way.
    A) 4 B) 3 C) 2 D) 1 E) 0 -points ▱

23. I consider debates on philosophical topics a waste of time.
    A) 4 B) 3 C) 2 D) 1 E) 0 -points ○

24. I would never call myself a sceptic or a cynic.
    A) 0 B) 1 C) 2 D) 3 E) 4 -points △

25. Conscientiousness is my top priority when I perform tasks assigned to me.
    A) 0 B) 1 C) 2 D) 3 E) 4 -points ▭

26. I often feel the symptoms of nervousness and strong internal tension.
    A) 0 B) 1 C) 2 D) 3 E) 4 -points □

736 I would like to thank Stark Verlagsgesellschaft for their permission to use and reproduce the German NEO-FFI test from: Jürgen Hesse and Hans Christian Schrader, *Persönlichkeitstests Verstehen–durchschauen–trainieren*, Stark Verlagsgesellschaft, Munich 2014, 89–94.

27. I am very receptive to humour and like to laugh.
    A) 0 B) 1 C) 2 D) 3 E) 4 -points

28. I like to play out unusual ideas or new theories in my head.
    A) 0 B) 1 C) 2 D) 3 E) 4 -points

29. I try to treat other people impartially and with friendliness.
    A) 0 B) 1 C) 2 D) 3 E) 4 -points

30. My workplace is always impeccably tidy and clean.
    A) 0 B) 1 C) 2 D) 3 E) 4 -points

31. I often suffer from the fact that people treat me badly.
    A) 0 B) 1 C) 2 D) 3 E) 4 -points

32. I am more of a pessimist.
    A) 4 B) 3 C) 2 D) 1 E) 0 -points

33. I believe that you should constantly broaden your knowledge.
    A) 0 B) 1 C) 2 D) 3 E) 4 -points

34. Many people think that I am cold or arrogant.
    A) 4 B) 3 C) 2 D) 1 E) 0 -points

35. I always keep my promises.
    A) 0 B) 1 C) 2 D) 3 E) 4 -points

36. I do not easily get worried.
    A) 4 B) 3 C) 2 D) 1 E) 0 -points

37. I like to be the centre of attention.
    A) 0 B) 1 C) 2 D) 3 E) 4 -points

38. I think daydreaming is a waste of time.
    A) 4 B) 3 C) 2 D) 1 E) 0 -points

39. I can sometimes be extremely ruthless to achieve a specific goal.
    A) 4 B) 3 C) 2 D) 1 E) 0 -points

40. I do not think I will ever be able to get my life in order.
    A) 4 B) 3 C) 2 D) 1 E) 0 -points

41. I am rarely overcome by sadness or depression.
    A) 4 B) 3 C) 2 D) 1 E) 0 -points

42. I would consider myself quite an active person.
    A) 0 B) 1 C) 2 D) 3 E) 4 -points

43. I believe that in the case of ethical issues it is important to also pay attention to the opinions of religious authorities.
A) 4 B) 3 C) 2 D) 1 E) 0 -points ○

44. Some people would describe me as egotistical and arrogant.
A) 4 B) 3 C) 2 D) 1 E) 0 -points △

45. I am a hardworking person who performs my tasks conscientiously.
A) 0 B) 1 C) 2 D) 3 E) 4 -points ▭

46. I have experienced such strong embarrassment that I could have crawled into a hole.
A) 0 B) 1 C) 2 D) 3 E) 4 -points □

47. I normally like to perform tasks on my own.
A) 4 B) 3 C) 2 D) 1 E) 0 -points ▱

48. I do not spend time thinking about the underlying topics of science or philosophy.
A) 4 B) 3 C) 2 D) 1 E) 0 -points ○

49. I prefer cooperation to competition.
A) 0 B) 1 C) 2 D) 3 E) 4 -points △

50. I often waste a lot of time before I start a task.
A) 4 B) 3 C) 2 D) 1 E) 0 -points ▭

SUM OF THE POINTS IN THE SINGLE FACTORS:
□ = Neuroticism:
▱ = Extroversion:
○ = Openess to Experience:
△ = Agreeableness:
▭ = Conscientiousness:

Each group of ten statements refers to each of the five factoring groups. The mean (2 points per statement) is 20 points for each factor. This is also the reference value. The maximum would be 40 points. From 25 or even 30 points per factor indicates that the corresponding trait is extremely pronounced.

Bibliography

Acs, Zoltan J., Pontus Braunerhjelm, David B. Audretsch, and Bo Carlsson. "The Knowledge Spillover Theory of Entrepreneurship." *Small Business Economics* 32 (2009): 15–30.

Agor, Weston H. "Using Intuition to Manage Organizations in the Future." *Business Horizons* (July/August 1984): 49–54.

Allinson, Christopher W., Elizabeth Chell, and John Hayes. "Intuition and Entrepreneurial Behaviour." *European Journal of Work and Organizational Psychology* 9, no. 1 (2009): 31–43.

Amit, Raphael, Kenneth R. MacCrimmon, Charlene Zietsma, and John M. Oesch. "Does Money Matter? Wealth Attainments as the Motive for Initiating Growth-Oriented Technology Ventures." *Journal of Business Venturing* 16 (2000): 119–143.

Andresen, Burghard. "Risikobereitschaft (R) – der sechste Basisfaktor der Persönlichkeit: Konvergenz multivariater Studien und Konstruktexplikation." *Zeitschrift für Differentielle und Diagnostische Psychologie* 16 (1995): 210–236.

Arnott, Robert, William Bernstein, and Lillian Wu. "The Rich Get Poorer: The Myth of Dynastic Wealth." *Cato Journal* 35, no. 3 (2015): 447 – 485.

Astebro, Thomas, and Samir Elhedhli. "The Effectiveness of Simple Decision Heuristics: Forecasting Commercial Success for Early-Stage Ventures." Management Science 52, no. 3 (2006): 395–409.

Astebro, Thomas, Holger Herz, Ramana Nanda, and Roberto A. Weber. "Seeking the Roots of Entrepreneurship: Insights from Behavioral Economics." *Journal of Economic Perspectives* 28, no. 3 (2014): 49–70.

Bandura, Albert. "The Role of Self-Efficacy in Goal-Based Motivation." In *New Developments in Goal Setting and Task Performance*, edited by Edwin A. Locke and Gary P. Latham, 147–157. New York: Routledge Taylor & Francis Group, 2013.

Baron, Robert A. "Opportunity Recognition as Pattern Recognition: How Entrepreneurs 'Connect the Dots' to Identify New Business Opportunities." *Academy of Management Perspectives* 20 (2006): 104–119.

Barrick, Murray R., Michael K. Mount, and Judy P. Strauss. "Conscientiousness and Performance of Sales Representatives: Test of the Mediating Effects of Goal Setting." *Journal of Applied Psychology* 78, no. 5 (1993): 715–722.

Baum, J. Robert. "Goals and Entrepreneurship." In *New Developments in Goal Setting and Task Performance*, edited by Edwin A. Locke and Gary P. Latham, 460–473. New York: Routledge Taylor & Francis Group, 2013.

Baum, J. Robert, Michael Frese, and Robert Baron, eds. *The Psychology of Entrepreneurship*. New York: Psychology Press Taylor & Francis Group, 2012.

Baum, J. Robert, and Edwin A. Locke. "The Relationship of Entrepreneurial Traits, Skill, and Motivation to Subsequent Venture Growth." *Journal of Applied Psychology* 89 (2004): 587–598.

Beck, Hanno. *Behavioral Economics: Eine Einführung.* Wiesbaden: Springer Gabler, 2014.

Becker, Irene. "Die Reichen und ihr Reichtum." In *Oberschichten – Eliten – Herrschende Klassen,* edited by Stefan Hradil and Peter Imbusch, 73–98. Wiesbaden: Springer Fachmedien, 2003.

Beierlein, Constanze, Anastassyia Kovaleva, Christoph J. Kemper, and Beatrice Rammstedt. "Ein Messinstrument zur Erfassung subjektiver Kompetenzerwartungen: Allgemeine Selbstwirksamkeit Kurzskala (ASKU)", Working Paper 17, gesis Leibniz Institut für Sozialwissenschaften, Mannheim, 2012.

Bernardo, Antonio E., and Ivo Welch. "On the Evolution of Overconfidence and Entrepreneurs." *Journal of Economics & Management Strategy* 10, no. 3 (2001): 301–330.

Bibb, Porter, and Ted Turner. *It Ain't as Easy as It Looks.* Boulder: Atlantik Books, 1993.

Billionaires: Master Architects of Great Wealth and Lasting Legacies. UBS and PwC, 2015.

Bird, Barbara J. *Entrepreneurial Behavior.* Glenview: Scott, Foresman and Company, 1989.

Birley, Sue, and Paul Westhead. "A Taxonomy of Business Start-Up Reasons and Their Impact on Firm Growth and Size." *Journal of Business Venturing* 9 (1994): 7–31.

Bloomberg, Michael. *Bloomberg by Bloomberg: With Invaluable Help from Matthew Winkler.* New York: John Wiley & Sons, 1997.

Bohnsack, Ralf. *Rekonstruktive Sozialforschung: Einführung in qualitative Methoden,* 9th ed. Opladen: Verlag Barbara Budrich, 2014.

Bourdieu, Pierre. *Distinction: A Social Critique of the Judgement of Taste.* Abingdon: Routledge, 2010.

Böwing-Schmalenbrock, Melanie. *Wege zum Reichtum: Die Bedeutung von Erbschaften, Erwerbstätigkeit und Persönlichkeit für die Entstehung von Reichtum.* Wiesbaden: Springer VS, 2012.

Brandstätter, Hermann. "Unternehmensgründung und Unternehmenserfolg aus persönlichkeitspsychologischer Sicht." In *Unternehmerisch erfolgreiches Handeln,* edited by Klaus Moser, Bernad Batinic, and Jeanette Zempel, 155–172. Göttingen: Verlag für Angewandte Psychologie, 1999.

Branson, Richard. *Screw It, Let's Do It: Lessons in Life and Business, Expanded.* London: Virgin Books, 2007.

Brenkert, George G. "Innovation, Rule Breaking and the Ethics of Entrepreneurship." *Journal of Business Venturing* (2008): doi:10.1016/j.jbusvent.2008.04.004.

Brink, Alexander. "Das riskante Unternehmer-Netzwerk." In *Unternehmertum. Vom Nutzen und Nachteil einer riskanten Lebensform,* edited by Ludger Heidbrink and Peter Seele, 129–152. Frankfurt-am-Main: Campus Verlag, 2010.

Buffett, Mary, and David Clark. *The Tao of Warren Buffett.* New York: Scribner, 2006.

Buffett, Mary, and David Clark. *Warren Buffett's Management Secrets.* London: Scribner, 2009.

Bull, Ivan, and Gary E. Willard. "Towards a Theory of Entrepreneurship." *Journal of Business Venturing* 8 (1993): 183–195.

"Bundesministerium für Arbeit und Soziales, Lebenslagen in Deutschland: Vierter Armuts- und Reichtumsbericht der Bundesregierung." Working Paper, Berlin 2013.

Burke, Lisa A., and Monica K. Miller. "Taking the Mystery Out of Intuitive Decision Making." *Academy of Management Executive* 13, no. 4 (1999): 91–99.

Bürklin, Wilhelm. "Die Potsdamer Elitestudie von 1995: Problemstellung und wissenschaftliches Programm." In *Eliten in Deutschland: Rekrutierung und Integration,* edited by Wilhelm Bürklin and Hilke Rebenstorf, 11–34. Wiesbaden: Springer Fachmedien, 1997.

Bürklin, Wilhelm, and Hilke Rebenstorf. *Eliten in Deutschland: Rekrutierung und Integration.* Wiesbaden: Springer Fachmedien, 1997.

Busenitz, Lowell W. "Entrepreneurial Risk and Strategic Decision Making: It's a Matter of Perspective." *Journal of Applied Behavioral Science* 35, no. 3 (1999): 325–340.

Buß, Eugen. *Die deutschen Spitzenmanager: Wie sie wurden, was sie sind – Herkunft, Wertvorstellungen, Erfolgsregeln.* Munich: R. Oldenbourg Verlag, 2007.

Caliendo, Maro, Frank Fossen, and Alexander Kritikos. "Selbstständige sind anders: Persönlichkeit beeinflusst unternehmerisches Handeln." *Wochenbericht des DIW Berlin* 11 (2011): 2–8.

Carter, Nancy M., William B. Gartner, Kelly G. Shaver, and Elizabeth J. Gatewood. "The Career Reasons of Nascent Entrepreneurs." *Journal of Business Venturing* 18 (2003): 13–39.

Cassar, Gavin, and Justin Craig. "An Investigation of Hindsight Bias in Nascent Venture Activity." *Journal of Business Venturing* 24 (2009): 149–164.

Cervone, Daniel, and Lawrence A. Pervin. *Personality: Theory and Research*, 12th ed. New York: John Wiley & Sons, 2013.

Chanel, Coco. *The Allure of Chanel: As Told by Her to Paul Morand.* London: Pushkin Press, 2008.

Charles-Roux, Edmonde. *Chanel: Her Life, Her World, the Woman Behind the Legend.* New York: Alfred A. Knopf, 1975.

Chell, Elizabeth, Jean Haworth, and Sally Brearley. *The Entrepreneurial Personality: Concepts, Cases and Categories.* London: Routledge 1991.

Chernow, Ron. *Titan: The Life of John D. Rockefeller, Sr.* New York: Vintage, 1998.

Claxton, Guy. "Knowing Without Knowing Why." *The Psychologist* (May 1998): 217–220.

Colombo, Massimo G., and Luca Grilli. "Founders' Human Capital and the Growth of New Technology-Based Firms: A Competence-Based View." *Research Policy* 34 (2005): 795–816.

Cooper, Arnold C., Carolyn Y. Woo, and William C. Dunkelberg. "Entrepreneurs' Perceived Chances for Success." *Journal of Business Venturing* 3 (1988): 97–108.

Cromie, Stanley. "Motivations of Aspiring Male and Female Entrepreneurs." *Journal of Occupational Behaviour* 8 (1987): 251–261.

Csikszentmihalyi, Mihaly. *Creativity: Flow and the Psychology of Discovery and Invention.* New York: Harper Collins Publishers, 2013.

Dahrendorf, Ralf. "Eine neue deutsche Oberschicht?" *Die neue Gesellschaft* 9 (1962): 18–31.

Dane, Erik, and Michael G. Pratt. "Exploring Intuition and Its Role in Managerial Decision Making." *Academy of Management Review* 32, no. 1 (2007): 33–54.

Deakins, David, and Mark Freel. "Entrepreneurial Learning and the Growth Process in SMEs." *Learning Organization* 5, no. 3 (1998): 144–155.

Denrell, Jerker. "Vicarious Learning, Undersampling of Failure, and the Myths of Management." *Organization Science* 14, no. 3 (2003): 227–243.

Denrell, Jerker, and Christina Fang. "Predicting the Next Big Thing: Success as a Signal of Poor Judgement." *Management Science* 56, no. 10 (2010): 1653–1667.

Denrell, Jerker, and Chengwei Liu. "Top Performers Are Not the Most Impressive when Extreme Performance Indicates Unreliability." *Proceedings of the National Academy of Sciences* 109, no. 24 (2012): 9331–9336.

Deutscher Bundestag. "Lebenslagen in Deutschland: Dritter Armuts- und Reichtumsbericht der Bundesregierung." Paper 16/9915, 2008.

Deutscher Bundestag. "Lebenslagen in Deutschland: Erster Armuts- und Reichtumsbericht der Bundesregierung." Paper 14/5990, 2001.

Deutscher Bundestag. "Lebenslagen in Deutschland: Zweiter Armuts- und Reichtumsbericht der Bundesregierung." Paper 15/5015, 2005.

"Die Top-Verdiener im MDax." Last modified 15 May 2014. http://www.wiwo.de/finanzen/boerse/vorstandsverguetung-die-top-verdiener-im-mdax/9897550.html.

Dobbins, Bill, and Arnold Schwarzenegger. *The New Encyclopedia of Modern Bodybuilding.* New York: Simon & Schuster, 1999.

Dohmen, Günther. *Das informelle Lernen: Die internationale Erschließung einer bisher vernachlässigten Grundform des menschlichen Lernens für das lebenslange Lernen aller,* Bundesministerium für Bildung und Forschung. Bonn: 2001.

Druyen, Thomas. "Über die Studie 'Vermögen in Deutschland' und die vermögenskulturelle Zukunft." In *Vermögen in Deutschland: Heterogenität und Verantwortung,* edited by Wolfgang Lauterbach, Thomas Druyen, and Matthias Grundmann, 215–222. Wiesbaden: Springer VS, 2011.

Druyen, Thomas. *Vermögenskultur: Verantwortung im 21. Jahrhundert.* Wiesbaden: VS Verlag, 2011.

Druyen, Thomas, Wolfgang Lauterbach, and Matthias Grundmann, eds. *Reichtum und Vermögen: Zur gesellschaftlichen Bedeutung der Reichtums- und Vermögensforschung.* Wiesbaden: Springer VS, 2009.

Düx, Wiebken, and Erich Sass. "Lernen in informellen Kontexten: Lernpotenziale in Settings des freiwilligen Engagements." *Zeitschrift für Erziehungswissenschaft* 8, no. 3 (2005): 394–411.

DW. "Transgender in Deutschland." Last modified 13 May 2014. http://www.dw.com/de/transgender-in-deutschland/a-17630664.

Eker, T. Harv. *Secrets of the Millionaire Mind: Mastering the Inner Game of Wealth.* New York: Harper International, 2007.

Ellsberg, Michael. *The Education of Millionaires: Everything You Won't Learn in College about How to Be Successful.* New York: Portfolio / Penguin, 2012.

Ernst, Dagobert. "Die meisten Rocker sind friedlich." *Der Westen* (2012). Accessed 27 October 2017. http://www.derwesten.de/region/rhein_ruhr/die-meisten-rocker-sind-friedlich-id6396863.html.

Ernst, Heiko. "Glück haben – wie sehr bestimmen Zufälle unser Leben?" *Psychologie heute* 4 (2012). Accessed 27 October 2017. https://www.psychologie-heute.de/archiv/detailansicht/news/glueck_haben_wie_sehr_bestimmen_zufaelle_unser_leben_glueck_haben_wie_sehr_bestimmen_zufael.

Faschingbauer, Michael. *Effectuation: Wie erfolgreiche Unternehmer denken, entscheiden und handeln,* 2nd ed. Stuttgart: Schäffer-Poeschel Verlag, 2013.

Felber, W. *Eliteforschung in der Bundesrepublik Deutschland.* Wiesbaden: Springer Fachmedien, 1986.

Festinger, Leon. *A Theory of Cognitive Dissonance.* Stanford: Stanford University Press, 1957.

Flick, Uwe, Ernst von Kardorff, and Ines Steinke. *Qualitative Forschung: Ein Handbuch,* 10th ed. Hamburg: Rowohlt, 2013.

Flick, Uwe, Ernst von Kardorff, and Ines Steinke. "Was ist qualitative Forschung? Einleitung und Überblick." In *Qualitative Forschung: Ein Handbuch,* 10th ed., edited by Uwe Flick, Ernst von Kardorff, and Ines Steinke, 13–29. Hamburg: Rowohlt, 2013.

Frank, Robert. *Richistan: A Journey through the American Wealth Boom and the Lives of the New Rich.* New York: Crown Publishers, 2007.

Freeland, Chrystia. *Plutocrats: The Rise of the New Global Super-Rich and the Fall of Everyone Else.* New York: Penguin Press, 2012.

Frese, Michael. "The Psychological Actions and Entrepreneurial Success: An Action Theory Approach." In *The Psychology of Entrepreneurship,* edited by J. Robert Baum, Michael Frese, and Robert Baron, 151–189. New York: Psychology Press Taylor & Francis Group, 2012.

Frese, Michael, ed. *Erfolgreiche Unternehmensgründer: Psychologische Analysen und praktische Anleitungen für Unternehmer in Ost- und Westdeutschland.* Göttingen: Verlag für Angewandte Psychologie, 1998.

Frese, Michael, Judith Stewart, and Bettina Hannover. "Goal Orientation and Planfulness: Action Styles as Personality Concepts." *Journal of Personality and Social Psychology* 52 (1987): 1182–1194.

Fridson, Martin S. *How to Be a Billionaire: Proven Strategies from the Titans of Wealth.* New York: John Wiley & Sons, 2000.

Friedman, Shlomit. "Priming Subconscious Goals." In *New Developments in Goal Setting and Task Performance,* edited by Edwin A. Locke and Gary P. Latham, 549–565. New York: Routledge Taylor & Francis Group, 2013.

Friedmann, Lauri S. *Business Leaders: Michael Dell.* Greensboro: Morgan Reynolds, 2009.

Friedrichs, Julia. *Wir Erben: Was Geld mit Menschen macht.* Berlin: Berlin Verlag, 2015.

Galais, Nathalie. "Motive und Beweggründe für die Selbständigkeit und ihre Bedeutung für den Erfolg." In *Erfolgreiche Unternehmensgründer: Psychologische Analysen und praktische Anleitungen für Unternehmer in Ost- und Westdeutschland,* edited by Michael Frese, 83–98. Göttingen: Verlag für Angewandte Psychologie, 1998.

Gartner, William B. "'Who Is an entrepreneur?' Is the Wrong Question." *Entrepreneurship Theory and Practice* 13 (1988): 47–68.

Gastmann, Dennis. *Geschlossene Gesellschaft: Ein Reichtumsbericht.* Berlin: Rowohlt Berlin Verlag, 2014.

Gavin, Cassar, and Justin Craig. "An Investigation of Hindsight Bias in Nascent Venture Activity." *Journal of Business Venturing* 24 (2009): 149–164.

Gigerenzer, Gerd. *Gut Feelings: The Intelligence of the Unconscious.* New York: Viking Penguin, 2007.

Gigerenzer, Gerd. *Risk Savvy: How to Make Good Decisions.* New York: Viking Penguin, 2014.

Ginn, Charles W., and Donald L. Sexton. "A Comparison of the Personality Type Dimensions of the 1987 Inc. 500 Company Founders/CEOs with Those of Slower-Growth Firms." *Journal of Business Venturing* 5 (1990): 313–326.

Gladwell, Malcolm. *Outliers: The Story of Success.* London: Penguin Books, 2008.

Gläser, Jochen, and Grit Laudel. *Experteninterviews und qualitative Inhaltsanalyse als Instrumente rekonstruierender Untersuchungen,* 4th ed. Wiesbaden: VS Verlag für Sozialwissenschaften, 2010.

Göbel, Sigrun. "Persönlichkeit, Handlungsstrategien und Erfolg." In *Erfolgreiche Unternehmensgründer: Psychologische Analysen und praktische Anleitungen für Unternehmer in Ost- und Westdeutschland,* edited by Michael Frese, 99–122. Göttingen: Verlag für Angewandte Psychologie, 1998.

Göbel, Sigrun, and Michael Frese. "Konsequenzen für die Praxis: Ein Leitfaden für erfolgreiches Unternehmertum." In *Erfolgreiche Unternehmensgründer: Psychologische Analysen und praktische Anleitungen für Unternehmer in Ost- und Westdeutschland,* edited by Michael Frese, 171–204. Göttingen: Verlag für Angewandte Psychologie, 1998.

Göbel, Sigrun, and Michael Frese. "Persönlichkeit, Strategien und Erfolg bei Kleinunternehmern." In *Unternehmerisch erfolgreiches Handeln,* edited by Klaus Moser, Bernad Batinic, and Jeanette Zempel, 93–114. Göttingen: Verlag für Angewandte Psychologie, 1999.

Golenia, Marion, and Nils Neuber. "Bildungschancen in der Kinder- und Jugendarbeit: Eine Studie zum informellen Lernen im Sportverein." In *Informelles Lernen im Sport: Beiträge zur allgemeinen Bildungsdebatte,* edited by Nils Neuber, 189–210. Wiesbaden: VS Verlag für Sozialwissenschaften, 2010.

Gosling, Samuel D., and Jeff Potter. "The Regional Distribution and Correlates of an Entrepreneurship-Prone Personality Profile in the United States, Germany, and the United Kingdom: A Socioecological Perspective." Working Paper 550, SOEP, Berlin, 2013.

Grabka, Markus M. "Verteilung und Struktur des Reichtums in Deutschland." In *Reichtum, Philanthropie und Zivilgesellschaft*, edited by Wolfgang Lauterbach, Michael Hartmann, and Miriam Ströing, 21–46. Wiesbaden: Springer VS, 2014.

Gunz, Hugh, and Maury Peiperl, eds. *Handbook of Career Studies*. Los Angeles: Sage Publications, 2007.

Hamilton, Barton H., "Does Entrepreneurship Pay? An Empirical Analysis of the Returns of Self-Employment." *Journal of Political Economy* 108, no. 3 (2000): 604–631.

Harper, David A. "How Entrepreneurs Learn: A Popperian Approach and Its Limitations." Working Paper prepared for the group in Research in Strategy, Process and Economic Organization, Department of Industrial Economics and Strategy, Copenhagen Business School, 1999.

Hartmann, Michael. *Der Mythos von den Leistungseliten: Spitzenkarrieren und soziale Herkunft in Wirtschaft, Politik, Justiz und Wissenschaft*. Frankfurt-am-Main: Campus, 2002.

Hartmann, Michael. *The Sociology of Elites*. New York: Routledge, 2006.

Hartmann, Petra. *Wunsch und Wirklichkeit: Theorie und Empirie sozialer Erwünschtheit*. Wiesbaden: Springer Fachmedien, 1991.

Hayashi, Alden M. "When to Trust Your Gut." *Harvard Business Review* (February 2001): 5–11.

Hayek, Friedrich August von. *The Constitution of Liberty: The Definitive Edition*. Chicago: University of Chicago Press, 2011.

Hayek, Friedrich August von. "Rules, Perception and Intelligibility." In *Studies in Philosophy, Politics and Economics*, 43–65. London: Routledge & Kegan Paul, 1967.

Hayek, Friedrich August von. "Economics and Knowledge" in *Individualism and Economic Order*, Chicago: The University of Chicago Press, 1948.

Hayward, Mathew L. A., Dean A. Shepherd, and Dale Griffin. "A Hubris Theory of Entrepreneurship." *Management Science* 52, no. 2 (2006): 160–172.

Helfferich, Cornelia. *Die Qualität qualitativer Daten: Manual für die Durchführung qualitativer Interviews*, 4th ed. Wiesbaden: Springer VS, 2011.

Hermanns, Harry. "Interviewen als Tätigkeit." In *Qualitative Forschung: Ein Handbuch*, 10th ed., edited by Uwe Flick, Ernst von Kardorff, and Ines Steinke, 360–368. Hamburg: Rowohlt, 2013.

Herzberg, Philipp Yorck, and Marcus Roth. *Persönlichkeitspsychologie*. Wiesbaden: Springer VS, 2014.

Hesse, Jürgen, and Hans Christian Schrader. *Persönlichkeitstest: Verstehen – Durchschauen – Trainieren*. Munich: Stark Verlagsgesellschaft, 2014.

Hiemann, Roland. "'Geplant war das alles nicht': Werdegänge deutscher Wirtschaftsführer." In *Sprachlose Elite? Wie Unternehmer Politik und Gesellschaft sehen*, edited by Franz Walter and Stine Marg, 30–68. Reinbek: BP Gesellschaftsstudie, 2015.

Hill, Napoleon. *Think and Grow Rich: Instant Aid to Riches – New and Revised Edition*. New York:, Wilshire Book Co, 1966.

Hisrich, Robert, Janice Langan-Fox, and Sharon Grant. "Entrepreneurship Research and Practice: A Call to Action for Psychology." *American Psychologist* 62, no. 6 (2007): 575–589.

Hmieleski, Keith M., and Robert A. Baron. "Entrepreneurs' Optimism and New Venture Performance: A Social Cognitive Perspective." *Academy of Management Journal* 52, no. 3 (2009): 473–488.

Hoffmann, Arnd. *Zufall und Kontingenz in der Geschichtstheorie: Mit zwei Studien zu Theorie und Praxis der Sozialgeschichte*. Frankfurt-am-Main: Vittorio Klostermann, 2005.

Hollenbeck, John R., and Howard J. Klein. "Goal Commitment and the Goal-Setting Process: Problems, Prospects, and Proposals for Future Research." *Journal of Applied Psychology* 72 (1987): 212–220.

Hopf, Christel. "Qualitative Interviews: Ein Überblick." In *Qualitative Forschung: Ein Handbuch*, 10th ed., edited by Uwe Flick, Ernst von Kardorff, and Ines Steinke, 349–360. Hamburg: Rowohlt, 2013.

Hornday, John A., Jeffrey A. Timmins, and Karl H. Vesper. *Frontiers of Entrepreneurship Research: Proceedings of the 1983 Conference on Entrepreneurship at Babson College, Wellesley, Massachusetts*, n.d.

Hradil, Stefan, and Peter Imbusch, eds. *Oberschichten – Eliten – Herrschende Klassen*. Wiesbaden: Springer Fachmedien, 2003.

Huerta de Soto, Jesus. *Socialism, Economic Calculation, and Entrepreneurship*. Cheltenham: Edward Elgar Publishing, 2010.

Hurst, Erick, and Annamaria Lusardi. "Liquidity Constraints and Entrepreneurship: Household Wealth, Parental Wealth, and the Transition In and Out of Entrepreneurship." *Journal of Political Economy* 112, no. 2 (2004): 319–347.

Huster, Ernst-Ulrich. "Enttabuisierung der sozialen Distanz: Reichtum in Deutschland." In *Reichtum in Deutschland: Die Gewinner in der sozialen Polarisierung*, edited by Ernst-Ulrich Huster, 7–34. Frankfurt-am-Main: Campus Verlag, 1997.

Huster, Ernst-Ulrich, ed. *Reichtum in Deutschland: Die Gewinner in der sozialen Polarisierung*. Frankfurt-am-Main: Campus Verlag, 1997.

Huster, Ernst-Ulrich, and Fritz Rüdiger Volz, eds. *Theorien des Reichtums*. Münster: LIT Verlag, 2002.

Imbusch, Peter. "Reichtum als Lebensstil." In *Theorien des Reichtums*, edited by Ernst-Ulrich Huster and Fritz Rüdiger Volz, 213–247. Münster: LIT Verlag, 2002.

Irle, Martin, and Volker Möntmann. "Die Theorie der kognitiven Dissonanz: Ein Resümee ihrer theoretischen Entwicklung und empirischen Ergebnisse 1957–1976." In *Festinger, Leon: Theorie der kognitiven Dissonanz*, edited by Martin Irle and Volker Möntmann, 274–363. Bern: Verlag Hans Huber, 2012.

Judge, Timothy A., and John D. Kammeyer-Mueller. "Personality and Career Success." In *Handbook of Career Studies*, edited by Hugh Gunz and Maury Peiperl, 59–78. Los Angeles: Sage Publications, 2007.

Jungbluth, Rüdiger. *Die 11 Geheimnisse des IKEA-Erfolgs*. Frankfurt-am-Main: Bastei Lübbe, 2008.

Kahneman, Daniel. *Thinking, Fast and Slow*. New York: Farrar, Strauss and Giroux, 2011.

Kaina, Viktoria. "Deutschlands Eliten zwischen Kontinuität und Wandel. Empirische Befunde zu Rekrutierungswegen, Karrierepfaden und Kommunikationsmustern." *Aus Politik und Zeitgeschichte B* 10 (2004): 8–16.

Keese, Christoph. *Silicon Valley: Was aus dem mächtigsten Tal der Welt auf uns zukommt*. Munich: Albrecht Knaus Verlag, 2014.

Kelle, Udo, and Christian Erzberger. "Qualitative und quantitative Methoden: Kein Gegensatz." In *Qualitative Forschung: Ein Handbuch*, 10th ed., edited by Uwe, Ernst von Kardorff, and Ines Steinke, 299–308. Hamburg: Rowohlt, 2013.

Kerr, Steve, and Douglas Lepelley. "Stretch Goals: Risks, Possibilities, and Best Practices." In *New Developments in Goal Setting and Task Performance*, edited by Edwin A. Locke and Gary P. Latham, 21–32. New York: Routledge Taylor & Francis Group, 2013.

Kestel, Christine. "Über Elite: Form und Funktion von Elite-Kommunikation in der Gesellschaft der Gegenwarten." PhD diss., Ludwig-Maximilians-Universität Munich, 2008.

Kets de Vries, Manfred F. R. "The Anatomy of the Entrepreneur: Clinical Observations." *Human Relations* 49, no. 7 (1996): 853–883.

Kets de Vries, Manfred F. R. "The Dark Side of Entrepreneurship." *Harvard Business Review* (November 1985). Accessed 27 October 2017. https://hbr.org/1985/11/the-dark-side-of-entrepreneurship/ar/1.

Khan, Riz. *Alwaleed: Businessman, Billionaire, Prince.* London: Harper Collins, 2006.

Khan, Shamus Rahman. "The Sociology of Elites." *Annual Review of Sociology* 38 (2012): 361–377.

Khatri, Naresh, and H. Alvin Ng. "The Role of Intuition in Strategic Decision Making." *Human Relations* 53, no. 1 (2000): 57–86.

King, Nigel, and Christina Horrocks. *Interviews in Qualitative Research.* London: Sage Publication, 2010.

Kirzner, Israel M. *Competition & Entrepreneurship.* Chicago: The University of Chicago Press, 1973.

Kiyosaki, Robert T., and Sharon L. Lechter. *Rich Dad Poor Dad: What the Rich Teach Their Kids about Money that the Poor and Middle Class Do Not!* New York: Tech Press, Inc., 1998.

Knight Frank, *The Wealth Report,* London, 2014.

Kortmann, Klaus. "Vermögen in Deutschland: Die methodischen Anlagen der Untersuchung." In *Vermögen in Deutschland: Heterogenität und Verantwortung,* edited by Wolfgang Lauterbach, Thomas Druyen, and Matthias Grundmann, 15–28. Wiesbaden: Springer VS, 2011.

Kowal, Sabine, and Daniel C. O'Connell. "Zur Transkription von Gesprächen." In *Qualitative Forschung: Ein Handbuch,* 10th ed., edited by Uwe Flick, Ernst von Kardorff, and Ines Steinke, 437–447. Hamburg: Rowohlt, 2013.

Krais, Beate. "Begriffliche und theoretische Zugänge zu den 'oberen Rängen' der Gesellschaft." In *Oberschichten – Eliten – Herrschende Klassen,* edited by Stefan Hradil and Peter Imbusch, 35–54. Wiesbaden: Springer Fachmedien, 2003.

Krais, Beate, and Gunter Gebauer. *Habitus.* Bielefeld: Transcript Verlag, 2014.

Krampe, Ralf T. "Hochbegabung oder Langstreckenlauf? Eliteleistungen aus Sicht der Expertiseforschung." In *Deutschlands Eliten im Wandel,* edited by Herfried Münkler, Grit Straßenberger, and Matthias Bohlender, 363–383. Frankfurt-am-Main: Campus Verlag, 2006.

La Pira, Frank. "Entrepreneurial Intuition, an Empirical Approach." *Journal of Management and Marketing Research.* Accessed 5 August 2016. http://www.aabri.com/manuscripts/10554.pdf.

Lackner, Stefan. *Voraussetzungen und Erfolgsfaktoren unternehmerischen Denkens und Handelns: Eine empirische Analyse mittelständischer Unternehmen.* Hamburg: Verlag Dr. Kovac, 2002.

Lauterbach, Wolfgang. "Reiche Parallelwelten? Soziale Mobilität in Deutschland bei Wohlhabenden und Reichen." In *Reichtum, Philanthropie und Zivilgesellschaft,* edited by Wolfgang Lauterbach, Michael Hartmann, and Miriam Ströing, 77–98. Wiesbaden: Springer VS, 2014.

Lauterbach, Wolfgang, Thomas Druyen, and Matthias Grundmann, eds. *Vermögen in Deutschland: Heterogenität und Verantwortung.* Wiesbaden: Springer VS, 2011.

Lauterbach, Wolfgang, Michael Hartmann, and Miriam Ströing. *Reichtum, Philanthropie und Zivilgesellschaft.* Wiesbaden: Springer VS, 2014.

Lauterbach, Wolfgang, and Melanie Kramer. "'Vermögen in Deutschland' (ViD): Eine quantitative Studie." In *Reichtum und Vermögen: Zur gesellschaftlichen Bedeutung der Reichtums- und Vermögensforschung,* edited by Thomas Druyen, Wolfgang Lauterbach, and Matthias Grundmann, 279–294. Wiesbaden: Springer VS, 2009.

Lauterbach, Wolfgang, and Alexander Tarvenkorn. "Homogenität und Heterogenität von Reichen im Vergleich zur gesellschaftlichen Mitte." In *Vermögen in Deutschland: Heterogenität und Verantwortung*, edited by Wolfgang Lauterbach, Thomas Druyen, and Matthias Grundmann, 57–94. Wiesbaden: Springer VS, 2011.

Lesinski, Jeanne M. *Bill Gates*. Minneapolis: Twenty-First-Century Books, 2007.

Lindemann, Gesa. *Das paradoxe Geschlecht: Transsexualität im Spannungsfeld von Körper, Leib und Gefühl*. Wiesbaden: Springer VS, 2011.

Locke, Edwin A., and J. Robert Baum. "Entrepreneurial Motivation." In *The Psychology of Entrepreneurship*, edited by J. Robert Baum, Michael Frese, and Robert Baron, 93–112. New York: Psychology Press Taylor & Francis Group, 2012.

Locke, Edwin A., and Gary P. Latham. "Goal Setting Theory: The Current State." In *New Developments in Goal Setting and Task Performance*, edited by Edwin A. Locke and Gary P. Latham, 623–630. New York: Routledge Taylor & Francis Group, 2013.

Locke, Edwin A., and Gary P. Latham. "Goal Setting Theory, 1990." In *New Developments in Goal Setting and Task Performance*, edited by Edwin A. Locke and Gary P. Latham, 3–15. New York: Routledge Taylor & Francis Group, 2013.

Locke, Edwin A., and Gary P. Latham, eds. *New Developments in Goal Setting and Task Performance*. New York: Routledge Taylor & Francis Group, 2013.

Locke, Edwin A., and Gary P. Latham, eds. *A Theory of Goal Setting & Task Performance*. Englewood Cliffs: Prentice Hall, 1990.

Locke, Edwin A., Karyll N. Shaw, Lise M. Saari, and Gary P. Latham. "Goal Setting and Task Performance: 1969–1980." *Psychological Bulletin* 90, no. 1 (1981): 125–152.

Love, John F. *McDonald's: Behind the Arches*. Rev. ed. New York: Bantam Books, 1995.

Lowenstein, Roger. *Buffett: The Making of an American Capitalist*. New York: Random House, 1995.

Lundberg, Ferdinand. *The Rich and the Super-Rich: A Study in the Power of Money Today*. New York: Lyle Stuart, 1968.

Machatzke, Jörg. "Die Potsdamer Elitestudie: Positionsauswahl und Ausschöpfung." In *Eliten in Deutschland: Rekrutierung und Integration*, edited by Wilhelm Bürklin, and Hilke Rebenstorf, 35–68. Wiesbaden: Springer Fachmedien, 1997.

Mäder, Ueli, Ganga Jey Aratnam, and Sarah Schillinger. *Wie Reiche denken und lenken: Reichtum in der Schweiz – Geschichte, Fakten, Gespräche*. Zürich: Rotpunktverlag, 2010.

Mauboussin, Michael J. *The Success Equation: Untangling Skill and Luck in Business, Sports, and Investing*. Boston: Harvard Business Review Press, 2012.

Mayer, Horst Otto. *Interview und schriftliche Befragung: Grundlagen und Methoden empirischer Sozialforschung*, 6th ed. Munich: Oldenburg Wissenschaftsverlag, 2013.

Mayring, Philipp. *Qualitative Inhaltsanalyse: Grundlagen und Techniken*, 12th rev. ed. Weinheim: Beltz Verlag, 2015.

McCrae, Robert R., and Paul T. Costa. *Personality in Adulthood: A Five-Factor Theory Perspective*. New York: The Guilford Press, 2003.

Meinefeld, Werner. "Hypothesen und Vorwissen in der qualitativen Sozialforschung." In *Qualitative Forschung: Ein Handbuch*, 10th ed., edited by Uwe Flick, Ernst von Kardorff, and Ines Steinke, 265–275. Hamburg: Rowohlt, 2013.

Merkens, Hans. "Auswahlverfahren, Sampling, Fallkonstruktion." In *Qualitative Forschung: Ein Handbuch*, 10th ed., edited by Uwe Flick, Ernst von Kardorff, and Ines Steinke, 286–299. Hamburg: Rowohlt, 2013.

Miner, John B. *The 4 Routes to Entrepreneurial Success.* San Francisco: Berrett-Koehler Publishers, 1996.

Moore, Don A., John M. Oesch, and Charlene Zietsma. "What Competition? Myopic Self-Focus in Market-Entry Decisions." *Organization Science* 18, no. 3 (2007): 440–454.

Morrison, Elizabeth W. "Doing the Job Well: An Investigation of Pro-Social Rule Breaking." *Journal of Management* 32, no. 10 (2006): 5–28.

Moser, Klaus, Bernad Batinic, and Jeanette Zempel, ed. *Unternehmerisch erfolgreiches Handeln.* Göttingen: Verlag für Angewandte Psychologie, 1999.

Müller, Günther F. "Dispositionelle und biographische Bedingungen beruflicher Selbständigkeit." In *Unternehmerisch erfolgreiches Handeln,* edited by Klaus Moser, Bernad Batinic, and Jeanette Zempel, 173–192. Göttingen: Verlag für Angewandte Psychologie, 1999.

Mummendey, Hans Dieter, and Ina Grau. *Die Fragebogen-Methode: Grundlagen und Anwendung in Persönlichkeits-, Einstellungs- und Selbstkonzeptforschung,* 6th ed. Göttingen: Hogrefe Verlag, 2014.

Münkler, Herfried, Grit Straßenberger, and Matthias Bohlender. "Einleitung." In *Dies: Deutschlands Eliten im Wandel,* 11–21. Frankfurt-am-Main: Campus Verlag, 2006.

Münkler, Herfried, Grit Straßenberger, and Matthias Bohlender, eds. *Deutschlands Eliten im Wandel.* Frankfurt-am-Main: Campus Verlag, 2006.

Näher, Anatol-Fiete, and Ivar Krumpal. "Asking Sensitive Questions: The Impact of Forgiving Wording and Question Context on Social Desirability Bias." *Quality & Quantity* 46, no. 5 (2012): 1601–1616.

Nahrendorf, Rainer. *Der Unternehmer-Code: Was Gründer und Familienunternehmer erfolgreich macht.* Wiesbaden: Gabler Verlag, 2008.

Naidu, G.M., and Chem L. Narayana. "Problem-Solving Skills and Growth in Successful Entrepreneurial Firms." In *Frontiers of Entrepreneurship Research,* edited by N.C. Churchill, 87–99, 1990.

Nassehi, Armin. "Differenzierungseliten in der 'Gesellschaft der Gegenwarten.'" In *Deutschlands Eliten im Wandel,* edited by Herfried Münkler, Grit Straßenberger, and Matthias Bohlender, 255–274. Frankfurt-am-Main: Campus Verlag, 2006.

Neuber, Nils, ed. *Informelles Lernen im Sport: Beiträge zur allgemeinen Bildungsdebatte.* Wiesbaden: VS Verlag für Sozialwissenschaften, 2010.

Neuber, Nils. "Informelles Lernen im Sport: Ein vernachlässigtes Feld der allgemeinen Bildungs-debatte." In *Informelles Lernen im Sport. Beiträge zur allgemeinen Bildungsdebatte,* 9–34. Wiesbaden: Springer VS, 2010.

Neuweg, Georg Hans. *Könnerschaft und implizites Wissen: Zur lehr- und lerntheoretischen Bedeutung der Erkenntnis- und Wissenstheorie Michael Polanyis.* Münster: Waxmann Verlag, 2001.

Nohl, Arnd-Michael. *Interview und dokumentarische Methode: Anleitungen für die Forschungspraxis,* 4th rev. ed. Wiesbaden: Springer VS, 2012.

O'Brien, Lucy. *Madonna: Like an Icon – The Definitive Biography.* London: Transworld Publishers, 2007.

Obschonka, Martin, Eva Schmitt-Rodermund, Rainer K. Silbereisen, Samuel D. Gosling, and Jeff Potter. "The Regional Distribution and Correlates of an Entrepreneurship-Prone Personality Profile in the United States, Germany, and the United Kingdom: A Socioecological Perspective." Working Paper 550, SOEP, 2013.

Obschonka, Martin, Rainer K. Silbereisen, and Eva Schmitt-Rodermund. "Explaining Entrepreneurial Behavior: Dispositional Personality Traits, Growth of Personal Entrepreneurial Resources, and Business Idea Generation." *Career Development Quarterly* 60 (2012): 178–190.

Oettingen, Gabriele, Gaby Hönig, and Peter M. Gollwitzer. "Effective Self-Regulation of Goal Attainment." *International Journal of Educational Research* 33 (2000): 705–732.

Oettingen, Gabriele, Marion Wittchen, and Peter M. Gollwitzer. "Regulating Goal Pursuit through Mental Contrasting with Implementation Intentions." In *New Developments in Goal Setting and Task Performance*, edited by Edwin A. Locke and Gary P. Latham, 523–548. New York: Routledge Taylor & Francis Group, 2013.

Ogilvy, David. *An Autobiography.* New York: John Wiley & Sons, 1997.

Ogilvy, David. *Confessions of an Advertising Man.* London: Athenenum, 1963.

Oguz, Fuat. "Hayek on Tacit Knowledge." *Journal of Institutional Economics* 6, no. 2 (2010): 145–165.

Opitz, Martin G. "Rocker im Spannungsfeld zwischen Clubinteressen und Gesellschaftsnormen, Constance 1990." PhD diss., Universität Bremen, 1989.

Otto, Werner. *Die Otto Gruppe. Der Weg zum Großunternehmen.* Düsseldorf: Econ Verlag, 1983.

Petersen, Thomas. *Der Fragebogen in der Sozialforschung.* Munich: UVK Verlagsgesellschaft, 2014.

Philipps, Kevin. *Wealth and Democracy: A Political History of the American Rich.* New York: Broadway Books, 2002.

Plaschka, Gerhard. *Unternehmenserfolg: Eine vergleichende empirische Untersuchung von erfolgreichen und nicht erfolgreichen Unternehmensgründern.* Vienna: Service Fachverlag an der Wirtschaftsuniversität Wien, 1986.

Platthaus, Andreas. *Von Mann & Maus: Die Welt des Walt Disney.* Berlin: Henschel Verlag, 2001.

Polanyi, Michael. *The Tacit Dimension.* London: Routledge, 1966.

Pontikes, Elizabeth G., and William P. Barnett. "When to Be a Nonconformist Entrepreneur? Organizational Responses to Vital Events." Working Paper 3003, Stanford Graduate School of Business, 2014. Accessed 7 July 2015. https://www.gsb.stanford.edu/faculty-research/working-papers/when-be-nonconformist-entrepreneur-organizational-responses-vital.

Priddat, Birger P. "Unternehmer als Cultural Entrepreneurs." In *Unternehmertum: Vom Nutzen und Nachteil einer riskanten Lebensform*, edited by Ludger Heidbrink and Peter Seele, 115–128. Frankfurt-am-Main: Campus Verlag, 2010.

Puri, Manju, and David T. Robinson. "Optimism and Economic Choice." *Journal of Financial Economics* 86 (2007): 71–99.

Rauch, Andreas, and Michael Frese. "Psychological Approaches to Entrepreneurial Success: A General Model and an Overview of Findings." In *International Review of Industrial and Organizational Psychology*, edited by C.L. Cooper and I.T. Robertson, 101–142. Chichester: Wiley, 2000.

Rauch, Andreas and Michael Frese. *Born to Be an Entrepreneur?, Revisting the Personality Approach to Entrepreneurship.* https://www.researchgate.net/publication/270820381_Born_to_Be_an_Entrepreneur_Revisiting_the_Personality_Approach_to_Entrepreneurship

Rauch, Andreas, and Michael Frese. "Was wissen wir über die Psychologie erfolgreichen Unternehmertums? Ein Literaturüberblick." In *Erfolgreiche Unternehmensgründer: Psychologische Analysen und praktische Anleitungen für Unternehmer in Ost- und Westdeutschland*, edited by Michael Frese, 5–34. Göttingen: Verlag für Angewandte Psychologie, 1998.

Raynor, Michael, Mumtaz Ahmed, and Andrew D. Henderson. "Are 'Great' Companies Just Lucky?" *Harvard Business Manager* (April 2009): 2–3.

Reber, Arthur S. "Implicit Learning and Tacit Knowledge." *Journal of Experimental Psychology* 118, no. 3 (1989): 219–235.

Reber, Arthur S., Faye F. Walkenfeld, and Ruth Hernstadt. "Implicit and Explicit Learning: Individual Differences and IQ." *Journal of Experimental Psychology* 17, no. 5 (1991): 888–896.

Reuber, A. Rebecca, and Eileen M. Fischer. "The Learning Experiences of Entrepreneurs."
In *Frontiers of Entrepreneurial Research*, edited by Neil C. Churchill, 234–247.
Massachusetts: Babson College, 1993.

Rickens, Christian. *Ganz oben: Wie Deutschlands Millionäre wirklich leben.*
Cologne: Kiepenheuer & Witsch, 2011.

Roman, Kenneth. *The King of Madison Avenue: David Ogilvy and the Making of Modern Advertising.*
New York: St. Martin's Griffin, 2009.

Ronstadt, Robert. "The Decision Not to Become an Entrepreneur." In *Frontiers of Entrepreneurship
Research,* edited by John A. Hornday, Jeffrey A. Timmins, and Karl H. Vesper, 192–212.
Massachusetts: Babson College, 1993.

Sarasvathy, Saras D. *Effectuation: Elements of Entrepreneurial Expertise – New Horizons
in Entrepreneurship.* Cheltenham: Edward Elger, 2008.

Saucier, Gerard, and Lewis R. Goldberg. "What Is Beyond the Big Five?" *Journal of Personality* 66,
no. 4 (1998): 495–524.

Schäfer, Bodo. *Der Weg zur finanziellen Freiheit. In sieben Jahren die erste Million.*
Frankfurt-am-Main: Campus Verlag, 1998.

Schenk, Roland. "Beurteilung des Unternehmenserfolgs." In *Erfolgreiche Unternehmensgründer:
Psychologische Analysen und praktische Anleitungen für Unternehmer in Ost- und Westdeutschland,*
edited by Michael Frese, 58–82. Göttingen: Verlag für Angewandte Psychologie, 1998.

Schervish, Paul G., Platon E. Coutsoukis, and Ethan Lewis. *Gospels of Wealth: How the Rich Portray
Their Lives.* Westport: Praeger Publishers, 1994.

Schmitt-Rodermund, Eva. "Pathways to Successful Entrepreneurship: Parenting, Personality,
Competence, and Interests." *Journal of Vocational Behavior* 65 (2004): 498–518.

Schmitt-Rodermund, Eva. "Wer wird Unternehmer? Persönlichkeit, Erziehungsstil sowie frühe
Interessen und Fähigkeiten als Vorläufer für unternehmerische Aktivität im Erwachsenenalter."
Wirtschaftspsychologie 2 (2005): 7–23.

Schmitt-Rodermund, Eva, and Rainer K. Silbereisen. "Erfolg von Unternehmern: Die Rolle von
Persönlichkeit und familiärer Sozialisation." In *Unternehmerisch erfolgreiches Handeln,*
edited by Klaus Moser, Bernad Batinic, and Jeanette Zempel, 115–144.
Göttingen: Verlag für Angewandte Psychologie, 1999.

Schmoock, Matthias. *Werner Otto. Der Jahrhundert-Mann.* Frankfurt-am-Main: Societäts-Verlag, 2009.

Schoeck, Helmut. *Envy: A Theory of Social Behaviour.* Indianapolis, Liberty Fund, 1966.

Schroeder, Alice. *The Snowball: Warren Buffett and the Business of Life.*
London: Bloomsbury Publishers, 2008.

Schuler, Thomas. *Die Mohns: Vom Provinzbuchhändler zum Weltkonzern –
Die Familie hinter Bertelsmann.* Frankfurt-am-Main: Campus, 2004.

Schultz, Howard, and Dori Jones Yang. *Pour Your Heart Into It: How Starbucks Built a Company
One Cup at a Time.* New York: Hyperion, 1997.

Schumpeter, Joseph. *Capitalism, Socialism and Democracy.*
London: George Allen & Unwin Publishers, 1976.

Schumpeter, Joseph. *Theory of Economic Development.* London: Routledge, 1981.

Schumpeter, Joseph. *Theorie der wirtschaftlichen Entwicklung.* Leipzig: Duncker & Humblot, 1912.

Schützenhöfer, Louis. *Vom Charme des Scheiterns: Krisen für einen Neustart nutzen.*
Vienna: Verlag Carl Ueberreuter, 2011.

Seger, Carol Augart. "Implicit Learning." *Psychological Bulletin* 115, no. 2 (1994): 163–196.

Segal, Gerry, Dan Borgia, and Jerry Schoenfeld. "Founder Human Capital and Small Firm Performance: An Empirical Study of Founder-Managed Natural Food Stores." *Journal of Management and Marketing Research* 4 (2009): 1–10.

Sehitiy, Tarek el, and Anna Schor-Tschudnowskaja. "Vermögende in Deutschland: Die Perspektiven der Vermögenskulturforschung." In *Vermögen in Deutschland: Heterogenität und Verantwortung,* edited by Wolfgang Lauterbach, Thomas Druyen, and Matthias Grundmann, 143–202. Wiesbaden: Springer VS, 2011.

Skopek, Nora. "Vermögen in Europa." In *Reichtum, Philanthropie und Zivilgesellschaft,* edited by Wolfgang Lauterbach, Michael Hartmann, and Miriam Ströing, 47–76. Wiesbaden: VS Verlag, 2014.

Slater, Robert. *George Soros: The World's Most Influential Investor.* New York: McGraw-Hill Companies, 2009.

Sombart, Werner. *Der moderne Kapitalismus, Vol. 1: Die vorkapitalistische Wirtschaft.* Munich: Duncker & Humblot, 1916.

Sombart, Werner. *Der moderne Kapitalismus, Vol. 3: Die vorkapitalistische Wirtschaft,* second half-volume. Munich: Duncker & Humblot, 1927.

Sombart, Werner. *The Quintessence of Capitalism: A Study of the History and Psychology of the Modern Business Man.* London: T. Fisher Unwin, Ltd., 1915.

Spannagel, Dorothee. *Reichtum in Deutschland: Empirische Analysen.* Wiesbaden: Springer VS, 2013.

Stadler, Christina. *Freude am Unternehmertum in kleineren und mittleren Unternehmen: Ergebnisse einer Quer- und Längsschnittanalyse.* Wiesbaden: Gabler Verlag, 2009.

Stanley, Thomas J. *The Millionaire Mind.* New York: Bantam Books, 2001.

Stanley, Thomas J., and William D. Danko. *The Millionaire Next Door.* Atlanta: Longstreet Press, 1996.

Statista. "Anzahl der Einkommensteuerpflichtigen mit mindestens einer Million Euro Einkünften in Deutschland von 2004 bis 2013." Last modified 2017. https://de.statista.com/statistik/daten/studie/162287/umfrage/einkommensmillionaere-in-deutschland.

Sternberg, Robert J. *Successful Intelligence: How Practical and Creative Intelligence Determine Success in Life.* New York: Penguin Group, 1997.

Ströing, Miriam, and Melanie Kramer. "Reichtum und die Übernahme gesellschaftlicher Verantwortung." In *Vermögen in Deutschland: Heterogenität und Verantwortung,* edited by Wolfgang Lauterbach, Thomas Druyen, and Matthias Grundmann, 95–142. Wiesbaden: Springer VS, 2011.

Teal, Elisabeth J., and Archie B. Carroll. "Moral Reasoning Skills: Are Entrepreneurs Different?" *Journal of Business Ethics* 19 (1999): 229–240.

Timmdorf, Jonas, ed. *Die Aldi-Brüder: Warum Karl und Theo Albrecht mit ihrem Discounter die reichsten Deutschen sind.* Mauritius: Fastbook Publishing, 2009.

Tracy, Brian. *Goals! How to Get Everything You Want – Faster Than You Ever Thought Possible.* San Francisco: Berrett-Koehler Publishers, 2010.

Utsch, Andreas. "Ein minimales Gesamtmodell von Erfolgsfaktoren: Ein Mediatorenmodell." In *Erfolgreiche Unternehmensgründer: Psychologische Analysen und praktische Anleitungen für Unternehmer in Ost- und Westdeutschland,* edited by Michael Frese, 133–148. Göttingen: Verlag für Angewandte Psychologie, 1998.

Utsch, Andreas. "Psychologische Einflussgrößen von Unternehmensgründung und Unternehmenserfolg." PhD diss., Justus-Liebig-Universität Gießen, 2004.

Vise, David A., and Mark Malseed. *The Google Story*. New York: Dell Publishing, 2005.

Wallace, James, and Jim Erickson. *Hard Drive. Bill Gates and the Making of the Microsoft Empire*. Chichester: Wiley, 1992.

Walter, Franz, and Stine Marg, eds. *Sprachlose Elite? Wie Unternehmer Politik und Gesellschaft sehen*. Reinbek: BP Gesellschaftsstudie, 2015.

Walton, Sam. *Made in America: My Story*. New York: Bantom Books, 1993.

Wasner, Barbara. *Eliten in Europa: Einführung in Theorien, Konzepte und Befunde*. Wiesbaden: Springer Fachmedien, 2006.

Watkins, Karen E., and Victoria J. Marsick. "Towards a Theory of Informal and Incidental Learning in Organizations." *International Journal of Lifelong Education* 11, no. 4 (1992): 287–300.

Welch, Jack, and John A. Byrne. *Straight from the Gut*. London: Warner Books, 2001.

Welch, Jack, and Suzy Welch. *Winning: The Answers – Confronting 74 of the Toughest Questions in Business Today*. New York: Harper Business, 2006.

Williams, Geoff. "No Rules." Entrepreneur (1999). Accessed 27 October 2017. https://www.entrepreneur.com/article/18298.

Wilson, Mike. *The Difference between God and Larry Ellison: Inside Oracle Corporation*. New York: Harper Business, 2002.

Wilson, Timothy D., and Jonathan W. Schooler. "Thinking Too Much: Introspection Can Reduce the Quality of Preferences and Decisions." *Journal of Personality and Social Psychology* 60, no. 2 (1991): 181–192.

Wolff, Michael. *The Man Who Owns the News: Inside the Secret World of Rupert Murdoch*. London: The Bodley Head, 2008.

Wolter, Felix. *Heikle Fragen in Interviews: Eine Validierung der Randomized Response-Technik*. Wiesbaden: Springer VS, 2012.

Woodward, Woody. *Millionaire Dropouts: Inspiring Stories of the World's Most Successful Failures*. Murrieta: Millionaire Dropouts, 2006.

Woolhouse, Leanne S., and Rowan Bayne. "Personality and the Use of Intuition: Individual Differences in Strategy and Performance on an Implicit Learning Task." *European Journal of Personality* 14 (2000): 157–169.

Wüllenweber, Walter. *Die Asozialen: Wie Ober- und Unterschicht unser Land ruinieren – und wer davon profitiert*. Munich: Deutsche Verlags Anstalt, 2012.

Young, Jeffrey S., and William L. Simon. *iCon Steve Jobs: The Greatest Second Act in the History of Business*. New Jersey: John Wiley & Sons, 2005.

Young, John E., and Donald L. Sexton. "Entrepreneurial Learning: A Conceptual Framework." *Journal of Enterprising Culture* 5, no. 3 (1997): 223–248.

Zhang, Zhen, and Richard D. Arvey. "Rule Breaking in Adolescence and Entrepreneurial Status: An Empirical Investigation." *Journal of Business Venturing* 24 (2009): 436–447.

Zhao, Hao, and Scott E. Seibert. "The Big Five Personality Dimensions and Entrepreneurial Status: A Meta-Analytical Review." *Journal of Applied Psychology* 91, no. 2 (2006): 259–271.

Zitelmann, Rainer. *Dare to Be Different and Grow Rich*. Mumbai: Indus Source Books, 2012.

Zitelmann, Rainer. *Reich werden und bleiben: Ihr Wegweiser zur finanziellen Freiheit*. Munich: FinanzBuch Verlag, 2015.

About the Author

DR. RAINER ZITELMANN

Rainer Zitelmann holds doctorates in History and Sociology. He is the author of 21 books. After working as a historian at the Freie Universität Berlin, he later served as section head at the daily newspaper *Die Welt*. In 2000, he founded his own company, which he subsequently sold in 2016. Today he lives in Berlin as an investor and publicist. The material in this book is based on his second doctoral dissertation.

Sharing knowledge since 1993

- 1993 Madrid
- 2008 Mexico DF and Monterrey
- 2010 London
- 2011 New York and Buenos Aires
- 2012 Bogotá
- 2014 Shanghai